NOVY MIR

Also edited and translated by Michael Glenny

REVOLUTIONARY SILHOUETTES by Anatoly Lunacharsky

THREE SOVIET PLAYS by Vladimir Mayakovsky, Isaac Babel and Yevgeny Schwartz

PLAYS by Mikhail Bulgakov (in preparation)

NOVY MIR
A Selection 1925-1967

Edited and introduced by MICHAEL GLENNY

Jonathan Cape Thirty Bedford Square London

First published 1972
Compilation and introductory matter © 1972 by Michael Glenny
A Tale of the Unextinguished Moon, by Boris Pilnyak © 1966 by Brian Pearce
One Day in the Life of Ivan Denisovich, by Alexander Solzhenitsyn © 1963 by Frederick A. Praeger Inc.
Black Snow, by Mikhail Bulgakov © 1967 by Michael Glenny
'The Reader' and 'The Spectator', by Rainer Maria Rilke, translated by J. B. Leishman © 1960 by the Hogarth Press
All other translations in this volume © 1972 by Jonathan Cape Ltd

Jonathan Cape Ltd, 30 Bedford Square, London WC1

ISBN 0 224 00707 6

PRINTED IN GREAT BRITAIN
BY EBENEZER BAYLIS AND SON LTD
THE TRINITY PRESS, WORCESTER, AND LONDON
ON PAPER MADE BY JOHN DICKINSON AND CO. LTD
BOUND BY G. AND J. KITCAT, LTD, LONDON

Contents

Acknowledgments

I should like to thank Mrs Olive Stevens, Mrs Tanya Forsyth, Mrs Vera Dixon, Max Hayward, Leonid Vladimirov, Dr Edward Braun and Nicholas Anning, for their most valuable collaboration and assistance.

For permission to reproduce copyright material, I gratefully acknowledge the following: *Stand* magazine and Brian Pearce, for 'A Tale of the Unextinguished Moon' by Boris Pilnyak, reprinted from *Stand*, 1966, no. 1; Pall Mall Press and Max Hayward and Ronald Hingley for the extract from *A Day in the Life of Ivan Denisovich* by Alexander Solzhenitsyn; Hodder and Stoughton for the chapter from *Black Snow* by Mikhail Bulgakov; Calder and Boyars for the extracts from *Rhinoceros* by Eugene Ionesco which appear in 'Rhinoceroses in New York' by Alexander Anikst; the Council of the Royal Society for Academician P. L. Kapitza's 'Recollections of Lord Rutherford', an address given in 1966; St John's College, Oxford, and the Hogarth Press for 'The Reader' and 'The Spectator' by Rainer Maria Rilke, translated by J. B. Leishman, which appear in 'People and Situations' by Boris Pasternak.

M.G.

NOVY MIR

Introduction

Outside the Soviet Union, *Novy Mir* is perhaps the best known example of a form of publication which has long been extinct in the West – the solid, serious, all-round literary-cum-political monthly with an average issue-size of 280 closely printed pages, a circulation of around 140,000, and which can print a whole novel at a time and still have room to spare. This type of journal is known in its homeland as a 'thick journal'; it represents a long and honourable tradition in Russian literature, going back to the early nineteenth century and such famous 'thick journals' as *The Moscow Telegraph, The Pole Star* and *The Northern Bee*, whose contributors included most of the great writers of the time. In 1836, Pushkin himself founded one, called *The Contemporary*, and edited it for a while, although it was not a wholly successful venture.

Perhaps the most important and influential figure of 'thick' journalism in the 'thirties and 'forties of the last century, and who gave it the basic character which *mutatis mutandis* it bears to this day, was the great critic Vissarion Belinsky (1811–48), the man who has also been called the founder of the 'intelligentsia'. This distinctly Russian socio-cultural phenomenon has proved so hardy that after 130 years it still provides the bulk of the readership for Russia's 'thick journals'.

To analyse the syndrome of causes which created and sustained the 'thick journal' is a major study in itself and too large a matter to deal with here in any but the most general terms. The intellectual avidity of the small but highly self-conscious educated class, the vast extent of Russia, the poor communications, the tedium and isolation of provincial life, were some of the factors which encouraged educated Russians to treasure their monthly or quarterly 'thick journal' as an intellectual lifeline to the outside world, and the journals themselves provided an appropriately varied and nourishing diet to sustain the intelligentsia's need for solid reading matter. Thus they not only published fiction and criticism, but were also the chief medium for popularizing and discussing the philosophical, scientific and political issues of the day. The latter were often camouflaged as polemics on literary or historical themes in order to evade the censorship, a feature which has of necessity persisted in the Soviet period.

Although the first two decades of the twentieth century saw a proliferation of journals, they tended to specialize in subject-matter, and thus largely forfeited the broadness of scope and heavyweight character which were the distinctive marks of the 'thick journal'. The species revived, however, after the revolution when in 1921, under the personal guidance of Lenin and with the collaboration of Maxim Gorky, a conscious attempt was made to create the first 'thick journal' of the new dispensation. Entitled *Krasnaya Nov'* ('Red Virgin Soil') and edited by A. K. Voronsky, it was dedicated to promoting a literary, political and educational line in conformity with Communist Party policy. It flourished in the early and mid 'twenties, but Voronsky was removed as a Trot-skyist in 1928 and *Krasnaya Nov'* declined rapidly after his de-parture. It had, however, shown the way for the foundation of many other similar Soviet journals which have proved longer lasting, such as *Oktyabr'* ('October'), *Zvezda* ('The Star') and *Novy Mir* ('New World'), the latter being launched in 1925 speci-fically as a forum for 'fellow-travelling' writers who were broadly in sympathy with the aims of the regime but who were not formally committed to any one of the many literary schools or groupings.

The first head of the editorial board was A. V. Lunacharsky, himself a prolific critic, playwright and journalist, who was the first People's Commissar for Education. It must be admitted that under Lunacharsky's short editorship *Novy Mir* was not a very interesting journal; it only came to life under the first of its two really great editors, Vyacheslav Polonsky, who chaired the editorial board from 1928 to 1934

After Polonsky came the barren years of Stalin's ever-tightening control of cultural policy, in which the contents of *Novy Mir*, as of all Soviet publications, became increasingly predictable, lifeless and to present-day eyes virtually unreadable, the occasional happy exception only serving to prove the rule. Apart from a slight revival during the Second World War, when ideological controls were a little relaxed, the greatest years of *Novy Mir* were to come, after a hesitant start in 1953, as a consequence of Khrushchev's de-Stalinization policy launched at the XX Party Congress in 1956. The man who was editor-in-chief of *Novy Mir* from 1953 to 1954, then again from 1958 to 1969, and who brought the journal to a height of vigour, influence and importance greater than ever before, greater even than under Polonsky, was the poet Alexander Tvardovsky. During his tenure not only was new Russian writing given an impetus which it had largely lost since the 'twenties, but a wealth of literature was published which had been suppressed during the previous twenty-five years. Then in late 1969, after stoutly supporting Solzhenitsyn against an officially sponsored attack, the courageous Tvardovsky was forced to resign his editorship, having made *Novy Mir* for several years the nearest equivalent to a liberal opposition forum which Soviet Russia had ever known since the relatively short-lived libertarian period of the mid-twenties.

When he died on December 18th, 1971, instead of being given the lavish public funeral accorded to 'establishment' literary figures, he was buried privately in the Novodevichy cemetery, Russia's equivalent of Père Lachaise. The occasion was made memorable by the presence of Alexander Solzhenitsyn, who paid one of his rare visits to Moscow. Soon afterwards, Solzhenitsyn's short, moving 'In Memoriam' was published in the West; for all its brevity it did infinitely more justice to Tvardovsky's real stature than the windy, evasive rhetoric of his official obituaries.

It should be made clear that it is not the purpose of this anthology to be a study in the politics of Soviet literature over the years since 1925. Such a work would be of the greatest interest and value, and it is to be hoped that one day it will be undertaken, but it is a project far outside the scope of this book. Instead, the prime criterion in the choice of material for inclusion has been literary. Almost without exception, the short introductory passages to each item touch in part on matters which are directly or indirectly political; this is an inevitable consequence of the politicization of literature which occurs in a country in whose ideology every aspect of public life—and especially literature—is considered legitimately subject to guidance and control.

Even the claim that literary considerations have been uppermost in compiling this anthology must be qualified by admitting the influence of a number of factors, some of them—such as space restrictions—common to all such collections, and others which are harder to define, because they spring from the difficulties inherent in presenting examples of writing from a cultural context which differs so profoundly, and to a degree often unrealized, from the social and intellectual climate familiar to Western readers. It is more from a feeling that certain features of this cultural gap are important and interesting, rather than from an urge to justify the apparent inconsistencies and omissions in this anthology, that the following *apologia* — using the word in its widest sense — is given.

On the strictly practical level, publishing considerations have as always been of foremost importance. Firstly, there is an upper limit to the size of such a volume, which imposes on an editor the overriding need to be firmly selective; whilst in some respects irksome, in that it often forces the compiler into the unhappy position of having to choose between the good and the good, it also serves, like the prospect of imminent peril, to concentrate the mind wonderfully and to make an editor more rigorously critical than he might otherwise be. Then there is the sheer volume of material to choose from — twelve issues a year for forty-five years. This has involved the effort to stand well back from the topics of the hour, which were often so fascinatingly reflected in the pages of *Novy Mir*, and to adopt a rather Olympian attitude in which the indefinable and subjective factor of taste has had to be ultimately decisive.

Another very marked inhibitor has been the fact that so much of the best and most important writing in *Novy Mir* has already been published in translation. This has necessitated the exclusion of much material of the greatest interest. At the same time, certain pieces have been included in the anthology which have already received wide publication in English and in many other languages. The most obvious example is the extract from Solzhenitsyn's *One Day in the Life of Ivan Denisovich*; here it was felt that by every appropriate moral and literary standard this work was of such outstanding significance that to have left it out on the grounds of previous publication would have been to distort the entire 'profile' of *Novy Mir* in the period in question. The editor's only regret is that the novella could not be included in its entirety; but this would have meant the exclusion of other passages of such intrinsic value that their omission, too, would have done excessive violence to the overall concept. The chapter here reproduced from Bulgakov's *Black Snow: A Theatrical Novel* has also been seen before; in this instance, whilst again deploring the need to extract only a part from the whole, the fact that this is a supremely polished example of a genre found all too infrequently in Soviet literature—satire—has made its inclusion desirable on grounds of both completeness and balance.

The need for balance has, indeed, been high on the list of priorities throughout, but it must be admitted that it has also been very hard to achieve. The causes for this relative lack of success are that either one or another of the limiting factors mentioned above tended to supervene; or that the quality of the material available in a particular genre (e.g. the novel) was insufficient to justify inclusion on straight literary grounds; or that an author who should by rights have been found a place in this collection was represented in *Novy Mir* by work which happened to fall well below his best standard. By contrast, the following pages contain what some may regard as rather too much from the pen of Boris Pasternak—and of which the bulk is prose rather than poetry. Here the editor must plead a degree of partiality, induced by the singular charm and sensitivity of Pasternak's prose writing, which shines out with such beacon-like brightness from the surrounding murk that the temptation to include two examples of his prose, in addition to a short poem, proved irresistible. There is however a real justification for this emphasis on Pasternak; he was one of the most frequent and prolific contributors to *Novy Mir* during Polonsky's editorship, and much of his writing published under Tvardovsky's aegis consists of material written, but suppressed, during the intervening years.

Strict balance has also perhaps been infringed a little, though it is hoped to advantage, by the need to give a certain stress to the role of *Novy Mir* as a forum for discussion of issues which lie outside the range of literature in the narrow sense of belles-lettres. Equally, a conscious bias has been applied towards themes which, more than others, are of direct interest to English-speaking readers. Both tendencies played a part, for instance, in prompting the inclusion of Academician Kapitza's *Reminiscences of Lord Rutherford*; this essay is an example of the way *Novy Mir* not infrequently publishes material aimed at bridging the gap between 'the two cultures' (a dichotomy felt in the Soviet Union as it is in the West), and at the same time is a record of an interesting and unusually positive episode in the rather chequered history of Anglo-Soviet relations. The theatre, too, is given a rather generous share in the whole, directly in Gladkov's *Meyerhold Speaks*, as a fictional element in Tarsis's *Desdemona*, rather more explicitly in Bulgakov's *Black Snow*, and centrally in Anikst's very subtle piece of Aesopian polemics entitled *Rhinoceroses in New York*. Finally, in the non-fiction category, there comes a historical document of considerable interest, Berezhkov's *On the Borderline of Peace and War*, written by the man who interpreted between Hitler and Molotov at the last meeting held between the Nazi and Soviet leaders before the German attack on Russia.

The very difficulty of producing an anthology of *Novy Mir* which is to be mainly literary yet also representative is perhaps the best indication of the essential vigour and variety of this journal — at least during the periods of its most inspired editorship. Elusive though the common denominator of these passages may appear to be if they are viewed over-schematically, it has been the editor's aim to bring together a collection in which as many as possible of the most important aspects of *Novy Mir* from 1926 to 1967 are reflected in writing that is a consistent pleasure to read.

MICHAEL GLENNY

Centre for Russian and East European Studies
University of Birmingham, England

A Tale of the Unextinguished Moon *by* Boris Pilnyak

Novy Mir, 1926/IV

Translated by Brian Pearce

A Tale of the Unextinguished Moon has a pedigree even more bizarre than most of the other extracts in this volume. Boris Vogau, alias Pilnyak, was one of the most original innovators in Russian writing of the 'twenties, which was a decade of stylistic experiment, and he influenced many of his contemporaries. In what is perhaps his best work, *The Naked Year* (1921), he drew an impressionistic picture of Russia in the midst of Civil War; his effects were achieved by boldly inventing and distorting words, by using words for their sound alone, by punning and by the use of repetition. His language has at times a rhythmic, incantatory, almost ritualistic quality.

The style of *A Tale of the Unextinguished Moon* (1926) is more restrained and conventional, though he still employs the device of repetition to press home strong images, and the images are usually direct, i.e. not couched in simile or metaphor.

The story caused a major political scandal. In October 1925, Mikhail Frunze, successor to Trotsky as Commissar for War, underwent an operation and died three days later. In the heated atmosphere of intrigue and jockeying for power within the leadership (Stalin had temporarily allied himself with Zinoviev in a move to oust Trotsky), the Frunze incident was inevitably regarded by some as a convenient medical murder. Without much camouflage, Pilnyak wrote his story for *Novy Mir* on that supposition, compounding the mystery by a disingenuous preface warning readers not to see in it 'genuine facts and living persons'. When the issue of *Novy Mir* appeared in mid-1926, Pilnyak was abroad, but it was brought to the attention of Stalin, who at once ordered the issue of the magazine to be withdrawn. A substitute issue was hastily printed and distributed, but not before a few of the offending copies had been sent out, mostly abroad. Pilnyak published a letter of apology in *Novy Mir*.

There seems little real evidence for Stalin's complicity in disposing of Frunze, indeed, Stalin favoured Frunze, who was an opponent of Trotsky. Pilnyak was not renowned for either his political shrewdness or for his resistance to pressure when attacked by the Party, but he was a powerful, original and idiosyncratic writer of prose.

It is greatly to the credit of the magazine *Stand* that this translation was published. Although other English translations have been made, none appears to have tackled the story's stylistic problems with such skill.

Chapter 1

As dawn broke, the factory hooters sounded across the city. The narrow streets were heavy with a mist compounded of fog, night and frost; it still lingered there, a sign that the morning would be joyless and grey. At this hour the rotary presses were hurling forth the last copies of the morning papers; soon afterwards, boys laden with bundles of these papers started out from the yards of the publishing offices and scattered among the streets. One after another the boys made their way to the still-deserted crossroads, where, as though clearing their throats, they began to shout, in the way they were to go on shouting all through the day, 'The Revolution in China! Arrival of C.-in-C. Gavrilov! C.-in-C.'s illness!'

And at that hour too a train pulled into the station where trains arrive from the South. It was a special train, with a blue saloon-car gleaming greyly at the end of it, silent, with sentries on the steps, and blinds pulled down behind the mirror-like glass of the windows. This train had come out of the black night, from the steppes which had squandered the summer luxuriously for the winter, the steppes pillaged in the summer and left to be aged by the snow. The train slowly crawled beneath the roof of the station, making no sound, and came to a standstill in a siding. The platform was deserted. At its gates there stood, doubtless by accident, stout ranks of green-tabbed militiamen. Three officers, with rhombus-shaped marks of

rank on their sleeves, approached the saloon-car. They exchanged
salutes with the sentries. One of the latter whispered something to
somebody inside the saloon-car; then the three men climbed in and
were hidden from view behind the blinds. The electric light was
switched on inside the carriage. Two army electricians had clam-
bered over it and led telephone cables from under the station roof
into the carriage. Yet another man approached the carriage, wearing
an old autumn overcoat and, inappropriately to the season, a fur
cap with ear-flaps. This man gave no salute, nor did anyone salute
him. He said to the sentry, 'Tell Nikolai Ivanovich that Popov's
here.'

The soldier slowly stared at Popov, looked him up and down,
took note of his shabby shoes, and slowly answered:

'The comrade Commander-in-Chief is not up yet.'

Popov smiled in a friendly way at the sentry, and going over to
the familiar second person singular, said in the same friendly way:

'Well now, chum, just you run along and tell him that Popov
says he's here.'

The soldier went off, and when he came back Popov entered the
carriage. Within it, because the blinds were down and the electric
light was on, the night still lingered. On the table there lay beside
the reading lamp an open book, and near that a plate with the
remains of some gruel. Behind the plate lay the unfastened holster
of an automatic revolver, the leather thong uncoiled in a spiral.
At the other end of the table stood a number of bottles which had
been opened. The three officers with the badged sleeves were
sitting well back from the table in leather armchairs along the
partition which separated the rooms; very modest, straight-backed,
their briefcases in their hands, they sat there in silence. Popov
walked behind the table, took off his overcoat and cap, put them
down beside him, picked up the book lying on the table and glanced
at it. The carriage waiter entered, his face expressing indifference
to everything that was going on in the world, and cleared the table.
He put the bottles away in a corner, brushed some pomegranate
peelings on to a tray, covered the table with a cloth, and set upon
it a glass in a metal stand, a plate with some stale bread, and an
egg-cup. Then he brought two eggs on a saucer, some salt, and some
little bottles of medicine. After pulling back one of the curtains and
looking out, he drew the blinds and turned off the light. The autumn

morning, the dreary frost-laden morning, stole into the room. In this sad light all faces were yellow; the thin and watery light resembled ichor. On the threshold, beside the departing waiter, an aide-de-camp appeared. The field orderly-room was already in operation; a telephone was ringing.

Then the commander-in-chief came in from the sleeping compartment. He was a man of medium height, broad-shouldered, with long fair hair brushed straight back. His army jacket, made of the same green material as the jackets the soldiers wore, but with four rhombus-shaped marks of rank on the rumpled sleeve, did not fit him. His spurred boots, though perfectly polished, showed by the worn state of their heels the long and arduous service they had given him. This was the man whose name called to memory all the heroic enthusiasm of the civil war, the thousands, the tens of thousands and hundreds of thousands of men who had marched behind him; the thousands, the tens of thousands and hundreds of thousands of dead, wounded and disabled; the chill, the frost and the heat of marches; the thunder of guns, the whistling of bullets and of night winds; camp fires, advances, victories and headlong retreats and, again, death.

This was the man who had commanded armies, thousands of men; who had commanded men, victories and death; powder, smoke, the scattered embers of camp-fires, torn flesh—victories that had set hundreds of red banners waving and multitudinous crowds roaring in the rear, victories that were broadcast all round the world, victories that were followed, in Russia's sandy steppes, by the digging of huge pits for the corpses, pits into which thousands of human bodies were cast. This was the man whose name was haloed with legends telling of his campaigns, his military virtues, his incomparable bravery and dash, his tenacity. This was the man who had the right and the will to send men into battle to kill their fellows, and themselves to die in their turn.

Into the sitting-room, then, came a man of medium height, broad-shouldered, with the kindly, rather weary face of a seminary student. He walked quickly, and his gait revealed at once the riding man and the civilian, having nothing in him of the soldier. The three callers from Army Headquarters sprang to attention. The C.-in-C. halted in front of them. He did not offer them his hand, but made the gesture which allowed them to stand at ease. And so, standing before them, the C.-in-C. received their reports. Each one stepped forward, faced him and delivered his report:

'In the army entrusted to my command ... In the service of the Revolution ... ' The C.-in-C., who seemed not to listen to what they had to say, shook hands with each in turn. Then he sat down in front of the glass that stood on the table, and the waiter came forward and poured tea for him from a gleaming tea-pot. The C.-in-C. picked up an egg.

'How are things?' he asked, quite simply, without using any official formulas. One of the Red officers spoke, telling him the latest news, and then in his turn asked:

'And how are you, Comrade Gavrilov?'

The C.-in-C.'s face grew unlike himself for a second. Then he said in a disgruntled tone:

'Well, here I am, you see, back from the Caucasus, where I went for my health. Now I'm all right.' He paused. 'I'm fit, now.' Another pause. 'Tell them over there not to lay on any formal reception; no guards of honour, nothing ... ' Another pause. 'That's all, comrades.'

The three officers rose to take their leave. Without getting up, the C.-in-C. gave each of them his hand, and they left the sitting-room in silence. When the C.-in-C. entered, Popov had not greeted him, but had picked up the book lying on the table, and, turning away from him, had begun leafing through it. The C.-in-C. had looked at Popov out of the corner of his eye and had not greeted him either, behaving as though he had not noticed him. As soon as the three officers had left, the C.-in-C., still without greeting his visitor, asked him, just as though they had seen each other the night before:

'Which would you prefer, Alyosha—tea or wine?'

But Popov had no chance to answer him, for the aide-de-camp appeared and reported to the Comrade Commander-in-Chief: The car had been off-loaded ... Communications were arriving in the orderly-room ... There was one from House No. 1, a secret missive from the General Secretary himself ... A suite of rooms at Army Headquarters had been made ready for the Commander-in-Chief ... There was a heap of telegrams and letters of greeting for the Commander-in-Chief ... etc., etc. The C.-in-C. dismissed the aide-de-camp, ordering him to remain in the carriage.

The waiter, without waiting for Popov's reply, set a glass of tea and another for wine upon the table. Popov came out of his corner and sat nearer the C.-in-C.

'And how are you, my dear Nikolai?' he asked solicitously, as though the object of his question were his own brother.

'I'm all right. Everything's fine; but I think you're going to have to take your stand soon in the guard of honour round my coffin,' answered Gavrilov, partly in earnest and partly in grim jest.

Popov and Gavrilov were bound together by old friendship, by the underground revolutionary work they had shared, by the same job in the distant years of their youth, when they were at the beginning of their careers as weavers in the mills of Orekhovo-Zuyevo. Later they had been in Bogorodsk prison at about the same time, and after that there began for both of them the typical life of a professional revolutionary: exile, escape, secret work, Tagansk transportation centre, exile, escape, emigration, Paris, Vienna, Chicago. And then the dark clouds of the 1914–1918 War: Brindisi, Salonika, Rumania, Kiev, Moscow, Petersburg. Then the tempests of 1917, Smolny, October, the bombardment of the Kremlin. After that, one of them had become the Chief of Staff of the Red Guard in Rostov-on-Don; and the other, as Rykov quipped, marshal of the proletarian nobility in Tula. For the former, life became a matter of war, victories, the command of guns, men and death; for the other, regional committees, executive committees, the Supreme Council of the National Economy, conferences, meetings, reports. Each of them devoted his whole life, all his thoughts, to the greatest revolution in the world, to the greatest truth and justice known to man. But they always remained to each other 'Nikolasha' and 'Alyosha', the weaver comrades of yore, without rank or ceremony between them.

'But tell me about your health, Nikolasha,' said Popov.

'Well, I had, and perhaps I still have, a stomach ulcer. The usual symptoms, you know, pains, bloody vomit, a frightful burning sensation – oh, all sorts of vile things,' said the C.-in-C., leaning towards Popov. 'They sent me to the Caucasus, I was given treatment, and the pains went away. That enabled me to take up work again. But six months later the pains and the vomiting began again, worse than ever, and I set off to the Caucasus once more. Down there the pains disappeared again and I even managed to drink a whole bottle of wine at one sitting, as a test of my recovery.'

He interrupted himself to ask:

'Look, Alyosha, wouldn't you like some wine? There is some there under the seat. I brought you a case. Uncork a bottle!'

Popov, not moving from his seat, his head resting in his palm, said:

'No, I never drink in the morning. Go on with what you were saying ... '

'Well, there you are; I tell you, I'm perfectly fit now.'

He fell silent, then began again after a short pause.

'Tell me, Alyosha, do you know why I have been recalled to Moscow?'

'I know nothing about it.'

'An order arrived summoning me to Moscow forthwith, and so off I went, without even stopping to see my wife. I can't imagine what the hell it can be about. Everything's all right in the Army, and there's no conference on or anything ... '

The Commander-in-Chief spoke about the army, about war; and he doubtless did not notice that when he spoke about the army he ceased to be a weaver and became a commander, a Red general of the Red Army. The Commander-in-Chief spoke about Orekhovo-Zuyevo and the years he had spent there; and he doubtless did not notice that then he became a weaver – the weaver who in those days loved a teacher from the other side of the river, so that he cleaned his boots to please her, walking barefoot to the school so as not to get them dirty and putting them on only when he reached a copse near the school. He had bought for her something extraordinary with ribbons on, and a saucy hat – but even so he never got beyond chats about books with the teacher: no romance came of all this; she wouldn't have him. The C.-in-C. who was a weaver was a genial, cheery man who could turn things into a joke and find something to laugh at in everything, and he laughed as he talked with his friend. Only from time to time did the C.-in-C. recollect himself and feel worried; remembering the unaccountable summons he felt ill at ease, and then the healthy weaver said of the sick C.-in-C.:

'A grandee, a field-marshal, a senator – and I can't eat buck-wheat gruel ... Yes, it's a fact, the Central Committee plays with a man – and you can't leave any words out of that song.' And he suffered in silence.

'But tell me frankly, Nikolasha, what do you suspect?' asked Popov. 'What was that nonsense just now, about a guard of honour round your coffin?'

The C.-in-C. hesitated, then said slowly:

'In Rostov, I ran into Potap.' This was the 'Party name' of a very outstanding revolutionary, one of the 'band of heroes' of 1918 ...

'He talked a lot about my illness, insisted I must have an operation ... assured me that it would be best for me to agree to be operated on; to have the ulcer removed, or sewn up, or something. Whatever it was, he tried to persuade me into it, in a very suspicious way.'

The C.-in-C. fell silent.

'I feel perfectly well, my whole being cries out against an operation. I don't want to be operated on; I'll get better all by myself. I tell you I don't feel any more pain, I've even put on weight ... and the devil alone knows what all this is about ... I'm grown up, I'm not a young man any more, I'm, so to speak, a sort of grandee— and here I am worrying about the state of my belly. It's disgraceful!'

He was silent again, and picked up the book.

'I'm reading Tolstoy now, old Tolstoy, his *Childhood and Boyhood*. He wrote well, did that old man, he had a feeling for life, for the blood ... I've seen no small amount of blood in my lifetime, yet ... yet ... all the same, I'm afraid of having an operation. I fear it like a child. They might murder me! How well old Tolstoy understood everything that has to do with man's blood!'

The aide-de-camp entered, came to attention, and announced that a messenger had arrived from Army Headquarters with a report; that a car, sent from House No. 1, was waiting to take the C.-in-C. there; that some more telegrams had arrived; and finally that somebody had been sent to fetch the packets they had brought from the South. The aide-de-camp placed a bundle of newspapers on the table. The C.-in-C. dismissed the aide-de-camp, telling him to get his greatcoat ready. He opened a newspaper. On the first page, where the most important events of the day are mentioned, was printed a headline: 'Arrival of C.-in-C. Gavrilov,' and on page three there appeared a report which began:

'Today sees the arrival in the capital of Commander-in-Chief Gavrilov, who has temporarily laid down his military responsibilities in order to undergo an operation for gastric ulcer.'

The report went on to indicate that the state of Comrade Gavrilov's health gave rise to grave anxiety but that the doctors were confident that his operation would be a success.

The old soldier of the Revolution, the Commander-in-Chief, the hero who had sent thousands of men to their deaths, the most highly perfected of military machines, designed expressly for killing, dying and conquering by means of blood – Gavrilov threw himself back in his chair, wiped his brow with the back of his hand and said, gazing fixedly at Popov:

'There, Alyosha, you see what I mean? There really is something very odd about all this. Ye-e-s ... What can be done about it though?' Then, calling to the aide-de-camp, he demanded that his greatcoat be brought.

Chapter 2

Where two of the main streets of the city crossed, at a point where vehicles, cart-horses and people flowed by in ceaseless succession, stood a house with a columned façade, behind a wooden fence. There was no name on the gate. On the threshold of the gateway surmounted by griffins two helmeted sentries stood stiffly on guard. Before them passed people, cars sounding their horns, crowds, human time, the dismal day, newspaper-sellers, men with briefcases, short-skirted women wearing transparent stockings so that their legs looked bare. But behind the griffins over the gateway, time slowed down and came to a stop. There was another house at the other end of the city, also in the classical style, and also hidden behind a wooden fence and some columns, also with adjoining smaller buildings, and with frightful mythological masks included in the bas-reliefs on its façade. This house had two gates, fauns grinned in the wrought-iron grilles; two shelters stood near the gates, and seated on stools beside these shelters were felt-booted porters in aprons with copper plaques on them. A closed car was drawn up beside one of the gates – black, with a red cross on it, and the word 'Ambulance'.

That day the leading article in the most important of the newspapers was devoted to the third anniversary of the Soviet currency reform. It said that the currency system could only survive on condition that the whole of economic life was based upon rigorously exact economic accounting, on a firm economic foundation. If the country's economic policy failed to correspond to the budget or to the real resources of the State, then without any doubt the financial system would be ruined, however strong it might be. There was also a headline: 'China's Struggle Against the Imperialists.' And other items too. The section 'Foreign News' included messages from Britain, France, Germany, Czechoslovakia, Latvia, America.

There was also a big article, under the fold, on 'The Question of Revolutionary Violence'. The paper further included two pages of advertisements, in which the reader's attention was particularly caught by the two most prominent announcements: 'The Truth About Life: Syphilis', and 'In A Lunatic Asylum, S. Broide's Latest Book.'

Exactly at noon a closed Rolls-Royce pulled up in front of the first house, the house where time slowed down. The sentry opened the door and the C.-in-C. stepped out.

In the office at the far end of the house, the curtains were half drawn across the windows, shutting out the traffic that hurried by on the other side of the panes. A fire was burning in the grate. Three telephones stood on the desk, which was covered with a red cloth, somehow confirming the stillness, along with the logs that crackled in the fireplace. Three telephones, three arteries running through the city into this office, by means of which the city could be controlled from this stillness, and everything known that happened within it. There was a massive bronze writing-set on the desk, and a dozen pencils, red and blue, protruded from the pen-stand. On the wall of the office, behind the desk, were a wireless set with two pairs of earphones, and a whole array of buttons for electric bells, with inscriptions ranging from 'Waiting Room' to 'Guard Alarm'. In front of the desk was an armchair; behind the desk a straight-backed man was sitting on a wooden chair. The curtains were half-drawn, and the electric lamp standing on the table was covered with a green shade, so that it was impossible to see the face of the straight-backed man.

The C.-in-C. crossed the carpet and seated himself in the leather armchair.

The straight-backed man began the conversation.

'Now look, Gavrilov, it's not for us to talk about the grinding-mill of the revolution and all that stuff. It's a pity, of course, but I suppose that history's wheels are to a very large extent set in motion by blood and death, especially where the wheel of revolution is concerned. As I say, it's not for you and me to talk about death and blood. Do you remember the day when we took command of the Red Guards, when they had lost everything, at Ekaterinov? You had a rifle, and so had I. A shell had blown your horse to pieces, but you kept going on foot. The troops began to fall back, but then you killed one of them with your revolver, and stopped a general stampede. Commander, you would have killed me too if I had lost my nerve; and I think you would have been right.'

The second man, the C.-in-C. replied:

'You're very comfortably installed here. Like a minister. Is it all right for me to smoke in here? I don't see any cigarette-ends.'

'Don't smoke; you shouldn't. Your health doesn't allow it. I don't smoke myself.'

'All right; now tell me what's up, without beating about the bush,' said the C.-in-C. in a sharp, harsh voice. 'Why have you summoned me? There's no point in your acting the diplomat. Tell me!'

'I've summoned you because it is imperative that you have an operation. The revolution needs you. I've consulted specialists, and they've told me that you would be fully recovered in a month. It is the Revolution that requires it. The specialists are waiting for you, they'll examine you and take care of everything. I've given orders already. There's even a German among them.'

'Just as you like, old man; but I'm going to smoke nevertheless,' said the C.-in-C. 'My doctors have told me that there's no need for an operation, and everything will clear up without resort to surgery. I feel quite fit, I've no need of an operation, and I don't want one.'

The man at the desk extended his hand behind him, felt for one of the buttons on the wall and pressed it. A secretary entered noiselessly. The first man asked him:

'Is anybody waiting to be seen?'

He made no comment on the secretary's affirmative reply, and dismissed him. Then he continued:

'Comrade Commander, do you remember our discussing the problem of whether or not to send four thousand men to certain death? You ordered that they be sent. And you were right. In three weeks' time you will be fully recovered. You must excuse me, but I have already given the necessary orders.'

A telephone rang. It was not an outside telephone but the inside one, which had only some thirty or forty lines. The man at the desk lifted the receiver, listened, answered and said: 'A note to the French? Ah yes, of course! Let it be done formally, as we decided yesterday. You know, the French are a very slippery lot, like the trout we used to fish for, remember? Eh? Yes, yes, squeeze them tight. That's all.' And he turned to his visitor.

'I'm sorry, Comrade Gavrilov, but there's nothing more to be said about it.'

The C.-in-C. finished his cigarette, stubbed the end of it in the stand of red and blue pencils, and rose from his armchair.

'Goodbye,' he said.

'Au revoir,' replied the other man.

The C.-in-C. walked across the red carpets and reached the outer door; the Rolls-Royce swept him away into the hubbub of the streets. The straight-backed man remained in his office. Nobody else came to see him. Straight-backed as ever, a big red pencil in his hand, he sat leaning over his papers. He rang; the secretary entered, and was told: 'Have this cigarette-end removed – there, in the pen-stand!' And then he fell silent again, leaning over his papers, red pencil in hand. An hour passed, then another. The man still sat over his papers. He was at work. Once, a telephone rang. He lifted the receiver and answered: 'Two million roubles' worth of rubber shoes and textiles to meet the shortage of goods in Turkestan? Yes, certainly. Yes, go ahead! That's all.'

A servant entered quite soundlessly, put on a small table by the window a tray with a glass of tea and a plate of cold meat covered with a napkin, and went out again.

Then the straight-backed man rang for his secretary once more and asked him:

'Is the confidential summary ready?'

The secretary replied that it was.

'Bring it to me, then.'

And once more, and now for a long time, the man fell silent, leaning over a large sheet of paper, over sections of the Commissariat of Foreign Affairs, the Political and Economic Departments of the O.G.P.U., the Commissariats of Finance, Foreign

Trade and Labour. Then, one after the other, there entered his office the two men who with him made up the triumvirate which ruled the whole country ...

At four in the afternoon a number of cars stopped outside the second house, which lay on the edge of the city. The house muffled itself in semi-darkness as though this semi-darkness could keep it warm against the musty damp. At the gate, beside the porters in aprons and felt boots, stood two militiamen. At the main entrance two more militiamen stood on guard, stiff as though on parade. An army officer wearing two Orders of the Red Banner, a man as supple as a withy, entered the house followed by two Red Army men. A man dressed in a long white coat came to meet them in the entrance hall. 'Yes, yes, of course ... '

The room was large and empty. In the middle stood a table covered with oilcloth and surrounded by high-backed chairs of imitation leather, the Government-issue sort, like those they have on the railways. Against one of the walls was a couch, also of imitation leather, covered with a sheet. Near the couch was a wooden stool. In a corner, over a wash-basin, containers with various preparations were set out—a big bottle of corrosive sub-limate, a pot of soft soap ... Yellow towels, which had not been blued by the laundry, hung beside the washbasin.

The first car to arrive brought the specialists—surgeons and physicians. They came into the room, greeting their colleague and host, a tall man, bearded, with a kindly face and a bald patch. Towards him walked Professor Lozovsky, a clean-shaven man of about thirty-five, wearing a frock coat; behind his pince-nez with the straight bridge-piece his eyes seemed banished to the corners of their sockets.

'Yes, yes, of course ... '

The clean-shaven man handed to the bearded one an opened envelope with blobs of sealing-wax on it.

The bearded man extracted a sheet of paper from the envelope, adjusted his glasses, read the paper, again fiddled with his glasses and, with a perplexed air, passed the paper to another of the doctors.

The clean-shaven man said solemnly:

'As you see, it is a secret document; and almost an order. It was brought to me this morning. You understand?'

Fragments of conversation were heard; subdued, anxious voices.
'But why hold a consultation?'

'I was summoned here by express order. The telegram was
signed by the director of the University.'

'Commander-in-Chief Gavrilov, you know, the one who ... '

'Yes, yes, of course ... the Revolution, the Army Commander ...
the regulations ... and ... well, so be it.'

'So there's to be a consultation.'

In this place the electric light threw sharply defined shadows.

One of the doctors buttonholed another; one doctor took another
by the arm and walked a few paces with him ... Suddenly the
rifle-butts of the Red Army men crashed down on the threshold,
there was a sharp click of heels, and the soldiers froze into immobility.
Tall, long as a withy, the young officer with the Orders of the Red
Banner appeared in the doorway and, supple as a whip, sprang to
attention. A moment later the C.-in-C. entered the waiting room,
walking quickly. He brushed his hair back with his hand, adjusted
the collar of his jacket and said:

'Good day, comrades. Do you want me to undress?'

The specialists slowly took their seats on the imitation leather
chairs, put their elbows on the table, spread out their hands upon it,
adjusted their glasses, and asked the patient to sit down. The one
who had handed over the envelope which had been sealed, the one
whose eyes were sunk in their sockets behind his upright pince-nez,
said to the man with the beard:

'Pavel Ivanovich, I presume you won't refuse, as *primus inter
pares*, to take the chair?'

'Am I to undress?' repeated the C.-in-C., putting his hand to
the collar of his jacket.

The man who had been asked to take the chair, Pavel Ivanovich,
pretended not to hear the C.-in-C.'s question and, seating himself
in the armchair, said gravely:

'I think we should begin by asking the patient when he first
noticed anything amiss, and what were the symptoms that told him
he was ill; then we will proceed to examine him ... '

When the consultation was over, a piece of paper lay there
covered with the doctor's illegible handwriting:

'Minutes of consultation between Professor —, Professor —,
Professor —' and so forth, seven times.

'The patient, Citizen Nikolai Ivanovich Gavrilov, complains of aches in the pit of the stomach, vomiting and burning pains. His illness began two years ago without his being aware of it. During this period he has been treated in field hospitals and has undergone courses of treatment at spas, without result. At the request of the patient, the specialists here present have been called into consultation.

Status praesens: The patient's general condition is satisfactory. Lungs: normal. Slight enlargement of the heart; pulse rapid. Some mild signs of neurasthenia. Nothing pathological in the other organs, except the stomach. The patient probably has an *ulcus ventriculi*, requiring operation.

The doctors in consultation propose that Professor Anatoly Kozmich Lozovsky operate on the patient.

'Professor Pavel Ivanovich Kokosov has agreed to assist.'

Place, date, seven signatures of professors.

Later, after the operation had taken place, it was established on the basis of private conversations that, actually, not one of the seven specialists had considered it necessary to operate on Gavrilov, whose illness was developing in a way that did not require surgical intervention; but at the consultation nobody said a word to this effect. The taciturn German alone had alluded to the needlessness of an operation, and he had not insisted after his colleagues had made comments and objections. It was further said that, when the consultation was over, at the very moment when he was getting into his car to go to the Scientists' Club, Professor Kokosov, the one with the bushy eyebrows, had remarked to Professor Lozovsky: 'Well, of course, if it were my brother who had our client's illness I wouldn't operate on him.' To which Professor Lozovsky had answered: 'Of course not, of course not … but, after all, this operation isn't at all dangerous.'

The car back-fired and set off.

The straight-backed man was still sitting in his office in the first house. The windows were carefully hidden by the curtains. Once more a fire was burning in the grate. The house was stiff with silence, as though this silence had been accumulating for a whole century. The man was seated on his wooden chair. Now he had some big books in German and English open on the table before him. In an upright hand he was writing in ink, in Russian, on German lined paper. The books opened before him dealt with the State, with Law, with Power. The light fell from the ceiling into the room and it was now possible to make out the man's face—a very ordinary face, a little on the hard side, perhaps, but concentrated, and not at all tired. The man remained seated for a long time, leaning over his books and his notebooks. Then he rang, and a shorthand-typist came in. He began dictating. The key points of his speech were: the USSR, America, Britain, the whole world and the USSR, the British pound sterling and Russian poods of wheat, American heavy industry, Chinese labour-power. The man spoke in a strong firm voice, and each of his phrases was a formula.

The moon was passing over the city.

Meanwhile, the C.-in-C. was at Popov's home in a room in a big hotel where only Communists lived. There were three of them; Gavrilov sat at the table, with little Natasha jumping about at his feet. Gavrilov was lighting matches, and Natasha, full of wonderment, as only children are, who can marvel at everything which is mysterious in the world—Natasha was rounding her lips and blowing at the flame. Her puff was not strong enough, the match did not go out at once; but in the end it died. And when that happened there was in Natasha's blue eyes so much amazement, joy and fear in the presence of mystery that it was impossible not to light another match, not to bow before this mystery that Natasha had within her.

Then Gavrilov put Natasha to bed. Sitting beside her cot he said to the little girl: 'Listen, close your eyes, and I'll sing you a song.' Thereupon he began singing, without knowing how or what to sing, making it up as he went along.

'The little goat came.
And the little goat said:
"You must be tired, tired, tired, tired, tired".'

He smiled, looked cunningly at Natasha, then at Popov, and sang what the sound of his own last words had put into his head:

'The little goat came
And the little goat said:
"You must be tired, tired, tired, tired, tired—
So sleep, and don't write, write, write, write, write ... ".'

Natasha opened her eyes and smiled, and Gavrilov went on

singing the last two lines in an awkward voice — he was a bad singer —
until Natasha fell asleep. Then Gavrilov and Popov drank tea alone
by themselves. Popov asked:

'Nikolai, would you like me to make some gruel?'

They were seated side by side, chatting in subdued voices,
slowly, without hurrying, and drinking a great deal of tea.

Gavrilov had unbuttoned the collar of his jacket and was drinking
his tea from the saucer. After talking about various matters of no
importance, Popov put aside his cup, still half full, paused and
said:

'Nikolai, I must tell you that my Zina has just left me. She's left
the child with me and gone off with some engineer or other whom
she was in love with before — the devil only knows why. I don't
want to blame her, I don't want to sully myself by abusing her;
but I must say, though, that she has run away like a bitch, without
saying anything to me, on the sly. I feel ashamed myself of what she
has done. You know all about it — how I picked her up in a ditch
at the front, how I cared for her, loved her and, fool that I was,
did everything I could for her. She turned out to be a little gentle-
woman, after all — I hadn't understood her, this woman I lived with
for five years.'

And Popov described all the details of the breach between himself
and his wife, all those foolish things which are grievous just because
of their pettiness, behind which nothing truly great is to be found.
Then they talked about their children, and Gavrilov talked about
his home life, his three big sons, his wife who, though already
getting on in years, remained the only woman in his life.

Before leaving, the C.-in-C. said:

'Lend me a book to read, something quite simple, about good
people and true love. Something like Tolstoy's *Childhood and
Boyhood*.'

All the corners of Popov's dwelling were stacked with books, but
it proved impossible to find a simple book about ordinary human
love, ordinary human relations, ordinary life, the sun shining on
people, and everyday joys. No, there were no such books there.

'Oho,' said Gavrilov, banteringly, 'so that's what your revolutionary literature is like! Well, all right, I'll have to read Tolstoy
once more. Ah, he wrote some fine pages about a pair of old kid
gloves at a ball!'

2

He became gloomy, fell silent, and after a second said, very quietly:

'Listen, Alyosha, I didn't want to talk about it, so as not to waste time in gossip, but still ... Today I went to the Centre, and then to the clinic, where a group of specialists were waiting for me.

'The specialists were full of their wisdom. I don't want to be operated on; of course I'm against it. Tomorrow, however, I am to go under the knife. Well, come along to the clinic. Don't forget our old times together. Don't write anything about it to my wife and children. Goodbye.'

Gavrilov left the room without shaking Popov's hand. There was a closed car standing near the hotel. Gavrilov got in and said: 'Home, to the station,' and the car was soon lost in the maze of streets. The moon glided along the rails in the sidings. A dog ran swiftly by, yelped and disappeared into the black and silent night. A sentry standing beside the steps of the carriage froze to attention as the C.-in-C. approached. The aide-de-camp appeared in the corridor, the waiter showed himself, the electric light came on, and silence—taciturn, blue, provincial—came over the carriage.

The C.-in-C. entered his bedroom, took his boots off and put on his slippers, unbuttoned the collar of his jacket, rang, and called for tea. Then he went into the sitting-room and sat down by the table lamp. The waiter brought tea, but the C.-in-C. did not even touch it. He stayed for a long time over his book, *Childhood and Boyhood*, reading and thinking. Then he went back to his bedroom, fetched a large writing pad, said to his aide-de-camp: 'Some ink, please,' and began writing, slowly, pondering over each phrase. He wrote a letter, read it through, sat deep in thought for a moment, then sealed the envelope. He wrote a second in the same way. Then he wrote a third letter, a very short one which he wrote hurriedly and sealed without reading. In the quiet carriage silence reigned undisturbed. The sentry remained motionless beside the steps. The aide-de-camp and the waiter remained motionless in the corridor. It seemed that time itself had come to a stop. The letters, in their white envelopes with the addresses on, lay for a long time on the table, before the C.-in-C. At last he took a large envelope put the three letters inside it and wrote on the outside: 'To be opened after my death.'

Chapter 3

The first snow fell the day that Gavrilov died. The city lay still in the white silence, all white and calm, and on the trees behind the windows were tomtits which had come to the city with the snow and were scattering snow about them.

Professor Pavel Ivanovich Kokosov always got up at seven, and that was the time he got up on the day of the operation. The professor put his head out from under the clothes, spat, stretched his hairy arm towards the bedside table, felt for his glasses with an habitual gesture, and put them on: they were lost under his bushy brows. Behind the window a tomtit perched on a birch tree was scattering snow all around it. The professor slipped on his dressing gown, slid his feet into his slippers and went into the bathroom.

At the time when he awoke, absolute silence prevailed in the house, but when he came out of the bathroom, grumbling and groaning, his wife Katerina Pavlovna was already in the dining-room noisily stirring sugar in the professor's glass with a tea-spoon, and the samovar was making itself heard.

'Good morning, Pavel Ivanovich,' said the wife.

'Good morning, Katerina Pavlovna,' said the husband.

The professor kissed his wife's hand, sat down facing her, and adjusted his glasses through his bushy brows. He silently gulped his tea and was about to make some routine remark when the traditional ritual of breakfast was disturbed by an unexpected telephone call.

The professor gazed severely at the door which led to his study, where the telephone was ringing; glanced suspiciously at his little tub of a wife, already past her youth, who was dressed in a Japanese kimono, got up, and made his way, still retaining his suspicious air, to the telephone. Shortly afterwards, words spoken by the professor in an unusually senile and querulous voice began to pass over the telephone.

'Well? Well? ... Yes, yes, I can hear you ... Who's speaking and what's it all about?'

The caller was saying that he was speaking from Army Headquarters, where they knew that the operation had been arranged for 8.30. Army Headquarters wished to know whether the professor needed anything. Would the professor like them to send a car for him?

The professor suddenly became angry, snorted and began talking in a shrill voice.

'I, of course, I serve society, not private persons ... Yes, yes, my dear sir, of course, I always take the tram to the clinic. I do my duty as my conscience tells me, if you'll pardon my saying so. I see no reason why I should not go by tram today as usual.'

And the professor hung up noisily, cutting off the caller. Then he sniffed, snorted, and turned back towards the table, his wife and the tea. He sniffed a little again, chewed his moustache, and quickly calmed down. Once more his eyes gleamed from behind his glasses and they were now very concentrated and intelligent. The professor said quietly:

'The peasant Ivan falls ill in the village of Drakiny Luzhi; he lies on the stove for three weeks, then, after praying and groaning and consulting all his relatives, he goes to the district hospital to see Doctor Pyotr Ivanovich. Pyotr Ivanovich has known Ivan for fifteen years, and over those fifteen years Ivan has paid some dozen and a half chickens to Pyotr Ivanovich and has got to know all Pyotr Ivanovich's children—he even pulled the ears of one of them when he was a boy, long ago. Ivan comes to Pyotr Ivanovich and presents him with a hen: Pyotr Ivanovich examines him, listens to his heart and if it's necessary, operates on him—calmly, quietly, sensibly and—no worse than I shall do. And if the operation isn't a success, Ivan dies, they put a cross over him, and that's that ... Or even suppose there comes to me the citizen, Anatoly Yurievich Svintsitsky. He tells me everything, down to the smallest symptom. I examine him, seven times perhaps. I study his case and I tell him: "Go, good sir, live with your ulcer; if you're careful you'll live another fifty years, and if you die—well there's nothing to be done about it. God has called you to him, that's all!" If he says to me: "Operate", then I operate; if he doesn't want me to, I don't.'

He fell silent.

'Today at the clinic I'm going to assist at an operation. They're going to operate on a Bolshevik, the Commander-in-Chief Gavrilov.'

'That's the one who ... ', said Katerina Pavlovna, 'that's the one who's often mentioned in the Bolshevik papers ... A terrible man. But tell me, Pavel Ivanovich, why aren't you operating on him yourself?'

'Well, there's nothing specially to worry about in that,' replied

the professor. 'Nowadays, you know, the young people have to be
brought to the fore, and it's Lozovsky who's going to operate. The
main thing is that, in the last analysis, after this consultation,
although all our great celebrities have examined him in all possible
ways, nobody really knows the patient. The chief difficulty is that
we don't know the man ... We're dealing with a formula, not with a
man, not with a living creature. General Number So-and-So,
whom they write about every day in the papers so as to frighten
people. And just let something go wrong with the operation —
you'll find yourself trailing all across Europe till you forget your
own father.'

Professor Anatoly Kuzmich Lozovsky's room was not in the
least like Kokosov's flat. Whereas the latter preserved and exemplified the Russian taste of the 1890's and early 1900's, Lozovsky's
room had come into being and been furnished between 1907 and
1916. That is to say, it had heavy curtains, a big sofa, bronze
figures of naked women acting as lamp-holders on the oaken desk,
and the walls were covered with hangings, these in their turn being
surmounted by second-rate paintings from the *Mir Iskusstva*
exhibitions.

Lozovsky was lying on the sofa, and he was not alone, but with a
young and pretty woman. His starched shirt-front lay on the carpet.
Lozovsky awoke, gently kissed the woman's shoulder, jumped
vigorously off the sofa, and pulled the curtain-cord. The heavy
hangings slid into the corner of the window and the snowy daylight
entered the room. With the happy air that people have who love
life passionately, Lozovsky gazed out into the street, the snow, the
sky.

At that moment the telephone rang. The professor's telephone
was hung above the sofa, behind the tapestry. He lifted the receiver.
'Yes, yes, I'm listening ... ' Army Headquarters was speaking, asking
if they should send a car for him.

'Yes, yes, please do. Don't worry about the operation, it will be a
splendid success, I assure you. As for the car, yes, please send it,
especially as I have some business to attend to before the operation.
Yes, please, eight o'clock.'

On the appointed day, early in the morning, Popov went to see
Gavrilov. It was not yet dawn, and lamps were still burning everywhere, but Popov was not able to talk with his friend, for the nurse

was taking Gavrilov away to the bathroom to have a last enema before the operation. As he went out, Gavrilov had the time to say only:

'Alyosha, read in Tolstoy's *Childhood and Boyhood* what he says about *comme il faut* and *pas comme il faut*! Ah, what a feeling the old man had for our blood!'

And these were the last words Popov heard Gavrilov utter before he died.

Before the operation, in the corridor linking the operating theatre with the ward where Gavrilov was, people walked about, hurrying, whispering, noiselessly busy. The night before the operation a rubber tube had been passed into the sick man's body; it was a siphon, used to aspirate the gastric juice and wash out the stomach — a hideous apparatus of rubber, the use of which makes one sick and sorry to think about it, and which strikes one as having been specially invented to humiliate human dignity. And so, that morning, immediately before the operation, Gavrilov was given a final enema.

Gavrilov entered the operating theatre wearing a long hospital gown, rough canvas drawers, a shirt with laces instead of buttons, and with numbered slippers on his bare feet. They had changed his garments for the last time that morning, giving him a sterilized set to put on. He arrived looking pale, thin and tired.

In the adjoining room spirit lamps were burning, long nickel boxes were boiling, men in white coats were silently waiting. The operating theatre was a very spacious room: all around, the floor, the walls, the ceiling were decorated with white oil paint. It was exceptionally light in there, for one of the walls was completely of glass and looked out over the river. In the middle of the room a long white table, the operating table. Kokosov and Lozovsky advanced to meet Gavrilov; both men, dressed in white coats, wore white caps upon their heads, like cooks. In addition, Kokosov had covered his beard with a bib, leaving visible only his eyes, and they were lost beneath his bushy brows. Along the wall a dozen men in white coats were lined up.

Accompanied by the nurse, Gavrilov came forward into the room very calmly. In silence he nodded to the professors and approached the table. He glanced out of the window, and clasped his hands behind his back. Another nurse brought in, holding it by a hook, a boiling sterilizer in which some instruments were shifting around, a long nickel box of them.

Lozovsky whispered to Kokosov:

'Shall we begin, Pavel Ivanovich?'

'Yes, yes, of course ... ' answered Kokosov.

And thereupon the professors washed their hands, again and again, drenched them in corrosive sublimate and covered them with tincture of iodine. The anaesthetist checked the mask and examined his bottle of chloroform.

'Let's begin, Comrade Gavrilov,' said Lozovsky. 'Would you mind lying on the table? Please take off your slippers.'

Gavrilov looked at the sister and with a slightly embarrassed air took off his shirt. The sister looked at Gavrilov as though he were an inanimate thing and smiled at him as one smiles at a child.

Gavrilov sat on the table, took off one slipper, then the other, quickly lay down, adjusted the bolster under his head, and closed his eyes. Then, with a swift, habitual, skilful movement, the nurse buckled the thongs over the patient's feet, fastening him to the table. The anaesthetist laid a towel over his eyes, smeared his nose and mouth with vaseline, placed the mask over his face, and took Gavrilov's hand to check his pulse. As soon as he began to pour chloroform over the mask a smell at once sweetish and astringent spread through the room.

The anaesthetist noted the time when the operation began. In silence the professors walked towards the window. While waiting, the sister arranged with forceps on a piece of sterilized gauze scalpels, swabs, forceps, Kocher's forceps, Péan's forceps, artery forceps, needles, silken threads. The anaesthetist added some more chloroform. A deathly silence reigned in the room.

Suddenly the sick man lifted his head and groaned:

'I'm suffocating, take off the mask,' he said, his teeth chattering.

'Just a little longer, please,' replied the assistant.

A few moments later, the patient started talking and singing.

'The ice has broken up ... The Volga is open again ... Darling mine, my darling ... I'm a silly young girl who has fallen in love,' sang the Commander-in-Chief, and then he whispered: 'You're tired, tired, tired.' He was silent for a while then said sternly: 'But never give me cranberry compote again. I'm fed up with it, and it's *pas comme il faut.*'

He fell silent, only to cry out immediately after, in a harsh voice, in that voice which must have rung out over the battlefields:

'No retreat! Not another step back! I'll shoot the lot of you! Alyosha, old man ... We're going at full speed, we can't see the ground any more ... I remember everything. Then I know what the Revolution is, I know its power. And I'm not afraid to die.'

And he began singing again:

'Over the Ural a carpenter lives, darling mine, my darling ... '

'How do you feel? You're not sleepy?' asked the anaesthetist in a low voice. And Gavrilov replied in his ordinary voice, quietly and conversationally:

'Nothing unusual — but I can't breathe.'

'Just a little longer,' said the anaesthetist, adding some more chloroform.

Kokosov looked at his watch in a worried manner and bent over the patient's record-sheet, perusing it once more. They had been putting Gavrilov to sleep for twenty-seven minutes now. Kokosov called a young assistant over and stuck out his face for his glasses to be adjusted on his nose. The anaesthetist, concerned, murmured to Lozovsky:

'Suppose we abandon the chloroform? We could try ether.'

Lozovsky replied:

'Let's carry on with the chloroform. If necessary, we'll have to postpone the operation. Though that wouldn't be convenient.'

Kokosov looked all round him with a stern look and, still worried, lowered his eyes. The anaesthetist added yet more liquid. The professors remained silent.

Gavrilov finally lost consciousness at the forty-eighth minute. Then the professors washed their hands in alcohol for the last time. A nurse exposed Gavrilov's belly, revealing thin ribs and a tight-drawn abdomen. With sweeping movements of his hands, Professor Kokosov washed with spirit, petrol and iodine the area to be operated on, the pit of the stomach. The sister held out towels to cover Gavrilov's head and feet, then poured half a bottle of iodine over Lozovsky's hands.

Lozovsky took a scalpel and drew it across the skin. Blood spurted forth and the skin folded back. From under it fat emerged, yellow like mutton-fat, in layers, veined with blood-vessels. Lozovsky cut again into the human flesh and sliced through the gleaming white fascia crossed by bluish nerves. Kokosov manipulated the Péan's and Kocher's forceps with a swiftness and skill that were surprising in view of his clumsy appearance, and promptly sealed off the bleeding-points.

Taking up another sharp instrument, Lozovsky opened the peritoneum. Then he put his knife aside and wiped away the blood with sterilized swabs. Within, through the incision, the gut and the milky-bluish bag of the stomach could be seen. Lozovsky inserted his hand into the abdominal cavity, delivered the stomach and squeezed it.

On the organ's gleaming flesh, just where the ulcer should have been, there was a white scar, as though modelled in wax and resembling the larva of a dung-beetle. The scar showed that the ulcer had healed already and that the operation had been quite pointless.

But suddenly, just at the moment when Gavrilov's stomach was between Professor Lozovsky's hands, a cry broke the silence ...

'Pulse!' cried the assistant.

'Breathing!' added Kokosov, as though mechanically.

And then Kokosov's malicious, terribly malicious eyes were seen to spring out from under his bushy brows and his glasses and dart this way and that.

As for Lozovsky's eyes, banished to the corners of their sockets near the bridge of his nose, they narrowed still more, sank deeply into his head, concentrated, fused, so to say, into a single eye with a terribly keen gaze.

The patient was pulseless, his heart was not beating, his breathing had ceased and his feet were already cold. It was cardiac shock. The organism was refusing chloroform, was intoxicated with it. It was plain the man would never wake again, that he was bound to die, and that artificial respiration, oxygen, camphor, saline solution or other methods could only put off death for an hour, ten hours, thirty hours, but not more. Strictly speaking, the man was dead already, and there was no way of restoring him to consciousness. It was obvious that Gavrilov was doomed to die under the knife, on the operating table. Professor Kokosov turned towards the nurse, held out his face to have his glasses adjusted, and shouted: 'Open the window! Inject camphor! Prepare the saline!'

The silent crowd of doctors suddenly became more silent than ever. As though nothing had happened, Kokosov bent over his

2*

instruments on the table and was silent, examining them. Lozovsky bent over them too, standing beside him.

'Pavel Ivanovich,' whispered Lozovsky, maliciously.

'Well?' replied Kokosov loudly.

'Pavel Ivanovich?' said Lozovsky in a still lower tone, and there was no longer any malice in his voice.

'Well?' replied Kokosov loudly and added: 'Continue the operation!'

The two professors straightened themselves and looked at each other; the eyes of one seemed to merge into a single eye, the eyes of the other stood out from under the thick hair of his brows. Lozovsky stepped back for a second from Kokosov, as though to avoid a blow, or to get things into perspective; his eye became two eyes again, and they began roving about; a second later they came together again in a look even sharper than before and which had become very penetrating. Lozovsky whispered:

'Pavel Ivanovich ... '

And he lowered his hands on to the wound: he did not sew up the divided tissues, but just tacked them together roughly, then pulled the edges of skin together and began suturing them, just at the surface of the wound. He ordered:

'Release the arms! Artificial respiration!'

They opened the huge window of the operating theatre, and the freshness of the first snow came into the room. Meanwhile camphor was being injected into the man's body. Kokosov, helped by the anaesthetist, pulled back Gavrilov's arms, then lifted them forward again, compelling the man to breathe artificially. Lozovsky was still stitching the wound. He cried out:

'Saline!'

An assistant stuck into the patient's chest two needles nearly as big as cigarettes, so as to introduce into the dying man's bloodstream a thousand cubic millimetres of saline solution, to maintain the blood pressure; Gavrilov's face was blue and lifeless, his lips livid.

Then they took Gavrilov off the table and put him on a trolley in order to take him back to his ward. His heart was beating, he was breathing, but he did not recover consciousness; perhaps he failed to recover consciousness right down to the last moment, when his heart, saturated with camphor and salt by artificial means, at last stopped beating; when, thirty-seven hours later, he died, the camphor and the doctors having given him up. It is possible that he died because, apart from the two professors and the sister, nobody had access to his room until after his last breath.

An hour before the C.-in-C.'s death was officially announced, a chance neighbour in the next ward heard strange sounds coming from the ward where Gavrilov was. It was as though somebody was knocking on the wall, as arrested persons do in prisons. There, in that ward, lay a man who was dead and yet alive, saturated with camphor because medicine holds to the ethical tradition that death cannot be allowed to occur under the surgeon's knife.

The operation had begun at 8.39 and at 11.11 Gavrilov had been removed from the operating theatre on the trolley. In the corridor the porter told Lozovsky that House No. 1 had telephoned for him twice. The professor went to the office, where the telephone was, stood for a moment by the window looking out at the first snow, chewed his fingers, then turned towards the telephone. A second later he was in the midst of that network of thirty or forty lines; he greeted the person at the other end, said that the operation had passed off favourably, but that the patient was still very weak; he and all his colleagues realized that the condition of the Commander-in-Chief was grave. He asked to be excused for not being able to come at once to House No. 1.

Gavrilov was dead. That is to say, Professor Lozovsky, a sheet of paper in his hand, emerged from his ward and, head bent, announced in sad and solemn tones that, to everyone's great regret, the patient, the Commander-in-Chief, Citizen Nikolai Ivanovich Gavrilov, had passed away at 1.17 a.m.

Three-quarters of an hour later, that is, at about 2 a.m. some parties of Red Army men entered the yard of the clinic and immediately took up positions at all the entrances and on all the staircases. At that hour clouds were climbing the sky, followed by the full moon, which seemed to have grown tired of chasing them.

At that hour, Professor Lozovsky, in a closed Rolls-Royce, was hastening to House No. 1. The Rolls glided noiselessly under the gateway with the griffins, past the sentries, and pulled up by the entrance. One of the guards opened the door. Lozovsky made his way to the office where three telephones stood on the red cloth on the desk and where, behind the desk, fixed to the wall, a battery of call-bells stood in line.

Nothing is known of the conversation that took place in the office. It lasted only three minutes; in any case Lozovsky came out very hurriedly from the office, the house and the courtyard, his overcoat over his arm and his hat in his hand, like one of Hoffmann's heroes. The car was not there any longer. Lozovsky staggered as though drunk. Beneath the moon, in the still desert of the night, the streets staggered together with Lozovsky.

Lozovsky, had left, à la Hoffmann, the office in House No. 1, and the man with the straight back remained there alone. The man was standing behind the table, leaning heavily upon it, his weight on his clenched fists. The man's head was bent. For a long time he remained motionless. He was being torn away from his papers, his formulas. Suddenly he began to bestir himself. His movements were angular and formal, like the formulas he dictated every night to his shorthand-typist. He moved very quickly. He pushed one of the bell-pushes behind him and lifted a telephone mouthpiece. To the guard who answered he said:

'A fast, closed car.' Then, over the telephone, he spoke to somebody who had evidently been asleep, somebody who was also a member of the supreme triumvirate. His voice was weak: 'Andrei, old man, another one has left us ... Kolya Gavrilov has died; we have lost our battle-comrade. Please ring Potap and tell him.'

The straight-backed man ordered his driver: 'To the clinic!'

In the dark corridors, sentinels stood on guard. The building kept silence, as silence must be kept in the presence of death. The straight-backed man made his way through the dark corridors to the ward where lay Commander-in-Chief Gavrilov. He passed into the ward where the corpse of the Commander-in-Chief lay on a bed amid a powerful stench of camphor.

Everyone went from the room, leaving only the straight-backed man and Gavrilov's body. The man sat down on the bed, at Gavrilov's feet. Gavrilov's hands lay on the bedclothes, beside his body. His head bent, silent, the man remained a long time beside the body. Silence reigned. The man took Gavrilov's hand, pressed it, and said:

'Farewell, comrade. Farewell, brother.' And he went out, head bent. Without looking at anyone, he said:

'The ventilator must be opened, one can't breathe in there.'
He disappeared quickly down a dark corridor.

Last Chapter

In the evening, after the funeral of Commander-in-Chief Gavrilov, after the military fanfares had died away and there had come an end to the dipping of flags in mourning before the coffin, after thousands and thousands of people had passed sorrowfully before the tomb, and when the corpse had begun to freeze in the ground like the ground itself, Popov fell asleep in his hotel room, waking up at an uncertain hour to find himself sitting at his table. It was dark, and Natasha was crying softly. Popov bent over his daughter, took her in his arms and walked about the room with her.

The white moon, tired of hurrying, was there outside the window. Popov went to the window, looked out at the snow, and the silent night. Natasha got down from her father's arms and stood leaning on the window-sill.

In his pocket Popov had Gavrilov's letter, the last words that the C.-in-C. had written, during the night before he had been taken to hospital. He had written in this letter:

'Alyosha, my old friend! I knew, after all, that I was going to die. Forgive me, but let me say that you are no longer very young. When I was rocking your little girl in my arms I suddenly had an idea. My wife too is already getting on, and you have known her for nearly twenty years. I have written to her. You write to her as well. Settle down together, the two of you, get married. Bring up the children. Forgive me, Alyosha.'

Natasha was standing at the window-sill and Popov saw that she was filling her cheeks with air, rounding her lips and, as she gazed at the moon, puffing at it.

'What are you doing, Natasha?' asked her father.

'I want to blow the moon out,' was Natasha's answer.

The full moon, looking like a merchant's wife, was gliding along behind the clouds, very weary from having hurried so much. It was the hour when the huge machine of the city was awaking, when the hooters of the factories, sounded, rending the air. They sounded long and slowly—one, two three; and merging together, they sent up a grey moaning over the city. Truly, it was the soul of the frozen city that through those hooters was moaning beneath the moon ...

An Adventure *by* Andrei Platonov

Novy Mir, 1928/VI

Translated by Olive Stevens

The change and uncertainty of the 1920s in Soviet Russia, when the Communist Party forced into effect a social and economic revolution with methods that were not only often harsh but involved many baffling reversals of policy, produced in literature a corresponding proliferation of trends and schools which now seem bewildering in their finely-shaded ideological differences and their loud claims to unique superiority. To use an expression coined by Mao Tse-tung in an analogous phase of the Chinese revolution, it was the period of 'a hundred flowers', when nearly as many theories of art and literature contended for primacy.

One of the least strident and most interesting of these literary factions which arose during the N.E.P. (New Economic Policy)* period was the so-called *Pereval* group, which took its name—meaning 'Mountain Pass'—from the title of an article by its guiding spirit and organizer, Alexander Voronsky. Founded in 1924, *Pereval* attracted a number of young aspirant writers, most of them already veterans of the Civil War, who felt that they had something to say but needed to learn how to say it. Their association rested on an acknowledged need to learn the craft of writing, whilst rejecting the brash dogmas and noisy polemics of other literary cliques. Unlike most such 'schools', *Pereval* was not politically exclusive: among its members were both sincere fellow travellers and Communist Party members

Apart from Voronsky himself (whose chief service to Soviet literature, was his inspiring editorship of the first Soviet 'thick' journal, *Krasnaya Nov'*), three of the most distinguished writers in the group were Artyom Vesyloy, Ivan Kataev and Andrei Platonov (1896–1951). All of them suffered varying degrees of

* The New Economic Policy (1921–27) was inaugurated by Lenin at the end of the Civil War. The policy was intended to restore the shattered Russian economy by a partial return to private enterprise in trade, industry and agriculture.

47

attack and persecution when a militant rival school known as RAPP mounted a fierce campaign against *Pereval* in 1930, which ended in 1932 with the dissolution of all the warring literary factions. In 1935 Voronsky was arrested as a Trotskyist and died in prison that year, while Vesyoly, Ivan Kataev and Platonov were all rounded up at the height of the purges in 1937. Platonov was the only one to survive and emerge from the prison camps. Some collections of his stories were published after his return, but they lacked much of the vigour, sensitivity and stylistic originality of his earlier writing.

Though he began his career as a poet, prose soon became Platonov's chosen medium, and the beginning of his *Pereval* period was strongly influenced by two classic writers of the early and late nineteenth century respectively—Gogol and Leskov. With them he shared a strong identification with the 'little man', the underdog, who struggles to maintain his identity and self-respect in a harsh and uncaring world. Whilst this remained his central preoccupation, Platonov's themes and styles adapted themselves to the harsh dynamics and fast-changing reality of Soviet society. At a time when the worth and the suffering of the individual seemed to count for less and less, Platonov's writing became a sustained plea for compassion towards the plight of the embattled individual. Simultaneously, in a search for a fixed point of moral reference and an unchanging value in a situation where all values were being overturned, Platonov looked to nature and the moral implications of man's need to maintain a healthy, stable *modus vivendi* with the forces of nature—something which he saw as fatally threatened by the violent pace of industrialization and social change.

Often, the central characters of Platonov's stories were obvious victim-figures of the accelerating Stalinist revolution—individual craftsmen, artisans or peasants hopelessly disorientated by the loss of their erstwhile place in society. But he was too subtle an observer to stick to this over-schematic political viewpoint, and in the story selected for this anthology, laconically entitled *An Adventure*, the suffering hero is a communist. A lonely, idealistic and intelligent man rather than the stock brutal commissar, he understands the real needs of the surly and uncooperative peasants whom it is his duty to help, and he wants to bring them to see the advantages of a rational, constructive approach to their problems in place of the lethargic fatalism which is causing the countryside to slither into dereliction. His efforts, however, are brutally nullified and he himself is killed by the terrible, elemental force of peasant anarchy which the revolution had awakened and which, ten years later, was still a force to be reckoned with.

This story, with its wide-ranging human and social implications, is told by Platonov with impressive concision and economy. The echoes of the author's apprenticeship as a poet can be heard in the frequent and rivetingly exact images, particularly where he expresses the subtle interplay of ambiguous relationships between man and nature. At this stage (1928) Platonov had left his nineteenth-century exemplars stylistically far behind, and was greatly influenced by his contemporary, Pilnyak, a writer who had developed an angular, oblique, allusive style (owing much to the theories of the Formalist school of criticism) which aimed at an effect of objectivity by the cool, rather detached building up of a mosaic of factual observation in place of the traditional realist method of direct narration. In the hands of a second-rate writer this method can become extremely tedious; its reappearance lately, for instance, in the French *nouveau roman* as practised by such writers as Alain Robbe-Grillet, can lead to the *reductio ad absurdum* of total unreadability. Such is Platonov's skill, however, that we are kept permanently aware of the human mainsprings of the action by the way he carefully laces the conscious 'objectivity' of the narrative with telling hints of the subjective reality beneath the surface.

Dvanov was a man used to wide horizons. Before his eyes there stretched the narrow valley of some ancient, long-dried-up river. In this valley was the village of Petropavlovka, a great herd of starving farmsteads jostling around a crowded waterhole.

Dvanov saw the boulders in the village street. Carried down here long ago by glaciers, they now lay strewn between the cottages and served as seats for ruminating old men.

Dvanov thought of these stones as he sat in the Petropavlovka village soviet. He had called there to get a night's lodging and write an article for the local paper. Dvanov wrote that nature cannot create anything ordinary, and that is why what nature does is good.

But nature never gives anything away; she demands patience. To build socialism in the steppe lands, water must be brought up to the high steppe from the few watercourses and dug deep out of the ground. By prospecting for water, Dvanov wrote, we shall at the same time also achieve our dearest aim—we shall be understood and loved by the peasants, who still do not care for us; because love is earned not by gifts but by constructive help.

Dvanov had the ability to combine human insight with political sense, and it was this which inspired his devotion to the common good.

Dvanov had begun to be tormented by the conviction that he already knew how a socialist order could be created in the steppe lands, yet nothing had so far been achieved. He could not long endure the gulf between vision and reality. The nerves running from his head were as live as hot wire, and what his head thought was quickly transformed into movement, manual work and action. Dvanov's perceptions were like hunger which can be neither denied nor forgotten.

The soviet refused to let Dvanov have a cart, and the peasant whom everybody called God pointed out to Dvanov the road to the village of Kaverino, which was twenty versts from the railway.

By midday Dvanov had reached a road that climbed out of the valley. Below him lay the dark gulley of a slow-moving steppe river. But he could see that the river was dying: it had silted up, and instead of flowing, it had spread itself out into marshland. An autumnal melancholy hung over these marshes. The fish had gone to the bottom, the birds had flown away, and the insects made no sound among the withered sedge. Living creatures love warmth and the stimulating light of the sun; here, in deep lairs, their cheerful noise was muffled and reduced to a whisper.

Dvanov believed in listening to nature, in drawing from it every sad or joyful sound from which to make songs that were as mighty as the forces of nature and as enticing as the wind. In this remote place Dvanov talked long and loud to himself. He liked talking to himself in open spaces. Talking to oneself is an art, while talking to other people is an amusement. That is why man seeks company and hence amusement, just as water runs downhill.

Turning his head through half a circle, Dvanov surveyed this field of vision and started talking again in order to think:

'Everything comes from nature. These hills and streams are not just things to write poetry about. They can be used to water the soil, feed cows and people and move machinery.'

Within sight of the smoke from the village chimneys of Kaverino the road ran high above a ravine. The air in the ravine was thickening into mist. Below were silent bogs, the retreat perhaps of strange folk who had turned aside from the confusion of life to the simplicity of contemplation.

From the depths of the ravine came the panting of tired horses. People were approaching, and their horses were struggling in the mud.

A brave young voice at the head of the cavalcade broke into song:

> 'There is a distant country
> Away on another shore,
> We live there in our dreams
> But the foe has gone before ... '

The horses' pace quickened. The detachment roared out a chorus, drowning the singer in front, but with their own refrain from a different song:

> 'Grow, grow, grow little apple
> Till you're golden ripe and fat,
> Till the Soviets come with their sickle
> And hammer to smash you flat.'

The solitary singer went on, out of tune with the others:

> 'My sword and my heart are with me here
> But my happiness lies far, far away ... '

The troop drowned the end of the verse with their chorus:

> 'Hey, little apple, see little apple,
> What a tasty morsel you'll be.
> Once you grew upon a tree
> And the tree belonged to me.
> But the Soviets have come
> And now you're gone ... '

The men whistled a chorus, then they finished the song with a great roar:

'Oh, little apple,
It's better to be free—
Don't let tsar or Soviet
Take what belongs to me.'

The singing faded. Dvanov stopped, interested by this cavalcade passing along the ravine.

'Hi, you up there,' someone shouted to Dvanov from the troop, 'come down and meet the Anarchists!'

Dvanov stayed where he was.

'Hurry up,' rang out a deep voice, probably the man who had led the singing. 'Move before I count ten, or I'll get you in my sights.'

Dvanov could not decide what to do, and said the first thing that came into his head

'Why don't you come up here? It's drier. Why bog your horses down in that ditch, you gang of kulaks?'

The men below him stopped.

'Put one through him, Nikita', ordered the deep voice.

Nikita raised his rifle, but first put himself right with God by shouting, 'By the scrotum of Jesus Christ, by the rib of the Holy Mother and by all the saints—take that!'

Without hearing a sound, Dvanov saw the tight spurt of flame and rolled down to the bottom of the ravine as if knocked off his feet by a crowbar. He did not lose consciousness, and as he rolled downward he heard a terrible roar coming from the ground as first one ear and then the other was pressed against it. Dvanov knew that he had been wounded in the right leg. It seemed that a metal bird had pierced it and was fluttering the sharp tips of its wings.

At the bottom of the ravine Dvanov clasped the warm leg of a horse, which comforted him. The leg was trembling slightly from fatigue, and smell of sweat and grass from the paths it had trodden.

'Put him out of his misery, Nikita. You can have his clothes.'

Dvanov heard this. He clutched the horse's leg with both hands, and the leg gave him the support of a living body. Dvanov's heart rose into his throat, and he cried out as he felt that delirium of the senses when life flows away from the heart and outward to the skin. Immediately he felt relief and a satisfying calm. Nature had drawn from Dvanov the substance for which she had created him: his seed. In that last moment of life, as he embraced the earth and the horse, for the first time Dvanov felt a clamorous lust for life, and was amazed at the impotence of his conscious mind compared with this bird of immortality which had brushed him with its tattered, quivering wing.

Nikita came up to Dvanov and touched his forehead to see if he were still warm. Nikita's hand was large and hot. Dvanov did not want this hand to be taken from him too soon, and he gently put the palm of his own hand over it. But Dvanov knew what Nikita was looking for, and to help him he said:

'Hit me on the head, Nikita. Split my skull as quick as you can.'

Nikita was not at all like his hand—Dvanov guessed this—and he shrieked in a thin, grating voice which had nothing in common with the gentle, life-giving warmth of his hand:

'So you're still alive. I'm not going to split you apart. I'm going to hack you to pieces—slowly. Why should you die quickly? You're a man, aren't you? So you lie there and suffer a bit. You won't like it, but when you do die you'll be glad of it.'

The legs of the leader's horse came up. The deep voice cut off Nikita sharply.

'If you start tormenting that man, you swine, I'll hack you to bits myself. Do as you're told—finish him off. You can have his clothes. How many times do I have to tell you this troop's not just a mob? We're Anarchists.'

'The creed of life, freedom and order!' said Dvanov as he lay there. 'What is your name?'

The leader laughed.

'Isn't that all the same to you now? Mrachinsky.'

Dvanov forgot about death. He had read Mrachinsky's *Adventures of a Modern Wandering Jew*.

'Are you the writer? I've read your book. Not that it matters to me now, but I liked your book.'

'Make him take his own clothes off. Why should I bother undressing a dead man? It'll be a job to turn him over,' said Nikita, bored with waiting. 'His clothes are tight-fitting, they'll get torn, and there'll be nothing left for me

Dvanov began to undress, so as not to disappoint Nikita. He was right; it is impossible to undress a dead man without tearing his clothes. The pain had stopped, but his right leg was numb and would not bend. Nikita noticed this, and gave him a friendly helping hand.

'Is this where I hit you?' he asked, carefully lifting Dvanov's leg.

'Yes, just there.'

'Well, never mind. The bone isn't broken and the wound will heal. You're a young fellow. Are your parents still alive?'

'Yes,' replied Dvanov.

'Well, you'll have to leave them,' said Nikita. 'They'll grieve a bit, and then they'll forget. Mourning's all parents do nowadays. You're a Communist, aren't you?'

'Yes, I'm a Communist.'

'That's your business. Everybody wants to be on the winning side.'

The leader was looking on in silence. The other Anarchists were busy with the horses and had begun to smoke, paying no attention to Dvanov and Nikita. The last gleam of twilight had faded above the ravine and night had fallen, as it must.

'So you liked my book?' asked the leader.

By now Dvanov had already taken off his waterproof cape and his trousers. Nikita was putting them into his bag.

'I've already said I liked it,' Dvanov repeated, looking at the oozing wound in his leg.

'And are you in sympathy with the idea of the book—with ever-lasting anarchy, what you might call man's wandering soul?' asked the leader searchingly.

'No,' Dvanov declared. 'The idea is nonsense, but the book is powerfully written. It happens like that sometimes. In this book you look on man as though you were a monkey looking at Robinson Crusoe. You get it all wrong, but it sounds splendid.'

The leader was so surprised that he rose up in his stirrups.

'That's very interesting. Nikita, we'll take this Communist as far as Limann's farm. He'll be all yours then.'

'But what about his clothes?' grumbled Nikita.

Dvanov made his peace with Nikita by agreeing to be naked for the short span of life that was left to him.

The leader did not object, but merely said to Nikita as a warning:

'Mind you don't do me out of him accidentally. This is a Bolshevik intellectual—a rare type.'

The troop set off. Dvanov held on to Nikita's stirrup and tried to hop on his left leg. His right leg did not actually hurt, but if he stood on it he felt the shot again and bits of metal pricking him from inside.

The ravine ran deep into the steppe until it narrowed and rose up to the level of the plain. A night wind blew steadily; naked, Dvanov hopped energetically on his one leg, and this warmed him.

As he rode along, Nikita went through Dvanov's clothes in a proprietary manner.

'You wetted yourself, you devil!' Nikita said without any ill-feeling. 'You're all like babies. I've never had a clean one yet. Even if you send them to the latrine first, they all shit themselves. Only had one good one, a district commissar. "Snuff out the candle," he said. "Goodbye to the Party, goodbye my children." He stayed clean. Amazing man ...'

Dvanov pictured this amazing man to himself, and he said to Nikita.

'It'll be your turn to be shot soon, clothes and all. We don't go in for wearing dead men's clothes.'

Nikita was not offended.

'You go on hopping. This is no time for you to be chattering your head off. I'm not going to dirty my pants, brother, you won't get the shit out of me.'

'I won't look,' Dvanov said soothingly to Nikita. 'And if you do, I won't hold it against you.'

'Nor do I hold it against anybody,' said Nikita with embarrassment. 'What does it matter to me? It's only their things I want.'

It took them about two hours to reach Limann's farm. While the Anarchists went around talking to the owners, Dvanov shivered in the wind. He pressed his chest against a horse to get warm. Then they began to lead the horses away, and Dvanov was left alone. As he led away his horse, Nikita said to him:

'Go where you like. You won't get far on one leg.'

Dvanov thought of hiding, but he was so weak that he could only sink to the ground. Alone in the darkened farmstead, he burst into tears. The farm was quiet, the bandits had all found billets and had gone to bed. Dvanov crawled to a shed and lay down in the millet straw. All night he dreamed the dreams that are more real than life itself and so cannot be remembered. He woke up in the silence of deepest night, the time when legend has it that children grow. There were tears in his eyes from crying in his sleep. He remembered that today he would die, and he hugged the straw as if it were a living body.

He fell asleep again.

In the morning Nikita only found him with great difficulty, and at first he thought that Dvanov was dead because he was smiling fixedly all over his face as he slept. But this was because Dvanov's unsmiling eyes were closed. Nikita knew dimly that a living man never laughs with the whole of his face: there is always sadness somewhere—in the eyes, or in the mouth.

Reminiscences of A. Blok *by* Andrei Biely

Novy Mir, 1933/III

Translated by Vera Dixon

The passage which follows, an extract from Andrei Biely's *Reminiscences of A. Blok*, contrasts strongly in mood, style and content with almost everything else in this anthology, with the possible exception of Pasternak's *People and Situations* (pp. 359–415). This element of sheer contrast is one of the reasons for its inclusion, since part of its interest is that it strikes a note very different from most Soviet literature of the period. Biely's *Reminiscences* are literally a voice from another age. Not only do they describe the years at the turn of the century; their very appearance in the *Novy Mir* of 1933 was an anachronism, for they were a reprint of a long essay which had first been published (in a very small edition) eleven years earlier. The fact, too, that they are so remarkably out of key with the Stalinist writing which was gaining the upper hand all around is an example of the courage shown by Polonsky in his editorial policy.

The extract, however, has much more to it than mere curiosity value. Both its subject, the poet Alexander Blok (1880–1921), and its author Andrei Biely (1880–1934)—whose real name was Boris Bugayev—are two of the most outstanding figures of the Russian symbolist movement. Despite the fact that the literature of the Soviet period could not possibly, it would seem, be more remote in spirit from the mysticism and the triple-distilled aestheticism of the symbolists, the influence of Blok on Soviet Russian poetry has been second only to Mayakovsky, while there is a case for holding that Biely's imaginative prose (in particular his novel *Petersburg*) exerted a powerful seminal influence on Soviet prose-writing in its most creative phase—the 'twenties and early 'thirties.

The symbolist movement, which dominated Russian letters in the first decade of this century, was a phenomenon so multiform, so rich, and yet so resistant to definition that to describe it succinctly is not merely difficult but self-defeating, since every statement made about it seems to require immediate qualification and, indeed, contradiction. In general terms, symbolism was the central and dynamic

element in the astonishing cultural renaissance which Russia experienced in every branch of the arts between the late 'nineties and
the First World War. Its spirit animated not only a *pléiade* of poets—
Balmont, Bryusov, Zinaida Gippius, Annensky, Vyacheslav Ivanov
—of whom Blok was, in a sense, only the first of his peers; it over-
flowed into music, and was the mainspring of the creative upsurge
in the theatre, ballet and painting. It was, in fact, from the fusion of
the latter two arts through the entrepreneurial genius of Diaghilev
that the outside world first became widely aware of that tremendous
artistic outburst in Russia of which symbolism was the inspiration
and exemplar.

Although intellectually and aesthetically linked with the movement
by countless indissoluble strands, Blok resisted attempts to include
him in a specifically symbolist 'school' of poetry and preferred to
see himself as an individualist struggling alone to master his destiny
through poetry. Whilst symbolism in Russia owed its initial impulse
to the French symbolist poets—Rimbaud, Verlaine, Mallarmé and
Baudelaire, the latter above all—the Russians with their apparently
ingrained urge to universalize ideas which in their Western European birthplace usually had a much narrower connotation, seized
upon symbolist theories and virtually elevated them to the all-
embracing significance of religion. Where Baudelaire had sought
refuge in a *rêve infini* of poetry as an escape from unbearable reality,
the Russian symbolists, and Blok in particular, took a much more
sanguine view of their art: for them it provided a channel to the
perception of a higher reality towards which they, as a kind of
priestly caste, were bound to point the way. It is from this aspect of
symbolist thought that derives the hieratic, even prophetic tone
which pervades so much of their poetry.

As an artist at a time when artists had very consciously donned
the mantle of the seer, Blok tended to function on such an elevated
plane that some of his most cherished ideas proved to be cruelly
out of tune with Russian reality, few of them more so than his perception of the Bolshevik revolution as a cleansing, apocalyptic
phenomenon which heralded a kind of mystical rebirth of the
Russian people purged of their erstwhile failings—a concept expressed in his masterpiece *The Twelve* (1918), in which a non-
descript band of Red Guards is symbolically identified with the
company of the Apostles. After that the collision between dream and

reality (because in a very real sense the universe of the symbolists had been a dream world) proved too much for Blok: for the remaining three years of his life he fell into creative sterility, and he died in a state of profound depression. Such was his poetic stature, however, that largely on the ambiguous evidence of *The Twelve* the Soviet ideologues have given Blok the posthumous status of a great *Soviet* poet—a piece of sleight-of-hand which has had the fortunate result of perpetuating the best of symbolist poetry in an age in which its mystical idealism would otherwise be anathema.

Andrei Biely, himself a poet, novelist, critic and theoretician of symbolism, which he preached with a greater intensity than Blok ever did, was for years Blok's close friend and admirer. At one point he was an even greater admirer of Blok's wife, the beautiful Lyubov Dmitrievna, who had been the inspiration of Blok's first volume of passionately elevated love poetry, *Verses on the Fair Lady.* As a thoroughgoing symbolist, Biely idealized his all too earthly feelings for Lyubov Dmitrievna and created around her a cult in which her being and her every action was invested with a higher, transcendent significance. In 1906 Biely fell in love with her, almost persuaded her to leave Blok, and challenged him to a duel, which Blok sensibly disregarded. Their friendship revived in time, and for a decade and a half Biely lived, worked and exchanged thoughts with Blok in something like intimacy.

Immediately after Blok's death, Biely set down his impressions of the years of their friendship, and in doing so created a unique record not so much of the factual aspect of their relationship as of the feel, the physical and emotional essence of a whole epoch of Russian literature—their private jokes, their amusements, their likes and dislikes, their connections with various journals and publishing houses, their friends, enemies and admirers. The result is a somewhat allusive, elliptical, indeed rather precious, yet charming and illuminating memoir. The footnotes, except for one on p. 84, are supplied by the present editor and replace those printed in *Novy Mir*.

On January 10th, 1904, which was a frosty, glowing sort of day, the front-door bell rang and I was called to the door. There I saw an elegantly dressed woman emerging from her furs, and a tall student hanging up his coat, his milk-white gloves gripped in one hand, his peaked cap already removed.

The Bloks had arrived!*

He wore a well-cut, close-fitting frock-coat, with wide shoulders and a narrow waist, its high blue collar propping up his chin. Lyubov Dmitrievna, the poet's wife, was dressed with stylish severity, and the air was rich with perfume. A gay, young and exquisitely elegant couple!

But ... was it possible that this was Alexander Blok—this young man with cheeks reddened by the weather rather than by sudden blushes? He looked more like the hero of some fairy tale, or a well-built military man, with his carefully controlled, economical movements and charmingly shy face. His head tilted a little to one side, he smilingly approached me, embarrassment in his blue eyes set deep within folds of skin and narrowed with the obvious strain of scrutinizing me. He stood there, shuffling his feet (rather like the young Gerhart Hauptmann):

'Boris Nikolayevich?'

We greeted each other, and kissed.

The image which I had conjured up after reading his poems was quite different. I had imagined him short, with a pale, sickly, heavily-jowled face, small feet, badly-tailored clothes, hair brushed back and troubled eyes, full of a phosphorescent glow, eternally gazing at distant horizons; that was the Blok of my daydreams:

> Oh, I am pale as palest snow,
> Hard of mind yet weak in heart.

A curly mop of thick, gingery hair, intelligent forehead with one deep furrow, smiling lips, and eyes peering closely at me and showing a surprising degree of embarrassment.

What a disappointment!

My mood transmitted itself to A.A. Disconcerted by my confusion, he lingered for some time by the coat-stand, smiling uncertainly and trying to push his gloves into his coat pocket, while I endeavoured to hang up his coat. His elegant wife, however, showed no embarrassment whatsoever. Carrying a huge fur muff, without taking off her small hat, her face glowing with the cold, her hair

* The meeting took place at the Moscow apartment of Sergei Solovyov.

glinting gold, she sailed into the room into which I was intending to usher my guests, and where my mother was already waiting for them.

We sat down in the drawing-room, not knowing what to do or what to say. Lyubov Dmitrievna sat a little apart and observed us silently.

I remember a rose-coloured, checkered ray of light filtering through the window-blind on to the poet's soft, gingery curls, his blue eyes, and an elbow resting on the arm of an oddly-shaped, old-fashioned chair. But I remember little of what was said—the talk was of ordinary, everyday matters ... about Moscow, about mutual friends, about 'The Griffin',* about Bryusov† and even about a subject we found difficult, yet knew had to be thoroughly discussed, namely paying calls. At this, we all three smiled.

The ice began to thaw, but as Blok was rather melancholy and I was an optimist, we both still had something to conceal from those around us. He felt a stranger to student life, to his stepfather,‡ to his relations, to the Mendeleyevs,§ to that very close military circle within which he moved (he lived in the barracks); he was often pained by people's lack of tact, and felt a revulsion towards frivolous gossip which he concealed under the guise of extra good manners or 'good form'. I can best describe it in poetic terms, as follows— being anapaestic in things intimate, he wore his coat like an iambic.

I could not master the iambic, but expressed myself in amphi-brachs; in alternating, intermittent, very short verse lines. My style of expressing myself was nervous confusion in the presence of others, combined with inner calm; his was the opposite—inwardly burning, outwardly calm.

A meeting of opposites.

On looking at me, anyone would say I was a native of Moscow; educated, if occasionally lacking in tact; my only luxury a rarely worn frock-coat; my everyday jacket was like a sack, because I did not bother to have it made to measure, but bought it off the peg in a cheap shop and was too lazy even to try it on. On looking at Blok, anyone might have said he was a member of the nobility, with his strained, good-mannered smile that was not unlike a politely

* Publishing house (1903–14) founded by Sergei Sokolov.
† See below, p. 69n.
‡ After divorce in 1889, Blok's mother married an army officer.
§ Blok's father-in-law was the celebrated physicist, Dmitry Mendeleyev.

stifled yawn. But his heart was gentle and compassionate towards
the poor and towards those close to him. I looked more cultured,
weaker, more nervy, more absentminded, more the middle-class
leftist than he; he seemed healthier and more intellectual than I.
Neither of us personified the style of our poetic writing; no one
would say, glancing at Blok, that he was the author of his cycle of
'visions';* he looked like an even tougher writer than Turgenev,
and like Turgenev he went shooting in hunting-boots and with a
red setter at his heels. A look at me, and people might guess: a
versifier, 'searching for the ideal'. To compound Blok's incomprehension of me, I was at that time distressed by the failure of the
'circle'† and my tangled relations with N.‡

Appearances are not reality.

Beneath Blok's nobleman's mask there undoubtedly lived both
Pestel§ and Lermontov;‖ whereas beneath my 'ideals' was a firmly
ensconced methodologist, always proving and looking for a sympathetic response, with an outgoing manner of speech which I
would specially adjust to my companion of the moment. Thus,
although I was always hurrying forward and tended to trip over my
own words, I was firmer, calmer and—yes—more patient. He could
not stand some conversations which I stoically endured.

Soon afterwards Blok confessed to me that there had been a
moment during that first meeting when he did not believe in me,
feeling that I was not the person he had imagined; I too felt this
reflection of myself in him. 'Bugayev is quite unlike what I thought
him to be', he wrote to his mother from Moscow.

That day I felt he was my senior (we were the same age).

Another point: if A.A. had been questioned about our meeting,
he would have briefly mentioned the inner rapport which arose
between us without going into psychological details and nuances.
He later wrote to his mother as follows: 'The door of the Solovyov
flat has a plate saying "Doctor Zatonsky". Bugayev and Petrovsky¶
say that he no longer exists—drowned in the bulrushes.' A some-

* Biely's name for Blok's cycle *Verses on the Fair Lady* (1903).

† Biely's literary coterie, 'The Argonauts', disrupted by his quarrel with Bryusov.

‡ Nina Petrovskaya, whose love affair with Biely ended in her attempt to
shoot him.

§ A leader of the abortive Decembrist revolt in 1825; executed by Nicholas I.

‖ M. Y. Lermontov (1814–41). The supreme lyric poet of Russian romanticism.

¶ A. S. Petrovsky. Friend of Biely; the Russian translator of Jakob Böhme.

what cryptic character-sketch. Or else: 'A gentleman ... whom I would define as "the man with the bandaged belly",' or, 'Bugayev, Petrovsky and I sit listening to the whistling wind. Rejoicing.'

As far as I was concerned, however, I listened to the overtones and the nuances, ignoring the words; I have forgotten the whole of our first conversation, only remembering that I had to admit how difficult it was to talk to him. He, however, dotted the 'i':

'*Very* difficult!'

As I tried to analyse the difficulties, I pulled myself up, suddenly realizing that such analysis is out of place at a first meeting; Blok endured it all with good grace and surprised me with the calm strength of his silence, emanating from his sunburnt, very healthy, pink-cheeked, young and extremely handsome face. There was no 'Knight of the Fair Lady'* about him, there was nothing of old stained-glass windows, of the Middle Ages, or of Dante about him; a touch of Faust, perhaps.

Thanks to this particular strength, he was able to bring light to any conversation, radiating great personal warmth; but any feeling of 'airiness' was missing.

He listened with his large head tilted a little, then nodding slightly to stress his words which he spoke in a loud but at the same time strangled and slightly wooden voice. Emitting little puffs of cigarette smoke, he screwed up his eyes and carefully examined the pale strips of light from the sun's rays.

He reminded me of a backwater from whose hidden depths a huge fish rises to the surface; there were no aphoristic ripples, or small, darting fish blowing up the tiny bubbles of paradoxes to which I had grown used while listening to Rachinsky† and Ellis.‡ He spoke in a rather weighty manner, briefly, positively, slightly hoarsely and with few gestures, only occasionally tapping the ash off his cigarette; and yet wisdom emanated from his laconic words. The ease with which he seemed to agree with everything so readily was merely inertia, laziness. Press him really hard when he said, 'Perhaps so', and he would take it back:

'On second thoughts, perhaps not ... You know, Borya, I disagree.' After that there was no changing his mind.

* Another reference to Blok's cycle *Verses on the Fair Lady*.
† Relative and guardian of Sergei Solovyov, q.v. below, p. 64.
‡ Pseudonym of L. L. Kobylinsky, poet and translator of Baudelaire.

Everything said at that first meeting has become clear to me, but it called for a sustained mental effort. I had expected him to have an airy quality of lightness about him, but his intellectuality crushed me.

The Bloks departed.

I remember the cold, the dim fading sunset, the pervading sadness, and I went to see Petrovsky, to share my impression of the Bloks with him. We found ourselves walking along the Nikitsky Boulevard and I suddenly burst out laughing.

'You know what!' I exclaimed. 'He is a carrot and his wife is a turnip!' and seizing on this schoolboy joke, we laughed away our sad, frivolous, confused thoughts.

Around the Samovar

During the first days of the Bloks' stay in Moscow, I tried to get to know them. That very same evening Petrovsky and I joined them at Seryozha's* cosy flat, which consisted of three small rooms crammed with all the furniture from the much larger flat on the Arbat.

There was now more ease and warmth between me and the Bloks. Seryozha, who was A.A.'s third cousin, was one of my closest friends, and he quickly put an end to formality, flitting from subject to subject, flinging out words, throwing his arms around—and even objects. He would jump up excitedly, raising his eyebrows and hunching his shoulders as he swayed over the tea-table, thrusting out his arm and jabbing the air with two fingers. Then he would stamp his feet, and nearly split his sides laughing. There was something very charming about him—still a boy, and yet a man matured by the strains and stresses of his life. With no one to lean on, and a horde of relatives who were a burden on his childlike shoulders; even his guardian, Rachinsky, a man of warmth, passion and great sincerity, was not unlike a blustering, scorching storm, a person who clearly needed a guardian himself.

Indeed, Petrovsky, who during those years often acted as nanny to Rachinsky, had already taken over the job of guardianship over Seryozha's 'guardian'. Over a cup of tea that evening, Petrovsky

* Sergei Solovyov; nephew of the philosopher Vladimir Solovyov.

exercised his wit on 'Dr Zatonsky', who was sinking in the back-water* of the apartment—sinking beneath the floorboards! Blok later described him in a letter as 'Very charming'.

We were a very merry quintet, sitting there drinking our tea.

Blok did some comic impersonations, pretending to be a visitor, gloves in hand, paying a call on one of the rich Moscow houses, keeping up the '*bon ton*' even when talking to dogs and caged jackdaws. Swivelling elegantly round, he would pass a remark to Lyubov Dmitrievna in his hoarse, smoker's voice:

'Do you know what, Lyuba—I think Seryozha is going to turn the table over.'

With dry humour he told us of his conjectures about Merezh-kovsky,† and it was all we could do not to burst out laughing at the concealed but very funny double meanings which he left half un-said, knocking the ash off his cigarette and innocently opening his blue eyes wider as he looked at us.

We discussed the magazine *Vesy* ('The Scales'),‡ the first sample issue of which was lying there, and which contained portraits of Bryusov and Gippius.§ Solovyov, who detested Gippius, tore out the portrait of the poetess with his usual capacity for taking things to their logical conclusion—not merely dotting the 'i' in 'Gippius', but piercing enormous holes all over it (his jokes were monstrous)— and then stamping on the portrait with his heel in honour of Blok's wife (later he became a friend of Gippius). After remarking on her uniqueness, Blok ironically mentioned her weakness for making mischief between people.

'Now, what about you?' we asked Blok's wife.

'Oh, no—I've no gift for making speeches.'

However, she listened intently, warming and expanding like cobalt, directing a searching gaze at everyone. Although the youngest there, she behaved like one of the oldest. Blok declared her to be very severe. When visiting a household where she did not feel at home, she would sit staring blankly at her enormous muff and rubbing it against her knees.

---

* A play on words, 'Zaton' being the Russian for backwater; the verb derived from it means 'to sink'.

† Dmitry Merezhkovsky (1886–1941). Poet, novelist, playwright, critic.

‡ Literary monthly (1904–09); publisher Polyakov, editor Bryusov.

§ Zinaida Gippius (1869–1945). Poet, editor, memoirist. Wife of Merezhkovsky.

Seryozha, who was still a schoolboy, was always making us laugh. For some unknown reason he put on a frock-coat formerly belonging to Vladimir Solovyov* and cut down to fit him, which made him look like a tradesman, and then tied a white scarf round his neck. The Bloks looked amazed at the way he flung himself about, at the way his eyebrows shot up and down in time with his scarf and his flapping ash-blond hair, for all the world like a tipsy usher at a tradesman's wedding. He almost tore himself apart with his grotesque performance 'à la Solovyov', stamping his feet, swooping like an eagle, pushing at the table and pulling at the tablecloth.

Petrovsky struck his little sturgeon-like nose into his pince-nez and, with his usual stammer, launched some of his stinging barbs. Lowering his eyes and blushing like an innocent maiden, he would veil his spiteful remarks as if they were delicate rosebuds.

I realized that Blok, Solovyov and Petrovsky were a trio of experienced wits, while my own 'lyrical' style (I had little time for jokes in those days) was hopelessly out of key. To entertain friends at a party, Alexander Alexandrovich Blok would mischievously spread his hands and poke gentle fun at the tortuousness of my lyrics. Then he would give an imitation of me being asked to give a reading, becoming shy and embarrassed, and refusing. I am told he parodied me perfectly, but he would never do it in my presence. However, at Shakhmatovo I used to caricature him to his face. Savagely grasping a pencil and trembling with eagerness, I would aim my glance at his pointed nose or at L.D.'s 'turnip' face, in order to scribble a maliciously grotesque drawing on some crumpled bit of paper. I would portray Alexander Alexandrovich with an idiotic look on his face as he turned Anna Schmidt† off her throne and installed his wife on it, while I, Rachinsky, Solovyov and his mother, dressed as an old peasant in cap and black shawl, would either fall about fainting or, rising to our feet, idiotically greet 'the empress'. Seryozha always provoked me into perpetuating these comic horrors, as in the game of Giant's Strides. I would not play jokes if left alone, but was quite often goaded into it by his malicious wit at the expense of Gippius or the mammoth outbursts of Seryozha's thunderous laughter.

* Vladimir Solovyov (1853–1900). Poet, mystic and philosopher, whose thought greatly influenced Biely.

† Disciple of Vladimir Solovyov. Writer on religion and mysticism.

REMINISCENCES OF A. BLOK 67

A.A.'s humour did not provoke me, and when Seryozha was not there I found being with the Bloks quiet, relaxed, but a little sad. A.A. did not joke, although occasionally he displayed his subtle humour without attempting character-drawing. He could strike home unerringly with a single stroke, using some apt, cutting word. Once he expressed the difference between us in one short phrase: 'You, Borya—are a spendthrift, and I—am a rake. A rake has the ability to give *himself*, while a spendthrift indulges in purely verbal largesse because he is vulnerable; this leads to handing out promissory notes—debts which can never be repaid.'

My mother used to say, 'Whenever Alexander Alexandrovich says something seriously, I want to burst out laughing.'

By the mere movement of his eyes or head, he could do a comic turn which would cause Seryozha to explode; but if he put anything into words, it was done with a grave, old-fashioned turn of phrase, like Dickens rather than Prutkov.*

The performance with the scarf that evening was typical of Seryozha, who was still a schoolboy; writing to his mother at the time Blok described the uproar we created: 'Woke up at mid-day from Seryozha's shouting'; 'Seryozha caused a disturbance in the omnibus, yelling his head off ... '; 'Seryozha departed, shouting loudly.' Blok always treated him with much affection.

His use of grammar amazed us that evening: short sentences constructed very simply, but with 'so as' or 'in order to' frequently inserted into ordinary, simple speech. Thus he would say, 'I shall go in order to buy', not, 'I shall go to buy', or, 'I am bringing some beer, so as to drink it'. He made no use of gerunds, and his language was not 'literary'—his sentences were like small blocks of wood, clear-cut and simple, yet with ripples of deeper meaning which evaporated like water. One's attention was concentrated on the meaning behind his actual words, and I later felt irritated by the paradox of this limpid ambiguity.

'Blok has no verbs!' growled Merezhkovsky.

Later on, having written 'Against Music', I attacked such misleading phrases, words which seem to say everything while saying nothing, make of them what you will; words which invite you to

---

* 'Kozma Prutkov' was the collective pseudonym of three writers—A. K. Tolstoy and the two brothers Zhemchuzhnikov—under which they published humorous, satirical parodies in the latter half of the 19th century.

search for a deeper, secret meaning and yet in fact are nothing but irresponsible clap-trap; words which, having promised you piles of gold, when you come to present your Bill of Exchange blink and announce with an innocent look, 'But we never promised that!'

One smiles at Anichkov and dines with him, then writes in all sincerity in one's diary: 'Idiot!' If you do not respond to hidden meanings, you will be thought a fool today; if you do respond, you will look a fool tomorrow, because the two meanings—the obscure hidden one and the plain one—will have turned a somersault in a year's time.

Blok and the Argonauts

Blok arrived on Saturday the tenth, and on Sunday the eleventh he and his wife found themselves in the company of the Argonauts, who were visiting me. It would probably be true to say that Blok's first ardent admirers in the Russia of that time were there to receive him. They were: the Ertels, Batyushkov, my mother, Chelishchev, Petrovsky, Pechkovsky, Vladimirov and his sisters, K. P. Khristoforova, Yanchin, Lesnov, Nina Petrovskaya,; also there were Balmont, Bryusov, the two Kobylinskys, Poyarkov, Madame Kistyakovskaya, outgrowing even her muff, with her one-eyed husband, and Chasovnikova, née A. V. Taneyeva; about twenty-five people in all.

The small dining-room seemed to explode with shouts and cigarette smoke. The poet was most affable, although a trifle apprehensive at having landed in the very heart of Moscow, where not only Belinsky and Ketcher,* but even Nozdrev† stretching out their arms from a not so distant past. The reflection of their brilliance glinted on the shabby wall-paper, ragged curtains and olive-coloured chairs in the drawing-room; where Lev Tolstoy once sat, where Maxim Kovalevsky‡ and Yanzhul§ displayed their oratory

* N. Kh. Ketcher (1809–86). Friend and collaborator of Belinsky; critic; translator of Schiller.

† A character in Gogol's *Dead Souls*.

‡ M. M. Kovalevsky (1851–1916). Professor of law at Moscow University and liberal politician.

§ I. I. Yanzhul (1845–1914). Statistician and economist; professor at Moscow University.

and where Blok's grandfather, Beketov, sat me on his knee: and now they were quoting ... Huysmans!

Dull and deadly arguments about Lotze,* which arose like the rising of a dead moon, were started by Sergei Kobylinsky. His face as white as a sheet, he battered people's minds and bored them almost to extinction, while his brother Lev, a great, thick-lipped vampire-like creature, insatiably sucked Blok's blood, constantly jumping up and making a loud crash with his chair. Blok tried in vain to take in what was being said, and unable to reply quickly enough, sat looking lost, with a strained smile on his lips. He seemed to stiffen, his face darkened, and bags appeared under his eyes. We took him into the study and Vladimirov, Ertel, Petrovsky, Malafeyev and I sat round him

Once again I had a chance to observe him. He did not move while he talked, but sat up straight, not leaning against the back of the chair. No creases appeared in his clothing when he bent his head with its mop of gingery-tawny curls, or crossed and uncrossed his legs, swinging his foot—otherwise he was very sparing in his gestures. At times, when he became agitated, he got up and shuffled his feet, or else walked slowly over to talk to someone; coming up close to them, opening wide his blue eyes, he would confide something to them, then click open his cigarette case, rap on it with two fingers, and silently offer a cigarette.

If someone came up and stood beside him, he would rise with polite hostility and stand listening with head slightly bent, smiling at his toes, and when that person sat down, he would sit down too.

These inborn good manners, with almost *mondain* self-restraint, engendered a wealth of kindly feeling towards him amongst the Argonauts, where he aroused much curiosity and became involved in a few intrigues. With the 'elders', like Bryusov† and K. D. Balmont,‡ Blok was polite and dignified, behaving simply, naturally and independently.

* Hermann Lotze (1817–81). German scientist and philosopher.
† Valery Bryusov (1873–1924). One of the founders and most influential exponents of Russian symbolism. Unemotional by nature, Bryusov's chief concern was with the forging of a new poetic style.
‡ Konstantin Balmont (1867–1942). Together with Bryusov, one of the founders of the Russian symbolist movement. Stylistically rich and subtle, his poetry was strongly marked with the 'decadent' strain of symbolism. Emigrated in 1921; died in Paris.

I remember Bryusov, with his Mongolian cheekbones and sharply-pointed little black beard, bending over the poet and, with his hand darting to and from his chest, discussing some poem, declaring that one of the lines was no good, while another was just right, and Blok, standing beside him, shook the ash off his cigarette and looked a trifle doubtful.

Some misunderstanding arose between him and L. L. Kobylinsky that evening and deepened with the years; Balmont did not care for Blok at all, so they hardly met, but his wife made a considerable impression on Balmont.

In spite of everything, Blok liked the Argonauts, and wrote to his mother on 15th December: 'Andrei Biely is inimitable'; and, 'a significant conversation ... very fine indeed' (with Seryozha and me). He wrote about Seryozha, ' ... my conversation with him — just the two of us, was ... important ... illuminating ... delightful ... ' and about Batyushkov, 'P. N. Batyushkov is coming to see us, a charming person'. Rachinsky was described as making 'an unparalleled impression', and he also wrote, ' ... there will be many pleasant memories of Moscow'.

He soon expressed his feelings in a poem, 'The Argonauts', in which the line, 'In silence let us link our arms', seemed to mean that he felt himself to belong to the Argonauts' brotherhood.

The 'elders', however, made a different impression: 'I felt an aversion to Balmont, and Bryusov's personality, also, did not seem particularly ... attractive.'

I recollect that he, Bryusov and I read poems aloud that evening. I read 'The Torah', he read 'To the Factory' and 'She arose in radiance', and Bryusov 'The Pale Steed', if I remember rightly.

Blok's slightly nasal manner of reading was very striking. He did not stress the third syllable in anapaests; it was as if he erased the music of the lines by his matter of fact, slightly strangled, sober and inexpressive voice, somehow swallowing the endings of words so that words which did not actually rhyme, like *granits* and *tsaritsu* and *obmanom — tumannye*, seemed to rhyme in his pronunciation. There was no change of pitch or variation in the length of pauses. One had the impression that he was trudging along in other people's footsteps, encased in heavy armour.

And his face would come to resemble his voice; it became heavy and frozen, his large nose looked sharper, and the moving outlines of his lips cast shadows on his clean-shaven chin. His eyes became opaque and it looked as if life was pouring out of them into words, as with the heavy tread of the 'Commendatore'* he slowly and harshly clumped along the lines of verse.

This poetry reading was rapturously received, and he wrote to his mother: 'I read "She arose in radiance", and a crowd of people in black frock-coats sighed loudly and jumped from their chairs shouting that I am Russia's greatest poet. We left after two o'clock in the morning. Everyone thanked me and shook hands.'

But I could understand from his reading that he was rejecting—incidentally very politely—the assertively *sans façon* style of some of his Moscow acquaintances, who were ready to clamour, embrace each other and swear allegiance while at the same time energetically elbowing their companions out of the way. Blok, too, could be crudely partial; thus, in the days when he poured out his affection for me and Seryozha, he wrote incredibly coarsely and, what is more, completely unfairly about a very cultured, respected and, as far as we were concerned, entirely inoffensive man called P. D. Boborykin: 'My poor mamma, whatever induced you to see that mangy swine.' Later on, I myself was insulted by Blok's very demeanour. It happened at a time when we had quarrelled and were not on speaking terms. While walking along a crowded Petersburg boulevard I saw Blok, who, wearing a pale-cream panama hat and clutching a cane, ran past me—looking as wooden and rigid as a board. His face was bloodless, and his offensively curved, supercilious lips glistened with coarse sensuality against a greyish-mauve background with a fading, greenish tinge.

I was outraged by his gesture of running past me with his foppish cane poking forward at people in front of him, while the very crease in his white panama seemed to crown his humiliation of me. It was like a slap in the face.

How dare he! I thought. Actually, he had not seen me.

And yet in the period when we were very close to each other, there was no limit to my desire to abase myself before him, to submit to him completely. He certainly did not demand this, and both my flaring anger and my inordinate rapture amazed him. The poet in him was intertwined with the sceptic, and one was struck by his aloofness to 'lyrical' influences, and by the way his mind,

* Blok's poem 'The Footsteps of the Commendatore' (1912).

completely foreign to these influences, observed them from a distance. His will-power seethed, but only in the hallucinatory world of his senses; it did not act on his intellect, which saw only its own duality and perceived the impossibility of self-knowledge. Knowledge was all: that he understood; yet it was incomprehensible. So there remained irony—a poison, as he observed later in an article on irony: 'The most sensitive beings of our age suffer from a disease unknown to medical men. This disease may be called 'irony' ... to its victims, there is no difference between Dante's Beatrice or Sologub's Nedotykomka ... * and all of us modern poets are close to the source of this terrible disease.'

Not suffering from the disease of irony, or anyway affected by it to a much lesser degree, I tried to transform this irony into a weapon with which to combat Heine, whom Blok had also quoted: 'I cannot understand where irony finishes and Heaven begins.'

I demanded a clearly perceptible division of the two spheres, and during the period of my strife with Blok, I wrote as follows about him: 'The most poisonous caterpillar of all was the "Fair Lady" (who later degenerated into a prostitute and a false quantity).' I further wrote about the 'witticisms' of his, to me at least, horrifying play *Balaganchik*:† 'One is amazed at the paper sky and the howl of a puppet, and that the victim's blood ... is cranberry juice.'

It was these attacks of my 'irony' against Blok's 'irony' that caused him in reply to call me 'mentally deranged'; and yet, when writing about irony a year later, he himself repeated my 'mentally deranged' remarks.

The cause of his irony was a sort of shock, which disrupted Blok's inner integrity; the shock was administered by a kind of joker inside him, who believed 'In vino veritas'.

We discover great truths through trivia, and I managed once to scent in him the aroma of the poison which destroyed him; very soon after that, although the boundary between humour and irony are supposed to be indiscernible, I discerned them.

The following incident happened outside St Mikola's Church one miserable, slushy day. The sledges rushing past spattered everyone, the houses looked murky and damp; everything seemed lower

---

* Fyodor Sologub (1863–1927). 'Nedotykomta' is a reference to his satirical novel *The Little Demon*.

† This title refers to a fairground puppet-show, not unlike Punch and Judy.

and closer than usual, and suddenly I saw Blok approaching me. He had on a very wet, dark green coat, a sodden peaked cap worn at an angle, and was carrying a bottle, all of which made him look like a student from Bronnaya Street. He showed me the bottle and spoke to me using the familiar form of address, which we had recently adopted between us.

'There you are ... in spite of everything, I've bought myself a bottle of beer, so as to drink it with my dinner.'

There was a needling irony and nothing of humour in the way he said those words, ' ... in spite of everything ... ', and 'so as ... '. I looked at him—etiolated, a crooked, forced smile on his lips, his hair an ashen-grey tinge instead of ginger-tawny, and a greenish bloom on his angular, waxen profile. He looked quite ordinary, yet quite hollow.

'Is this really Blok?' passed through my thoughts.

I was at that time completely overwhelmed by my tragic experience with N., and could not bother to concern myself with 'in spite of' or 'so as ... '. I felt hurt, as if he had given me a jab with his elbow. After bidding me goodbye, he turned into a side street, in order to ... 'so as ... '; would there be a corkscrew, though? It was dripping wet; the brooms were scraping at the slush, and dark, bluish-grey clouds hung low.

Utter Nonsense

We behaved like hosts anxious to entertain our guest, regaling him with friends as though with food. We trailed him round everywhere with us, including, for some reason, a visit to Father Antony: 'He always talks a lot and very well when we visit him.' The schoolboy Seryozha acted as Master of Ceremonies, rushing in, his coat wide open, wearing his tunic, a white rag flapping round his neck, and carrying an enormous hat, just like a tipsy usher at a shopkeeper's wedding. I saw him once going along in a cab, his fur coat wide open, the white rag streaming in the wind and snow falling on his chest.

During our many noisy journeys, dragging around the already exhausted Blok couple, he caught scarlet fever.

Here are some excerpts from Blok's letters:

3*

'Monday, 12th. Seryozha arrived and the three of us went to visit the Novodevichy Convent. Afterwards, wandered round the fields beyond the Moscow River, near the Vorobyov Hills. Went into the Kremlin. Fatigue and intoxication. Went to the Rachinsky's flat ... Bugayev arrived in the evening ... We drank wine and clinked our glasses ... Night.'

'Tuesday, 13th. Seryozha came in the morning ... We went to Sokolniki, with much merriment and some brawling ... Went to Sasha Markonet's ... Had dinner at Seryozha's and bumped into Rachinsky and Misha Kovalensky ... * Rushed off to see Bugayev in order to go to The Scorpion,† but he was not in, so I went on my own but left with Bugayev. Went to a meeting of The Griffin and exchanged embraces with Sokolov. The following people present at the meeting: The Sokolovs, Kobylinsky, Batyushkov, the Bugayevs (with mother), Koiransky and Kursinsky ... Supper ... Balmont came in drunk, and after a row with him, Kobylinsky left ... We left after two. Rather depressing and strange.' And so it goes on: 'Wednesday, 14th. In the morning, Bugayev, Petrovsky, Sokolova and the two of us went off to the Donskoi Monastery to visit Father Antony ... Very thin, with blazing eyes ... and with a tinge of irony ... We went on foot.'

This dragging around went on every day. How did he survive it? And he wrote, as a result, 'We try to avoid the people here.'

On the anniversary of the deaths of M. S. and O. M. Solovyov, 'We arrived at the Novodevichy Convent ... ' he wrote to his mother. 'After the memorial mass (the nuns sang very well), the whole crowd of us went to the Popovs, where it was very noisy. We ate pancakes and drank a lot of toasts.' 'That day,' he wrote, 'Bugayev and I began to use "thou" to each other.'

The snow was crunchy; tiny, powdery snowflakes dropped down the fir trees; it was a dull, subdued day with a mild snowfall. I remember the frescoes in the cathedral of 'somersaulting saints' (Blok's description of their postures); a stream of black-garbed, whispering, round-shouldered, elderly nuns in trailing habits emerging from the shadows, their figures bent with the weight of huge, lighted candles flickering above their billowing cowls.

The snow rustled softly, with a sound like watered silk, through

* A Marxist historian, Blok's second cousin.
† Publishing house founded in 1900 by S. Polyakov, closed down in 1916.

the branches of the fir trees and above the modest porcelain wreath on the gravestone and the shining 'eye' of the amber icon-lamp, which cast its gentle light over the windy cemetery. Blok was serious and withdrawn; he was not with us.

L. L. Kobylínsky (pen-name 'Ellis'), a slightly dishevelled dandy, clung to him, slipping his arm through Blok's and spluttering loudly into his face some nonsense of his own which was quite unsuitable for the occasion. He was pale, elegant, brilliant with flashing eyes and hysterically twitching elbows ... he disturbed Blok with his high-pitched giggle, and later, at the Popovs, he still pestered him, twirling his moustache, mouthing high-flown generalizations and demanding precise, immediate and lengthy answers to his questions.

Alexander Alexandrovich endured it for a long time, although his face grew paler, as if the last traces of his sunburn were being consumed. He smoked and said nothing, then suddenly and not without provocation, he made a bold effort to shake Ellis off. He drew an imaginary line upwards with his face, and blew out a vertical, curling, double-barrelled column of cigarette smoke. He seemed about to make some capricious remark, but it died within him.

It would have been 'not quite done', no doubt!

Ellis, devil and buffoon, in his little braided frock-coat, waved his arm with its rubber cuff up towards the ceiling, waved it over the poetry of Dante, at cathedral roofs and at the gargoyles with their downcurved beaks.

'Now do you understand?'

But Blok no longer understood anything; he only winced at his own hypocrisy, and his face darkened with the shadows that sharply outlined his long Pierrot's nose. Afterwards, he confessed to me:

'You know, Borya, I simply can't stand Lev Lvovich!'

And for years this was the annual toast at the Popov's house.

I was more patient, although I suffered as he did. He would curl up and turn away, while I offered myself to be torn to pieces, although I occasionally flared up in protest. There were times when I defended Ellis; at others, I attacked him. At that particular time I was quarrelling with Balmont for having insulted Ellis; 'Andrei Biely has written immediately to Balmont to say that until he apologizes to Kobylinsky, Bugayev will have nothing to do with him.'

This happened on the fourteenth, but on the sixteenth, seeing the way Ellis seemed to be sucking Blok dry by clinging to him like a leech, I was ready to wring his neck. Yet I had to stand up for Ellis even against Blok. Although in my heart of hearts on Blok's side, I was outwardly at daggers drawn with him because of Ellis. As host and master of ceremonies, I restrained my feelings and somehow managed to free the poet from the ghastly Ellis. Blok could understand nothing of Ellis's scholarly yet stimulating views on history. (Blok showed a stony indifference to history.) In Ellis's vivid and lively sense of history—although naturally with a Marxist slant—there was a lot that the poet could have learned to his advantage. Blok's cosmic 'splendours' lacked their cross, their pain (this came later), while I hung from my cross at that time, obstinately trying to extract the 'rhythms' from the howling chaos around me.

The evening at The Griffin, following the visit to the Popovs, caused me even greater pain. Yet Blok described it quite calmly in a letter, as follows: 'S. A. Sokolov created an impression of falsity; the evening was a failure.'

I think that for me, that evening was one of disaster, focusing as it did on the utter falsity of people stupidly banging their heads together in an effort to produce 'rhythms', and not realizing that those rhythms were nothing more than 'seeing stars' after this idiotic clash of foreheads, until they were all bruises and bumps. A little monster awoke in each one, and, like the imps in bottles sold at Moscow fairs, jumped out of their wide-open mouths and ran about among the guests as though possessed of an independent existence.

Blok also noticed the terrible depression—which I fully understood—of Nina Petrovskaya. Her husband, Sokolov, having bawled out a torrent of rhyming drivel (such as ' ... his blood from passion was so black, that now to red it has gone back'!), blew out his cheeks (so that they looked as if they were stuffed with eiderdown) and banged his fist on the table.

'The table!' he yelled, goggling at Blok with his boot-button eyes.

'What about the table?'

And staring at Batyushkov, towering like one of the pillars of Hercules, he roared in his deep bass voice:

'Look!'

Everyone stared at the table, panting with excitement, but the table merely stayed as it was.

'?!?'

On seeing that everyone was waiting for an explanation, Sokolov, who was a barrister, and had recently discovered spiritualism, adjusted his pince-nez with much dignity, and, slightly embarrassed at what he had just done, proceeded in the same deep voice:

'The table ... er ... I think ... in our flat, we have recently ... '

Everyone stood and waited.

'We have recently heard ... "knocks" ... '

He meant spiritualist knocks.

What did all this have to do with the table? The table did not seem to have any intention of jumping or tilting; like an obedient donkey, it was carrying a load of plates, fruit and wine. Petrovskaya put her hands over her ears at this senseless lack of taste. She was so ashamed at her husband behaving in this fashion, that she flinched as though someone had slapped her face.

We stood, and then sat down, as though we were on a bed of nails, and felt uneasy for the rest of the evening. Then there arose a most ridiculous conversation; Sokolov propounded his 'mystical' opinions, to which no one responded, except for the gentle little 'ladybird' Batyushkov, a grey-haired infant. Pathetically clutching the hands of someone near him, he pump-handled them up to his armpits one moment and below his belly the next, almost tearing them off; all this was in order to demonstrate his sympathy towards the owner of the hands and towards Sokolov.

Mishenka Ertel, with a glint in his small green eyes, looking like a moulting cuckoo, his short, bristly moustache quivering, swayed as he expressed his utter rapture to Sokolov:

'Se'gei A'ekseyich ... has seized ... ha, ha, the bull by the ho'ns!'

To which Sokolov drawled in his velvety bass voice, putting on his pince-nez:

'Thank you so much, my dear—you understand me!'

Like Petrovskaya, I nearly fell through the floor. Was this simply a display of the Argonauts nonsensical fireworks, or was it—a madhouse?

> Everyone shouted at the round tables,
> Anxiously changing their places.

That evening played a decisive part in my life, finally killing off that 'style' out of which I had wanted to create a melody of sparkling social tact. So this was the new quality in the chemistry of souls, in the counterpoint of human interaction? Not harmony, but table-tapping! The mystery of life? Mystery has given birth to a mouse — possibly the word *mus* is derived from *musterion; ter* means a beast in Greek, and this beast emerged that evening.

As I advance in years, I only wince on hearing the word 'mystery', and in 1906, remembering those ravings, I wrote: 'The mountain brought forth a mouse ... To the hostess's question, "Looking for tea?", someone shouted in reply, "I look for the resurrection of the dead!" ... There was candied furniture in the house; you could not sit in a chair ... it was sticky all over.'

The Bloks saw the Argonaut circle fail dismally that evening, while I had long ago failed in my own eyes, in my affair with N.

In his heart of hearts, Alexander Alexandrovich felt this in me, and this Griffin evening linked us together. He glanced at me anxiously over the heads of all the little monsters and very soon we left and came out on to the midnight Znamenka, powdered over with soft snow.

Shakhmatovo

At the beginning of July, I set off for Shakhmatovo, and quite un-expectedly Petrovsky came with me. While travelling along in our railway carriage, we were suddenly overcome with fear: I because I suddenly realized that I was going for the first time to stay with a family I did not know, without Seryozha, and with the uninvited Petrovsky in tow, while he sat hunched up in embarrassment, knowing that he was intruding.

On reaching Podsolnechnaya station we hired a shaky and un-comfortable trap and jogged along in it for about twelve miles over bogs and corduroy roads and through frequent patches of immature woodland. Then we saw the rising, wooded hills. This landscape was more reminiscent of Tver than of the Moscow region, and was the same as near Klin. The sight of this landscape brought Blok's poetry to mind. The nearby railway stations seemed to me connected with the names of friends: Khimki—with the Zakharins; Kryukovo—with the Solovyovs or the Kovalenskys; Povorovka—with Petrovsky; Podsolnechanaya—with Bloks and the Beketovs; and further on—with Mendeleyev: Klin, or Maidanovo; Frolovskoye, where Tchaikovsky, the Kuvshinnikovs and that strange lady Novikova used to live; and what about Demyanovo, where I and all the Taneyevs grew up? And Dulepovo—the home of the Kostromitinovs, distant relations of my mother? and Nagornoye (halfway between Podsolnechnaya and Demyanovo), where we lit bonfires and went mushroom-picking, where Grigori Avetovich Dzhanshiev used to cook kebab.

Suddenly there was a clearing in the wood, and quite unexpectedly, we rolled into the spacious grass-grown courtyard of a country-house with several outbuildings. There was also the little house, half concealed in greenery, where the Bloks themselves lived. We drove up to the main house. It was single-storeyed, and if I remember rightly, grey in colour with seven windows and a gable entirely taken up by one very large semi-circular window. The front door was shut and there was no one about. We opened the door and saw two, slim, short, bustling, middle-aged ladies, who appeared somewhat embarrassed to see us. They were Alexandra Andreyevna Kublitskaya and Maria Andreyevna Beketova, A.A.'s mother and aunt. Petrovsky wilted, and out of embarrassment I started talking nonsense. The four of us found ourselves in the drawing-room, and for a long time could think of nothing to do.

I was greatly astonished by Alexandra Andreyevna, with her greying hair, her tiny, red, radish-like nose; she was modestly dressed in a grey blouse and skirt, sharp-eyed, fluttery, a little bird caught in a trap. She looked like a student-teacher, and this made her seem extremely young. Not so much her features, but her alertness, her attitude to others made her look less like a mother than her own sister; this, and her agitation lest we feel nervous at being faced by the older generation was what made her so distinctive.

In that comfortable, spacious, sun-filled room, with every piece of well-polished furniture in its proper place, we felt as though we were being inspected by our tremulous hostess. I remember the trembling, but not the banal things we said.

Then two thin, fine-drawn law students entered and clicked their heels, followed by a pale, slight, elegant and very pleasant

blue-eyed woman, their mother. This was the third Beketov sister
Sophia Andreyevna.

We walked along the terrace and down the steep garden paths,
sloping into the woods, then through the wood and into the fields,
where we immediately saw husband and wife returning from a walk.
There was Lyubov Dmitrievna, young and rosy-cheeked, in her
light pink wrap, fluttering in the breeze, a white parasol held over
her smooth sun-gold hair. She was coming towards us with a slow,
slightly swaying walk through the flowers and tall, waving grass.
Alexander Alexandrovich, walking with her, was slim, tall, broad-
shouldered and very sunburnt. He wore a snow-white shirt
embroidered with purple swans and tied with an embroidered sash
with swinging, tasselled ends. He wore high boots but no hat, and
his curly mop of hair glinted ginger in the sun. Every inch a brave,
fairytale hero—not Blok!

With the shrill cries of the swallows all round us, he stopped,
amongst the flowers, and, shading his eyes with his hand, scruti-
nized us from a distance and then ran towards us, a little breath-
less, but not in the least surprised, and on reaching us shook hands.

'So—you've come!' And looking at Petrovsky, he added kindly.
'I'm so glad you came too!'

Feeling confused, Petrovsky cut his reply short with a wave of
the hand. But Alexander Alexandrovich's whole manner seemed
designed to stress that Alexei Sergeyevich's arrival was quite natural
and proper.

L.D. came up too, smiling, greeting us like old friends. We all
wondered about the disappearance of S. M. Solovyov, chatted
about mutual friends in Moscow and about all kinds of trivia, the
importance of which constantly changes, flaring up with an inner
flame one moment and dimming the next. A.A. illuminated our
chatter and our pleasure in each other's company with a comfortable
silence. There was a spicy richness in the air from the breeze, the
plants and the cries of the swallows. Being a good host, he managed
to create a sense of comfort and homely simplicity, showing consideration and care, not fussily but firmly, down to the smallest
trifles. He breathed a worldly, Epicurean wisdom and warm affection
for the surrounding countryside. He seemed to have grown roots
here, and the woods and fields and the wild roses which climbed all
over one wing of the house and were a mass of deep crimson, gold-

centred flowers (such as I'd never seen before), all seemed a part of his work-room.

We returned to the terrace, and with a neat but powerful leap Blok jumped up the three steps. Bending down a little, and with her slightly swaying gait, L.D. went up the steps, hunching her broad, rounded shoulders and gathering up her loose wrap at the knee. As she went up, she screwed up her Kirghiz-Kaisatz eyes at us. They were blue and slanting and outlined with black lashes, in sharp contrast to her round, rose-white face and large, ugly mouth. Aiming her words in my direction, and so tense that it made her look unattractive, she asked me in a hollow, chesty contralto:

'And how is N.?'

In the country she looked not like a lady but like a robust peasant woman in blooming health, while in her slow, lazy movements, I perceived a sort of secret reckless daring.

We sat down feeling slightly overpowered. Alexandra Andreyevna darted here and there with her restless little brown eyes; when she spoke, her words darted out like scurrying mice. Maria Andreyevna in a speckled dress, sat down next to her and joined her in blinking and pulling faces. 'Sasha' sat down, crossing his legs and fingering the tassel of his sash. He sat sprawled out, a benign look on his face, and his mouth open as if he was about to say something but thought better of it, 'h'm' being the only sound emerging, while the tilt of his head expressed a frank desire to listen—but not to talk.

I was amazed by his physical bulk: it reminded one of another, earlier poet who was a Tula landowner named Shenshin, and who signed his poems about roses and dawns with the name of 'A.A. Fet'.*

Against the background of this comfortably seated man, whom we had perhaps interrupted in the carrying out of his domestic duties, the 'Moscow' Blok seemed to be entirely the right alias for someone who was used to sitting on a mossy log in the evenings, in a cloud of bluish cigarette-smoke, discussing household matters in a slightly cracked voice. On taking me to the neatly hoed kitchen garden, he picked up a spade and sticking it into the ground, said:

'Do you know, Borya, I dug this ditch myself, in the spring ... I work here every spring.'

All the letters to his relatives dating from this time are filled with domestic affairs. He wrote to his mother: 'Here is the key for you,

* A. A. Shenshin, alias Fet (1820–92). Lyric poet.

Mama ... ' 'the piglets are splendid little beasts ... ' 'We've kept two heifers for breeding ... ' 'I've written two reviews ... ' 'We're planting potatoes near the hazel grove ... ' 'There is a new garden gate ... ' 'Why did you give orders to spoil the meadow ... ' 'The trees have been felled in several parts of the wood at Proslovo ... ' 'The boar cost 21 roubles ... ' 'The cattle pen is simply excellent ... ' and so on.

His letters were full of this domesticity. Writing reviews and 'talking to Solovyov', who paid an unexpected visit in the spring, were mere chance occurrences. Here Blok was earthy, excessively so—going to the extremes of the later Dutch painters, who merely painted hares. 'They have just brought in a tea-loaf and sponge-cake made by Darya ... tea, and ham of pale dawn-pink with a sunset-coloured surround, mild, not salty ... Went for a walk after eating ... ' 'Darya is an aristocratic housekeeper, providing whatever people fancy, such as ham, mincemeat with sour cream, cream cheese ... milk ... stock with boiled beef, or vegetable soup ... ' There is something definitely Flemish in the ham with a 'sunset-coloured surround'. 'After eating our fill, we went for a walk'; ' ... we eat plenty and it's all very tasty ... ' Then the description of the food follows: ' ... Eggs, milk, tea, bread, beef soups, mincemeat, ham, cream cheese ... etc.' Details of the food and appreciation of it were the leitmotifs of all the letters to his relatives. This conjures up not the poet Fet, but a replete Shenshin in front of a picture, again painted by one of the late Flemish masters. 'Sixteen pink piglets being suckled by two excellent sows ... a boar with a calm and intelligent expression on his face.' What? Face!?! And what do *people* have—'faces' or 'snouts'?

The reverse of all this domesticity was the Blok who could write:

'Mangy swine', 'a little yid', 'bandaged belly', 'a lady with a grating voice, due to excessive drinking', etc. 'I consider that I have a right to wash my hands of it all and devote myself to art. Let the scoundrels crucify me and let them choke in their own swill.' Later on, when he was quarrelling with us (with Seryozha and me), he wrote, 'Seryozha has grown very fat and plain.'

A Dutch artist would have been quite right to portray Blok as Shenshin: the truth of this impression was fully revealed in later years, when his diaries, biography and correspondence with relatives were released. Everything became quite clear—he was 'Shenshin the landowner', married to Botkina, formerly a hussar and bosom friend of Apollon Grigoriev.

In Shakhmatovo as in Moscow, in the first moment of complete trust ('Sasha' and 'Borya'), we clearly also aroused a certain apprehension in each other. For my part, it was due to his naturalism, to his 'Shenshin' self who took notice of what he ate; even during the first, romantic visit to Moscow, he noted, ' ... during a late supper', 'We are going to have dinner at the "Slavyansky Bazaar",' 'Seryozha paid ... ', or ' ... we ate pancakes'.

For his part, he probably feared that I could not keep count of all the dishes consumed at Shakhmatovo. Alexandra Andreyevna conveyed Blok's impressions of the first evening to S. Solovyov (who told them to me).

'What sort of a person is he? He doesn't eat and he doesn't drink!' This was about me.

I did both, of course, but worn out because of the affair with N., and thoroughly fatigued by the ceaseless reading I had been doing during the previous few weeks, I most certainly did not look like a healthy child of nature. I was willing my senses to perceive and my mind to think clearly, to work out convictions and opinions just as A.A. worked in his vegetable garden. One's will has muscles, as well as one's body.

I was more sinewy and that is where strength lies—in sinews, not in flesh.

Later, my feelings about Blok were divided. Whilst warming to him as to a kind friend, I nevertheless concealed from him the fact that I knew all the details of last summer's correspondence. Under the skull of this sturdy, healthy fellow, this intelligent man, there was much that was trivial and banal. He himself could have no conception of it, having been spoilt from childhood by relatives who considered that he was already a Goethe, and who treated what he said in moments of pique as prophecy. (Sudden thought: who can tell how much of this was the natural ebullience of a healthy man, and how much was arrogance?)

Friendship with the poet was a great comfort to me, in the sense that all personal friendships are a comfort and a help; but through it all ran the worrying knowledge, like a mouse scratching beyond the threshold of consciousness, of the complete bankruptcy of ideas, which was, so to speak, secretly creeping up on Alexander Blok from behind. It was this which caused a split in my mind. The theme of 'dawn', for instance, became merely a piece of hollow jargon in our conversation—a metaphor that had lost its true meaning. It was this that depressed me and made me seem to Blok to be neither eating nor drinking. It is hard to live in tight boots, and I felt constricted at having to live without the 'feast of consciousness'. Medtner had taught me to feast. Through contact with him and his cultural interests I felt happy and in my element, in spite of having been so badly and so recently scarred by life; whereas here, in Shakhmatovo, where nature was at its most gorgeous, sensual, tender best, and where I felt so warm and comfortable with the Bloks, one half of me suddenly felt itself to be suffocating and in mortal anguish, as if for the past two years I had been experiencing in all its profundity the conflict which broke out between me and the poet in 1906.*

This was the cause of my inner discomfort. Without being able to have a frank showdown over the matter, I realized that Blok was a man of literary culture and taste, but that he did not possess that higher culture, that expansion of consciousness in the style of Goethe; there was no many-sided diversity in him, no striving for higher things. Because of this, in spite of his seeming breadth of mind there was a narrowness about his interests, and too much of what gravely disturbed both Medtner and me was completely foreign and incomprehensible to him.

I can best explain myself in the words of Tchaikovsky, since they reflect exactly what I myself had experienced and barely managed to suppress, something that was becoming the misanthropic, reverse side of all my friendships:

'I do not know how to be myself. As soon as I am with people ... new people that is, I immediately assume the part of a courteous, gentle and modest man, who is seemingly delighted to make new acquaintances, and who instinctively tries to charm, and in the

---

* In revising this part of my reminiscences, which were first published in *Epic* in 1922, I am including a few realistic points which were unsuitable for publication at the time of the poet's death, when all of us who loved him were filled with the romanticism of remembrance. Now, however, nearly ten years after his death, one can speak of many things in a calmer and more outspoken manner. (Author's note.)

main succeeds, but all this at the price of extreme tension combined with revulsion at one's own play-acting.'*

I was not play-acting, however. With one half of my consciousness I was seeking friendship with Blok and union with him in silent companionship, while with the other half I was applying to Blok the yardstick of Medtner's attitude to romantics. My mind would critically examine Blok's elaborately concealed fads and cults, which neither I nor Seryozha could share. I wanted to arrive at a solid, intelligible comprehension of whether the allegory of the dawn referred to the pink cape worn by Lyubov Dmitrievna, in which she sometimes 'enveloped herself' or 'was enveloped'. That this was so could be inferred from her self-conscious pose, her knowing attitude towards us. Blok wrote to his mother that 'Anna Nikolayevna† regards herself as the incarnation ... of the "World Spirit" ... She wants to play the same role in Petersburg as Lyuba (Lyubov Dmitrievna) played in Moscow.'

Oh, really?!

... I remember how during tea Blok absentmindedly put a tumbler over a fly as he listened to chatter about Moscow, about Seryozha, about Bryusov and G. A. Rachinsky. He sat with a barely visible smile on his lips, breathing slightly noisily, tripping over his own words as though resorting to clumsiness out of condescension, something that a year later greatly irritated me. There was also a note of slight cruelty when he mentioned A. G. Kovalenskaya's Griffin. When he said 'Aunt Sasha' his voice became hollow, but on saying 'Aunt Sonia' it was melodious.

It is difficult to give the exact text of what he said. In our trios and quartets his remarks were like a footnote to the main text, or a variant of it in the form of a suggested metaphor on the margins of a book he happened to be reading at the time. Without the actual text of Seryozha, Alexandra Andreyevna and myself, Blok's sketchy remarks, made as it were on the tracing paper over the drawing, are faint and indistinct.

I remember his words about Rozanov:‡

* Modest Tchaikovsky, *Life and Letters of Peter Illyich Tchaikovsky* (London, 1906).
† Anna Nikolayevna Schmidt; see above, p. 66n.
‡ V. V. Rozanov (1856–1919). Philosopher and critic.

'Now, about Vasili Vasilievich ... hmph ... with his little beard ...
You know ... He lisps ... always in a tiny panic ... '

The entire meaning was in the gestures, the cigarette-puffing, the
head nodding, the foot swinging.

He provoked us to play games with people's surnames, in order
to demonstrate the extent of Bryusov's influence on us. As I remember it came out as follows: Bryusov—or 'Bryu' '-sov'—had
such an effect on us that he changed our poetry. The letter 'k' was
all that was left of Blok—he became 'Bryuk' ('Bryu' being Bryusov's influence on him); whereas 'Biely' became 'Biesov' ('-sov'
because of the effect of Bryu-sov).

He was quite inimitable when it came to buffoonery or parodies.
Legs crossed, one hand hanging down loose, the other holding a
tumbler over a buzzing fly. His mouth gaping with amusement, calm
and mute. It is almost impossible to convey Blok's playful tone.
It was not a matter of words but of those mischievous gestures and
looks to which he resorted instead of speech.

Thus on listening to me telling a story of meeting someone I
knew, and remembering I had once said that the sound of all words
ending in '-ak—Kulak (fist) or dur-ak (fool)—made me think of a
goat dancing, on hearing someone exclaim kak (how), he recrossed
his legs and, shaking the ash off his cigarette, remarked with sombre
dryness:

'Not kak—simply -ak!'

Solovyov, who was a very impressionable boy, flared up like
a powder-magazine. Blok's mimicry set light to him like a
match.

At times Blok became kind and gentle, though hardly uttering a
word. Conversation became almost non-existent, more like a rippling
brook: words like crystals flowed and evaporated into a landscape of
cumulus clouds, constantly changing their shape, and the meaning
of it became fluid and beyond sense. How often I used to swear at
this shapeless babble: 'Absolute nonsense!' And yet how many
times I gave myself up to it, creating verbal rainbows as though
the Bloks were sitting beside a fountain. L.D. answered me with
flashing eyes, covering her shoulders with a shawl, and Blok listened,
looking like a cat being scratched behind the ear.

To be presented with the text of Blok's words is like reading
Eckermann's record of Goethe's sayings. It is just like a gramophone

record, and both volumes, without the third describing Goethe's gestures, are lifeless.

I did not want to be Eckermann to Blok's Goethe, and so will not report the conversations at Shakhmatovo, which lasted for hours, and only snatches of which can be remembered.

Through the tangle of wild roses, the Bloks took us to one of the wings of the house. Clutching at a bush, A.A. picked a crimson flower and with a sarcastic grin handed it to me, as if it were an invitation to something wonderful. Or else, breaking off what he was saying, he slowly walked up to me, again with a grin, and again invitingly, took me into a corner: 'Come on, Borya!' ... he stood there for a while shuffling his feet and bringing his eyes closer to mine, then said 'Oh, well ... doesn't matter!' and led me back.

The first day passed in chatter. At dinner, the two law students, after bowing politely and clicking their heels, sat down stiff as ramrods and passed plates with exaggerated courtesy. The poet's other aunt, Sophia Andreyevna, sat at a distance and with inaudible lip-movements spoke to her third son, a frightened-looking deaf-mute. The little dog, Crabb, was also present. Alexandra Andreyevna and Maria Andreyevna stayed close together. The Piottukhs* left after dinner.

'They are positivists ... ' explained Blok, 'they come without disturbing anything or anyone ... But inwardly, they despise us ... however, they are always polite.'

Thus, after warning us of the rift which separated the two families living under the same roof, he took us across the meadow to the swampy, moss-grown woods, with patches of marshy water looking like blue window-panes. A rose-coloured, golden-tinted sky was spread out above a nearby hill, and L.D. pointed to the rosy part of it: 'That's where I used to live!'

Boblovo, belonging to the Mendeleyevs, was beyond the hill.

'There's a pose for you!' said A. S. Petrovsky, at my elbow.

She threw herself into the part. We were all intrigued by this couple's almost royal aloofness, and Petrovsky noted the way this was stressed by the intonation of her words. There was a certain '*Noli me tangere*' about A.A. and L.D., which caused people to wink knowingly 'Come on, tell us,' as though there were something odd about them. Both Lyuba and Sasha were *special people* — and

* Blok's mother and stepfather.

we tried all sorts of devices, using drills and chisels (crafty questions) to break open this locked chest with all its treasures. What was in it? Was it inarticulacy, shared beliefs, playfulness, shyness? This meaningful silence and the rather childish pose of L.D. was noted by Petrovsky, who confessed to me in the evening.

'I understand now why you and Seryozha pester them.'

He was incidentally completely charmed by his hosts and became like a high-spirited boy, his cap stuck askew on his head; he was cheerful and sociable. Blok took us to our room in the gable with the semicircular window (over the roof of the terrace). We sat talking till dawn, unable to sleep, discussing our experiences during the day.

The turquoise-greenish sky gilded the edges of the small grey clouds, and the east quivered with flashes of summer lightning.

The Quiet Life

Lazily, we woke up about nine, went downstairs around ten and drank coffee with cream with Alexandra Andreyevna. I often caught her sharply observant glance directed at me, a glance which said, 'Please explain—what does it all mean?' Obviously she did not understand our symbolic world of cryptic references, preferring Lyuba to be a wife rather than 'The Fair Lady'. Here was something hard to understand, something to do with metaphysics, with countless references to quotations, but people do not marry quotations; they are cut out and stuck into books (Blok liked to cut out pictures from various magazines and stick them into albums). Metaphysics—is that the physics of Meta? Is that what it is? Someone had written: 'I will pour my life into a scream ... ' (what about?); or else, ' ... the prophet's burning coal has been thrust into my heart'. He reproached me with covering my face with a mask in my article 'Art Forms'; yet he wrote the following himself: 'St Petersburg was unprepared for our arrival from Moscow; we demanded realism in life.'

Life was realistic for Blok in his roles as the young husband, as the student attending lectures by Professor Shlyapkin, and as the householder concerned about his pigs; but there was little that was realistic in the words of the ironic poet, with the prophet's burning coal in place of his heart, pouring his life either into 'The Fair Lady' or into the mystical piece of ham, 'pale dawn-pink with sun-set-coloured surround, tender, mildly-cured and not salty'. The irony of life is: has the girl a blonde plait of hair, or is she holding a scythe ... or maybe she squints?*

Blok himself counted irony among the grievous sins but was himself an ironist: 'I am getting some bookshelves constructed to reach right up to the ceiling—so the books can only be reached by those whose stature is sufficient to understand them.'

But to build symbolic poetry on a foundation of irony?

Sometimes I found it very difficult to be with Alexandra Andreyevna.

The Bloks put in their appearance after eleven. A.A. in his shirt with the purple swans, and L.D. in a loose, 'dawn-pink, sunset-glowing' wrap. After coffee, everyone lazed about in the bright, comfortable drawing-room. Everything followed a certain order, everything had its right time. No doubt all arranged by the capable hands of Alexandra Andreyevna.

She disappeared after coffee to attend to domestic matters, while the four of us—the Bloks, Petrovsky and I—lounged about in easy-chairs. Standing over a chair, I would set the ball rolling by making some 'theoretical' remark as an opening gambit, aiming my words at Blok, so that he could qualify them with his: 'That's right', or 'No, not like that'. Once he flung at me:

'No more, that's enough!'

This referred to style—not to words.

Once, while listening, he bent his head very low, and both the angle of the head and position of the nose showed confused perplexity, which he expressed by muttering 'h'm' or 'ha'—a combination of irony with the groundless fear of a blind man who is sprawling not in an easy-chair but on a marshy tussock, and playing not with the tassel of a sash but on a lute, badly out of tune. Suddenly he got up, and taking me by the elbow, led me out on to the terrace and down into the garden, where steep paths led down into the trees. We stopped in a field, in the tall grass, and there, chewing a wheatstalk, with twisted lips, he slowly spoke his thoughts. He

* A pun from the play *Balganchik*, based on the fact that the Russian word *kosa* means either a 'plait of hair' or a 'scythe'. The related verb *Kosit'* means 'to mow' or 'to squint'.

stressed that these were not mere whims; no, he knew and understood himself well and we were wrong in regarding him as a shining
light—this was not true, he was an ignorant creature of darkness:

'You make a mistake in thinking of me as a creature of light ...
I do not understand the meaning of life ... '

His voice sounded dry, nasal, slightly foggy and a little cracked;
he seemed to chop his words with a hatchet and the unseeing gaze
of his blue eyes seemed consciously to beg my forgiveness for
something: 'I am ignorant!'

We stood hatless in the blazing sun, then walked along slowly,
casting short, dark shadows. He told me of a feeling of stagnation
in his everyday life, and that he did not believe in any kind of happy
future. At times it seemed to him that the human race was going to
perish, and it depressed him to realize that he, Blok, was stagnant
and inactive and that this was probably due to bad heredity (the
weight of many generations): that all his efforts to find some way of
expressing himself in this life were in vain, and that death always
tips the balance. We would all be snuffed out—and to believe anything else was mere illusion.

His smile was strained and he forced out his words, talking past
me disjointedly yet urgently as if his mind were in a muddle. I
can remember that agitation and that tone of conviction as if
this was an age-old theme on which he had been reflecting for
years.

This theme later appeared in the poem 'Retribution',* retribution
being his father, Alexander Lvovich Blok, whom he felt within
himself. I must confess, I felt completely lost in all this. That
sombre mood, with its overtones of both scepticism and sensuality,
seemed out of keeping with his healthy appearance, his naturalism,
sunburn, strong muscles, and the lofty pose of a stately elder, a
venerable Goethe from a new Weimar, which relatives tried to foist
upon him.

By making an intellectual effort I have rejected the idea of the
power of fate and of a boundary between everyday life and thought;
but I fully realized that philosophy was of little use in grappling
with this earthy, slow and stagnant intellect, concerned with pigs and
ham. Thinking of the poetry of 'The Fair Lady' and his words about

* A long poem which Blok began in 1911 and which remained unfinished at
his death.

the 'prophet's burning coal' in his heart, one wondered how it was possible to reconcile with all this his relatives' assertions that 'Sasha and Lyuba were special people'. He was Shenshin, a sceptic, an old sensualist, a former hussar, who drove Lev Tolstoy and V. S. Solovyov to despair. In view of all this, what sense was there in the cult of Solovyov's poetry, which he was trying to develop?

All this swirled up within me like a hurricane at the sudden appearance of the 'ignorant' Blok on my horizon. I remember that we were walking across some fields while I struggled with myself to find an answer. What was needed in order to understand his precise but limited intellect, which shunned even the approaches to gnosiological consciousness?

I looked at the blue expanse of sky, and it seemed to darken. Much later, I described the impression of this black hell of the soul in 'The Silver Dove'.* 'But it is in the black air of hell that the artist finds ... other worlds ... ' wrote Blok, later still. My description of the black sky striking terror was appreciated and mentioned by the poet in his article, because it was a true impression left in me from the moment when the veil of 'Blok the romantic', was torn away (if only for a moment) and I saw the 'black midday sky' within him.

He stood before me, with a broken stalk of wheat in his hand: 'You've had this sort of experience yourself, Borya!' he said.

However, I did not know it – then. I knew the sombre darkness of life, but the grim self-destructiveness of a purely sensuous existence was as yet unknown to me.

Could I have been aware, for one brief moment, of our future relationship? Blok later wrote: 'How I scolded Borya and Ellis ... ' (Letters to his mother.) And then: 'Rode twenty-four miles on our bicycles, although we had been drunk as lords the day before ... ' 'Rozanov ... seemed very close to me ... '; ' ... we've been drinking ... '; 'I am tired of bachelor life ... '; 'I get drunk every evening ... '; ' ... waste a lot of my energy ... on women ... '; 'terrible loneliness and despair ... '; ' ... little actresses, by whose side one wrinkles one's nose, as if one expects them to stink of sweat ... '; 'I have not seen A. Biely. It seems we cannot stand each other.'

This was written only four years later. Very soon, he was writing a poem glorifying the lady's heel which had pierced his heart,

* A novel by Biely, first published in 1909.

whereas I wrote a bold article directed against 'mystical anarchism', for which I held Blok responsible.*

I found the ideology of Blok, the blind man, completely untenable, not because he could not see any logical way out, but because living in appalling spiritual gloom, he dared to write haughtily from Moscow that 'Sasha and Lyuba' would shortly descend upon the capital of what was then the Russian Empire.

The feeling of protest against him once more flared up for a moment in my subconscious as I looked at him and sensed something like a blind beggar, trudging slowly along the roads and plaintively chanting some psalm-like tune. I remembered his proud fanfares when writing to me in the summer of 1903, and although only a year had passed, something in him had changed.

After this conversation, we returned to the house and went indoors, sitting down feeling completely overwhelmed. Knitting her eyebrows and puckering her little forehead, Lyubov Dmitrievna appeared to be anxiously listening to our silence. She looked extremely plain, and once again she seemed to be possessed by some reckless daring, which she managed to stifle. Alexandra Andreyevna fussed around, while Maria Andreyevna, sitting quietly, dressed in her speckled frock, started to blink. Somewhere in the distance one could hear a voice singing about Vanka the wicked seducer.

I asked A.A. if he liked Russian songs.

'No ... there's too much anguish in them!'

During those years, he considered everything Russian as anguished. The style of the songs, the kerchiefs, the topical ballads, they all seemed hostile to him. The minute you allow a kerchief to intrude, Dostoievsky's Grushenka appears, and he detested everything connected with Dostoievsky. There one found riot and debauch ... and there also was ... Katka from 'The Twelve'.† The poem 'Troika', which I had just published in the *Journal for All* and which was a folk-poem in spirit, was still completely alien to him.

> I, a clown at the shining footlights,
> Spring up through the open trap-door.

I felt sad at the thought of Anna Andreyevna, in her mouse-grey frock, placing her hands, palms outwards, on each side of her head,

* Refers to Biely's hostile review of Blok's volume of *Lyrical Dramas* (1908).
† A prostitute in Blok's long, enigmatic poem on the revolution.

her little, pink nose sticking forward and her brown eyes darting here and there, with Maria Andreyevna bustling in her wake.

That night I told Petrovsky about my interpretation of Blok. Petrovsky sighed, rubbing his pince-nez: 'That's right, he's all burnt up ... failed completely!'

However, we tried to brush this aside, and the days passed in delightful idleness. The two law students clicked their heels at lunchtime; we lounged about, then separated. We met again at dinner. I used to go wandering along the roads to the village of Tarakanovo. Beyond Tarakanovo, I would walk whistling with my hands behind my back, along the sun-scorched road, the wheel-ruts full of dust. The ground had gone very hard because of the drought; there was a slight burnt smell over the fields, and clouds of dust whirled about in the distance.

I felt very sad whenever I thought about Blok. I seemed to have had a foreboding of the tragedy that was to happen between us and separate us for five long years. And in fact, my relationship with the poet did not return to normal until 1910. In the period I have described there already seemed to be a jarring note in the very psychology of our friendship.

Desdemona *by* Valery Tarsis

Novy Mir, 1938/IX

Translated by Jacqueline Mitchell

Valery Yakovlevich Tarsis was born at Kiev in 1906 into a family of Greek origin. Apart from some juvenilia in the form of short stories published in the 'twenties, his literary career was founded on translation from the classics of Western European literature, including Sterne, Stendhal and Flaubert; he also wrote a critical study of modern Western writers. Until 1937 he was a publisher's editor, specializing in foreign literature. While serving in the Red Army during the Second World War, he was twice severely wounded.

Prevented by the regimes of both Stalin and Khrushchev from having his writing published, in 1960 Tarsis despairingly sent abroad the MSS of two novels, *The Bluebottle* and *The Red and the Black*, first published in England in 1962 in one volume under the title *The Bluebottle*. They subsequently appeared in many other countries. For this he was put into a lunatic asylum. The incident received considerable publicity in the West, and he was released in 1963. The outcome was the book which has made his name abroad, the autobiographical account of his experiences as a 'political lunatic' entitled *Ward 7*, a title devised with conscious reference to Chekhov's famous short story *Ward 6*. In 1966, while on an officially sanctioned visit to England, Tarsis was deprived of his Soviet passport and remained in the West, settling in Switzerland.

In addition to its intrinsic merit, the short novella *Desdemona*, published here in translation for the first time, occupies a special place in Tarsis's career as a writer, as he has described in a note specially written for this edition:

I am very pleased that my first story, written when I was a young man, should be appearing in England and America. It is very dear to me and has a certain autobiographical significance. From my earliest youth I have greatly loved the Caucasus, and Daghestan in particular, and once spent some time travelling all over the Caucasus. One day during a halt in my journey I

94

met a troupe of actors which became the subject of my story *Desdemona*. The actors trudged on foot from one mountain village to another, carrying their scenery, props and costumes on their backs. I was so fascinated by this encounter that I changed my itinerary and spent about three weeks with them. Thus my story came into being. Its plot is based on something that really happened, though I altered it slightly.

The then editor-in-chief of *Novy Mir*, Vladimir Stavsky, liked the story very much indeed. A Cossack by origin, he loved everything to do with the Caucasus, but thought that publishing it might be too risky. He was helped to make up his mind by the novelist and playwright, Leonid Leonov, who was then the fiction editor. He was delighted with the story. Two years after its publication he said to me, 'Whenever I read any new works, I compare them with your *Desdemona*, and not one of them stands up to the comparison.'

The readers, too, liked it a great deal, and the editors received many letters hailing this unknown new writer. Soon after the story appeared, however, it was reviewed in *Pravda* by someone called Belyaev, who criticized it sharply, calling it 'snobbish and devoid of ideas' and full of 'obvious bourgeois tendencies'. Naturally, after that no one else reviewed it, although I knew that several critics had been preparing to print laudatory reviews.

This success inspired me, and it was as a result of it that I conceived the idea of writing a large-scale novel about life in Soviet Russia. Until the outbreak of war I travelled the country, gathering material; I visited factories, state and collective farms, and I met countless interesting people. After that came twenty-four years of work, at the end of which I had completed my ten-volume epic: *The Dangerous Life of Valentin Almazov*. The first volume, entitled *Confrontation with a Mirror*, has been published; the second is shortly to appear.

I

The ground was soft and untouched by the January cold. The steps of passers-by sounded like faint sighs. Above the sheer peak, a waning moon cast its radiance over the distant mountain range like a mantle of snow, though there was still no snow on the mountains.

From the narrow, passage-like street of a Caucasian mountain village several people emerged into a little square, and were then engulfed once more by the darkness of an alleyway where the upper balconies of the houses leaned so close together that they seemed to be whispering to each other. Just as in summer, clouds of dust were stirred up under their heavy boots. A multitude of bright stars clustered in the thin ribbon of sky.

Lowering their heads, they climbed to the first floor of a white house up a narrow stairway of sun-baked clay. Hearing their steps, the owner of the house flung open the door. They went in and were enveloped by such heat after the cold night air that for a moment they gasped for breath. A red-hot iron stove was humming and crackling. The faces of the host and hostess were as red as the pattern on the rugs which covered the floor and walls of the room. Water was bubbling in a large cast-iron pot on the stove, and a small kerosene lamp was flickering on the table.

The guests, in their overcoats, felt cloaks and sheepskins, stood jostling in the doorway. Their hosts seized three chairs and arranged them around the room, but there were too few of them for the guests, and Kurban Emirov, a man with shaggy red hair, took off his tall sheepskin hat, banged it against his hand and shouted, 'Lord, you're like a lot of sheep—you can't even wag your tails without your shepherd.'

He lowered himself ponderously on to the rug. He was wearing a curly, ginger-coloured sheepskin coat, and as he sat on the floor he looked like a pile of sheepskins.

'You're certainly unique, anyway,' laughed Mikail Aliyev. 'I'll bet you're the only red-headed Avar in the whole of Daghestan.'

'Kindly don't make fun of our theatre director and my guest,' said the host sedately.

'Thank you, Shapi. You're the only one who sticks up for me among all these miserable wretches.'

The visitors sat down on the carpet. For greater comfort they removed their coats and cloaks and tossed them into the corner. They talked so fast that it sounded as if thousands of tiny sea-borne pebbles were being dashed against the shore. Short, harsh words, apparently made up of nothing but consonants, rattled down like flails.

Little Khabibat was asleep in one corner in a narrow wooden cot. Although only five months old, she had already grown used to the ceaseless surge of people's voices, the wood crackling in the stove and the wind howling on the Khunzakh plateau.

'I hope you don't mind us all crowding into your house like this, Shapi,' said Kurban. 'The devil himself would freeze to death in the theatre, let alone your wife Aishat and little Khabi.'

'Anyway, you can't drag a baby around in the cold and dark,' said Rukiat, her words sounding like the patter of falling shingle.

And then, in a voice like a faraway bell carried down from the mountains by a gust of wind, Aishat said, 'I'm such a nuisance to you.'

They all instinctively stopped talking for a moment, caressed by the tender breeze of Aishat's words. Mikail then said thoughtfully, 'When communism comes to the whole world every girl will speak like you, Aishat.'

'I swear I did right to choose you, Mikail. You're just the right man to run the literary side of the Avar Theatre,' said Kurban in a loud voice.

'Officially I'm the prompter. It's becoming a habit ...'

'And I say that fine words are flattering, but flattering words are false,' said Shapi hoarsely.

'You must have done quite a bit of flattery yourself in your time, to have enticed such a beautiful woman,' said Kurban, with a cheerful wink.

Shapi stood up. He was a stocky, broad-shouldered, thickset man with a short, fat neck. He silently rolled himself a cigarette, lit it, spat juicily and said to his wife, 'Are you going to make us some khinkal?'

Aishat went out and returned after a minute with a copper basin and a bag of flour. Carefully pushing aside the books and papers, she began preparing the dish on the table.

'Meanwhile we can start our meeting, which is what we came here for, Shapi. There's only one item on the agenda—to cast the parts for *Othello*, a play written by that world-famous playwright Shakespeare, with the help of a writer who is no less famous in these parts and who is also artist, scene-painter, translator and prompter—Mikail Aliyev. Any objections or other suggestions?' Kurban tossed back his ginger forelock above his freckled, brick-red face. He was sitting closest to the stove and his damp forehead glistened and shone.

Aishat looked round. She turned pale, which made her unusually white face look almost translucent. She looked at Kurban's flushed complexion and then turned towards Shapi, whose eyes were shining like two sparks of green fire in a face of lacquered bronze. Aishat lowered her head again and went back to her work. Only her shoulders could be seen quivering beneath her long black headscarf.

'I have an objection,' said Mikail. 'I won't let you have the play unless you pay me royalties.'

'Will someone please take this great brain away from me and give it to someone else?' said Kurban with a despairing gesture. 'As actor and prompter you're getting two hundred roubles. Since when has our theatre paid fees? It's ridiculous. Think of the glory of it: your name printed in red on the posters alongside Shakespeare's —it's you who ought to be paying me!'

'Am I supposed to do the scenery for nothing as well?'

'Please yourself, comrade. If you act without scenery or costumes you'll look as much like Othello as a Khunsakh ass looks like a motor-car.'

'Kurban,' said Shapi, breathing heavily, 'I have a say in this meeting too, and I tell you *I'm* going to play Othello, not Mikail. It's no better than capitalism if one person gets everything and the others get nothing.'

'Capitalism, indeed! If you can't think of anything better than that to say at this meeting, I advise you to stuff your mouth with khinkal and keep quiet for the rest of your life. Have you ever seen *Othello*? Don't you realize you can't possibly play Othello? You're too short. That great empty head of yours would only come up to Othello's stomach.'

'What does height matter?' said Shapi, breathing heavily. 'I'm dark-skinned, like a real Moor—that's much more important.'

'Please!' said Kurban imploringly. He looked round at everyone in turn, his bobbing ginger quiff pecking like a rooster at the clouds of blue-grey tobacco smoke. 'Please,' Kurban repeated, 'will some-body take this Moor away from me and give him to someone else?'

'All right, I give in,' said Mikail.

He was about to say something else, but Aishat turned around quickly; her scarf fluttered like a blackbird's wing and brushed lightly over Mikail's hand. It happened in a brief moment, and then her head was once more bent low over the table and her little fingers working furiously as she kneaded the lumps of heavy dough.

'Listen, have we come here to have a working meeting or to start haggling? Mikail's playing Othello, because there's no one else who can do it. Maybe next season I'll invite Kachalov down from the Moscow Art Theatre. Mikail must be made to earn his pay, after all. He's so lazy that he'd be quite willing to give up the part. And you, Shapi, will play Cassio.'

'Did you know, Kurban, I've got four quilted blankets with beautiful patterns on them—the very thing we need for the bedroom scene,' said Shapi.

'Well, go and cover yourself up with them and then we'll have something pleasant to look at for a change.'

'Just what I was going to do. I'll cover myself up in them, but of course Aishat will be lying under them too, right beside me. I'd be interested to know how you're going to put a pleasant sight like that on stage!'

Things were taking a nasty turn, and everyone began to feel embarrassed. They all knew about Shapi's touchiness and obstinacy.

'Aishat's the only one who can play Desdemona. Do you want to spoil the play?' asked Rukiat timidly.

Shapi sat down on the rug in silence. Breathing heavily, he began to fill the air around him with smoke rings.

Kurban moved his lips silently. If he was sure of one thing, it was that *Othello* would be ruined without Aishat. How could they stage any play without her?

Little Aishat stood there with her head lowered, curls piled up above her white forehead, her face, pale but for flushed cheeks, glowing faintly, and her girlish breasts heaving convulsively as she breathed. What did she see in that sullen, obstinate, vindictive creature Shapi? His mind was as small and inflexible as his fat neck. It was absurd for these two to be in love. How could they be made to quarrel or divorce?

Kurban had visited Aishat soon after the baby had been born. He was impatient for her to get fit again. The collective farmers and shepherds from Chokh, the bricklayers from Sogratl, the mechanics from Gergebil and the market-gardeners from Tlokh and Botlikh all wore gloomy expressions in the theatre when they were deprived of that unique, special voice which held sway over their hearts and fantasies. Pale and hollow-cheeked, she looked like an ailing child. Kurban and Aishat had a brief talk.

'Aishat, do you think if you put a good Kuban saddle on to a little donkey you could fool a crack rider into thinking it was a fine horse?'

'You're so fond of making fun of everything, Kurban, even a real horse would seem a donkey to you.'

'But your heart's as soft as wax and you've wrapped it round your eyes and blinded yourself, so you can't see that you've become no more than a pile of bedding-straw for a donkey.'

'I don't know what you're talking about, Kurban. I love my husband and I'm happy to be a mother, but I shall go on being an actress to my dying day.'

'It's like putting straw and burning coals into one shed.'

'But that shed is my heart and that won't catch fire.'

'You believe in yourself as much as a saint believes in Allah. Don't you see you're in hell? I swear I mean to drag you out of it.'

'No, don't touch me; it's paradise, and I don't want you to take it away from me.'

'Shakespeare would have had a good laugh at you.'

'And when he'd had his laugh he would have written a sad play which would make everyone cry, even you, Kurban.'

'I can see I'm not going to convince you, but don't forget what I've said. You're walking a tightrope and you think it's the broad highroad ... Goodbye.'

Kurban remembered that conversation now. He had thought of it many times. Why did she love that damned Shapi? He was stubborn, and had no talent. Kurban would have sacked him from the theatre long ago, but then Shapi would have forbidden Aishat to act. True, Aishat might have disobeyed him, but it was better not to think about that. What starts as a quiet talk between man and wife can end in a sharp answer from a dagger, and Kurban did not care for scenes like that.

He knew that Shapi did not like the theatre; he was far more interested in his market-garden where he grew his beloved potatoes, but besides his other qualities he was greedy and mean and it was the salary of 150 roubles a month which tied him to the theatre. He was not too bad at playing character parts and was not without one or two skills—he had a good memory and the ability to appear relaxed on stage. Of course, this was not really enough to earn him such a high salary, but whenever people hinted to Kurban that Shapi was overpaid, he would say, 'You don't understand. A man who has managed to get himself a wife like that deserves the same rate as a lead player.' This was all very well, but it was going too far when this man had the insolence to want to play Othello! He had obviously gone out of his little mind. Kurban finally decided on a last resort. This red-headed psychologist knew that greed is as strong as passionate love ...

Kurban smiled at his own thoughts. His red quiff bobbed up as he raised his head.

The boiling water was bubbling away in the pot. Aishat was putting the dark, steaming khinkal out on to a plate, her face on fire.

Trying to smooth things over, a young actor called Akhmet-Nami said, 'I'm sure our host will change his mind and agree to play Cassio. It's a good part too.'

'Now I suppose you're going to ask me to play that scoundrel Iago or that idle woman-chaser Rodrigo,' said Shapi sullenly.

'Oh, be quiet, you two! What's the use of this pointless argument? We'll cancel the play and move on to the next item on the agenda: khinkal and wine, which Akhmet-Nami is now going to serve us, as a little exercise in professional training ... he shall play the waiter— but no servility, mind, Akhmet-Nami. To do it properly you must pull a disagreeable face, swear at me in a loud voice and see to it that we have a quart of red wine in ten minutes from now.'

Akhmet-Nami jumped up, put on his felt cloak, grabbed a large copper kettle and went out.

'Kurban,' said Aishat in a scarcely audible voice, 'you can't cancel *Othello*.'

Although she spoke as quietly as the rustle of a bird's wings, everyone pricked up their ears, and even Kurban gave a forced, nervous smile as he replied. 'What do you mean—"you can't"? Next you'll say I can make a roast turkey out of this maize khinkal, or sauce provençale, like you get in restaurants in Moscow. Well,

I had some of that sauce once – on the day I graduated – but I've forgotten what it tastes like by now.'

'No, you won't do it, Kurban,' said Mikail firmly.

'Won't I? – Go and report me to Shakespeare, if you like. Why should I rack my brains and quarrel with my friend Shapi just because of some Moor of Venice? My father would have done the same, by God.'

'I can play Othello as well as anyone else,' said Shapi, 'but if you don't want to put it on then I won't play it. It's no loss to me; I get my pay just the same.'

'Quite right, Shapi,' said Kurban, 'you won't lose money and Othello won't be any richer for your help, either. Othello had riches enough heaped on him for all his brave deeds.'

Puzzled smiles appeared on the actor's faces. No one could say for sure what was in Kurban's cunning mind. A great deal of work had already been put into the play and the actors had fallen in love with it.

Aishat was more upset than anyone. She would have been quite unmoved by the thought of the house burning down, of Shapi not loving her any more, of wolves killing the sheep and the potatoes being frostbitten – by anything, in fact, except that she might not play Desdemona.

As soon as Mikail had translated it she had copied out the whole play. Evening after evening, except when her husband had shouted angrily at her 'That's enough oil you've burnt. We don't keep a shop, you know,' she had carefully written out every word in her childish handwriting. As the words crept along the paper in black rows, the lines came to be a long, delightful road beckoning her on to some promised land. It was as if she were following a steep upward path, and the higher she went the brighter the world became. Each new speech of Desdemona poured into her heart like a springtime torrent. Streams were gurgling, exotic birds from beyond the sea were singing and she could already hear the sound of her own voice as it spoke those gorgeous words. It was she who was singing a song about a willow tree to her little Khabi, she who was gazing at her husband with mixed fear and tenderness. Perhaps dark suspicions were already stirring in his mind, too … ?

Aishat was eighteen that spring. She could only dimly remember her mother, a worn-out old woman who had died a long time ago when Aishat was still a little girl. She had only one clear, unforgettable memory of her, when the whole family was once returning home to their village. Her mother was carrying an iron bedstead on her back. Great drops of sweat were running down her wrinkled, sunburnt face. The little girl was walking by her side, taking quick little steps and holding on to the cold iron rods with her tiny hands. It was as if they were burning her soft little palms. She so desperately wanted to help, but how was she to find the strength?

She had sat down on the grass verge and started crying at the top of her voice.

Her father, who was walking behind them with a large clay pipe between his teeth, had looked puzzled, stopped and smacked her, while her mother called out angrily, 'You should be ashamed of yourself ... You're a big girl now ... !'

She had wiped away her tears with her little fist and walked on. Yes, she really was a big girl. She was wearing a long dress down to her ankles and a white scarf which fell down her back to below her knees. She was seven years old.

That autumn her mother took to her bed and never got up again. Old Magoma, her father, did not re-marry, and so Aishat became the housekeeper. She looked after the sheep, worked in the garden and cooked the dinner.

Her life went on in this unhurried fashion until one day at school she saw a play for the first time. It was Mikail's play *Sisters*. She was twelve years old at the time.

She repeated to herself the strange, moving words spoken by the younger sister who was the heroine of the play. With her she galloped off on horseback, hastening to tell the Red partisans that the Whites were approaching their native village; she it was who carefully dressed the officer's wounds, spoke tender words to him, sang songs and danced when they celebrated May Day, and, even though she was a little puzzled by them, she thrilled as she spoke her words of love.

That night she tossed and turned for a long time in her bed, and the next day as soon as school was over she went to the theatre.

She was met by Mikail, and for a long time she could say nothing, but only gaze with her big, frightened eyes at this tall, elegant young man with his white skin and smooth, pink, girlish cheeks. He had a finely chiselled nose, high, delicately arched eyebrows, and was altogether unlike the young Avars.

'Well, what have you got to say to me, little girl?' asked Mikail with a smile. Aishat's fear suddenly left her and she gave a word-perfect recitation of the younger sister's speech from the second act.

She stopped as suddenly as she had begun, and Mikail said nothing, listening to the silence, as though not he but some unknown magician had written those resounding words.

'Who are you?' he said in a voice that could scarcely be heard.

'My father's called Magoma and my mother's dead.'

'Do you want to act with us?'

'My father won't let me. I have to keep house.'

'Do you go to school?'

'Yes, but how can I do any school work if you go away? Can't you stay here?'

'No we can't, little girl, but when you finish school you can come and join us. We'll persuade your father.'

'Are you coming again?'

'Of course, often.'

Aishat ran home.

Humdrum life began once more. But Aishat lived a special, secret life which other people did not notice. She would go far away into the mountains and recite her favourite poems in a sing-song voice. She found Russian difficult. Her book was often splashed with tears, but when she had cried her fill she would set about her work again with great determination, and in her tear-swollen eyes there appeared an expression of angry, obstinate perseverance, as if she had been driving off a gang of children intent on teasing her.

A year later she managed to get hold of a newly published copy of Mikail's translation of *Romeo and Juliet*. Aishat was so moved by it that at times she lost all sense of reality. She twice forgot to give old Magoma his dinner, she neglected her homework and avoided her friends.

Aishat would lie for hours on the grass. Before her eyes there flickered the tattered pages of her book and the fantastic visions which they conjured up, but she saw nothing of what was around her. Faraway images came to life on the mountains of Khunzakh. She thumbed through the book without reading it, because she knew every page by heart and only needed to glance at the top line to see before her eyes a market square, a palace or a darkened crypt.

The theatre was temporarily closed. Half the troupe had to be dismissed for lack of funds and all summer Aishat watched the main road in vain for a sight of their familiar faces.

Once when she was reciting *Romeo and Juliet* she was startled by a stocky little man hung about with pheasants.

'What's all that rubbish you're shouting? You'll never get an answer from the wind,' said the hunter.

Startled at first, Aishat calmed down when she recognized Shapi.

'What do you want? Go away,' she answered crossly.

'My way passes right beside you,' said Shapi, and sat down heavily. 'Instead of shouting all that nonsense into the air you should come hunting with me in the forest. It's full of wolves, jackals and hares, and every kind of bird you've ever seen—and plenty you haven't.'

'Aren't you afraid of them?' asked Aishat suspiciously.

'Has Shapi ever been afraid of anything? If you can keep a secret I'll tell you something to show you how brave some men are.'

'You won't lie to me, will you?'

'Why should I? What would be the use? Nothing's worth doing if there's no use in it, especially telling lies.'

'All right, I won't tell anyone.'

'Once I used to ride with some bandits to rob the rich, and I was never once afraid. Two of them attacked me, but I tossed them aside like puppies. No one has ever beaten me in a fight, although I was nearly caught once. We went into a house and I saw the man's wife lying there—she was beautiful, just like you—so I stopped, and while I was looking at her, her husband crept up behind me. A second longer and I would have been caught, but I came to my senses and grabbed him by the arms ... You're the most beautiful girl in our village. I want to go to your father and ask him to let me marry you.'

Aishat suddenly stood up, and before Shapi realized what was happening she had run off.

But they met many more times. Shapi used to tell her about his strange escapades and adventures when he went hunting, and Aishat would listen quietly and attentively.

When she was sixteen Shapi went to old Magoma and said to him, 'Listen, Magoma, all's well now that the Soviets are in power.

4*

My parents are dead and you're a good man — give me your daughter.'

Magoma looked at him from under his bushy grey eyebrows and said slowly and deliberately, 'If you want to see which is stronger, your bones or my stick, then go on talking.'

'But Aishat won't refuse.'

'You might as well say that my sheep have written a letter to you to say they want to be moved into your sheepfold. There aren't many liars hereabouts as barefaced as you.'

'I'll give her a good home.'

'Yes — the same way you give that herd of lice a good home in your one and only shirt. Get out, my hands are itching for a fight.'

Shapi went away.

One day he said to Aishat, 'Shall I carry you off in the night?'

'Yes,' Aishat replied.

Aishat liked Shapi. He knew so many strange stories, and besides his fierce eyes were so tender when they looked at her. She could not understand where this strange tenderness of Shapi's came from.

She also liked him because he was very strong. Aishat did not know what love was, but she liked being with Shapi, and after all she was sixteen and therefore grown up; old Magoma would probably try and find her a husband soon in any case. Better marry Shapi, or else before she knew where she was she would find herself married off to an old man with a wagging beard like a goat.

Occasionally Aishat thought of Mikail, and when she did she suddenly felt freezing cold and then a few moments later so hot that her cheeks seemed to be on fire, and her heart started beating furiously. She once dreamed that she felt his hand on her breast, and she thought she was dying. Her breathing became difficult and she woke up with a pain in her heart. She did not want to think about it again and tried to banish these thoughts from her mind. She sometimes had the fleeting, almost unconscious notion that if Mikail came, picked her up and carried her off, no matter where, she would not resist but would obey in silence. But these ideas were just flashes of lightning or perhaps heralds of a storm, and on the whole Aishat felt happy and at peace.

'Let Shapi take me away,' she thought, 'I'll be a good wife to him.'

And so he carried her off.

Old Magoma heaped abuse on him, cursed him with all the foul language he knew, and then ate a plateful of home-made fried sausage and drank a tankard of wine at his new son-in-law's house, cursed him again, but with a considerably diminished assortment of invective, and went home to bed.

The young couple lived quietly, and to all appearances happily, but soon something happened which cast a dark shadow over their newly-wed serenity.

A troupe of actors led by Kurban Emirov arrived in Khunzakh to found a new permanent theatre.

Aishat was crossing the yard with a bundle of firewood when she looked over the low stone wall and suddenly saw Mikail walking slowly towards her.

The firewood fell from her grasp and she stopped in the middle of the yard, confused and dumbfounded. Mikail was coming straight towards her. She could not take her eyes from him and kept staring at him, although she knew she ought not to be doing this. He walked on towards her.

Her icy hand was in his firm, warm grasp, and no sooner had he spoken his first words than she gave up the struggle against herself.

'Aishat, how beautiful you've become, yet you're still as tiny as ever,' said Mikail.

'I'm married to Shapi. He's waiting for me at home.'

'Aishat, your voice still sounds like a stream in spring. Your heart isn't still covered with ice, is it? I've never forgotten you.'

'Don't talk about it, Mikail. You're a sensible grown man.'

'I've made a terrible mistake, Aishat.'

'I don't know what you've done, Mikail, but if you can't put the mistake right why make yourself and other people unhappy by talking about it?'

'No, I'm not going to leave it at that. You're going to ... '

'You have no right to tell me what to do, Mikail.'

'You don't understand, Aishat. I wanted to come and tell you about my latest success, I thought ... '

'Just keep thinking how successful you are, Mikail. You've already started out on the highroad and I'm still on a narrow mountain footpath. We have nothing in common.'

'Aishat, I swear you're making a mistake. I've been told to come here by Kurban Emirov, the director of our theatre. We're inviting you to join our troupe. I've told him so much about you, and today you're going to come and meet all our friends at the House of Socialist Culture.'

'All right, I'll come. But I must say goodbye for now, my husband is expecting me.'

Before supper Aishat went along to the House of Socialist Culture where the Avar Theatre was to stage its plays. The actors had gathered in a small room and Kurban's fiery ginger quiff was bobbing up and down.

They welcomed her noisily. Mikail took her up to Kurban and said, 'Well, Kurban, this is our future leading lady. If I'm wrong, you can call me an ass.'

'Why, aren't there enough asses here already? Or have they exchanged all their donkeys for cars? Anyway,' he said, turning to Aishat, 'recite something, and don't be afraid of me, I won't eat you.'

Aishat was silent for a few moments, and then recited Juliet's opening speech in a low voice.

At once everyone stopped talking. Kurban lowered his ginger quiff and stood stock still.

Aishat looked up only once and saw Mikail's eyes glinting with joy. Her heart was full of Juliet's suffering. Poor Juliet! She would never be happy, but how much she wanted to live, to look into those flashing eyes, to sing, to lie on the soft grass and float away into the infinite blue sky. Aishat's voice grew firmer and more confident, and her words rang out ... When she had finished and was standing silent, her hands clenched beneath her long white scarf, she suddenly felt cold. The actors said nothing for several minutes.

At last Kurban raised his red quiff. He was obviously moved. 'Give me your hand, Mikail.' He took Mikail's hand firmly in his and shook it for a long time.

'As for you, little girl, I'm making you a member of our troupe and paying you the highest rate, two hundred roubles a month, starting from today,' he said turning to Aishat.

'I'm very happy to hear that, but I'm afraid my husband won't let me.'

'Don't you worry. If your husband hasn't enough brains, I'll kill a calf and serve him the brains with sauce jardinière, like they do in restaurants in Moscow. No one who's not blind has ever seen Kurban not get his own way.'

The next day Kurban invited Shapi to see the new building which had been allocated to the theatre. Rukiat, his actress wife, had made some khinkal from white wheat flour, and two jugs of wine stood on a table set with an embroidered tablecloth. Kurban placed Shapi next to himself, while the other actors sat around primly. Rukiat stood modestly in a corner awaiting her husband's orders.

Kurban raised his glass: 'I drink my first glass to our distinguished guest, Shapi, and if anyone says there is a man more honourable and brave than our Shapi, may the bones of that impudent fellow turn as soft as this wheaten khinkal. Isn't that right, comrades?'

The room was filled with noisy approval and the clinking of glasses.

Shapi liked this red-headed director who was entertaining him with such courtesy, and the other actors seemed nice enough too. His brow furrowed slightly, however, when he looked at Mikail. He disliked this quiet man with his ingratiating manners. He was too pale, too much like a fine gentleman from the big city, and he spent too much time talking to Aishat ... There was nothing wrong in this, of course, he was only talking theatrical shop with her, but he did not quite like the way she was looking at him.

I suppose it's understandable, he thought to himself. She's scared by this unexpected offer. That must be why she's looking at him in that strange way. All the same ...

Kurban kept enthusiastically pouring out more drink for Shapi, and when Shapi was fairly drunk he said to him:

'Tell me, Shapi my friend, what would you call a man who had a good horse but kept it in the stable all the time, never rode it, never put it to work?'

'I'd call a man like that an ass.'

'And I tell you you're insulting yourself, Shapi. Why call yourself an ass?'

'But I haven't got a horse. What are you talking about?'

'You may not have a horse, but you have got a wife and she's worth more than a whole herd of Arab horses. Your wife will be famous throughout Daghestan and I'm giving her two hundred roubles a month just for a start. Work it out for yourself. Shapi.'

'Two hundred roubles is good money. But whoever heard of a wife acting in a theatre?'

'My wife does.'

'Agreed. I'd already thought of that, Kurban. Now you tell me something. You say my wife's going to be famous, so does that mean that I have to do the housework instead of her and let everyone laugh at me?'

'May the man who laughs at my friend Shapi choke to death on a bone.'

'I've had an idea. If you want my wife to act you can take me on as well. I can act just as well as she can, and besides, two hundred roubles is good money but four hundred is even better.'

'Aha!' cried Kurban. 'Who said Kurban had a good head on his shoulders? Better kill an ox and give me some of its brains with sauce piquante before I can compete with a mind like my good friend Shapi's!'

'Shapi, how are you going to act if you haven't been trained?' Mikail asked.

'What about her? She hasn't been trained in Moscow, has she? I can hit a bear first shot. How about that? That's better than talking your head off dressed up in funny clothes. But four hundred roubles isn't bad money. Otherwise I wouldn't consider it.'

'Well, my friends, what shall we do? I begrudge nothing to a man who can drive a bargain like my friend Shapi. All right—done. Three hundred roubles is good money,' said Kurban.

'But I said four hundred was good money.'

'Do you mean to say that three hundred roubles in Soviet money are just worthless pieces of paper? Only a kulak talks like that, not my good friend Shapi.'

'I didn't say that. But if you're my friend I can have the last word in your house: three hundred and fifty roubles is good money too.'

'Let's shake on it.'

So this was how Aishat and Shapi became members of the troupe.

For a long time afterwards, Kurban regretted paying Shapi's one hundred and fifty roubles, which he considered wasted. Then the idea of breaking up the marriage first came into his head. He could not imagine the theatre without Aishat; but Shapi was stubborn, and they were to have several nasty surprises from him yet.

Aishat was happy. For Shapi to have agreed so quickly was more than she had hoped for, and all that evening she was especially kind and affectionate to him. To Aishat the theatre was still a new and strange yet fascinating world. Everything in it delighted her, and she did not notice the dirt backstage, the cold, the holes and patches in the costumes and the makeshift scenery.

The public took to her at once and before long her fame had spread to the surrounding villages. Although her husband and her father were always scolding her for neglecting her household duties, this no longer worried her. The short break from work, one month in all, when Khabibat was born, was agony for her. At first she did not even feel any joy in motherhood, and it was only after a few months that she began to love the baby passionately and to croon lullabies to her for hours on end.

Only her occasional meetings with Mikail embarrassed her, and then for a long time she would lose all self-confidence. But she tried to avoid meeting him, and sometimes Shapi was amazed at the intensity of his wife's sudden tenderness and the passion of her caresses, as she was usually such a quiet, reserved creature.

The days went by peacefully.

When Mikail read out his translation of *Othello* Aishat did not say a word during the discussion that followed, but she could not sleep all that night. The next day she asked Mikail for his manuscript book and spent two weeks laboriously copying out the play.

She was caught up in a storm of conflicting feelings. She thought ceaselessly about Desdemona, who fascinated yet at the same time disturbed her. A month later she could no longer distinguish herself from that pale maid of Venice. She talked to her as if she were her own heart and soul. She was enraptured by the everlasting power of love and indignant at the gentle, uncomplaining way in which the falsely accused Desdemona endured her husband's insults. However much I loved him I wouldn't have let him order me about like that, she thought to herself.

She wanted to play Desdemona as a strong, self-willed woman who could not bear mistrust.

There's no love without trust, she thought. If Desdemona had been more determined in rejecting his accusations and had stood up bravely against Othello's suspicions, she could have overcome that villain Iago and spoiled his wicked plans.

To Aishat it seemed like years since she had first come to know Desdemona, for in that time she had come to understand so many things and had grown up a great deal. She became even more silent and reserved; a harsh note crept into her voice and Shapi often looked at her darkening eyes in silence.

And now this unexpected obstacle had arisen ...

It was not only Mikail who noticed Aishat's fingers trembling slightly as she put the plate of khinkal on to the table.

The door opened. Everyone thought it was Shapi coming back from fetching firewood, but instead old Magoma came groaning and wheezing into the room. He stood on the threshold as if undecided.

'I seem to have come at the wrong time—you have so many guests. Well, I can come and see you another day.'

'Sit down, Father. You're not disturbing us,' said Aishat, 'and the khinkal's just ready.'

'Sit down, old man, sit down,' said Kurban, giving him a slap on the arm of his fur coat. 'We've got some good news for you. We're letting your daughter go, so that she can get on with the housework to please you and her husband.'

Shapi came in with an armful of firewood. The thin branches fell and scattered about the floor. As he heard Kurban's words he said nothing, but only sighed deeply.

'Please have some khinkal,' said Aishat in a barely audible voice, her lips scarcely moving and her head bowed.

Akhmet-Nami came back, put the kettleful of wine on the table and looked around in astonishment.

'What's this—a funeral?'

'Yes, it is, Akhmet-Nami,' said Kurban with a sigh, 'we're burying the famous actress Aishat.'

'That's an undertaker's joke, Kurban. I like that kind of joke on the stage, but I prefer something a bit more cheerful in real life.'

'You're wrong if you think I'm joking. I'm not in a joking mood,' said Kurban, as he put a large piece of khinkal dripping with aromatic garlic sauce into his mouth.

'What are you talking about, Kurban?' asked Rukiat, looking

anxiously at her husband. 'You may as well close the theatre down without Aishat.'

'And what about you? You'll play not only Desdemona but the devil in a skirt if I tell you to. Oh, you women, what's the good of you? All you can do is wag your tongues, and sigh when you're in bed.'

'Kurban,' said Mikail from the corner of the room, 'I respect your wife Rukiat, but she can't play Desdemona.'

'Of course I can't. He's making fun of me,' said Rukiat.

'Aren't you clever! Do you think I don't know that? Good. Let's drink a glass of wine to Aishat the housewife.'

Kurban stretched out his glass towards Aishat: 'Your very good health, Aishat! I hope you have a dozen more children.'

Aishat raised her hand. The rapid movement made her scarf fall to the ground, showing everyone her hot, pale face and her unnaturally big eyes. The next moment she hit the glass of wine which Kurban was holding in his outstretched hand. The wine spilled, splashing the people sitting nearby, and the glass fell on to the rug with a dull thud.

'You will not drink that toast, Kurban. Pour yourself out another glass,' she said.

For a moment there was general embarrassment.

Shapi picked up the glass, wiped it with a towel, poured some wine into it and offered it to Kurban without a word.

The director's ginger quiff bobbed up, and his eyes were dancing as he called out, 'I swear that was the most interesting toast I've ever made in my life. I can see I shouldn't be drinking to Aishat the housewife and I'm glad of it. We're now waiting for our friend Shapi to say something.'

Kurban poured out some wine and handed it to Shapi.

'Kurban,' said Shapi slowly, 'if you want my wife and me to leave the theatre we won't come begging to you to keep us. Isn't that right, Aishat?'

'Yes, that's right,' said Aishat, and her voice sounded unusually affectionate.

'Do I want them to leave the theatre? Did you hear that, my friends?' said Kurban, shrugging his shoulders in mock resignation. 'The next thing you'll be saying, Shapi, is that I want to eat my own liver with khinkal sauce.'

'You mean you don't want us to leave the theatre? In that case, this is what I say: let Aishat play Desdemona, and I won't take a part in the play. I'll be prompter. Is that right, Aishat?'

'Yes, quite right,' said Aishat, again in a ringing voice, and Shapi felt a sense of relief, as though he was driving fast along a straight, smooth road with the bells jingling on the harness and luring him towards the distant mountains.

To hell with that long, lanky creature Mikail, thought Shapi. Let him play Othello if he likes, but I'm not going to lower myself by playing any stupid part. But it's not worth leaving the theatre for that; it would be ridiculous when your own wife's a famous actress and you certainly won't find three hundred and fifty roubles a month lying around on the roadside, no matter how hard you look.

Aishat came to life again and her cheeks and ears turned pink. She had forgotten to put back her scarf, so that Mikail could now feast his eyes on her girlish face, her glittering eyes and her high forehead. She could feel his hungry looks, and this made her blush still more with embarrassment and annoyance. She whispered softly, 'What a good man Shapi is. It wasn't easy for him to make that sacrifice for me, and that means he loves me. So I must always love him, I must, I must! ...

'Well, my friends,' shouted Kurban, 'now that we've come to a peaceful agreement we can at last get on with the meeting.'

'It's a shame that Shapi gave in so quickly,' sighed old Magoma, wiping his greasy fingers on his sleeves. 'I always said there was no rhyme nor reason in your way of life. The money's good, of course, but what sort of a job is it?'

'Don't you worry, old fellow. You'll understand when you get older. Your son-in-law's making good money.'

'You're always making fun of people. All right, live your life. May Allah be your judge.' The old man went out.

'Before we start casting the play we must discuss what cuts we have to make,' said Kurban. 'The play's too long to put on in one evening, so my suggestions are as follows ... ' Kurban went through all the possible cuts in detail.

There was no argument about the first act, but passions rose when it came to the second act. When Kurban suggested leaving out the scene where they are waiting for Othello on the quayside in Cyprus, they cut him off before he could finish what he was saying.

'I'll never agree to that,' said Mikail, jumping up. 'That scene is vital – it illustrates Iago's character so well, how he despises women, how he hates people.'

'It's an important scene for Desdemona, too,' said Aishat. 'She's uneasy because she's afraid for Othello, yet at the same time she listens calmly and proudly to the malicious things that Iago is saying, calls him a vile slanderer and shows how much she despises him. It takes a brave woman to face danger with a smile like that.'

'And listen to Iago's marvellous lines:

> She that was ever fair, and never proud;
> Had tongue at will, and yet was never loud;
> Never lack'd gold, and yet went never gay;
> Fled from her wish, and yet said "Now I may";
> She that being anger'd, her revenge being nigh,
> Bade her wrong stay, and her displeasure fly ...

Don't you see how this reveals Iago's mixture of intelligence and malice? No, we can't do without those lines,' said Mikail hotly.

'That's enough from counsel for the defence. I'm the one who's playing Iago and I'm not so attached to his every word as you are.'

'Are you playing Iago?' asked Rukiat in astonishment.

'And who else? Which of you is a bigger villain than Kurban? If I eat your horrible stale bread without complaining and fail to murder you for it, it's not because I'm an angel, it's just that by the evening I forget what you fed me on in the morning. All right, I agree to leave the scene in.'

Aishat asked for Scene 1 of Act III to be shortened.

'We could begin straight away with Scene 3. The essential part is when Desdemona begs Othello to forgive Cassio, and that doesn't come until Scene 3. And then that Clown in Scene 1 gets on my nerves.'

'You've obviously missed the point,' said Mikail.

'No, I haven't missed the point. A clown may not have looked out of place in Shakespeare's day, but I think he's just a nuisance.'

'The audience must have something to laugh at,' said Kurban. 'What would you do without me, for instance? You would all go sour like Rukiat's pickled cabbage.'

'Your jokes make me want to cry,' said Rukiat.

'Oh, you silly little fool—when you've had a good laugh even tears taste sweet. It's like that in the theatre, and that's how it is in life, too ... Don't you worry, Aishat, you'll have enough tragedies in your life. Shapi will see to that.'

'I can see you're bargaining over my wife's future. Well, it's not market day today,' said Shapi sullenly.

'All right, Shapi. Let's stop bargaining and make up our minds: we'll cut that scene.'

At Aishat's insistence, Desdemona's conversation with the Clown in Scene 4 of Act III was also cut out.

'I've no time for him,' said Aishat trying to justify herself. 'Just think—the moment after that stupid argument with him I have the handkerchief scene.'

There was no more discussion. Everyone agreed to shorten Scene 1, Act V. 'They always shorten it in Moscow, too,' said Kurban.

Then they moved on to casting, which only took a few minutes. Akhmet-Nami was overjoyed to be given the part of Cassio. They were getting ready to go when a man from the telegraph office came into the room.

'I decided to bring you this nice telegram myself. It was late and there was no one to deliver it, so as I was just going home from work I thought I'd bring you the good news myself.'

'Give it to me,' shouted Kurban. 'Listen: "Permission granted cast *Othello* after tour Botlikh spend month Makhach-Kala work Daghestan State Theatre. Ministry of Arts".'

The messenger was given a noisy welcome, and he swallowed some khinkal, swilling it down with cloudy wine. Khabibat started crying.

'Now look, you've woken up the baby,' said Kurban angrily. 'It's amazing. I've been shouting my head off for the past two hours and she's only just realized that I have a voice that wakens the dead. Oh, what clever little creatures children are! Come on, quick, let's be off!'

Stooping to avoid hitting their heads, the guests crowded out of the room. Khabibat started crying even louder. Aishat picked up the baby and soon there came a loud and satisfied sucking noise.

2

The moon had risen higher still. It was surrounded by a huge, bright disc-like halo which covered half the sky and looked as if it had been woven out of mist. The pale stars winked dimly and wearily, and the earth was bathed in a gentle glow.

'We shall probably have snow,' said Rukiat, looking at the sky.

'Don't be such a pessimist. We have to go to Botlikh in a few days' time, and she wants it to snow.'

'It's not my fault. Look at that ring round the moon.'

The actors stopped at the corner and arranged to meet at ten o'clock the next morning for rehearsal. Kurban, Mikail and Akhmet-Nami went off together as they lived in the same house.

Rukiat felt embarrassed walking through the village with men. She quickened her pace and was soon a long way in front of them, while the men walked slowly, sometimes stopping to roll or light a cigarette.

They sat down on some logs in the square in front of the District Committee building.

The square was surrounded on all sides by mountains whose sharply indented ridges stood out against the sky. Here and there the peaks were draped in clouds like cast-off fur coats. The distance was hazy with moonlit mist, and away to the right glimmered the lights of the fortress. The silence was so immense, so complete that one dared not speak for fear of disturbing the deep sleep of this midnight world.

Such might have been the thoughts of a stranger entranced by this astonishing, motionless silence, but Kurban had grown up here and in any case he was not the sort of person who notices the silence of the sleeping night. Instead, he was already thinking of the next day, as if the sun had already risen and people were up and about.

Kurban was thinking of everything at once—about their tour to Botlikh, about Makhach-Kala, about the grant for building the theatre, about having to get a good comedy actor at all costs, and about buying a hundred yards of artificial silk, but most of all he was worrying about Shapi. The latest disagreement over the part of Othello had barely been settled when a new problem arose, and so it went on. Yes, he would really have to get rid of that bull of a

man, but at the same time — and this was the most important thing —
he must keep Aishat in the troupe.

'What are you thinking about, Kurban?' asked Mikail, interrupting his meditation.

'I'm doing some arithmetic,' answered Kurban. 'I bet Shapi's
already imagining himself walking around Makhach-Kala convinced that he's the most indispensable member of the troupe.
And the cost of getting there, the hotel and the food is all running
out of the second hole in my pocket.'

'What do you mean — the second hole?' asked Akhmet-Nami
curiously.

'I mean that eighteen hundred roubles a year is already running
out of the first hole to this Shapi, and since he's got a wide throat
he's not likely to choke himself. Arithmetic's a boring subject, my
friend. You can thank your stars you don't have to do as much of it
as your boss, who has to be the chief accountant, book-keeper and
cashier whether he likes it or not.'

'Yes, of course,' said Mikail thoughtfully. 'He won't let Aishat
go alone.'

'Now instead of coming to such brilliantly obvious conclusions,
it would be a great deal better if you got on with *your* part of the
job.'

'What has it to do with me?'

'Well, if I were you I shouldn't be wasting any time in persuading
that beautiful little creature to come and warm my bed for me. If
you're going to play the noble Moor in real life too, Mikail, then I
wouldn't give a brass kopeck for your boring existence.'

'You're wrong, Kurban. Aishat loves her husband.'

'Ah, Mikail, I'm older than you are and I know more about this
not very funny comedy called life. Believe me, all our women love
their husbands. But if you tell her she loves *you*, she'll believe you
and obey you. A woman's heart only has in it what men write there.
They're not very literate and not too rational.'

'Aishat has progressed from that stage,' said Mikail. 'And not
only Aishat. You're out of date, Kurban. Soviet women are pilots,
engineers, partisans' widows and Komsomol members, and they
can write their own lives. Their hearts are like Khunsakh stone
nowadays, not beeswax. It's hard to get any honey out of stone
honeycombs like those.'

'I'm still convinced she loves you. Have you ever heard of a Caucasian girl telling you such a thing herself? She'll keep persuading herself until she dies that she loves Shapi unless you get on with the job.'

'I don't like the way you're talking, Kurban,' said Akhmet-Nami. 'If wives start falling in love with other men, what are we going to do? Suppose your Rukiat ... '

'There's no comparison. If you think that Rukiat can find herself another director, there's no point in my wasting time giving you at least three portions of extra brains with any sauce you like. You'll die a donkey without the help of any sauce at all.'

'So you think Aishat doesn't love ... ' Mikail began, but he was interrupted by Kurban as he stood up:

'Now you just be sensible. When young men of your age start thinking they've got something of a future ... '

They began to walk towards the house in silence. Kurban went upstairs to his room, and Akhmet-Nami slipped into the door next to it. Mikail stood for a while longer on the veranda looking out at the pale glow in the night sky before going upstairs to his room.

He felt for his matches in the dark, lit the tin lamp, undressed and turned back the covers on his bed. The sheets and pillows felt colder than ice. The little stove was on the floor below where the food was cooked and where an old couple slept. The upstairs rooms were not heated. Mikail pulled the bedclothes over his head and breathed rapidly in and out to warm the bed. The cold made it even harder than usual to think, and it was only when warmth began to penetrate him that fleeting thoughts started slowly to form in his mind. At first vague and confused, they gradually became more distinct and meaningful.

Surely it can't be ... Aishat has never given the slightest sign or hint that she might leave Shapi. She knows I love her, of course. I even think she could have been my wife if I hadn't been so stupid and missed my chance. Still, Kurban's as clever as the devil and its worth listening to what he says. Besides, he has nothing against me—on the contrary, he has often shown how much he likes me. Anyway, he's a good friend, he loves the theatre and the actors, and he works like a slave. What if he is right and I'm missing my chance? ...

Mikail now felt very warm. He pushed his head out of the bed-clothes, gulped in the freezing air and at once started coughing.

The silvery glow of starlight suffused the darkness, and in the play of faint light and shadow he saw the dim figure of Aishat ...

Aishat was not asleep either. She had fed Khabibat and was trying to lull her to sleep, but the little girl stayed awake for a long time. Softly, Aishat began singing a little song about a willow tree. She had learned this sad song and grown fond of it when she had first read *Othello*. She sang it to the tune of an old Avar love song which she had heard when she was a child.

'The poor soul sat sighing by a sycamore tree,
    Sing all a green willow;
Her hand on her bosom, her head on her knee,
    Sing willow, willow, willow:
The fresh streams ran by her, and murmur'd her moans;
    Sing willow, willow, willow:
Her salt tears fell from her, and soften'd the stones;
    Sing willow, willow willow:
Sing all a green willow must be my garland ... '

The gentle flow of the song lulled Khabibat to sleep. Aishat could hear her gentle, regular breathing, and when she had put her to bed she fell into a reflective mood. Sadness came over her, and she imagined that it was the girl Barbara who had just sung the song, not she herself. Then she remembered the lines that Desdemona speaks just before the song:

My mother had a maid call'd Barbara;
She was in love, and he she lov'd prov'd mad
And did forsake her; she had a song of 'willow';
An old thing 'twas, but it express'd her fortune,
And she died singing it ...

' "Forsake her ... " What am I saying? No, no, just some silly ideas creeping into my head.'

The door gave a creak and Shapi came into the room. He squatted down and threw some dry logs into the stove. The fire crackled more vigorously and the stove-pipe began to roar.

'If we go to town for a whole month, who's going to look after the farm? I don't know what they're all so pleased about ... You too.'

Shapi spoke slowly, as though to no one in particular. Aishat kept quiet.

'People who haven't got farms, they're the ones who should be actors — like those wandering conjurors from Tsovkra.'

'No one has forced you into anything, Shapi.'

'What do you mean, no one has forced me?' Shapi stood up and moved towards her. 'And don't play the innocent with me. If ever I let you out of my sight you'd be making love to any man you fancied and I'd have to kill them to wipe out the shame.'

'I've done nothing to hurt you, Shapi. But it would be better if you looked after the farm. It's a different matter with someone like Mikail. He hasn't got a farm, his hands are soft.'

'So you even think about his nice soft hands at night, do you?'

'What are you talking about? I simply meant that he's not used to working on a farm. He's a single man. He hasn't even got a stove and he sits freezing in his room like a wolf in the forest.'

Shapi moved closer.

'And you feel sorry for him. Well, why don't you go and warm him up? He won't refuse you. Go, before it's too late. My hands still know how to hold a dagger.'

Aishat looked up at her husband and immediately looked down again. His quivering chin and his face, distorted with rage, terrified her.

'Please, Shapi, put that nonsense out of your head. You've thought up all those terrible things to frighten me and you're torturing yourself and me for nothing.'

'Of course, I'm much older than you and he's young. I haven't got rosy cheeks and soft hands.'

'Now that's enough ... please.'

Aishat caressed his shoulder and looked at him with such an imploring smile that Shapi could not help falling silent, and all the vicious things he had meant to say stuck in his throat. But his anger and his vague, unquenched desire for revenge did not leave him.

'What if we don't go?'

Frightened, Aishat looked up quickly.

'How can I not go, Shapi? How can I miss an opportunity of learning from such famous actors?'

'But you can't go without me. The whole village will laugh at me.'

'Why don't you trust me, Shapi?'

'I know you like your freedom. You don't care if people laugh at me.'

Aishat got up, walked over to the corner, unrolled a bright quilted blanket and threw it on to the bed.

'All right, I won't go,' she said angrily as she smoothed out the blanket. 'All right. So what if I do become the worst actress in the troupe, I won't go.'

Shapi could not see her face and said amiably, 'Don't worry, it doesn't matter. You'll act well even if you don't go. Kurban himself says there's no other actress like you.'

Shapi took off his boots with a grunt, put out the light and went to bed.

Aishat got in quietly beside him. It was late. They usually went to bed much earlier and it was not long before Shapi was snoring. Aishat very much wanted to cry, and she could feel the tears welling up and tickling her long eyelashes. The insult she had suffered lay like a heavy stone upon her heart. She was annoyed with herself, as well; she much disliked being weak and submissive, and yet she had given in again.

She curled herself up into a ball. Shapi was snoring and whistling. She did not want to touch this man who was interfering with her life. Then she suddenly thought—was he just interfering? Wasn't it that he loved her? He did not want to leave her alone in the town because she was dear to him, and he was afraid of losing her. He never looked at other women, but what about her? When Mikail came she so much wanted him to lay his long white fingers on her hair ... and she had looked at him in a way that was dangerous.

She was hot now and found it difficult to breathe.

What shall I do? she thought to herself. I love Shapi. He's a good man, honest and straightforward. There aren't many like him. Why does he hinder me, though? I want to be an actress and nothing else. How am I going to sort out this business? What is the right thing to do?

Her thoughts became more and more blurred. She imagined that Mikail was bending over her so closely that his breath was tickling her ear. He was telling her terrible things, when Shapi suddenly shook his fist at her. She implored him not to beat her, she was completely innocent, she had not asked Mikail to come. Oh no, it wasn't Shapi, it was Othello shouting 'Are not you a strumpet?' What was she supposed to say to him? And she remembered her lines:

> 'No, as I am a Christian.
> If to preserve this vessel for my lord
> From any other foul unlawful touch
> Be not to be a strumpet, I am none.'

3

The sun had almost set and was sinking into the soft, grey cobweb of Tlokh. The thin, bare trees seemed to shrink in the February cold, and the faint hoar-frost patterns on their stiff branches were gilded by the last rays of the sun. It was quiet, and the only movement was the orange globe of the sun sinking down slowly and noiselessly behind its screen of frosted tracery.

A group of people were coming down to the village of Tlokh from the last sharp bend in the road. Sometimes the village looked quite near, and then it would seem far away again. The road hugged the cold rock of the overhanging mountains, which now hid the nearby village once again from the weary eyes of the travellers.

There were about twenty of them, mostly men. Tightly packed, heavy goatskin rucksacks, bags and large bundles swayed on their backs as they trudged along. Only one woman, who was carrying a child in her arms, had a comparatively small pack on her back.

They were all wearing heavy fur coats, with long, almost ground-length sleeves, or felt cloaks. It was hard going, and the steam from their breath swirled in front of them in thick clouds. Passers-by looked at the unusual caravan of people in astonishment. An occasional man with a pipe between his teeth, sauntering along behind his small overloaded donkey, would look at the travellers with an ironical smile, calling out to them as they passed, 'Can't you manage one donkey between so many of you?'

To which would come the instant reply, 'We've been looking for a donkey all week but we couldn't find one. You're the first one we've come across. Let us hire you, there's a good fellow.' Or else, 'What could we do? There aren't any more donkeys to be had, they've all got wise like you.'

At last Tlokh came in sight. The dark blue haze of twilight was already thickening in the valley. The travellers stopped at the gates of a canning factory, where everything was quiet and deserted, and asked the nightwatchman for a bucket of water. After that they went up to a clearing behind some orchards, threw their baggage down on to the ground, straightened their shoulders and started collecting twigs and branches for a camp-fire.

While the men were making the fire the women untied the bundles spread out the rugs and blankets, carefully inspected the creased silk dresses and the wigs, checked to see if the boxes of make-up were safe and that the tins of paint were not damaged—if they were, then there would be trouble from Mikail.

Mikail did not go collecting firewood. He was so tired he could not stand up. Apart from his own baggage and a large piece of scenery, he had also been carrying a bundle containing Aishat's costumes. At the start, Shapi had shown no intention of carrying her bundle; she had stood there smiling helplessly, with Khabibat tightly swathed and pressed closely to her breast, not daring to ask for help. It was then that Mikail took her bundle without a word and strode on ahead. Everyone noticed it immediately, but no one said a word. Shapi said nothing either, but he obviously felt cut to the quick. He said nothing throughout the journey, and when Aishat spoke to him he did not answer, pretending not to notice her.

Aishat did not speak to him again. She was very afraid of having arguments in public. People would start saying that they did not get on, just when she wanted to convince them that the opposite was true. She had not spoken a word to Mikail on the journey either, and it was only now when he lowered himself heavily to the ground that she looked at him tenderly and shyly like a guilty schoolgirl.

Mikail saw her sudden, timid look and wanted to say something but could not find the right words. He simply felt more exhausted than before.

'Are you very tired, Mikail? Walking is easier in spring, isn't it?'

'Yes, I am tired. I don't know why. I've never felt so tired.'

'You've been carrying a heavy load.'

'No, no, that's nothing. It's my thoughts that are making me tired.'

'Are you still thinking about Othello?' Aishat interrupted in a frightened voice. 'It's a difficult part.'

'Yes, you're right. It's dreadful when a thought obsesses you and completely takes possession of you. It saps your strength, your staying power and your peace of mind and makes you do crazy things.'

'So you don't want to play Othello as a man blinded by jealousy, but as someone obsessed by an idea? That's very interesting.'

'Yes, when I play Othello, Aishat, I don't want to be jealous of Desdemona. You see, I want to love her, love her madly, and only give in to this terrible jealousy for one short second. Then it vanishes like smoke and I love the enchanting Desdemona again. To me the most important thing is to show in the last scene that I'm cured of this madness for ever. I want to play someone who is crazed by love, not a jealous husband. I can't be jealous, Aishat. I only know how to love.'

'What a shame Desdemona dies and you can't prove it to her.'

'But suppose she didn't die?'

'She wouldn't have enough strength to fight and defend herself.'

'Are you sure about that, Aishat? Desdemona's not a weak woman, you said that yourself.'

'If Othello was the kind of man you intend him to be, his love would have conquered his madness and they would have been happy ... oh, how happy they would have been, Mikail ... '

'Love is stronger than jealousy, Aishat. I'll prove that.'

'To do that you would have to kill the jealous Othello and play him so that everyone in the audience could see that love had triumphed.'

'I shall kill him, Aishat, you'll see.'

'It's a pity Othello wasn't like you. Then there would have been no woman on earth happier than Desdemona.'

By now Mikail had forgotten about being tired. He leaped to his feet and strode up and down without noticing the cold.

The men's voices could be heard in the distance as they trudged slowly back, weighed down with armfuls of brushwood. Kurban and Shapi were walking in front, engaged in lively conversation. When they were still some distance from the camp-site, Kurban said to no one in particular, 'When you load up a donkey with twice as much baggage as usual, he just accepts it. What else can he do? He's the poor slave of an uncaring master and he can't protest. But when a man acts like that donkey and carries a double load of his own free

will, and not his own load at that, but someone else's, then the
question is—who is the donkey and who is the master? What would
you say, my friends?'

'Perhaps he's a thief, who's fooling the owner because he wants to
steal the baggage for himself?' asked Akhmet-Nami tentatively. 'In
that case the master would certainly be the donkey for having
entrusted his baggage to a thief.'

Kurban burst out laughing. 'Ha, ha! I declare you're not as
stupid as you look, Akhmet. You've hit the nail on the head. The
master walks about in broad daylight with a light pack on his back
and doesn't see that his property has already been stolen.'

'What are you getting at?' asked Radzhab, the comic of the troupe
and a simpleton, whom Kurban had been wanting to replace for a
long time. 'If you're thinking of Mikail, then you're wrong. He's a
very honest fellow and he carried Aishat's things out of kindness.
Shapi can sleep soundly. Mikail wouldn't be interested in taking so
much as a needle and thread if it didn't belong to him.'

Kurban laughed even louder. 'Why should I ever want to upset
my friend Shapi? He can sleep soundly—it's others who can't sleep.
Don't forget, though, that it's the sound sleepers who are the easiest
of all to rob. That's what my old father always used to teach me.'

'Why are you talking like this, Kurban?' asked Shapi angrily.
'I don't know whether you're just having a joke or making me a
laughing-stock. There are people listening and heaven knows what
they may be thinking.'

'Can't I have a laugh to warm myself up?' said Kurban, quicken-
ing his step in order to get ahead of his friends.

'But you're laughing about something that concerns *me*,' said
Shapi, still on the offensive.

Kurban looked around. The others were lagging behind. He bent
his head closer to Shapi and started whispering in the tone of a
sympathetic friend: 'Listen, Shapi, you and I aren't young. We
ought to be able to see a bit further than the others. I wouldn't like
my best friend Shapi to find himself in the same position as the
mullah I'm going to tell you about now:

'A certain mullah lived in Sogratl. He was an educated man and
he spent his days in learned conversation with the many Arabic
scholars for which Sogratl has always been famous. Everything
went well for this mullah. He had a rich farm, his servants respected

him and the amount of his learning and wisdom increased not daily but hourly. He also had a beautiful clever wife, and they lived very happily together. The mullah only had one worry, namely, that a young relative of his whose parents had died had come to live with him. The lad was tall and handsome, but he was a young rake. He drank wine, kept company with bandits, and to cut a long story short he caused the mullah a great deal of distress. What was he to do? The mullah asked his beautiful, clever wife for some advice and she said to him, "You don't know how to deal with a young man like him. Leave it to me, and I'll take this young rogue in hand." And what do you think? Within a month this incorrigible scoundrel had changed beyond recognition. He quietened down, stayed at home more and read books. The mullah could not have been more delighted. But this is what had happened: as soon as the mullah went off to the mosque in the morning, the young man would immediately jump into bed with his beautiful, clever wife. In the evening the mullah, exhausted with praying, with learned discussion and generous hospitality, came home and soon fell asleep. While he was sleeping soundly his wife spent her time with the young man, and if the mullah woke up she would answer him from the next room and say she was reading a book and would be coming to bed shortly. Now the mullah's servant-girl, although she was being well paid by her mistress to hold her tongue, was after all only human. And is there a woman in the world who can hold her tongue, even if you were to cover her in gold from head to foot? A woman's greatest delight is to give away someone else's secret, especially if it's about a close friend or about her mistress. All was revealed. And so one day the Arabic scholars summoned the mullah and decided to open his eyes for him. They were offended for their friend's sake. He listened calmly to their story, and said, "That is all lies and gossip, spread about by jealous people. It has never happened and never can happen. If Allah had seen a sin like that he would have given me warning and I would have seen it too. Never listen to scandal-mongers." The learned Arabic scholars were amazed at the mullah's wisdom. And thus they continued to live: his wife swore that she was faithful and the mullah was content with his life.

'And so, my dear Shapi, I don't want you to be like that mullah. If you want to wait for Allah to enlighten you, that is your business.

But you've got to be blind not to see the way Aishat and Mikail look at each other.'

They were approaching the camp-site when Kurban said, 'Just look at them talking together. It's a pity it's dark and we can't see their faces properly. He's excited, that's why he's walking up and down and she's gazing at him like that. Of course, it's stupid to be jealous, Shapi. We've both read *Othello* and we know it's wrong. But you've still got to keep a look-out—not from jealousy, you understand, but out of plain common sense.'

Kurban and Shapi threw down the firewood on to the ground. Aishat had not noticed them approaching and gave a start. Shapi went right up to her, and although it was quite dark he could clearly see that her cheeks were burning and she was trembling slightly.

'What are you trembling for?' he asked in a hoarse voice.

'It's cold.'

'You should have put on warmer clothes. Give me the matches.'

He snatched the matches out of her hand and felt it shaking. He said nothing, but started to light the fire.

The women brewed the tea and fried slices of home-made sausage, which everyone devoured hungrily. The talk was dull and lifeless at supper. They were all overcome with exhaustion and soon lay down to sleep, covering themselves with whatever they could find.

Shapi tossed about under his fur coat and could not sleep. Lying by his side, Aishat realized that something was wrong. He always went to sleep immediately and his wakefulness was a bad sign. She did not feel like sleeping either, and looked at the distant stars, listening anxiously to every sound as if she were expecting something; but there was absolute silence round about and the only sound was the sleepers' breathing. Suddenly she heard Shapi's cautious whisper: 'Why did he carry your pack? Are you ill or something?'

'I was carrying the baby. Anyway, he took it of his own accord. I didn't ask him to.'

'Why did you give it to him? What are people going to say? It's funny he only took your pack and no one else's. He's your lover, you filthy bitch. And I thought I could trust you.'

'You should be ashamed of yourself, Shapi. *You* should have taken my pack.'

'You can look for someone else to be your donkey. If I see that sort of thing again, you'd both better watch out.'

'You've got nothing whatever to get angry about. He's never even touched me.'

'Sticking up for him, eh? I'm not blind, you know.' He turned his back on her and stopped talking.

Day breaks early in the mountains. The morning mist had dispersed and the warm, golden-tinged blue sky was shining into the actors' eyes, still half-closed with sleep. They got up quickly, breakfasted and set off ...

The troupe arrived in Botlikh at midday, and turned down a narrow, winding street to the club. The village lay stretched along the bank of a river, hemmed in all around by the mountains. Children ran out of the houses, shouting and chattering as they skipped along behind the actors. Everywhere they were met by men in fur coats who bowed in greeting and welcomed them as friends.

The club was uncomfortable and cold, but in the office the actors were greeted by the cheering warmth of an iron stove. Kurban put his foot on a chair, took off his fur hat and raised his hand. 'There'll be no show today, comrades, because we have to get the place ready. So choose yourself a room to share with your family or friends, and after that we'll get on with the scenery. Men only. The women can do the washing and mending and other vital matters of that sort. The office, rehearsal room, wardrobe and dressing-room for all actors, men and women, will be this room, because there isn't another one. But there is one considerable advantage, which makes up for a great deal: in the daytime the auditorium will be used for a meeting of Party organizers and others to prepare for next season's campaign, so the building will be heated and you won't freeze. You have your tireless director to thank for that. Now, let's get down to work.'

Everyone jumped up and they all began talking at once.

At that moment a young man in an army greatcoat came into the room. He was tall, clean-shaven and had an obvious soldierly air about him.

'Comrade Rizhanov, welcome to you in your own land!' Kurban shouted from the other side of the room. 'Comrades, allow me to

5

introduce you to the new secretary of the District Party Committee.'

'Well, what was the journey like?' inquired Rizhanov, looking round at the actors with great curiosity. He had just come back from ten years in the Red Army, during which time he had largely lost contact with his home town. Everything now seemed new and interesting, as though he was seeing it all for the first time.

'Wonderful journey,' replied Kurban. 'Seventy kilometres on foot with all our baggage. Our engines worked without a single breakdown. The donkeys were bursting with envy and we covered every passing car with dust!'

'Do you really mean you came on foot?' asked Rizhanov in amazement. 'And carrying all your stuff, as well?'

'This makes the seventeenth tour we've done this season, comrade secretary. One hundred and fifty-three performances, apart from other happenings. But we can't afford to hire carts. Work it out for yourself—we get thirty-five thousand roubles a year for production costs, actors' and assistants' salaries, scenery, costumes, heating, lighting, machinery, ventilation, publicity and so on. You can't travel far on that kind of money, but you can walk as far as you like. And so we've walked here.'

'Right, let's find these people some rooms and then feed them,' said Rizhanov, 'then we'll have another little talk.'

He said a few words to the District Committee officials who had come in with him, and who now went off round the village with the actors. Rizhanov arranged for the visitors to have free board and lodging, which the District Committee would pay for out of its funds. He also personally saw to it that everything was organized for the actors, and waited until they were all installed in their lodgings before asking Kurban and Mikail to supper with him at his home.

Thus they were all able to spend the evening in warmth and comfort, and everything would have been fine if a chance event had not spoiled the cheerful atmosphere.

Kurban had asked if they could have dinner in the main room, which was heated. While the secretary's wife was roasting a lamb, the men brought crockery and chairs from the next room, cut up the bread and drank a glass of wine apiece.

Rizhanov was listening with intense interest to Kurban's stories about the theatre and the life of an actor. It sometimes occurred to him that Kurban's imagination was apt to get the better of him, but Mikail's calm, sober comments dispelled his doubts.

'You people are heroic—there's no other word for it. I'm surprised you haven't given up the job long ago. You'd be better off doing almost anything else,' said Rizhanov.

'No, you're wrong, my dear friend. Give up the job, leave the stage? You're joking. I don't mind travelling on foot. Even if my legs dropped off I'd tie them on with string and set off again, and the tour would start on time. And my actors feel just as I do. We'll soon be living in warmth and comfort, and there'll be a stove in every room. We'll have everything we need. It's already begun—we've been invited to Makhach-Kala, and the state theatre is going to help us stage *Othello*.'

'You're playing *Othello*?' asked Rizhanov in amazement.

'And why not?' said Kurban with a shrug of his shoulders. 'This is the man who translated it and he's going to play *Othello*. And our Desdemona is a real star! I bet if old Shakespeare could see our Aishat, he'd say, "It was worthwhile writing the play to have someone like her act in it!" '

'And how are rehearsals going?'

'They're not going, they're flying. My brilliant company has already learnt the play by heart—I really don't know why I pay a prompter.'

Mikail gave him an angry look.

'Listen, Mikail, instead of glaring at your producer, the man who pays a slacker like you the top salary rate, you'd do better to bring Aishat over here and go through a short scene from *Othello* with her to show our kind host.'

Rizhanov waved this suggestion aside and said, 'No need for that right now. The actors are tired. Some other time.'

'My dear secretary, from tomorrow onwards we shall be acting every day and there won't be time. Surely you aren't tired after that little stroll in the mountains, are you, Mikail? If you are, then no Avar girl is going to marry you!'

Mikail gave a wave of his hand and hurried out.

As soon as he entered the house where Aishat and Shapi had been lodged, he could hear Shapi's loud snoring. Aishat was sitting at the table sewing a little dress for Khabibat. She was soon ready, and went out after Mikail after asking her hostess to mind the baby.

She flushed with embarrassment when Rizhanov got up from the table to greet her, and when his wife complimented her on her beauty Aishat became thoroughly confused and did not know where to hide her burning face. She sat in silence with her white shawl pulled round her as though she was cold ...

Then Aishat and Mikail stood up, went into the middle of the room and were silent for a few seconds.

Suddenly Aishat raised her head and threw off her shawl. Everyone now saw a new face, completely different from the Aishat who had been sitting at the table. She looked somehow younger, and her round childish face was lit up with a radiant smile. Her first words sounded like a distant bell:

'How is't with you, my lord?'

Instinctively Mikail reached out towards her:

'Give me your hand. This hand is moist, my lady.'

Aishat leaned her head to one side and said in the same melodious voice:

'It yet has felt no age nor known no sorrow.'

At that moment the door creaked and Shapi appeared on the threshold. He stopped, looked at everyone there, muttered, 'Beg pardon,' took off his hat and put it on again.

Rizhanov was about to get up, but Kurban motioned him down with an abrupt gesture. Aishat saw Shapi at once, but Mikail had not yet seen him. He noticed that Aishat's expression had changed suddenly, as if she were overcome with pain and vexation, perhaps because he had squeezed her hand too hard. He began saying his next lines with passionate feeling:

'This argues fruitfulness and liberal heart;
Hot, hot, and moist; this hand of yours requires
A sequester from liberty, fasting and prayer,
Much castigation, exercise devout;
For here's a young and sweating devil here,
That commonly rebels ...'

Everyone could see how tightly Mikail's long fingers were squeezing Aishat's little hand. He was excited, but there was no shadow of suspicion, malice or torment on his face as he spoke the lines:

> ' ... 'Tis a good hand,
> A frank one.'

Mikail was keeping to his word and not playing Othello as jealous, but as a man in love. However, to the people watching, the logic of his reading of Othello was not immediately clear. Greatly embarrassed, Rizhanov and his wife looked at the actors and at Shapi. Kurban managed to whisper to them that Shapi was Aishat's husband, but they were so delighted by Aishat's acting that they soon forgot about everything else. At last she said:

> 'In sooth, you are to blame.'

Mikail did not even say his last word, 'Away!' which ended the handkerchief scene. He and Aishat stood facing each other, breathing hard and not knowing what to do next.

Rizhanov was the first to break the silence. 'Wonderful,' he said. 'I've never heard a voice like yours before.'

'Believe me, Allah himself does not have such a voice in his choir of angels.'

Shapi was still standing in the doorway. Rizhanov stood up and said to him in a welcoming tone, 'Please sit down.'

'No thank you. Beg your pardon, but I've come for my wife. The baby's crying.'

Aishat quickly put on her shawl, having just noticed that it was lying on a chair. She tied it under her chin and, with a nod to Rizhanov and his wife, hurried out of the room followed by Shapi.

It was already dark outside. Although there were few people about, Shapi glanced around several times. He did not want anyone to see him walking alongside his wife, as this would humiliate him. When they turned left off the main street and walked up a narrow footpath, he looked round again. There was not a soul about. In the huge vault of the sky the pale stars were winking, each time in a different place, as if they were piercing the thick, dark-blue velvet sky and the rays of the departed sun were peeping through the tiny holes.

Walking a few paces behind her, Shapi said, 'You went without telling me. Standing there without a shawl—you might as well have taken your dress off too and showed them what the rest of you looked like. That stallion was licking his lips at you the whole time. You disgusting, shameless woman.'

'Shapi, you're wrong. We were acting.'

'Be quiet, you slut. He's meant to be angry with you in that scene, to suspect you of being unfaithful to him, yet he was looking at you like a hungry ram. You're shameless, the pair of you, and in public, too ...'

'It's just Mikail's interpretation of the part. You remember what he said at the meeting.'

'I suppose you think you can disgrace me in front of everyone just because I'm old. He almost tore your hand off, the way he was squeezing it.'

Aishat remembered how passionately Mikail had pressed her hand and could think of no answer.

'Why don't you say something, you bitch?' he said in a threatening whisper. Shapi came closer to her, so that she could hear his heavy breathing. 'Well, say something.'

Aishat had the feeling he had guessed at her secret thought of how good it had been when Mikail had squeezed her hand tightly ... She gave her husband a look of terrified entreaty.

Her glance finally convinced Shapi that his suspicions were right. That pathetic look confirmed her guilt, and with it terrible vicious thoughts came pouring into his feverish brain and stung him like a swarm of wasps. Choking with rage and emotion, Shapi could hardly breathe and was unable to speak. Then he hit Aishat on the head. He saw her fall slowly to the ground as though melting into the mist. He raised his arm to hit her again, but it suddenly went weak and fell to his side ... Aishat was no longer there, only a vague heap on the mauve-grey stone of the pathway.

Shapi gave a sudden cry. His hoarse, choking groans broke the silence of the dusk. It was as though a wolf had come out of the distant forest and had begun to howl in fear at the unfamiliar emptiness, at the vast sky and the hostile silence.

Aishat lay there motionless, and only regained her senses when Akhmet-Nami bent over her. Without a word he picked her up and carried her on his outstretched arms. Aishat's lips and chin were covered in blood. Shapi trudged behind as if his feet were tied to the ground and it was hard for him to drag them along.

The following day Aishat acted in the show as usual. She had difficulty in walking, she felt dizzy, and offstage she several times hit her head painfully against bits of scenery. In the last interval she fainted for several minutes, and when she came to she found Kurban bending over her, his ginger quiff tickling her cold, damp forehead. Aishat looked at him in fear and pleading, as if expecting him to be furious with her. She raised her hand to ward off the imminent blow, but Kurban smiled and said in a voice of uncharacteristic gentleness, 'You can't let us down, Aishat. The show must go on, you know that. The second bell's gone already. Please, Aishat.'

Slowly Aishat got up. The crowd of frightened actors stared at her in expectation. Their made-up faces faces looked strange to her. She went over to the table, looked at herself in the mirror, touched up her make-up and said without looking round, 'I'm ready, Kurban. You can sound the third bell.'

4

The solid grey and black mass of the mountains soared up, their peaks, like pointed hats, seeming to move against the blue dome of the sky. The road ran between them, clinging to alternate sides of a gorge. The sky was lit by the glow of the hidden sun, although its rays had not yet reached the road. Down there in the dim, cool twilight beneath the misty blue of the precipice, between mountainsides strewn with boulders, the delicate arch of the bridge seemed to have come alive in the dusk.

A little crowd of people was standing by the parapet, sitting on rocks and on small suitcases. As soon as the far-off noise of an approaching engine was heard they jumped up, grabbed their cases in their left hands, raised their right hands and waited for the vehicle to appear round the corner. Sad and disappointed, they watched a small car go by, shrugged in resignation and sat down again on their rocks and suitcases. Several lorries passed by with no seats to spare. The travellers sat there for hours, the weary, interminable wait made tolerable only by Kurban's ceaseless flow of cheerful banter.

At last a lorry roared up, raising a cloud of dust, and stopped about ten paces past them. The driver leaned out of his cab and said in a lazy drawl, 'O.K., jump on, lords and ladies.'

There were considerably more people than seats available, and Kurban shouted threateningly, 'No one may get on until the actors are seated.' But the others would not have dreamt of getting aboard before the actors, anyway. They all knew Kurban and his company.

The driver poked his head out of the cabin and shouted, 'Hold hard—we haven't done a deal yet. I want at least fifty kopecks per head.'

'Why?' asked Kurban in surprise. 'Won't the engine make it all the way otherwise?'

'No, it's *me* that won't make it,' answered the driver. 'If you don't like the price you can wait for the bus.'

'All right, there you are,' said Kurban. 'Telling us to wait for the bus, indeed! We're not just anybody, you know—we're actors!' And the lorry rumbled off to a chorus of cheerful shouts.

They arrived at Makhach-Kala at dusk. Dense low clouds blanketed the town, drizzling rain was slanting down; a muffled roar could be heard coming from the sea and every passing car threw up twin sprays of muddy water. The travellers were exhausted, and even Kurban was in low spirits. At last they stopped outside a hotel in Buinakskaya Street. Kurban came to terms with the receptionist and then said to the actors, 'I've taken two rooms, one for the women and the other for the men. O.K.? Let's go and settle down.'

So began their stay in Makhach-Kala.

In the mornings they would have a leisurely breakfast of tea and maize *churek* before going to the theatre for rehearsals. They drank more tea later in the morning, in the evening some of them watched the play and some took part in the crowd scenes. Then they had tea again, sang songs to the *gumuz* and went to bed …

On their free days the woman made khinkal and in the afternoon they all sat on one of their rugs in the men's room, ate the khinkal and held heated discussions about the happenings of the past week.

And a great deal had happened. But whenever the actors were engrossed in their discussions, Shapi remained taciturn and sullen. He never missed a rehearsal or a performance, so as to look as busy as everyone else. He went along to the production meetings but rarely said anything, and when he did make a contribution it was said off-handedly, grudgingly and mostly in a disapproving tone of voice. He took badly to this enforced idleness, which increased his animosity towards his wife, for it was her fault that he had been made to leave his home and his work to come to this useless and, to him, boring town. He also harboured a growing sense of malice towards the rest of the troupe, as if they too were indirectly responsible for the mess he was in.

Kurban had decided to take him to Makhach-Kala at his own expense, but now he thought to himself, Kurban, you'll look a proper fool if that money turns out to have been wasted. He had a very long talk with Mikail after this, and they devised a plan. Several times Shapi noticed them giving him nasty looks, and concluded that something unpleasant was being cooked up for him. After what had happened in Botlikh all the actors disliked him even more, and did not hide it. Aishat scarcely spoke to him, and only answered his questions in curt monosyllables. There was something about her attitude which he could not understand and which he therefore felt to be dangerous, but he could not tell from which direction the danger threatened, and because of this he grew more and more uneasy.

Outwardly Aishat treated him as she had always done. They were both naturally taciturn and as a rule rarely spoke to each other, but in her normal silence there had never been this element of latent hostility which he clearly sensed now. Several times at night he had made love to her with unusual and, as it seemed to her, agonized passion. Then they would lie for a long time with their eyes open. Aishat caught his imploring looks, but she said nothing, although she felt sorry for him. She thought he was regretting his brutality, that he was unhappy and hurt, and that she ought to say something kind to him, but as soon as she was about to speak a strange force gripped her throat and the words died on her lips.

This agonizing duel continued in Makhach-Kala, except that Aishat felt even more estranged from her husband. She sensed his anguish. One day he got drunk with some of his cronies, came home late and sat outside the door of the women's room until morning, looking so ghastly that the duty concierge was afraid to speak to him.

Their estrangement increased daily. Shapi felt a permanent, almost physical pain in his breast. Everything that happened, however apparently trivial, made the pain worse and brought

5*

closer the unknown danger, the disaster which Shapi now regarded as inevitable. Aishat was moving away from him and he felt he had less and less strength to hold on to her.

From the very first everyone at the Russian-language Municipal Theatre fell in love with Aishat. Although her Russian was not particularly good, and she was often at a loss for a word, she nevertheless amazed the Russian actors and Verkhovtsev, the artistic director, by her detailed knowledge of *Othello* and her original interpretation of Desdemona. They had expected an illiterate amateur, and were amazed by the extraordinary artistic sensitivity of this little woman with her shawl always tied round her head.

Work at the theatre went on apace. Verkhovtsev and his assistants had more than enough to do in clearing away the mass of prejudices which inhibited the Avar actors, and this was not achieved without some unpleasant incidents. Till then, the actors had thought it indecent for men and women to touch each other, and they only pretended to embrace and kiss onstage. It looked comical, and the audience often used to laugh during the performance when there was nothing funny in the script. This annoyed Aishat, and she complained to Mikail that this ridiculous laughter was upsetting her acting. She realized that it was the affected clowning, their substitute for real embraces, which made the audience laugh, but she dared not say this openly.

When they rehearsed the scene in the second act on the quayside in Cyprus, Verkhovtsev, a short, fat man, began shaking with laughter as Aishat and Mikail clumsily held out their arms to each other. 'My dear Othello!' murmured Aishat, casting a terrified sidelong glance at Verkhovtsev, who was laughing aloud. Eventually he stopped, wiped the sweat from his brow and said:

'My dear Aishat, I nearly died laughing. The way you stand in front of Othello like a schoolmarm—it's a farce! Your beloved husband has just arrived, you've been sick with anxiety about him because he might have died in a violent storm, and instead of throwing yourself into his arms you just flutter your hands in that coy way!'

'We can't do it any other way,' Aishat replied, greatly embarrassed. 'It's the way we do it ... '

'Well, you can stop all that nonsense. An actor must act, not just pull faces. Now please embrace at once. Go on, Mikail!'

Verkhovtsev went up to her, embraced her heartily and threw her arms around his neck. 'That's how it should be done, only look at me, not at the wings.'

Aishat was burning all over and did not even notice when Mikail approached her. Shapi was standing in the wings as if petrified. Just as Mikail was about to embrace Aishat he stumped forward and said, 'Aishat, I'm telling you ... '

Aishat looked round and stepped away from Mikail, who gave a despairing gesture and withdrew to a corner.

'You're disturbing our work, Shapi. Go away,' said Verkhovtsev.

'You've forgotten she's my wife,' said Shapi. 'I won't allow it.'

'Stop playing the fool. This is serious, and you're making a frivolous interruption.'

Kurban walked over to Verkhovtsev and said with a groan, 'Comrade Verkhovtsev, this man Shapi is making my hair turn grey.'

'I won't allow it,' Shapi repeated sullenly.

'There you are—what did I tell you?' said Kurban. 'Comrade Verkhovtsev, please remove this ox', he said pointing to Shapi, 'and make a lamb out of him if you're gifted in that direction.'

'Oh Shapi, I never thought you were such a coward that you're afraid of losing your wife if she so much as touches another man,' said Mikail angrily.

'You're saying that because you haven't got a wife of your own and you want to steal a bit of everyone else's.'

An ugly scene was so imminent that the rehearsal had to be abandoned.

During subsequent rehearsals Shapi stood there glowering, with his eyes riveted to Aishat. The other actors soon agreed to stop making their absurd grimaces and stilted gestures and to embrace realistically on stage. Kurban could not help saying to Rukiat as they were going home, 'You must admit that no one can hug and kiss as well as your husband. Now do you appreciate me?'

'Shut up, you old lecher,' said Rukiat with a sigh of pretended despair.

Kurban now devised a clever move. Aishat was to rehearse her scenes with Mikail at a time when Shapi was taking part in the crowd scenes at the evening performance. Kurban arranged it all with Verkhovtsev and they kept Shapi busy every evening, even when there was nothing particular for him to do.

'That's all very well, but what happens when it comes to the performance? You can't hide him away then,' Verkhovtsev said to Kurban one day.

'But by then ... Comrade Verkhovtsev, you forget that I'm playing Iago. What sort of a villain do you think I am if everything stays as it is?'

'I see.'

'I have a plan ... Othello has to save Desdemona for our theatre.'

'That'll be a hard task.'

'But they interpret their parts like that. It's not my fault. Believe me, it's much better to be a midwife than a gravedigger.'

'It seems you want to be both.'

'You've guessed right, my dear sir. I want to be a midwife when love is born and a gravedigger for jealousy.'

'Iago did the opposite.'

'My dear Verkhovtsev, everything's upside down—that's what the whole affair is about. I'll remove Shapi, I'll

Make the Moor thank me, love me and reward me,
For making him egregiously an ass,
And practising upon his peace and quiet,
Even to madness ... '

On their way home Rukiat began hurriedly whispering to Kurban, stretching up towards his face, though even on tiptoe she scarcely came up to his shoulder.

'I'm afraid for Mikail in case Shapi does something to him. I'm afraid for Aishat, too.'

'Now don't bother your head about that. Listen to me. You know Mikail has a large silk shawl, a beautiful shawl. It would make a magnificent white dress for Desdemona. It would be positively indecent for Desdemona to act in any other dress. Aishat hasn't any silk, and can't afford to buy any. Do you see what I mean?'

'No, I don't. Wouldn't it be better to give her my white silk dress? We're the same size.'

'I swear that only Tsudakhar donkeys can be stupider than you are. Go and tell Mikail, the rest doesn't concern you.'

Kurban strode on angrily without looking round. Puzzled, Rukiat hurried along behind him.

At home she chose a suitable moment to stop Mikail on the staircase and whisper to him about the shawl. Mikail was about to reply to her, but she had run down the stairs before he could open his mouth.

In the evening Mikail and Aishat were rehearsing *Othello* as usual. Shapi had a part in that evening's performance, and they were alone in the little room. Mikail brought with him a small parcel, which he put down on the table. They started rehearsing. Aishat's hot hand lay obediently in Mikail's big, cold hand ... Aishat felt as if she were sinking deliciously into a cool stream, and her heart too was gripped by a sensation of cold as though Mikail's long, slim fingers were touching it. Aishat took a step forward and looked up but she did not see Mikail's eyes, his half-opened lips and his slightly trembling chin. Mikail was coming to the end of his speech:

> ' ... 'Tis a good hand,
> A frank one.'

Although Aishat's thoughts were on his hands, on hearing her cue she instinctively spoke her line:

> ' ... You may, indeed, say so,
> For 'twas that hand that gave away my heart.'

Mikail looked reproachfully into her eyes. He was blaming her for something, but for what? She had done him no wrong. He said sadly:

> 'A liberal hand; the hearts of old gave hands,
> But our new heraldry is hands not hearts.'

The words stunned her. She was distraught, inconsolable. Her hand was in Mikail's, but where was her heart? She could feel only pain and an agonizing void. Her heart belonged to Shapi—but had he not thrown it away? He had beaten her, sworn at her, and she was perpetually haunted by his grim, suspicious stare. How dare he call her pure heart a nest of vipers! He could see nothing in it but lies and treachery, that was why Desdemona had died. She had picked up her heart, which Othello had thrown into the mud and dust of the wayside, and offered it to him again, and because of that he believed in his own terrible accusation. It was slavish obedience which had killed Desdemona. If she had stood up to Othello everything would have been different. Love must be proud and unbending. That was the sort of Desdemona she would be. She would still love Othello alone, but Othello was Mikail, not Shapi. She whispered her next line in a state of sheer exhaustion:

'I cannot speak of this ... '

Mikail saw her eyes begging him for mercy and he let her hand go. Now their lines followed each other in quick succession. They were both hurrying in order to drown their thoughts in a flood of words, but the thoughts welled up in spite of it. Then Mikail took the parcel from the table and within a moment the long white shawl was draped around Aishat's shoulders, reaching all the way down to her feet.

Stern and unsmiling, Mikail looked at her and went on with his lines:

'That handkerchief
Did an Egyptian to my mother give:
She was a charmer, and could almost read
The thoughts of people; she told her, while she kept it,
'Twould make her amiable and subdue my father
Entirely to her love, but if she lost it
Or made a gift of it, my father's eye
Should hold her loathed, and his spirits should hunt
After new fancies. She dying gave it me;
And bid me, when my fate would have me wive,
To give it her. I did so: and take heed on't;
Make it a darling like your precious eye;
To lose't or give't away were such perdition
As nothing else could match.'

Aishat wrapped the shawl tightly round herself. The silk was heavy, slippery and cool and smelt of dried herbs. She stretched her hand out to Mikail. Once again those long fingers reached out for her heart and Aishat looked timorously, imploringly into his big eyes. Someone else's voice seemed to say her words:

'Is't possible?'

Mikail seized on her words as though they were a long dreamt-of promise, and said to her with great feeling:

' 'Tis true; there's magic in the web of it ... '

Her eyes said to him, 'I know it's true,' and with even greater
passion he said to her:

'The worms were hallow'd that did breed the silk,
And it was dy'd in mummy, which the skilful
Conserv'd of maidens' hearts.'

Yes, she could feel that the silk was special. She wanted to rest
her head on Mikail's chest, the heavy, smooth shawl was drawing
her to him, her heart was full of hopeless, unthinkable, impossible
feelings. Faintly she said:

'Indeed! Is't true?'

And Mikail replied in a passionate whisper:

'Most veritable; therefore look to't well.'

Aishat was almost unconscious as she spoke the remaining lines
of that scene, and when it was over she sat down exhausted on the
edge of a chair.

She sat there in silence, not looking at Mikail. Verkhovtsev
looked in and shouted, 'Come on, come on, get on with it!' and
banging the door he ran off down the corridor, clattering noisily
along the stone slabs of the floor.

Frightened, Aishat pulled the shawl from her shoulders and held
it out to Mikail. He shook his head and said, 'No, Aishat, don't.
It's for you. You can make a dress for Desdemona out of it. It's
my mother's shawl. When she was dying she left it to my future
wife, and said, "This shawl will bring happiness to your wife.
Tell her to take care of it." '

'How can you go against your mother's dying wishes? How can
you take away your future wife's happiness?'

'I'm doing neither, Aishat. I shall never marry.'

'Why, Mikail? You're not old and ugly, are you?'

'Let's not talk about it, Aishat ... Take the shawl, you'll need it
for the dress. And if I ever do marry, the shawl will belong to my
wife.'

'Thank you, Mikail,' answered Aishat softly. She stood up,
walked over to him and caressed his forehead and hair, then ran
quickly out of the room.

She found herself in a crowd of people which blocked her way to the doors as they jostled her from side to side. The audience was rushing to the cloakrooms to get their coats. She felt dizzy and was about to burst into tears of frustration when she suddenly saw Shapi in front of her. He said nothing, but merely gave her a sullen look. He turned round and walked off, elbowing his way through the crowd. Aishat meekly followed after him.

After the brightly lit theatre they were plunged into the damp gloom of the street. The sticky mud squelched under their feet. The people streaming out of the theatre were at once swallowed up by the streets and their dark shadows disappeared in the fog. The roar of the surf was quite near and sounded like heavy iron wheels rolling along a cobbled road.

Aishat asked Shapi to take a walk with her along the shore, as she had a bad headache. Shapi silently agreed and turned off down a side street. Every moment the sea crashed against the shore with a deep, thunderous sigh and then retreated into the darkness of the night with a dull rumble. A solitary light winked in the grey-white mist. Aishat felt that she was on stage and that none of this really existed, but she could not remember which play it was and what part she was playing. Aishat racked her brains to remember, but out of the darkness only the great waves charged forward like a herd of shaggy black beasts, and ran away again, roaring and whistling. The lines which Mikail had spoken not long ago seemed like an impossible dream. Aishat was now waiting for a miracle – for Shapi suddenly to turn round towards her, embrace her and say some simple, childish words to her. These words could save them both. But he walked on in silence, holding himself erect and seeming as inscrutable as the night. It was clear to Aishat that her hopes were in vain. Her mind a despairing blank, she let her head fall and clasped her hands to her breast in doomed silence. After walking like this for a long time she found, without knowing why, that she was afraid to unclasp her hands. Suddenly the thought came to her that she only had to let her hands go and she could drop her life like a heavy stone whose weight had become intolerable. She slowly lowered her right hand and the parcel fell into a puddle. It was only now that she remembered she had been carrying the shawl, Mikail's present, under her arm.

She quickly bent down, tore off the damp newspaper in which it was wrapped and hid the shawl under her coat. They were now climbing up some wide stone steps and could see the dim lights of Buinakskaya Street.

'Have you been with him the whole evening again?' asked Shapi, without looking at her. His words had no more effect on her now. She no longer felt frightened and lonely, as she had a few minutes before when she had dropped the parcel. All the time she felt its warmth against her, and it was perhaps because of this that her voice was now gentle and soft.

'I can't help it, Shapi. Comrade Verkhovtsev insists on us rehearsing every day.'

'You know the part by heart now.'

'That isn't enough ... '

'Of course it isn't enough for *you*. *You've* got to embrace each other all night long.'

'It's no use accusing him, Shapi. He's much shyer and more reserved than any of the other actors, and he's very kind to me. Look, he's even given me a silk shawl to make a dress for Desdemona.'

'A shawl ... He'll be sending you the bridal money before long. And you took it, you shameless creature.'

'But he's our friend.'

'How dare you accept a shawl from him? Now everyone will laugh at me!'

'No one has a word to say against Mikail. He's a decent, honest man.'

'A shawl from your lover to make everyone point their fingers at me!'

'He treats you very well, and believe me he hasn't an unkind thought in his head.'

'This is the limit! Openly accepting expensive presents. A shawl from your lover—you worthless slut!'

'You can call me what you like, but he's done nothing.'

They were walking along a deserted street and within a minute had arrived at their hotel. Shapi pulled angrily at the door, making such a noise that all the dogs in the neighbourhood started barking. Kurban and Akhmet-Nami were standing by the banister on the landing, a blue cloud of tobacco smoke drifting around their heads. When Shapi and Aishat reached the landing, Kurban shook his finger at them:

'What have you two been up to?'

Shapi stopped and said to Aishat, 'Go on, show them your present.'

Aishat slowly took out the shawl and held it out to Shapi.

'We know. We hear you have an admirer, Aishat,' said Kurban with a laugh.

Shapi turned red and hit Aishat with the shawl. It fell to the floor. Aishat quickly bent down, picked it up and went to her room.

'Oh Shapi, you have fried meat-balls in your head instead of brains. If you hit her again she can get a free divorce. And besides, remember that every time you hit her you're driving her closer to the other man, whose hands are so soft.'

'I'll tear his hands off.'

'You donkey, that'll make the equation even worse: minus wife, plus prison.'

Shapi turned round and went out again.

Kurban yawned, and said thoughtfully, 'Tell me, Akhmet-Nami, where can I find a market to sell off this bull at a small loss? I ask you: will the Avar theatre flourish? Yes, it will. Then let me ask you again: how is it going to flourish when that bull can trample all over our choicest flowers?'

5

The roads branched away from Khunzakh fortress in several directions. One road wound down towards the Arakansk ravine like a twisting ribbon, another curved in an arc up to the village, thrusting its way in a series of hairpin bends through the Tsad uplands where they were topped by the huddle of high, narrow peasant houses. The spring sunshine had warmed the cold rock of the mountain tops, where ragged scraps of dissolving cloud and wisps of fog were swirling downward into the valleys below. A liquid blue torrent seemed to stream from the sky, as though blue water was flowing slowly from the Tsumadinsk horizon out of a trout-mere and into the bottomless black of Arakansk.

People from the surrounding villages were walking along these roads, people who had got up at the crack of dawn to be in Khunzakh by dusk. Tomorrow they would be hard at work again, but today ...

Everybody in Khunzakh knew that today was a special day. Instead of just loafing about the village as usual, the children were crowding round the entrance to the House of Socialist Culture, whose doors were open wide. Large canvas flats painted with exotic landscapes were propped against the wall, and men were carrying them with great care into the building.

An enormous cloth placard had been fastened to a telegraph pole in the square, proclaiming in large blue and red letters:

HOUSE OF SOCIALIST CULTURE

First performance of

OTHELLO
A Tragedy in Five Acts

TODAY

THE CURTAIN WILL RISE AT 6 O'CLOCK

Tickets on sale from 12 noon onwards

Mikail, wearing a brown sweater, was constantly dashing in and out. His hands were covered in paint and his cheeks were feverishly red as he shouted to the workmen handling the scenery. As they waited for the next exciting incident, the village boys fought among themselves, but idly and without their usual enthusiasm. They knocked each other's caps off, exchanged insults with the grown-ups and peeped impatiently into the building. Throughout the day people were arriving from the neighbouring villages. They seated themselves on logs and boulders, took out loaves of bread, garlic and pieces of cold mutton from their knapsacks and ate their leisurely meals. Others went to the restaurant, which was as noisy as a fairground. Two waiters with perspiring red faces rushed about among the tables, customers shouting at them from all sides:

'Give us some lamb, Ibrahim.'

'Hey, Ali—vodka!'

The officials from the Ministry of Arts were lunching there too. They behaved very solemnly, and teased Kurban with mysterious, veiled hints. Kurban could only guess that they were preparing some kind of pleasant surprise, but they would divulge no more, although he never stopped plying them with the local liqueur, a cloudy brew made from pears.

By evening the whole village had gathered around the House of Socialist Culture. All tickets were sold. Kurban closed the box-office, counted the money and put it in the inside pocket of his jacket, where he usually kept the petty cash, and went to the actors' dressing-room.

Here it was much warmer than outside, as the actors had been heating it up with their breath for several hours. Aishat was dressing. Over her usual black dress and warm bodice, she wore the white silk dress which she had made from Mikail's shawl. As a result she looked considerably plumper, very like Desdemona as she was painted by English artists of the eighteenth century. Aishat had spent hours studying the engravings in the copies of Shakespeare which Mikail had lent her. More than anything else she was fasci-nated by an engraving by John Boydell, showing the scene of Des-demona's murder. Othello is standing by her couch with a dagger in his right hand and staring at Desdemona, who is lying among the tangled bedclothes, her eyes gleaming like white-hot coals. Her knee and right breast are bare, her long eyelashes stand out clearly against her pale face and her delicate pink ear seems to hear in anticipation the sounds of the terrible act about to take place and which is already latent in the air. Desdemona seems to press her ear to the pillow to catch the least sound ...

Shapi, who was hanging around in the dressing-room although he had no business to be there, looked at Aishat in astonishment. No, this was not Aishat but a beautiful Venetian lady. How lovely she looked with her blonde hair and her white dress! Shapi felt with a sudden shiver of horror that he had lost this beautiful proud woman and that it was his own fault. His damned greed! He should never have allowed her to act and to share the actors' life, but he had been tempted by the money, and now all was lost. This woman was no longer his wife, she herself had forgotten that her name had once been Aishat.

Mikail came over to her. He was already made up and in costume. How handsome he is, damn him, Shapi thought, clenching his fists. He'll soon be embracing her, touching her breasts and her shoulders. I've got to put an end to it!

Mikail stopped, looked at Aishat admiringly, and recited in a low voice:

> 'Thou cunning pattern of excelling nature,
> I know not where is that Promethean heat
> That can thy light relume ... '

Shapi clenched his fists. They weren't even embarrassed any longer, damn them.

Kurban inspected the actors.

'Right, we're ready. Shapi, on stage please. Time for curtain up.'

Shapi went out without a word.

The actors put the finishing touches to their make-up. The men's costumes were made out of black and coloured velveteen, which looked like velvet from a distance, the women were dressed in silk.

'Cassio and Montano on stage!' shouted Kurban. 'How beautiful you look, Aishat. Believe me, if I were Mikail I'd suffocate you with kisses—after Act V, of course!'

Aishat blushed.

'You know, Kurban,' said Mikail, 'that is why Othello suffocates Desdemona—because she so entrances him. Look how passionately he kissed her before he does it.'

'Very well, do as you like—as long as everyone enjoys it. But you're both so proper that even that villain Iago can't help you.'

Aishat went on stage.

In the semi-darkness of the hall the audience, wearing sheepskin coats, furs and tall sheepskin hats, were sitting packed together like sardines on the narrow benches, all craning their necks to hear better. They were amazingly quiet, and at the slightest cry from her child a mother would quickly push her breast into its mouth lest it break the tense silence even for a second.

The audience was enraptured by Aishat from her very first lines. She had never before been in such good voice. The shepherds from Khunzakh and Tsad, the smallholders from Tlokh and the bricklayers from Sogratl had never heard such beautiful, tender, sweet-sounding words. Speechless with delight, their smiles of innocent enjoyment chased the wrinkles away towards their eyes where they were met by tears running unbidden down their cheeks. 'Mikail must have been to paradise—where else could he have learned such tender words?'

Iago, however, had a fierce reception, and Kurban was met by a hail of choice invective. Even when he came out to take a bow in the interval the audience hissed and shouted abuse at him. After the third act, when it was obvious to everyone that the play was an amazing success, the senior official from the Ministry of Arts came on stage and solemnly announced, 'Due to their remarkably successful production there will be a premium of five hundred roubles each for Kurban Emirov, Mikail Aliyev, Aishat—' his words were interrupted by thunderous applause—'besides which, the theatre will receive an extra grant of twenty thousand roubles to repair the building, for new scenery and so on—'

Act IV went with tremendous verve. Because she was excited and happy, Aishat acted so well that she was interrupted every minute by enthusiastic applause.

Shapi was sitting morosely in the prompter's box, angry and forgotten by everybody. He did not even come out in the intervals. It seemed to him that when telling Emilia that she had no husband, Aishat had spoken her lines with special defiance:

> DES.: Who is thy lord?
> EMIL.:   He that is yours, sweet lady.
> DES.: I ha' none, do not talk to me, Emilia,
>   I cannot weep, nor answer have I none,
>   But what should go by water ...

There was even something defiant in the way she looked at him. 'Just wait, I'll make you cry all right,' he thought to himself.

Act V began, and the tension in the audience reached its climax. Aishat was lying in bed in the same dress, but in her mind's eye she could see the half-naked Desdemona in John Boydell's picture, and she felt ashamed and fearful because Mikail was moving towards her and he would see her unclothed. He was coming closer now, and her eyes were closed in sleep. He bent down and said in a trembling voice:

> 'When I have pluck'd the rose,
> I cannot give it vital growth again,
> It needs must wither: I'll smell it on the tree.
> (*Kisses her.*)
> O balmy breath, that dost almost persuade
> Justice to break her sword! ... '

Mikail bent down to her lips. Aishat closed her eyes tightly, and suddenly her breathing stopped. She felt as if she were stifling, she could remember nothing any more and only knew that this first kiss of her life would never end, and that if it did her life would end too. At last Mikail tore his lips from hers and said:

'I must weep,
But they are cruel tears ... '

She heard muffled sobs from the audience and Mikail's words:

' ... She wakes.'

But she could neither speak nor move. Mikail repeated the line slightly louder:

'She wakes.'

Shapi prompted her from the box:

'Who's there? Othello?'

But in vain ... she lay as if struck by lightning. Shapi said in a hoarse whisper, 'Wake up, you slut!' This brought her to her senses; she raised herself up and the scene went on. Shapi shook his fist at her and said in a choking voice:

'Think on thy sins.'

When Mikail repeated the line, however, his voice sounded uncertain, yet affectionate, as though he were talking to a mischievous little girl. Although Shapi was still furious, Aishat's fear had gone, and she answered Mikail with the utmost tenderness:

'They are the loves I bear to you.'

At this Shapi shouted, 'And for that thou diest!' so loudly that several voices in the front row were heard saying, 'Quiet, prompter!' Shapi was enraged. He shouted the lines, waving his arms and stamping his feet, while Mikail repeated them in a tender, loving voice that belied what he was saying. But Aishat seemed so anxious and fearful when she looked at him that the audience was thoroughly convinced of the danger that was threatening her. She knew that at any moment Mikail would lean over her and put his hands round her neck. She was already suffocating at the mere thought of it and could hardly say her line:

'Kill me tomorrow; let me live tonight.'

As he stifled her the audience cried and sobbed. The rest of the scene was played only with great difficulty. Women were weeping aloud when Mikail stabbed himself with his dagger, fell across the motionless body of Aishat and said:

'I kiss'd thee ere I kill'd thee, no way but this,
Killing myself to die upon a kiss'.

At this the curtain had to be rung down: the final lines, spoken by Cassio and Lodovico, were forgotten. There was pandemonium in the audience, but neither Mikail nor Aishat noticed that the curtain had fallen.

Aishat lay where she was, suffering but happy from Othello's last, agonized caress. Nothing could make her believe that she was not Desdemona. Suddenly she was being violently punched all over, a familiar hairy fist was beating her face, her head and her breasts, washing off Desdemona's make-up with blood. For a second her eyes met Shapi's and it was only then that she realized the play was over.

Aishat lost consciousness. It had all happened in no more than a minute. By the time Mikail was on his feet, the others were already holding Shapi by the arms and pulling him towards the exit. He was snarling, biting the hands of the people who were holding him, kicking and spitting.

A thunderous roar could be heard in the auditorium, people were shouting 'Aishat! Mikail!' They all wanted to see their favourite actors again, but there were no curtain calls.

Aishat was lying in a narrow hospital bed. On that sunny day everything was dazzling white, and through the window she could see the deep-blue, gold-trimmed curtain of the sky rolling down towards the first delicate, springtime greenery on the mountains. She knew that Shapi would be coming at any moment. She felt calm, and when he appeared in the doorway she frowned at him in grim expectancy. Shapi stooped down and said in a faint, unsteady voice, 'I was wrong, Aishat, I made a mistake ... '

Aishat pulled the bedclothes up to her chin and replied calmly and unemotionally, 'It's no use coming to see me, Shapi. You've killed your wife. You have no wife now. Go and find yourself another one, a better one. Goodbye.'

'Aishat ... '

'I've told you, you've killed your wife.'

Shapi jerked up his head, clenched his fists and said, 'No, I haven't killed her yet, but I will.'

A short, slim nurse appeared noiselessly behind him, took hold of Shapi by the sleeve and led him out as though she were much stronger than he was. Aishat lay without a sound. Time moved slowly, as if weighed down by the heat of the sun. She felt suffocated, and threw off the bedclothes. Lying like this, she looked exactly like the Desdemona in Boydell's picture. She pulled her nightdress off her shoulders until she was naked to the waist, and threw back her head.

Strands of sunlight covered her with a network of golden patterns, intricate as lace, and as she lay there she felt at peace, as if she had been dead but had come back to life and would now live the eternal, never-fading youth of Desdemona. She felt such joy in being young and in the thought that she would soon be wearing Desdemona's white dress again. When Mikail came in she threw up her hands to hide her naked breasts, but instead she unthinkingly flung her arms around Othello's neck. Nor could she explain why Othello was not in his costume and was wearing no make-up—he was completely white, and had such limpid, dark-blue eyes. The only thing she knew was that she wanted to sing and caress this strange Othello. And she began to sing softly:

> 'The poor soul sat sighing by a sycamore tree,
> Sing all a green willow ... '

Bread *by* Boris Pasternak

Novy Mir, 1956/x

Translated by Ewald Osers

Something of the development of Pasternak's poetic gift is described
in his autobiographical essay *People and Situations*, which is included in this anthology (see pp. 359–415). In his youth his creative
urge was undirected: first music and then philosophy appeared to
be his true bent, both soon rejected. As the result of a profound
emotional shock while he was a philosophy student at Marburg
University, he found his true vocation as a poet. Beginning in the
afterglow of symbolism, in the 'twenties Pasternak belonged to the
more (artistically) radical wing of the futurist movement; but he
always shunned the involvement in polemics and propaganda
characteristic of such futurists as Mayakovsky. Bukharin, the party
theoretician (later purged by Stalin after a show trial) in a speech
to the First Congress of Soviet Writers in 1934, described Pasternak
as 'the greatest poetic master of our times'. With a perceptivity
rare in a communist politician, Bukharin also remarked that Pasternak's intensely subjective approach resulted in a poetry of original
but over-personal images. In the chaste seclusion of his poetic
laboratory, Pasternak worked like a dedicated craftsman over the
verbal forms of his verse, which emerged rich in language though too
narrow in its range of content.

This is a fair critique of Pasternak from an avowed political
viewpoint; a non-communist critic, however, would not call into
question the poet's rights to a highly personal vision. It was to some
extent by restricting his field of vision that Pasternak achieved a
degree of concentration unattained by any other Russian lyric poet
of this century.

The few examples of his work which appeared in *Novy Mir* are
not wholly typical of his best lyrics, and they present difficulties in
translation owing to Pasternak's reliance on the interaction and
associative overtones of Russian words which inevitably evaporate
in translation. Nevertheless the three poems included are good
illustrations of his philosophical approach to nature; of his reflections

on the history of his time; and of her personal feelings over the fate of another Russian poet. The other two poems appear in their chronological position in order of publication in *Novy Mir*, on pp. 250–51.

Bread

You chart a half-century's findings
But you keep them out of your books;
And if you're not hopelessly stupid,
Then surely you've grasped certain things.

That work, honest toil, makes you happy
And paves the way to success,
That idleness equals torture,
Achievement alone gives you bliss.

That the silent kingdom of nature,
Of minerals, plants and of beasts,
Has its secrets, its own revelations,
Its heroes and men of renown.

That the first of these revelations
Lies in the chain of man's fate:
From our ancestor to all his descendants —
The ever-renewed gift of bread.

That the field under rye, wheat and barley
Not only calls for the flail:
It is also a page in a book which
Your forefather wrote for you.

That here is his word, as he wrote it,
His first untutored attempt:
'Midst the hardship of earthly existence,
'Midst birth and labour and death.

Meyerhold Speaks *by* A. Gladkov

Novy Mir, 1961/VIII

Translated by Olive Stevens

It is notoriously unwise to try to classify relative achievement in
the arts. Yet there is a good case for claiming that Russia's greatest,
most influential and enduring contribution to the arts in the
twentieth century has been in the theatre. If in addition to theatre
proper the ballet and the ancillary theatre arts—painting and
music—are included, the influence of the Russian theatrical genius
is clear: names like Chekhov, Diaghilev, Bakst, Nijinsky, Stravinsky
are fundamental to our experience of theatre in the widest sense.
Since they bypass the language barrier, Russian ballet, theatre
design and music have perhaps had the most obvious and widely
felt impact; but in the 'straight' theatre too the predominant
influence on acting technique throughout the world has been
Russian—namely, that of Stanislavsky and the Moscow Art Theatre
which he created together with Nemirovich-Danchenko.

Compared with the widespread recognition accorded to Stanislavsky, the name of Vsevolod Emilievich Meyerhold has been
somewhat eclipsed in the general consciousness; and yet this
dynamic, endlessly creative man dominated the Russian theatre
and inspired the theatrical avant-garde of the world for nearly two
decades at a time when Stanislavsky had ceased in any sense to be
an innovator. Although as artistic director and producer Meyerhold
had by turns shocked and delighted the select audiences of St
Petersburg and Moscow from the turn of the century onwards, it
was only after the Revolution, when the theatre became widely
democratized and the arts flourished in the libertarian climate of
the 'twenties, that his protean talents were given full play. More
than any other individual, Meyerhold was responsible for Moscow
becoming the theatrical capital of the world in those years.

Although trained as an actor and director by Stanislavsky and
Nemirovich-Danchenko, during his years of ceaseless experimenta-
tion before 1917 the constant tendency of Meyerhold's staging was
to move away from Moscow Art Theatre *verismo* in search of a non-

naturalistic and stylized form of theatre—towards what he called 'theatrical theatre' or, as it has since come to be known, expressionism. Meyerhold abhorred naturalism as being alien to the true nature of the theatre; his fundamental critique of naturalistic staging was that the 'fourth wall' convention of the proscenium-arch theatre treated the audience as voyeurs who were being allowed a peep into a world of apparent, though false, reality—a technique whose visual literalism tended to stultify rather than excite the spectator's imagination. In place of this, Meyerhold stressed *à l'outrance* the theatre's power of selection, emphasis and abstraction; he insisted that its proper function as an art-form was to express a poetic or 'theatrical' reality beyond the scope of naturalism, and which by emphasizing rather than suppressing that most 'theatrical' of all its elements—artifice—should heighten the audience's receptivity to the powerful kind of imagery which only the theatre could create.

Meyerhold's compulsive drive to innovate and to shock people into an enhancement of their perceptions in the theatre was such that he not infrequently rejected even his own novel ideas of the recent past as outdated. Virtually every technique that is still looked upon as 'avante-garde' in today's theatre—alienation, absurdity, audience involvement, stylized mime, dance, abstract design—was tried out, exploited and then often cast aside by Meyerhold as he restlessly pushed back the frontiers of the theatrically possible. There were, however, two constant elements in his search for the ultimate in non-realistic theatre: constructivism and bio-mechanics. His constructivist sets were a total rejection of all the canons of realism, usually consisting of a ramp or two, a few stark uprights and a series of platforms, together with the direct use of graphics to announce rather than portray the stage locale. The object of such sets was to stress the centrality of the actor by providing him with a series of visually neutral platforms in space. Since this also entailed great precision on the part of the actor and the most rigid directorial control, Meyerhold 'choreographed' all his productions like a ballet-master, plotting every movement and gesture. The system by which he trained his actors to execute this most demanding method of production was called 'bio-mechanics'; in essence it was a schooling in all the physical skills of circus, ballet and pantomime in addition to the conventional techniques of drama. Its ultimate aim was to give the actor's body an expressive validity equal to that of speech.

Temperamentally and artistically, Meyerhold was very close to the futurist movement in art and literature, above all to Mayakovsky. In 1918, at the very start of Meyerhold's post-revolutionary career, he first produced Mayakovsky's bold, iconoclastic political farce called *Mystery-Bouffe*; ten years later he was responsible for the premieres of Mayakovsky's satirical comedies *The Bedbug* and *The Bath-house*. In the intervening years, however, one of his chief problems was the shortage of suitable new plays by Soviet authors, and some of his most startlingly original productions were his re-interpretations of nineteenth-century classics such as Gogol and Ostrovsky.

This questing, independent spirit did not long survive Stalin's assumption of supreme power. Conservative and philistine, Stalin was as determined to induce uniformity into the style and form of the arts as he was to ensure orthodoxy in their content, and Meyerhold fell into increasing disfavour as Stalin forced the Soviet theatre to accept Stanislavskian naturalism and his System as the sole acceptable canons of style. While Meyerhold's wings were progressively clipped in the 'thirties, Stanislavsky somehow managed to protect his friend and erstwhile pupil from the worst consequences of Stalin's persecution. But when Stanislavsky died in 1938, Meyerhold was left defenceless; stoutly refusing to kow-tow to the shoddy dictates of Stalinist mediocrity, Meyerhold was arrested in 1939 and died an unrecorded death in a labour camp—a shameful, tragic finale to the life of Russia's outstanding man of the theatre.

The jokes, comments and aphorisms of Meyerhold recorded in the following pages by his amanuensis Gladkov are taken from the early to mid 'thirties, the years of Meyerhold's gradual enforced eclipse. In consequence they lack some of the vigour, bite and assertiveness of his style of the 'twenties; in spite of this, these passages speak with his authentic voice, charged with the wit, sensibility, dedication and wisdom of an artist of genius. (The footnotes are all supplied by the present editor.)

I spent three years with Vsevolod Emilievich Meyerhold. During those three years I saw him daily, sometimes even twice a day; there

*were days when we met in the morning and did not part until evening.
Even after I had left the theatre which bears his name, I still continued
to see him from time to time. Occasionally he would ring me up and
ask me to come round, but more often the initiative came from me.
Those were the last years of his life.* He was working on Pushkin's
Boris Godunov, *Chekhov's one-act plays,* Seifullina's* Natasha, *the
dramatization of* How the Steel was Tempered,† *and he was revising
and updating his old productions of* Woe from Wit,‡ The Forest,§
Gogol's The Government Inspector *and others.*

*I tried to note down the most interesting things he said, and my own
observations about him. Here they are in front of me, the tattered old
notebooks which I always carried about with me during those years.
Some of these notes were published in the journal* Teatralnaya Zhizn'
('Theatre Life'), No. 5 of 1960.

*Meyerhold was highly articulate. It is true that at rehearsals he
preferred expressive demonstrations to lengthy explanations, but
many of the remarks he flung at actors were as concise and witty as
aphorisms. A couple of inspired sentences thrown out at random would
bear the imprint of his vast creative experience and would be the
outcome of his habit of deep reflection. At times he would get carried
away and describe his many encounters with writers, artists and
musicians and all the many remarkable people connected with the
theatre whom he had met. In the course of his long life his friends,
colleagues and occasional adversaries included Stanislavsky, Komissarzhevskaya, Blok, Mayakovsky and Yesenin, and he had lively
memories of Tolstoy, Chekhov, Serov,‖ Eleonora Duse and Lensky.¶*

* Lydia Seifullina (1889–1954). Soviet playwright, whose main themes were
revolution and social change.

† Novel by Nikolai Ostrovsky (1904–36), published in English under the
title *The Making of a Hero*, translated by Alec Brown (London, Secker and
Warburg, 1937).

‡ The classic play by A. S. Griboyedov (1795–1829). Translated into English
by Joshua Cooper and published under the title *Chatsky* (Harmondsworth,
Penguin, 1972).

§ Play by A. N. Ostrovsky (1823–86), Russia's greatest nineteenth-century
playwright.

‖ V. A. Serov (1865–1911). Russian impressionist painter. Also painted
scenery for the stage, particularly opera.

¶ Alexander Pavlovich Lensky (1847–1908). Illegitimate son of Prince
P. I. Gagarin. Distinguished actor and director, spent most of his career at the
Maly Theatre. Famous as a teacher of acting.

My notebooks of 1934–39 have preserved most of Meyerhold's chance remarks on countless subjects, as well as some of the stories he told. Journalism had taught me to write quickly and more or less accurately. Most of these notes were taken during rehearsals, others after conversations with Meyerhold, and some of them are his answers to my questions. In those years I was very young and inquisitive. He was always very friendly to me, and he trusted me; I took advantage of this to ask him about many things. He would always respond, sometimes with a joke.

Here are some of these notes:

I would re-phrase Chekhov's well-known dictum about the gun hanging on the wall in the first act like this: if there is a rifle on the wall in the first act, then in the last act there should be a machine-gun.

In order to cry real tears on the stage, you have to experience the joy of creation, a kind of inner elation, in fact the same sort of emotion that you really need to experience in order to burst out laughing. Stage tears and stage laughter have exactly the same psychological foundation. Behind them there must be the joy of the artist and his creative urge, and nothing else. All the other methods of producing tears are neurotic, pathological and anti-artistic.

Don't shout like that! Everything must be much quieter. When actors shout, there can be no nuances. When I was young and worked with Konstantin Sergeyevich,* he thought I shouted too much and he always made me speak more quietly; I did not understand why, and I was my own worst enemy.

Yours is the Korsh† style of acting, not the Meyerhold style. You only think of yourself when you act, forgetting the general plan of the production. Korsh did not allow actors to mask their partners, but that was the only limiting factor. If you alter my exact plan for

* Stanislavsky.
† F. A. Korsh (1852–1921). Impresario who founded the Korsh Theatre in 1882. Closed in 1932, the building is now used by the Moscow Art Theatre.

the production by half a metre, you ruin the whole thing. You must submit to the artistic discipline of sensing where you stand in the general composition, otherwise you'd better exchange me for Korsh! One or the other!

The fundamental problem of the contemporary theatre is the preservation of the actor's power of improvisation within the complex and tight framework constructed by the director. It usually works like the fable: free the nose, and the tail will get stuck. I was talking to Konstantin Sergeyevich recently, and he was also thinking about the problem. He and I are working towards a solution, but it is rather like making a tunnel through the Alps: I am tunnelling from one side and he is coming towards me from the other side, and somewhere in the middle we are bound to meet.

It is precisely in the ability to improvise that drama differs from opera. In opera, the conductor cannot allow any passage to be extended; the only thing he can do is to alter the tempo of the whole piece. Chaliapin, who was essentially an actor, felt the need to improvise, and altered the tempo accordingly. These attempts to alter the tempo were the cause of his many conflicts with conductors. I personally will never renounce the right to encourage actors to improvise. The only important thing to remember with improvisation is that the main action should not be overshadowed by something of secondary importance; there is also the problem of timing and the time-relationship between the different sections of the production.

The director's theatre is the actor's theatre plus the art of creating an ensemble.

An actor ought not to stick to the narrow confines of his profession in his personal friendships; this still happens too often. The confined world of the stage can be very harmful. Shchepkin*was friends with Herzen and Gogol, Lensky with Chekhov. All my life I have

---

* M. S. Shchepkin (1788–1863). Famous actor, born a serf and first acted in a theatrical company composed of serfs. Then transferred to the professional stage, and only received his freedom, on the initiative of S. G. Volkonsky, one of the Decembrists, in 1821 when he was already famous.

6

tried to meet writers, musicians and artists. This enlarges one's
horizon and keeps one free from the narrow conservatism of our
inbred profession.

An actor is at the peak of his artistry when he is forty or forty-five.
By that age his professional experience has been fortified by his
rich experience of life.

What distinguishes a good actor from a bad actor is that he doesn't
act on Thursday the way he did on Tuesday. An actor does not find
satisfaction in repeating a success, but in varying his performance
and improvising within the bounds of the production as a whole.
Self-discipline within the space-time framework of a production
or an ensemble imposes a sacrifice on the actor for the sake of the
whole production, and the director makes a similar sacrifice in
allowing improvisation. But if these sacrifices are to be fruitful,
they must be mutual.

I have often noticed that when a talented actor alters my plan, I
don't just ignore it: I usually don't even notice it. Sometimes I am
told afterwards, 'Look, so-and-so has completely altered your
interpretation,' and then I am genuinely surprised. 'Really? Has
he?' I almost always feel that I have worked it out like that or
thought of it all myself.

I would strictly forbid actors to drink wine or coffee, or take valerian
drops. All these affect the nervous system, and an actor must have
the strongest nerves. There was a poet who wrote to Flaubert
saying he had written a poem while weeping, and Flaubert laughed
at him. Contrary to the generally accepted belief, Yesenin never
wrote poetry when he was drunk; I happen to know this. An actor's,
or for that matter anybody else's creativity is the act of a clear,
happy mind and a healthy, unclouded will. At the beginning of
the century there was a type of actor who was called a 'neurasthenic
hero' (Orlenev* was one of them), but it it significant that no one
ever disqualified themselves professionally as quickly as actors of
this type. Most of them were mental and physical wrecks by the

* P. N. Orlenev (1869–1932). Trained at Maly Theatre. Played mostly in
the provinces, but also at the Korsh Theatre, Moscow. Specialized in a psychological approach to his parts.

time they were forty-five, which is the age at which a dramatic actor reaches his peak.

Individuality is an actor's most prized asset. Individuality must show through even the most skilled acting. There was once an actor called Petrovsky who was technically the most amazing character-actor, yet he did not become a great actor because he lacked individuality. Perhaps at one time he did possess an embryonic individuality, but he not only failed to develop it—he suppressed it altogether. It seems to me that every one of us starts out with individuality: after all, no child is like any other child. Our upbringing wipes out our individuality, but an actor must protect his individuality and develop it. I have the habit, whenever I meet someone for the first time, of imagining what he must have been like as a child. Try it. It's very interesting and instructive. Well now, we have an actor in our company whom, try as I may, I cannot imagine as a child. He's like an onion. Peel a bit off him, and there's another skin underneath, and under that layer there's another, and another, and so on till the end. His individuality has been completely erased, and despite his excellent technique he is mediocre in every part he plays. You want to know who it is? As if I'd tell you! ...

Observation! Curiosity! Attention! Yesterday I asked several of our young actors in turn what sort of street lamps there were in front of the theatre, and nobody gave the right reply. This is awful! When you read the classics you should start by reading those which can teach you to be observant. Gogol in *Dead Souls* is wonderfully observant.

Costume is a part of the body. Look at the Caucasian mountain tribesmen. You would think that their *burkas* [long felt cloaks] would conceal their bodies, but on a true Caucasian the cloak is so made that it is almost a living thing, it pulsates with life, and through it you can see the rippling movement of the body. I saw Fokine in a ballet, and went backstage specially to see how his costume was made; he was wearing a lot of thick material, padding and God knows what else, and yet onstage I saw every line of his body. Stanislavsky studied dressmaking in Paris in order to understand the nature of stage costume.

'Stop!' (*To an actor, K., who was sitting on a tall ladder.*) 'Change your position. Sit more firmly, more comfortably.' (ACTOR: 'But I am quite comfortable.') I don't care whether you're comfortable or not. What matters is that the audience shouldn't feel worried about you, or wonder if you are comfortable up there. This irrelevant anxiety might stop them from concentrating on the scene we're playing ... There, that's better. Thank you.

I forgot who it was who said, 'Art is to reality as wine is to grapes.' What a brilliant remark!

Whenever I come across a street brawl, I stop and watch it. In street brawls and rows you can observe an enormous variety of the most profound human characteristics. Don't listen to the policeman when he says, 'Move on, there.' Walk round the crowd, take up a position on the other side, and watch. When I was young and first went to Italy, I meant to see all the museums and palaces I could, but I soon dropped all that as I was fascinated by the teeming life of the Milan streets. I wandered about with my mouth open, drinking everything in. If I'm late for a rehearsal, and you can see out of the window some incident going on in Gorky Street, then you can be sure that Meyerhold is there.

I don't like make-up. When I was young I loved it; but that passed. Now I can't stand it. Actors often argue with me about this when I start removing their make-up before a first night, but I don't say anything, as I know that the time will come when they won't like it either. Make-up should be minimal. Lensky was brilliant at using minimal, but completely convincing, make-up. There were many theories put forward about why I used hardly any make-up in *The Magnanimous Cuckold*, and I was responsible for some of them myself, but the explanation is quite simple: I don't like make-up, that's all. And why should the young use make-up? All great actors — Ilinsky,* Babanova† — have used very little make-up; it only

* Igor Vladimirovich Ilinsky (b. 1901). Comic actor of exceptional talent and range, who worked in Meyerhold's theatre from 1920–35, and also acted in films. He was particularly successful in satirical roles. Created the role of Prisypkin, the absurd anti-hero of Mayakovsky's *The Bedbug* (1929).

† Maria Ivanovna Babanova (b. 1900). Worked in Meyerhold's theatre 1920–1927. Acted in an exceptionally wide range of romantic and comedy parts.

hampered them. Enthusiasm for make-up is an infantile disease in an actor.

Have you ever wondered why there is always music playing during the acrobat's turn in a circus? You'll say it is for atmosphere, or to make it all more cheerful, but that would be a superficial answer. Circus performers need music for the rhythm, to help calculate time. Their work is based on the most precise timing, and the slightest deviation may lead to a breakdown and catastrophe. Against a background of familiar music, the timing is usually faultless. Without music, it is difficult, but not impossible. If the orchestra were suddenly to play some other music, which the acrobat wasn't used to, this might easily cause a disaster. To some extent it is the same in the theatre. If an actor depends on the rhythm of background music, his acting acquires precision. In eastern theatres, a stage-hand hits a board at crucial points; this helps the actor to be exact in his performance. An actor needs background music to teach him to listen to the passing of time on stage. If an actor has got used to working with background music, then his timing will be quite different without it. As well as developing the ability to improvise, our school of training demands that the actor should develop a talent for self-discipline. Nothing helps the discipline of playing within a time-limit as much as background music.

A pause in the action is very tempting for a good actor who can mime, but if an actor has no sense of time, it can be intolerable. This is where the development of self-discipline comes in. In production after production I have experimented in my directorial scores with devices for self-discipline. In *Bubus the Teacher** background music helped the actors achieve discipline in timing. In *The Government Inspector* the reason for having a small truck stage was discipline in space. Both these productions were tremendously instructive for the actors as exercises in discipline. I noticed that those concerned showed a sharp improvement in their professional abilities.

Once, in Constantinople, I found myself in a Moslem school

* A play by A. M. Faiko (b. 1893). Faiko had been an actor and producer before he began to write plays. See footnote p. 193.

attached to a mosque, and I was surprised to see that while learning the Koran by heart the pupil would hold his teacher's hand, and they would both sway rhythmically. And then I realized that a strict rhythm makes the pupil concentrate and helps him to remember better. Rhythm is a great help.

Good actors always improvise, even within the framework of the most rigid production. Before I saw Mikhail Chekhov as Khlestakov, I had heard that in one place he parodied the portrait of Nicholas I which is hanging on stage, and on my way to the play I savoured this ingenious bit of 'business' in anticipation; but during the performance I did not see it, although Chekhov was in good form and acted splendidly. Moreover, during the performance I completely forgot that I was waiting to see this bit. That evening Chekhov played that passage differently, and he had an absolute right to do so. It was not that he forgot; he did something else instead, and the absence of this clever piece of 'business' was only noticed by those who had seen the play several times running. And when afterwards people said to me, 'Isn't Chekhov's "business" with the portrait marvellous!' I would say, 'Yes, yes,' without in the least feeling I had been cheated.

An actor can only improvise when he is inwardly happy. Without an atmosphere of creative joy and artistic triumph an actor can never reveal himself to the fullest extent. That is why at rehearsals I so often shout 'Good!' at the actors, even when they are far from good. When an actor hears you shout 'Good!' you find that he actually does start acting well. Work should be cheerful and happy. When I have been irritable and angry at rehearsals (and this sometimes happens), at home afterwards I have cursed myself and been very sorry. The director's irritability immediately paralyses the actor, and is as inadmissible as haughty silence. If you cannot feel the actor's expectant eyes upon you, you are no director.

The seasoned actor should be able to play both on a big stage, in a large-scale production like my *Don Juan*, and, like Varlamov*

* Konstantin Alexandrovich Varlamov (1848–1915). Distinguished comic actor of the Alexandrinsky Theatre, St Petersburg, where he worked for forty years.

and Davydov,* sitting for a long time on a sofa (which is what I was aiming at in *The Government Inspector*). In one production (I have forgotten the name of the play) Varlamov was alone on stage for nearly twenty minutes, lying motionless in bed, and it was brilliant. This was what the play required, but it was also a virtuoso example of acting discipline. Without discipline there can be no mastery.

Nothing ever happens on stage by chance. At one performance I saw an actor accidentally drop a flower as he made his exit. An actress remaining on stage unobtrusively picked it up. It seemed to be of no importance, but I looked round and saw that the audience had begun whispering to each other. They had already assumed God knows what about the relationship between these two persons and they were expecting it to develop further.

During dress rehearsals old-time prompters always used to mark in their copies how long each act should take: say, thirty-four minutes for the first act, forty-three minutes for the second, twenty-five for the third ... I used to see these notes in old prompt copies which had been preserved, and for a long time I did not understand why this was done, until the old-timers in the theatre explained it to me. Apparently a good, experienced prompter was responsible for controlling the running-time of the play. We now talk about time-study, and think we have discovered America, but this was being done long ago. The prompter was obliged to make a report after the performance: the act took so long today because someone or other spent too long on a minor scene, or someone rushed a scene, or the stage manager was slow on cues. It was a most important function. A performance can be distorted if an act is prolonged or hurried. Play Maeterlinck too fast and you get vaudeville. Play a comedy slowly, and it will seem like Leonid Andreyev.

A director sometimes has to be cunning in order to achieve what he wants. When I put on *Tantris the Jester* at the Alexandrinsky Theatre I had a big crowd scene, which was always being wrecked by overacting on the part of the extras, who had been trained by

* Vladimir Nikolaevich **Davydov** (1849-1925). Distinguished and versatile actor of the Alexandrinsky Theatre. Teacher of Komissarzhevskaya.

Sanin.* They did their best; every one of them was acting flat out in order to impress his girlfriend sitting in a complimentary seat in the thirteenth or fourteenth row. I could do nothing with them. Then I made all the extras in the crowd scenes join hands. I don't remember how I persuaded them (they were supposed to be a crowd of prison guards), but as soon as they did it I no longer had to restrain them—I even had to shout 'More movement! More action!', smiling to myself as I did so. If I had just told them to be quiet and control themselves they would have stood stock still and left it at that...

I consider that the day of gunpowder in art is not yet over, and that tears make the powder damp. That is why I dislike sentimental art.

We are right to be proud of our theatre, but whenever I'm abroad I always try and see if there is anything good there that we might copy. There may be worthless plays and old-fashioned productions, but I am always impressed by a particular quality of musicality in foreign actors, their professionalism and their discipline, and by that sense of responsibility for every routine performance which they have and which we seem to be losing. At the Théâtre de la Madeleine in Paris I was delighted with one particular actor, and was taken backstage to see him. And just imagine, after a most difficult performance, he was not having a rest, nor was he hurrying off to supper, but was making himself some coffee on a spirit stove and rehearsing a certain scene which he thought had not gone too well that day. Nobody forced him to do this; he himself realized it should be done. In our theatre we are rather weak on professional discipline; we rather let ourselves go, we become passive, we don't go to see other plays or rehearsals, and—to put it very mildly—we don't pull our weight. In my opinion, enemy No. 1 in our theatre companies is the Oblomov complex. What we need is constant discipline, to be kept on our toes, to put more energy into our work. Our performances should be redolent of will-power. The first purpose of the theatre, as of music, is to act as a stimulus to live

* Alexander Akimovich Sanin, real name Schönberg (1869–1956). Early collaborator and co-director at the Moscow Art Theatre with Stanislavsky. Actor, director and teacher at the Alexandrinsky Theatre, 1902–7. Emigrated in 1922.

more fully. The right conditions? Forget it! In 1920, half-starving and with a tubercular lesion in my shoulder, I felt splendid and even fell in love ...

You ask me who was the best actor I ever saw in my life. Yes, I have seen all the great actors of the last fifty years or thereabouts, but I'm not going to hum and haw and say, 'On the one hand ... but on the other ... ' I'll tell you straightaway, because I have thought about this—the best actor I ever saw was Alexander Pavlovich Lensky. He had all the qualities I prize in an actor, and he was a true artist.

Lensky had the priceless gift of lightness of touch, which is quite different from being a lightweight or being frivolous. He could bring lightness to such heavyweight parts as Famusov* or Hamlet. He was able to convey the most complex ideas and the most tragic situations amazingly lightly, without any apparent effort, yet preserving all the nuances; constantly mobile on stage, yet achieving an astonishing depth of interpretation. Like no one else he was able at one and the same time to be serious, tragic, deep—yet light of touch. Even Stanislavsky was nowhere near him in the ease with which he played Famusov. Whatever he played (and I must have seen him in at least twenty roles), I never saw him show a trace of the effort which lay behind his technique, and it would be almost blasphemy to presume that he consciously concealed it. A light touch adds an electrifying quality to tragedy, to comedy, to kitchen-sink drama, to everything, in fact. I think this is why vaudeville is such great training: it is a splendid school for comedy, and it is even a school for tragedy. Orlenev, Moskvin,† Stanislavsky and Komissarzhevskaya all passed through this school.

An actor's work really starts after the first night. I am convinced that a production is never ready by the first night, and not because there has not been enough time but because it only 'matures' in front of an audience. At least, in my experience I have never seen

---

* Character in Griboyedov's *The Mischief of Being Clever*.

† I. M. Moskvin (1874–1946). Soviet actor of great virtuosity. One of the founder-members of the Moscow Art Theatre, of which he became director in 1943.

a production that was ready by the first night. Salvini* used to say that he understood Othello only after his two-hundredth performance. Time nowadays moves at a different pace, and therefore we can cut that down to a tenth, and say to the critics: judge us only after the twentieth performance. Only then will the actors' parts ring true, as they should. I hear that Nemirovich-Danchenko† recently argued the same way. But whatever I, Nemirovich-Danchenko, Stanislavsky, Gordon Craig, Mei Lan-fang‡ or Moissi§ may say, theatre managers are so pig-headed that they will continue to invite critics to the first night.

I have seen fifteen or twenty Hamlets in my lifetime, and they were all different; the only thing they had in common was that they all wore black.

Training and creative art are two completely different things. The actor who does well at drama school does not always become a great actor; I even fear that he may never become a great actor. People don't learn writing just to acquire neat handwriting, which is only practised by army clerks. But that doesn't mean that writing lessons aren't necessary. Calligraphy does not create an individual style of handwriting, but it provides a foundation for it, like any training. Serov was quite right when he asserted that a portrait is only any good when it contains some magical error. I have talked to many people whose portraits Serov painted, and I was fascinated by the process of their creation. The odd thing is that all the sitters considered that something unexpected and unusual happened to their portrait while Serov was painting it, but since this happened with all his portraits it must have been Serov's usual method of working. At first he would take a long time over it, and the result was simply a good likeness; the client was pleased and so was his

* Tommaso Salvini (1829–1915). Italian actor, famous as Othello. Fought under Garibaldi.

† Vladimir Ivanovich Nemirovich-Danchenko (1858–1943). Writer, actor, director. In 1898 co-founder with Stanislavsky of the Moscow Art Theatre.

‡ Mei Lan-fang (1894–1961). Chinese actor and director, who combined a career in the traditional Chinese theatre with the introduction of Western-style drama.

§ Alexander Moissi (1880–1935). Austrian actor of Albanian origin. Acted in Berlin, Prague and Vienna. Visited U.S.S.R. several times.

mother-in-law. Then suddenly Serov would dash in, wipe every-thing off, start all over again on the same canvas and produce a new portrait, this time containing that magical error of which he spoke. It is interesting that in order to achieve such a portrait he first had to rough out an exact likeness. Funnily enough, some of his sitters preferred the more 'correct' version of the portrait.

I was once told how Lenin, during a very serious political argument (and *how* he could argue), while listening to an opponent, fondled a dog under the table. This detail convinced me of the strength of Lenin's inner equilibrium. He was at peace with himself. For an actor, this sort of information is priceless. Once you have it, the job is done, the role created. For a good actor, that is.

Have you noticed how similar are the endings of two of Pushkin's masterpieces, *Boris Godunov* and *The Feast during the Plague*? They both end in silence: 'The people are silent' (*Boris*), and 'The chairman remains sunk in deep thought' (*The Feast*). Clearly this is not just a pause, but a tempo-marking for a directorial score. In Pushkin's day the art of the director did not exist, but he brilliantly foresaw it. That is why I am right when I say that Pushkin's dramas are the theatre of the future.

All my life I have been lucky in my teachers. Stanislavsky, Fedotov,* Nemirovich-Danchenko, the masters of the old Maly Theatre, Chekhov, Gorky, Dalmatov,† Savina,‡ Varlamov, Golovin,§ Blok, Komissarzhevskaya—I learned as much as I could from them all. I could even add another dozen names. You can never be a master

* A. F. Fedotov (1841–95). Acted at the Maly Theatre with Stanislavsky with whom he organized the semi-amateur Moscow Society for Art and Literature. Produced several plays for this society and taught acting.

† Stage name of Vasily Luchich (1852–1912). Of Serbian origin, born in Dalmatia. Playwright and actor, particularly famous for his aristocratic roles.

‡ Maria Savina (1854–1915). Russian actress of Italian origin. Began acting at the age of eight. One of the Alexandrinsky Theatre's most versatile character actresses.

§ Alexander Yakovlevich Golovin (1863–1930). Painter and stage designer. Aimed at making decor and costumes an intrinsic part of the production. His vigorous, colourful sets and costumes for the European tours of Diaghilev's ballet had a worldwide influence on theatre design. Between 1908 and 1917 designed most of Meyerhold's productions.

unless you have the ability to be a pupil. I was greedy for knowledge and full of curiosity. And I'll give you one more piece of advice: be inquisitive and be grateful, learn to marvel and to admire.

Vrubel* did a drawing called 'Insomnia'. It is just a rumpled bed and a rumpled pillow. There is no one there, but what has happened is absolutely clear from the drawing. The person is not there — and yet he is ...

Komissarzhevskaya† was a wonderful actress, but people wanted her to be a Joan of Arc at the same time. She did not, in fact, die of smallpox, but of the same thing that Gogol died of — melancholy. Her constitution was weakened by anguish at the disparity between the strength of her vocation and the reality of the artistic problems she had to face, and she became prone to infection by smallpox. Gogol, too, had some sort of illness with a long Latin name, but that wasn't what killed him. Komissarzhevskaya is remembered for her dramatic roles, but she was a lovely Mirandolina, and excellent in one-act sketches. There was a tremendous joie-de-vivre in her acting, but at the time no one wanted this. She was very gifted. She was musical in the highest degree, by which I mean that she not only sang well but created her parts with a sense of musicality. She had the gift of co-ordinating the whole apparatus of her body quite naturally; her arms would droop as the tone of a speech was lowered — generally speaking, a rare accomplishment. Her acting technique was not a matter of craftsmanship but of individuality, and she therefore seemed to have no technique. Young people of my generation used to regard Garshin‡ as their favourite writer; nowadays this seems almost incomprehensible. I myself changed my un-Russian Christian name§ to Vsevolod in honour of Garshin. Garshin carried within him the music of his time. I don't know why, talking about

* Mikhail Alexandrovich Vrubel (1856–1910). An artist of great spiritual intensity and unique style; died in a lunatic asylum.

† Vera Fyodorovna Komissarzhevskaya (1864–1910). Leading Russian interpreter of turn-of-the-century social drama (Ibsen, Hauptmann, etc.).

‡ V. M. Garshin (1855–88). His first story, *Four Days*, brought him immediate fame in 1877. Most of his work reflected his acute sense of alienation.

§ Born into a German Lutheran family, Meyerhold was first christened Karl-Theodor, but changed his name to Vsevolod when he adopted Russian Orthodoxy in his teens.

Komissarzhevskaya, I suddenly thought of Garshin. It can't be accidental.

Mayakovsky said somewhere, 'In order to laugh, one has to have a face.' That was well said, very well said.

Having known Stanislavsky only when he was old, you cannot imagine what an actor he was. If I've ever managed to achieve anything, it is only because I spent years with him. So put that in your pipe and smoke it! If anyone thinks that I am pleased when people are rude about Stanislavsky, they are wrong. We differed occasionally, but I always respected and loved him deeply. He was a wonderful actor with amazing technique. After all, he was not particularly well endowed with what are regarded as the necessary professional attributes. He was too tall, his voice was somewhat hollow, his diction was not absolutely perfect, and he even refused to shave off his moustache out of naive vanity. But all this was forgotten as soon as he walked on stage. Sometimes when I used to go back to my little room after a performance with him, or after a rehearsal, I could not sleep all night. To achieve anything one must first learn to admire and be amazed.

In the 'twenties I fought against the Maly Theatre, but while I was a student I spent nearly every evening up in the gallery there. The ushers of the top tiers knew my friends and me so well by sight that if they met us in the public baths, they would greet us as friends. We went into raptures over Yermolova*— and Fedotova,† Lensky, the Muzils‡ and the two elder Sadovskys. Before you set yourself up as a critic, you ought to know something about what you are criticizing. I would like to know whether those who run me down have actually seen my productions. When one checks up on them, one usually finds that they have seen one or two, and there have been

* Maria Nikolaevna Yermolova (1853–1928). A great Russian actress who played over three hundred roles in half a century at the Maly Theatre. A theatre named after her was opened in Moscow in 1937.

† G. N. Fedotova (1846–1925). Began acting at the Maly Theatre in 1862, retired owing to ill health in 1905, but continued teaching until her death. Her autobiography, *My Life and Art*, was published in Moscow in 1933.

‡ Borozdin-Muzil, a theatrical family of which four generations in succession acted at the Maly Theatre from 1828 until the 1930s.

instances of them not even seeing one performance through to the end ...

An artist has no need to know whether he is a realist or a romantic. And in any case, these terms have different meanings for different people. You must bring your own vision of the world, whatever it may be, into your art, and then after that you'll be pigeon-holed, and perhaps moved from one pigeon-hole to another several times over. Often these classifications do not so much describe as endow. When someone wrote that I had at last produced a realistic play I was delighted, not because it was true, but because I knew that someone wanted to say something pleasant about me. It's like being made a full general when you have been a lieutenant-general.

You ask whether the Moscow Art Theatre's *Seagull* was naturalistic, and you think you have asked me a tricky question, because I reject naturalism, and yet it was in that production that with much trepidation I played my favourite part. One must admit that there were certain elements of naturalism, but this is not important. The main thing is that it had in it a poetic sensitivity, and the hidden poetry of Chekhov's prose was made into wonderful theatre by the genius of Stanislavsky's direction. Before Stanislavsky began producing, only the subject-matter in Chekhov was performed; they used to forget that in his plays there is the sound of rain outside the window, the clatter of a fallen bucket, early morning behind the shutters, mist on the lake, and that all this (previously to be found only in prose writing) was inextricably linked with the actions of his characters. At that time it was the latest discovery, and 'naturalism' only appeared when it had become a cliché. And all clichés are bad, whether they are naturalistic or Meyerholdistic.

It is only bad directors who think the plays of Ibsen are calm. Read them carefully, and you will find as much action in them as in an American Western.

All my life I have dreamed of producing a Greek tragedy in Leningrad in the square in front of the Kazan Cathedral. Even in Greece itself there is not such a suitable, even, one might say, ideal spot, with the colonnade enclosing the central square on two sides, and the great depth between the pillars giving the actors somewhere to hide before their entrances.

A one-act play is always built symmetrically; no hint of asymmetry in this genre is permissible. That's why we repeat the waltz in Chekhov's *Jubilee*; the audience gets a feeling of balance, and this is, as it were, the musical way of apprehending the structure of the piece.

I like the dramatic form of the old Spanish theatre, with the false finale at the end of the second act and the heightened pace of the third act which equals the two first acts in content. It is amazing to see how the laws of audience-perception are observed in this three-part formula. I learnt a lot from this, although I am not a dramatist.

Pushkin was a student of Shakespeare, and that was revolutionary enough for a theatre weighed down by the legacy of pseudo-classicism; but the spirit of his *Boris Godunov* is even more revolutionary than the formal structure of the play. To comply with the censor's demands, he altered the people's cry 'Hail, Tsar Dmitry Ivanovich' to the famous stage direction 'The people are silent,' and in so doing he outwitted the censor, as this did not diminish but rather increased the part played by the people. The difference between a mob shouting 'hail' first to one tsar and then to another, and a mob expressing its opinion by silence, is enormous. Besides this, Pushkin set the Russian theatre of the future an interesting problem of unusual difficulty: how should silence be played so that it is louder than shouting? I solved this problem for myself, and I am grateful to the stupid censor for prompting Pushkin to make this remarkable discovery.

What is most theatrically effective in drama is to see the process by which the hero makes a decision. This is far more effective than listening at keyholes, slaps on the face, or duels, and is precisely why *Hamlet* is the most popular play of all ages and all countries. It is far more powerful than 'finding out', although there is plenty of that, too, in *Hamlet*. *Hamlet* has everything and for the less sophisticated and more naive it is also a splendid melodrama.

Ghosts is a good play, but compare it with *Hamlet* and you see how much more there is in *Hamlet*.

The essence of drama lies in the inevitability of the unexpected.

Carlo Gozzi won his struggle with Goldoni not because he revived (admittedly not for long) the *commedia dell'arte*, which was languishing under the onslaught of the literary theatre, but because he made his masked characters talk in the language of his day. The problems of trying to revive a stylized art-form are foreign to real art.

When I was imprisoned by Wrangel in Novorossisk,* I had a little volume of Pushkin's dramas in the Educational Press edition. I got so used to it that when I started work again on *Boris Godunov*, *The Stone Guest* and *Rusalka*, for some reason or other I felt a compulsive need to have this edition, which is so compact and convenient. Or perhaps it was because it was so closely associated with my fantasies. While in prison I imagined the script of a play about the False Dmitry, following in Pushkin's footsteps. I was already beginning to compose it in my head when the Red Army stormed the town and I was set free. Later I offered the theme I had worked out to Sergei Yesenin and Marina Tsvetaeva, but poets are proud people and like to think things out for themselves. But have you noticed that in that famous list of projects drawn up by Pushkin there are both *Antony and Cleopatra* and *Dmitry and Marina*? Do you think this is accidental? No, I am sure there was a touch of genius in the fact that Pushkin associated them, and we ought to bear this in mind ... †

* General Wrangel was the anti-communist 'White' Russian general who controlled much of Southern Russia during the later stages of the Civil War (1920). Meyerhold happened to be in Novorossisk when, in the ebb and flow of the Civil War battlefront, the town was temporarily held by Wrangel's forces. As a Communist Party member, Meyerhold was lucky to have escaped with his life.

† Dmitry ('The False Dmitry') was the name assumed by the Pretender who, with Polish backing, defeated Boris Godunov's forces and was proclaimed tsar in 1605. The traditional view of his wife, the Polish princess Marina, is that she was an ambitious woman who drove Dmitry to destruction through his infatuation with her; hence the parallel with *Antony and Cleopatra* suggested by Meyerhold.

Re-reading Belinsky, this is what I found in his article *Russian Literature in 1843*: 'It is more difficult in art to amuse than to move ... ' What do you think? Is this true? Despite all the reservations one may make, I think it is nevertheless true. Comedy survives through the ages longer than tragedy ... Comedy absorbs the truth of its own time more completely. Is this a paradox? Well, think it over ...

Mayakovsky was nearly twenty years younger than me, but from our very first meeting there was none of the distance between us that there might be between a 'senior' and a 'junior'. From the first moment of our friendship he treated me with no particular deference; this was natural as we immediately agreed on politics, and this was what was most important in 1918. For both of us the October Revolution was the way out of an intellectual blind alley. And when we both began work on *Mystery-Bouffe** we never had a moment's misunderstanding. Even as a young man Mayakovsky was remarkably politically mature, and although I was the older I was able to learn from him. Besides that, he was amazingly tactful, despite his reputation for rudeness. There was one very difficult situation when we began work on Selvinsky's† play *The Second Army Commander*, and certain literary trouble-makers tried to play off Mayakovsky and Selvinsky against each other; although I could sometimes sense his unspoken, suppressed jealousy, he always behaved absolutely correctly, even though he did not particularly like *The Second Army Commander*.

Leconte de Lisle used to say: 'Strictly speaking, the concept of "form" does not exist in language. Form is simply the most natural expression of thought.' I subscribe entirely to that.

There are gaps in the careful and thorough biography N. D. Volkov wrote of me. For instance, there is no mention of that important moment of maturity which occurred when I made my first acquaintance with Lenin's *Iskra* in Italy in May 1902, and with his book

---

* A satirical pantomime on revolutionary themes by Mayakovsky, first produced by Meyerhold in 1918.

† Ilya Selvinsky (b. 1899). Poet of the constructivist school. Took part in an expedition to the North Polar ice-cap in 1933–4. His play, *The Second Army Commander* (1929), deals with the defeat of a band of anarchist outlaws.

What is to be done? which had only just been published abroad.
I had come to Milan to look at cathedrals and museums, and I spent
whole days wandering about the streets admiring the Italian crowds,
and then when I returned to the hotel, I would bury myself in
illegal newspapers and pamphlets and read and read without cease.
At that time there were already differences between Lenin and
Plekhanov, and émigré students whom I knew would almost choke
as they argued over the tactics of the Russian Social-Democratic
Party. The terms 'Bolshevik' and 'Menshevik' did not yet exist, if
I'm not mistaken, but the split was already there.

Of course, Dostoevsky was a natural dramatist. In his novels one
glimpses fragments of unwritten tragedies. In spite of all the
mistakes made by his adaptors we have the right to use the expression 'the theatre of Dostoevsky' as we would 'the theatre of
Gogol', 'the theatre of Pushkin', 'the theatre of Ostrovsky', 'the
theatre of Lermontov'. I regret not having been able to work on
Dostoevsky, as I think I understand his 'fantastic realism'.

What can I tell you about my relationship with Blok? It was very
complex and constantly changing, particularly on his side. After
*Balaganchik** we disagreed, then we became reconciled to the point
of intimate friendship. But we broke away from each other again,
not so much for personal reasons but because of our principles.
When I read Blok's diary and correspondence I was surprised by
the variations in his attitude towards me: there was respect and
bitterness, sympathy and coldness. I think the reason for this was
that when Blok criticized me, he was at the same time struggling
against certain traits in his own character. We had a great deal in
common, and, of course, one's own defects are never so obnoxious
as when observed in someone else. Everything that Blok criticized
in me, he saw in himself, try as he might to get rid of it. Incidentally, I did not understand this at the time, and I was annoyed
because I was fond of him. We rarely argued. Blok could not argue.
After deep consideration he would say what he thought and then
he would be silent. But he was a wonderful listener—a rare gift.

* A verse play written by Blok in 1906 and first produced in that year by
Meyerhold at Komissarzhevskaya's theatre in St Petersburg. Cf., p. 72n.

In Mayakovsky's plays there is something of Mayakovsky in each of his characters, just as there is something of Shakespeare in Shakespeare's heroes. If we want to imagine the legendary personality of Shakespeare, we should not search old church records or his genealogy, but study his characters. I can even imagine his voice, just as I can always hear Mayakovsky's voice in the characters of his comedies.

I was the first to put on all three of Mayakovsky's plays, but I would very much like to work on them again. By some wretched coincidence, I had to hurry with all three, because of the production schedule in the theatre. That is why I consider my productions only as a director's first draft, like *The Mischief of Being Clever*, opus 1928. I think that my best was *The Bath-house*. I dream of going back to them and working on them again, this time without being hurried.

Child

Chekhov was fond of me. This is the pride of my life, and one of my dearest memories. We used to write to each other. He liked my letters. He was always advising me to write myself, and even gave me letters of introduction to various publishing houses. I had quite a lot of his letters—about eight or nine, I think, but they were all lost, except one, which I allowed to be published. The others were more flattering, and I was too embarrassed to show them to anyone. When I left Leningrad I gave them to a museum for safe keeping, and when I returned I found that the man I had given them to had died. I cannot forgive myself for this. I lost what I treasured; what I did not treasure was preserved. This happens so often in life.

When I first visited Chekhov, I was surprised to see a completely bare table in his room. There were a few sheets of paper, an inkwell, and that was all. I even thought that perhaps the table was going to be laid for dinner, and, being shy, I hastily said that I had already dined. But apparently the Chekhovs had also dined; the empty table was essential for his work, as it helped him to concentrate.

Chekhov had a habit of laughing quite suddenly in the wrong place when he was being told a story. At first this was very confusing, and it was only after some time that the person talking to him would realize that Chekhov was listening to the story as it were along parallel lines, that he was already mentally altering it, reconstructing it, sharpening it up, filling in the details, seizing on the humorous possibilities, and revelling in them. He listened, thought and imagined far more quickly than anyone with whom he talked. This parallel mental activity of his thrived on conversation, but was far more impetuous and effective. He would listen attentively, and at the same time his creative ability would transform what he heard. I also noticed this amazing characteristic in Ilinsky, who frequently surprised me in conversation with his unexpected laughter. I sometimes even used to stop, until I got used to his laughing not at my words but, like Chekhov, at his own imagination working alongside. This was a sign of spiritual health and of intensely active, creative thought.

It was when I was studying at Moscow University that I first saw Lev Tolstoy at close quarters. Like all young people, my friends embraced one doctrine after another, and as Tolstoy's followers were persecuted by the government, we instinctively sympathized with them, without thinking very deeply. In those days one out of every three students was bound to be a Tolstoyan. One day, together with several of my friends, I went to see Tolstoy in his house in Khamovniki. We rang. We went in. We were asked to wait in the drawing-room. There we sat, feeling rather nervous. Until then I had never seen Tolstoy. People looked upon him as they did upon — I was going to say Gorky or Romain Rolland, but no, it was more than that. We waited for quite a long time, and I remember that my palms began to sweat. We looked at the door through which Tolstoy would enter. And then the door opened. Tolstoy came in. And immediately one had to lower one's gaze. For some reason, and quite involuntarily, I had been looking at the top panel of the door, and it turned out that he was quite small. Like this ... half a metre shorter. I remember that for a moment I was disappointed. He was just a little old man. Very ordinary, like the porter at the university. No, even more ordinary. And then he began talking, and everything changed. And again I was surprised. He had an authoritative, upper-class voice, with a throaty way of pronouncing his r's. White Army generals talk like that on the stage now. He spoke to us sternly, and his manner was almost unfriendly. I was surprised by the fact that he did not in the least try to curry favour with the young, as so many did in those days. I soon realized that there was more respect for us in his attitude than there was in that of other 'influential thinkers' who invariably joked and smiled when they talked to students. Those of us who were brave enough, of course, began to ask him questions about the meaning of life and so on. I kept quiet. All the time I kept thinking that he would tell us that all this was nonsense, and that he would ring for the footman to show us out. But he went on replying patiently, even though not very willingly. When he was sitting, one did not notice how small he was, but when he got up to say goodbye to us, I was again surprised that he was such a little old man. A few years later I went to see Tolstoy once more, but it is the first impression that is always strongest.

When I was working with Vishnevsky,* I was very pleased that he seemed to be afraid of words. He gave us a splendid script, *The Last and Decisive*, and then he would come to rehearsals and scatter a few extra words in small pinches. We would say to him, 'Vsevolod, give us some more words,' but he seemed to hug them to his bosom and would only hand them out sparingly. And this was not in the least because he had too few words—he had a tremendous stock of them—but his economy in words was an aspect of his taste and his sense of what is good theatre. I think it is better to have to beg a dramatist for words that are essential than to have to cross out whole pages written by playwrights for whom words are cheap.

Pushkin strove to imitate Shakespeare, but he is better than Shakespeare. He is more transparent and more fragrant. The most important thing about Pushkin is that he achieves everything by the most economical means. This is the height of genius.

Critics would very much like artists to mature somewhere in a laboratory behind drawn curtains and locked doors. But we grow, mature, seek, make our mistakes and our discoveries in the public gaze and with the collaboration of an audience. Generals learn by blood being spilt on the battlefield, but artists learn by spilling

---

* V. V. Vishnevsky (1900–1951). Wrote plays about the Revolution and Civil War. *The Last and Decisive* was produced in 1931; the title is taken from a line of the 'Internationale' in Russian.

their own blood. Yes, and what's a mistake, after all? Very often
tomorrow's success springs from today's mistake.

Gorky made some very wise remarks about the way in which
people behave in private. When I visited him in Sorrento in 1925,
he read them out to me, and I was amazed by their subtlety and wit.
They tell you much more about the histrionic nature of human
behaviour than in Yevreinov's* affected and flowery treatises. Every
person has something of an actor in him. Watch yourself when
you're at home. If you have come back from a meeting where you
made a speech, or from an amorous encounter, or from a river where
you helped to save a child from drowning, when you get home you
will go on for some time being an orator, or a lover or a hero.
People would not love actors so much if they weren't all partly
actors themselves.

In my life, before every step upward, there has always been a
tragic interval of indecision and doubt, which sometimes led me to
the brink of despair. On only two occasions in my life (and they
were the two most important) did I come to a decision without
wavering. The first was when I graduated from the Philharmonic.†
I rejected the well-paid and flattering offers from two important
provincial impresarios and accepted a small salary in the Moscow
Art Theatre, which was only just starting. (As a way of earning
one's living this was extremely risky!) The other occasion was when
I immediately understood the meaning of the October seizure of
power, and flung myself into the Revolution. I had been prepared
for these decisions by all my past life, and they came to me naturally
and simply. But I shall never forget my inner conflict during the
autumn and early winter of 1905. There was a violent revolutionary
ferment in the country, and we were preparing to open a studio
theatre on Povarskaya Street. *The Children of the Sun*‡ had a shock-
ing first night at the Moscow Art Theatre. Stanislavsky decided
not to open the studio. Everything seemed to have collapsed around

---

* Nikolai Nikolaevich Yevreinov (1879–1953). Playwright, director,
theoretician of the nature of drama and the psychology of acting.

† The Academy of Music and Drama of the Moscow Philharmonic Society, at
which Meyerhold studied acting under Nemirovich-Danchenko from 1896–98.

‡ Play by Gorky, written in 1905.

me. At Stanislavsky's invitation I played Treplev again for a short
time in a revival of *The Seagull* at the Art Theatre. This was something in the nature of a bridge for my possible return to the Moscow
Art Theatre, and Stanislavsky hinted as much. But there were
obstacles: Nemirovich-Danchenko was rather cool about the idea;
and at that time I myself did not know what I wanted—I had completely lost my bearings. Eventually I did not have to take any
decision at all: everything was decided for me by the fact that there
was a complete absence of friendly contact between me and my
former colleagues, the cast of *The Seagull*, whom I used to meet
backstage during the show. They irritated me, and I appeared
strange to them. This was the time of the Moscow armed rising.
I lived in a district where the barricades were up. I shall never
forget the terrible impressions of those days: Moscow blacked-out,
Presnya* wrecked. The tragedy of the defeated revolution was then
somehow more important than anything personal, and my disappointment at the death of the stillborn theatre passed very quickly.
Very soon I quite sincerely stopped worrying about it. After that I
went to St Petersburg and there were new contacts and friendships,
then there was the attempt to found a popular new theatre in
Tiflis, and finally an unexpected letter from Komissarzhevskaya.

I know now that when the periodic crash comes, the only thing to
do is to wait patiently and calmly for a miracle—for the friendly
hand that will save me. After the studio on Povarskaya Street failed,
I got a letter from Komissarzhevskaya. After I left her, there was a
hiatus for a time, and then a letter came from Telyakovsky,†
written at the instigation of Golovin. And immediately after the
closing of GOSTIM‡ I was rung up by Stanislavsky. (*Noted in 1938.*)

* Presnya, a working-class district of Moscow, which was the scene of heavy
fighting in the 1905 revolution.

† Vladimir Telyakovsky (1861–1924). Director of Imperial Theatres; engaged
Meyerhold as actor and stage-director at the Alexandrinsky Theatre, St Petersburg, in April 1908.

‡ Meyerhold's theatre in Moscow, which he ran from 1920 to 1938. After
several changes of name, in 1926 it received the title of GOSTIM—an abbreviation
of the full name Gosudarstvenny Teatr imeni Meierkholda (State theatre
in the name of Meyerhold). It was closed by Stalin, who could not tolerate
Meyerhold's unquenchable urge to experiment and innovate. On the closure
of GOSTIM, Stanislavsky invited Meyerhold to work at the Stanislavsky Opera
Theatre.

When you see a tree lose its leaves in autumn, it seems to be dying. But it is not dying, it is getting ready for its renewal the following spring. There are no trees that produce green leaves the whole year round, and there are no artists who do not experience crises, depression, doubts. But what would you say about gardeners who chopped down the trees that had lost their leaves in the autumn? Surely artists should be treated as patiently and kindly as we treat trees.

The so-called 'success' of a first night should not be the chief aim of the theatre. Sometimes you must keep going with your eyes open even when you know you're heading for failure. When I put on Selvinsky's *The Second Army Commander* I was convinced of its inevitable failure; but this did not influence my decision. Besides various short-term tactical aims, I had long-term strategic objectives too. I wanted that splendid poet Selvinsky to smell greasepaint, and I hoped that in the future he would write us a new and wonderful play. *The Second Army Commander* had strong scenes and lively poetry, but it made one fatal mistake: the chief character, Okonny, could not be the hero of a Soviet tragedy; he was too insignificant for it. But all the same, I am not sorry that I put on this play. Without defeat there is no victory. In that production there were some discoveries which I prize very much, as well as some first-class acting. Isn't that something? I consider that there are situations in which the theatre must face up bravely to a flop and not retreat. It was that sort of situation.

I am often asked what I think of Okhlopkov's* productions, where the audience sits all round the stage, and so on. I have not seen these productions, but I think an artistic director has the right to seat the audience in this way if he needs to. The only thing that worries me is that this experiment is taking place in such a small auditorium. In my opinion an arrangement like this demands a larger cubic capacity of air above the stage, a special arrangement for the orchestra and special acoustics in the hall. If these conditions

* Nikolai Pavlovich Okhlopkov (b. 1900). Actor and director. Worked as an actor in Meyerhold's theatre from 1923 to 1929. From 1930 to 1937 ran the Realistic Theatre, where he introduced 'theatre in the round'. Famous for his simple, forceful style of production.

do not exist and this good idea is carried out in a tiny building, it may not work. (*Meyerhold had in mind the theatre on Mayakovsky Square which at that time housed the Realistic Theatre, directed by N. P. Okhlopkov. Obraztsov's* puppet theatre is there now.*)

When I see the productions put on by the youngest of my pupils, I am dizzied by the continuous changes of scenery and tempo. I wonder anxiously whether it was really I who taught them this. And then I console myself: 'No, it's their youth and lack of experience exaggerating my defects, which they have assimilated only too well.' And then I want to put on productions that are even quieter and more restrained. That is how I learn from my pupils.

The two poles of theatrical Moscow are said to be my theatre and the Moscow Art Theatre. I would be prepared to consider myself as one of the poles, but if I were to name the other it would be the Kamerny Theatre.† No theatre can be more alien and more opposed to mine than the Kamerny. The Moscow Art Theatre at one time had four studios. With a great stretch of the imagination it might be said that my theatre also is one of the Moscow Art Theatre studios; not the fifth, of course, but let us say, bearing in mind the distance between us, the 255th. After all, I too am a pupil of Stanislavsky's, and the M.A.T. was my alma mater. I can find links between my theatre and the M.A.T. and even with the Maly, but between us and the Kamerny there is a deep gulf. It is only Intourist guides who place Meyerhold and Tairov side by side. Incidentally, they are also rather fond of linking us with St Basil's Cathedral, too, but I am more inclined to accept St Basil's as a neighbour than Tairov.

---

* Sergei Obraztsov (b. 1901). Joined the Musical Workshop of the Moscow Art Theatre in 1922 and the Nemirovich-Danchenko Theatre in 1926. Started producing puppet plays in 1923, and in 1931 founded his own puppet theatre which he still directs.

† Kamerny ('Chamber') Theatre, Moscow. Founded in 1914 by Alexander Tairov, who apart from a short break in the 'forties, ran the theatre until his death in 1950. In the 'twenties, Tairov rivalled Meyerhold as the most daring innovator of the Soviet theatre, but unlike Meyerhold he later adapted himself successfully to Stalin's dictates on theatrical style. It is to this that Meyerhold is chiefly referring when he talks of the deep gulf between himself and Tairov.

More often than not, a director's inexperience shows itself by blurring the exposition of a play. If you don't 'announce' the exposition with absolute clarity, the audience will not understand the rest of the play, or will still be guessing at the meaning long after they ought to have grasped it.

It is wrong to contrast the stylized theatre with the realistic theatre. A stylized realistic theatre—that is our aim.

Read more! Read unceasingly! Read! Read with a pencil in your hand. Make extracts. Leave lists in your books of all the passages that have caught your attention. This is essential. All the books in my library contain lists like that and are annotated. For instance, I have read all of Wagner in German. Everybody knows him as a composer and a librettist, but besides that he also wrote ten volumes of the most interesting articles. I have studied them all. In those volumes you can find the lists I have made and you will immediately understand what interests me. Have no respect for the margins of books. Write all over them. A book which I have written in is ten times more valuable to me than a new one.

It was a personal tragedy for me that Stanislavsky shut down the studio theatre on Povarskaya Street in 1905, but in fact he was right to do so. With characteristic haste and impetuosity I had tried to unite in it the most diverse elements: symbolist drama, stylizing designers, and young actors trained in the school of the early days of the Moscow Art Theatre. Whatever our objectives might have been, all these elements simply could not be co-ordinated, and roughly speaking it was like the fable of the swan, the crayfish and the pike.* With his instinct and sound taste, Stanislavsky understood this, and after I had recovered from the bitterness of failure, this was a lesson to me: first of all, one has to educate a new kind of actor, and only then set him new problems. This was the conclusion that Stanislavsky came to as well, and he was already developing the basic principles of his 'Method', which was then in its first draft.

* In Krylov's fable the swan, the crayfish and the pike simultaneously pull a boat in different directions, and so can make no progress.

The new technique of the theatre was dictated by the dramatists. In Maeterlinck's *Death of Tintagiles* there are some scenes which take ten or twelve minutes to play, the action taking place in a medieval castle. But in order to put up the scenery representing the castle the intervals have to be twice as long as the scenes, and this is ridiculous. Inevitably we had to devise a stylized castle. This is how the dramatist pushes the theatre into new techniques.

Round a table there may be agreement between the director and the actors, but it is deceptive. It is impossible to walk onstage with the same sense of assurance that is generated round a table. Once onstage, practically everything has to be worked out again from the beginning in any case. Often there is not enough time; the management is hurrying us on. As a result the production is staged with many rhythmic and psycho-physical defects—all because there was too much sitting round a table, and we got too used to the decisions taken there. Directors like Sakhnovsky* actually make their actors create their parts twice over, once at the table and then again on stage. These two different methods only clash and hinder each other. I advise young directors to try from the very beginning to rehearse in conditions as close as possible to those of the actual performance. I would have failed with *Masquerade*† if I had agreed to the producer's request to start rehearsals in a small foyer. I had to get the actors used from the very beginning to large-scale rhythms. Yurev,‡ a wise man and a masterly actor, entirely understood this and supported me.

With me, anger often turns out to be a stimulus to creative action. That is why I wanted to put on *The Queen of Spades* after I had

* Vasily Grigorievich Sakhnovsky (1886–1945). Became a director at the Moscow Art Theatre in 1926, where he co-directed the dramatized version of Gogol's *Dead Souls* with Stanislavsky. Author of a number of books on playwrights and the theatre.

† Romantic verse drama by Lermontov, written in 1835–6. Meyerhold directed a brilliant version of it at the Alexandrinsky (now the Pushkin) Theatre in 1917.

‡ Y. M. Yurev (1872–1948). Trained at the Moscow Philharmonic Society and the Maly Theatre. Spent most of his career at the Alexandrinsky Theatre. In Meyerhold's production of *Masquerade* he played the hero, Arbenin.

copious

footnotes voluminous, fill in background

seen and heard Pechkovsky* play Herman. I was so furious with him that if I had met him at night in a dark alleyway, it might have been the worse for him. Having got angry and grumbled for a while, I began to think and dream, and that is how I conceived this production.

I always know when I have failed. For instance, there was the experimental production of Chekhov's *The Proposal* which the audience did not take to, although we had all worked on it with loving enjoyment. But we had been too clever, and the result was that we lost the humour. One must be brutally frank—there is usually more laughter at an amateur performance of *The Proposal* than there was in our theatre, although Ilinsky was acting and Meyerhold directing. Chekhov's light, transparent humour could not bear the weight of our excessive ingenuity, and so we failed. One must never deceive oneself. You may not admit it to the critics, but tell yourself everything.

In my first production of *The Mischief of Being Clever*, I made many mistakes; I was greatly helped in this by the artist Shestakov.† The production was soaked in pseudo-erudition. Separate episodes grew out of proportion and did not fuse with each other. In 1935 I put on another production, in which I corrected some of my mistakes. The alterations hardly concerned the actors (except for the inevitable re-polishing where they had grown rusty), as we had been on the right road with them even in 1928. Shestakov and I must bear the full responsibility for the mistakes of that production, and I do not blame the actors at all.

Beware of using metaphors with pedants. They understand everything literally and then give us no rest. I once said that words were a decorative pattern on the canvas of movement. This was an ordinary metaphor of the sort that one frequently produces while

* Nikolai Konstantinovich Pechkovsky (b. 1896). Lyric tenor; leading opera singer at the Kirov Theatre, Leningrad, from 1924 to 1941. From 1939 to 1941, artistic director of the Kirov opera. Herman in *The Queen of Spades* was his most celebrated role.

† V. A. Shestakov (b. 1898). Scenic designer; was chief artist at the Moscow Art Theatre 1922–27, and at Meyerhold's theatre 1927–29.

talking to pupils. But the pedants took it literally, and for the last two decades they have been scientifically refuting this fragile aphorism of mine. Similarly, many things have long been laid at Gordon Craig's door, because he once compared actors to puppets. Goethe (whom incidentally I do not like) once said that actors should become like tightrope-walkers. But does that mean that he advised Hamlet to walk on a wire? Of course not. It was simply that he wanted to advise actors to aim for faultless precision in their every movement.

I had a great range as an actor: I played in comedy and in tragedy, and was even prepared to take women's parts. I was trained in music and choreography. I also studied law, wrote for the newspapers, and translated foreign languages. I consider myself a writer and a teacher. And all this was useful to me as a director. Had I been an expert in anything else, that too would have been useful. A director has to be very knowledgeable. There is the expression 'narrow specialization'. A director has to specialize more widely than anyone on earth.

A director must know all the disciplines which go to make up the art of the theatre. I had occasion to watch Edward Gordon Craig at rehearsals, and I was always impressed by the way he did not shout, 'Give me a blue light,' but specified exactly, 'Switch on no. 3 spot and no. 8 spot.' He could even talk to carpenters professionally, although I don't suppose he could ever have made a chair. One should spend hours with the electricians before one has the right to give them orders. When the wardrobe mistress brings the costumes the director must not mumble, 'A little tighter here, a little wider there,' but should give precise instructions: 'Undo that seam, and put a wire in here.' Only then will lazy colleagues stop making objections and claiming, as they usually do, that it is impossible to alter anything; you don't have to take them at their word. Stanislavsky learned dressmaking in Paris so as to have a better understanding of theatrical design.

A director must be able to direct anything. He has no right to be like a doctor, who specializes in children's ailments, or in venereal disease, or in ear, nose and throat infections. A director who claims that he can only produce tragedies and cannot put on comedy or vaudeville will certainly fail, because in real art the high and the low, the sad and the funny, light and darkness are so close as to be inseparable.

A director must sense the passage of time without having to take his watch out of his waistcoat pocket. A performance is an alternation of dynamics and statics, but also of dynamics of different orders. That is why I think a sense of rhythm is one of the most important gifts a director can have. Without an acute feeling for stage time it is impossible to put on a good production.

I think it was Scriabin who said that rhythm was 'time bewitched'. That was brilliantly put.

A director must be able to interpret the written text of the play he is producing; but that is not enough; he must be able to build what I call the 'second floor' of the play in his imagination. Whatever you may say, a play is only raw material for the theatre. I can interpret a play without altering a word of it, but I can pervert the author's intention simply by misplacing a few stresses. The effort to preserve and embody the author's meaning is not merely a matter of keeping to the letter of the script.

In Russia in the first half of the nineteenth century there were cases when the censor took plays out of the repertoire, although on being read they had aroused no suspicions and had been passed. Actors like Mochalov* put into their interpretation things that were not in the text. They mimed, paused, stopped, gestured, cut passages short and varied the stress. The audience understood this perfectly, and reacted to it. This is what I call the 'second floor' of the play. And this was more or less casual and semi-improvised, as the art of the director did not exist then. The censors were appalled by these performances, and a play that until then had been passed as acceptable was banned after the performance. This shows that they under-

* Pavel Stepanovich Mochalov (1800–48). Famous tragedian, who came of a family of serf actors. A controversial figure, he was ardently supported by the critic Belinsky; his other admirers included Gogol, Lermontov and Turgenev.

stood the nature of the theatre better than our present-day critics, who are only concerned with the letter of the text.

The fundamental law of bio-mechanics* is very simple: the whole of the body takes part in every one of our movements. The rest is practice, exercises, study. Tell me, what is there in this that upsets people so much, arouses such protests and seems so heretical, so unacceptable? It's as if there were a kind of curse on me — the simplest things I say turn out to be paradoxes or heresies which must be punished by burning at the stake. I am sure that if I were to say tomorrow that the Volga flows into the Caspian Sea, the day after tomorrow there would be demands that I acknowledge all the errors in that statement.

Association is the key ... Devise your moves on stage for the associations they can evoke. I have only just begun to realize the immense power of associative images in the theatre. There is a wealth of possibilities.

You are listening to *The Queen of Spades*, and you suddenly remember some episode from Stendhal — or rather you don't exactly remember, but something half-recollected flickers across your consciousness. The image of Herman and the heroes of Stendhal are a true form of association. True association reinforces a performance and increases its effectiveness beyond bounds, but a false association can wreck it. A production may stick precisely to the letter of the play — the wigs worn just so, the noses stuck on properly, and the script correctly spoken, yet the associations evoked in the audience can be quite alien to the author's idea and the spirit of his work. The only way to read the classics is to take them not in isolation, but together with the whole library shelf on which they stand. Pushkin may hardly have known Stendhal, and it appears that Byron, who knew him well, did not suspect what a great writer Stendhal was. But for us today, Herman, the heroes of Lermontov's stories, Stendhal's heroes and Byron's heroes all belong together,

---

* Bio-mechanics was the name given by Meyerhold to his system of training actors; the aim was for the actor to achieve total control over his body as an instrument of expression. Critics of the method held that the real purpose was to turn actors into little more than obedient puppets.

and associated memories of them inevitably pass across our mind's eye, provided we ourselves do not close the door on these associations. If we make use of associations we can leave things unsaid, and the audience themselves will fill them in for us.

Two examples from the Moscow Art Theatre will demonstrate how much more powerful associative images are than the text of the play. Ibsen's *An Enemy of the People* is intended by the author to be the most conservative and anti-social play, propagating social isolation. But it had an immense revolutionary success in Russia on the eve of 1905, because the situation was such that the audience, inflamed with revolutionary excitement, interpreted the theme as the struggle between the individual and the majority. The associations aroused in the audience put a completely different emphasis on the subject of the play. The same thing happened with Hamsun's* *At the Gates of the Kingdom*. The audience was in no mood to listen carefully to the text of Kareno's monologue preaching poverty. Yet because of the power of association in their own minds, which linked the struggle of an active minority against the majority with the idea of revolution in general, Kareno's fight against the liberals, which the author had written from a very right-wing viewpoint, became identified with the revolutionary struggle and was decked out by the audience in their own left-wing colours. I remember this very well, as I played Kareno many times.

There is nothing mysterious about the grotesque. It is quite simply a stage style which plays on sharp contrasts, and produces a constant shifting of the planes of perception. An example is Gogol's *The Nose*. In art there can be no forbidden devices; it is simply that they must be used in a timely and appropriate way.

An audience's impression is all the richer if it is perceived subconsciously — I myself have several devices which I conceal from

* Knut Hamsun (1859–1952). Norwegian novelist and playwright; Nobel prize winner (1920). Strongly influenced by Nietzsche and Strindberg, Hamsun was attracted by the Nietzschean elements in Nazi ideology, and collaborated with the Germans during the Second World War occupation of Norway. In 1945 he was convicted of high treason, but his sentence was commuted in view of his advanced age.

the audience. Ilinsky's 'business' as Prisypkin in the hostel scene in *The Bedbug* was a means of creating the necessary tension throughout that scene, but I did not in the least want the audience to notice it.

I am afraid that we have conditioned our audiences to react with thoughtless, stupid laughter — to laugh at all costs, in fact. Don't you think people laugh too much in our theatre nowadays? The moment may come, perhaps tomorrow, when the audience, corrupted by our desperate efforts to amuse them, will either guffaw or be coldly silent when they see a subtle, complex, intelligent play. That is why I always attack playwright X so passionately. He may be an able man, but he actively participates in corrupting the audience with idiotic laughter. That is the only reason why I hate him with all my heart and soul!

If you start reading a play, don't put it down; if you must do so, when you pick it up again re-start on the first page. I have noticed that one can only properly appreciate a play if one reads it through at one go.

It seems to me that the current argument in the theatrical journals as to who is more important in creating a production, the director or the playwright, is very naive. I think the most important thing is the *idea* behind the production, whoever its originator may be. Whichever member of the partnership, director or playwright has the most significant, lively, witty ideas is the 'leader' in this situation. When I worked with Faiko,* and I suppose with Erdman,† I was the 'leader', but when it came to Mayakovsky, I must admit it was a different story. But I do not see anything humiliating to the playwright or the director in either case.

---

* Alexei Faiko (b. 1893). Actor, director, playwright. Meyerhold produced two of Faiko's plays: *Lake Lyul* in 1923, and *Bubus The Teacher* in 1925. In itself an unoriginal satire on decadent capitalist society, *Bubus* was memorable for being one of Meyerhold's most ingenious and highly stylized productions.

† Nikolai Erdman (1902–72). Playwright, author of satirical comedies, of which Meyerhold produced *The Warrant* in 1925. Meyerhold's production of Erdman's *The Suicide* was banned in rehearsal. Erdman was sent to a labour camp during the purges of 1936–8; he survived, but no more of his plays have been staged.

Before the first night of *The Lady of the Camellias* I was in a very agitated state, as well I might have been: at the dress rehearsals the performance had lasted for about five hours. The management were glaring at me like wolves. I hastily cut out what I could, but it was still too long, and, what was worse, the quality of the production entirely depended on its stylishness. Any attempt at drastic cutting would have turned out like those American digests of Tolstoy's great novels, like cans of literary corned beef. I awaited the audience's reaction with unusual anxiety. Would they be prepared to listen to my unhurried story? And at the first night I was moved to tears (real tears, not a rhetorical phrase) when I saw that the audience was watching and listening without any visible signs of strain. This was my greatest moment of joy and triumph. And then these thoughts came into my head: an audience in a hurry is the enemy of the theatre. We gulp down bitter medicine, but we savour good food. It is not worth taxing an audience's patience, but on the other hand it is not necessary to pander to an audience which can never 'spare the time'. If the theatre cannot make the audience forget about time, then what right has the theatre to exist?

I love the theatre, and I am sometimes sorry that the torch of the actor's craft is beginning to pass to the film actor. I am not talking about Chaplin, whom with some sort of magic foresight we loved even before we saw him. But just think of Buster Keaton! His films were absolutely unique for their subtlety, their clear-cut scenic design, their tactful characterization and stylish discipline of gesture.

When I was in Kislovodsk and heard of the death of Stanislavsky* from Livanov,† I wanted to run right away from everybody and cry like a boy who has lost his father.

The modern aeroplane is light and streamlined and looks as if it has been made all in one piece; at first glance it appears to be a much less complicated machine than the old Farmans and Blériots. It is the same with art. The perfect creation of a master seems simple

---

* Stanislavsky died on August 7th, 1938.
† Boris Livanov (b. 1904). Soviet actor.

and elementary compared to the cumbersome work of the striving amateur.

Now here is a paradox: I sometimes need better and more experienced actors for small parts than for the main ones. *The Queen of Spades* was so successful because I insisted that the Countess, who has only one song, and Eletsky should be sung by the best singers, who in other productions would have had the main roles. Recently in the theatre I was annoyed when somebody said that the part of Luka in Chekhov's *The Bear* was hardly a part at all, but just a useful stage prop. Had I not long ago stopped acting, I would have loved to play Luka myself, and then I would have shown them whether it is a part or not. The secret of producing *Boris Godunov* lies in the casting of the so-called small parts.

I got the main idea for my stage interpretation of *The Mischief of Being Clever* from a letter which Pushkin wrote to Bestuzhev after he had read the play. This letter is now quite forgotten, and that is why the stage characteristics which I gave to Sofia, Molchalin, Chatsky and the others caused such amazement. I put into effect what Pushkin had said a hundred years before, and I was accused of striving after mere originality for its own sake!

It is not true that directors do not need to understand typecasting. The problem is how one uses this knowledge. Now here is another paradox: I have to know which actors in my company are the 'lover' type, so that I shall *not* give them 'lover' parts. I have often noticed that an actor will unexpectedly reveal something in himself when he is forced to work 'against the grain' of his own more obvious characteristics. He cannot get rid of these, of course, so they remain in the background as a kind of accompaniment to the image he is creating. There is nothing so dull as a provincial heroine playing Katerina. The chief fascination of Komissarzhevskaya lay precisely in the fact that she played heroines without being a 'heroine'. An actor is so constituted, alas, that whenever he is type-cast he generally stops working, apparently imagining that he can get by on his voice or his looks. In order to induce an actor to work hard, one must sometimes consciously give him a paradoxical problem, which he will have to solve by abandoning his 'standard' techniques. In my experience this method of casting has almost always been justified. I do not like Ferdinands who declaim unctuously, deep-voiced Katerinas and Khlestakovs who gabble.

I am certain that if an actor adopts the right physical pose, he will speak his lines properly. But the choice of the right stance is in itself a conscious act, an act of creative thought. The way an actor holds himself can be incorrect or approximate in relation to the part he is playing, or it can be almost right, or casual, or precisely right and so on. The range of possibilities is enormous. But just as the writer searches for the exact word, so I search for the most exact stance.

Stage design is emphatically not a matter of static composition, but a process: a process in which time acts upon space. In addition to a plastic element it also contains a time element, i.e. a rhythmic and musical element.

When you look at a bridge, you see as it were a leap which has been solidified in metal, and that is a process, and not something static. The stress which is expressed in a bridge is the main thing about it, not the ornaments that decorate its balustrade. It is the same with staging. Using another kind of simile, I might say that if acting is the melody, then staging is the harmony.

A director must not be afraid of creative conflicts with actors at rehearsals, even if this leads to fisticuffs. The director's strength lies in the fact that in contrast to the actor he always knows (or should know!) what the production is going to look like tomorrow. He is in charge of the *whole* production, and therefore he is in-evitably in a stronger position than the actor. So don't be afraid of quarrels and fights!

It is very bad when a director is blinkered by the preliminary sketch of a production and cannot make use of whatever happens to turn up in the course of rehearsals. Often something occurs by chance which can lead to a completely unforeseen effect, and one must know how to make use of it. This has happened constantly in my experience. Here are two examples from the work on some of our recent productions. At one of the dress rehearsals of *The Lady of the Camellias*, in Scene ii of Act I, the actors accidentally threw up the paper carnival streamers so high that instead of falling down again they got stuck on the steel ropes, and this was so unexpectedly pretty that a murmur of delight ran through the entire audience. Strictly speaking this was a mistake and shouldn't have happened, but it provided a delightful touch. The actor who was playing Gaston made use of it; without my direction, he took the ends of the streamers in his hands and absent-mindedly played with them in his scene with Marguerite. All I had to do was to give my approval, and develop and formalize it slightly. While rehearsing the restaurant scene in *The Prelude** there was also an unforeseen event when an actor who was not on stage jumped heavily on to the floor from a bit of scenery backstage. The crash of this jump corresponded rhythmically with a pause in the music of the dance composed by Shebalin,† and I realized that here was a possibility of altering Hugo Numbach's entry from upstage to downstage right, which I had already thought out; this enabled me to give the dance to Sverdlin‡ to perform, and it gets a round of applause whenever he does it.

Allow me to inform you, my brothers-in-arms and pupils, that the idea of a director's theatre is absolute nonsense and must not be believed in. There is no director, that is, there is no good director, who would put his art above the interests of the actor as the chief person in the theatre. The director's skill lies in the art of the staging, of timing the alternations in the lighting and the music. All this is only there to serve our excellent, highly-trained actors.

I cannot understand why our opera houses still retain this clumsy anachronism of placing the orchestra in front of the stage. It surely makes singers force their voices, and robs the singing of subtlety

---

* A dramatization of his own novel of the same name by the Soviet novelist and playwright Yury Pavlovich German (b. 1910). His first work for the stage, it was produced by Meyerhold in 1933.

† V. Y. Shebalin (b. 1902). Soviet composer. Wrote music for Mayakovsky's *Lenin*, and set to music poems by Pushkin, Blok, Yesenin and others.

‡ Lev Naumovich Sverdlin (b. 1901). Soviet actor. Famous for his physical agility and grace, he was a leading exponent and teacher of Meyerhold's system of bio-mechanics. Worked in Meyerhold's theatre 1926–37. The part of Hugo Numbach is regarded as having been the best of his career.

and nuance. It is very difficult for singers to penetrate the powerful musical curtain of the orchestra. In the theatre at Bayreuth the orchestra is placed much lower down than in our theatres, and this has a tremendous effect. When Wagner put four to six *forte* signs in his score he naturally had this kind of orchestra placing in mind, but our conductors, in quite different conditions, blindly follow these directions and allow the orchestra to blast away, creating an unbearable din. I cannot bear shouting in opera, so I have stopped going to our productions of Wagner. In the Mariinsky Theatre, because of this shouting, singers strained their throats beyond endurance and crippled their vocal chords, while Yershov* had to retire early. The opera needs many reforms. The architects should find another place for the orchestra, and the singers should learn their parts so that they don't need to keep their eyes fixed on the conductor. I have promised myself that if ever again I produce an opera, I shall work myself to a standstill if necessary but I will put the orchestra somewhere else. (*Noted in 1936. At the beginning of 1939 I asked Meyerhold, who had by then started directing at the Stanislavsky Opera Theatre, whether he still intended to carry out this reform, and he replied, 'Yes, of course, but just let me get a little more firmly entrenched here first.'*)

Simplicity is the most precious thing in art. But every artist has his own conception of simplicity. There is Pushkin's simplicity, and there is the simplicity of a primitive. There is no such thing as a universal simplicity, which can be achieved and understood by everyone, just as there is no 'golden mean' in art. An artist must strive to attain his own form of simplicity, which will not be in the least like the simplicity of any of his fellow-artists. The highest form of simplicity in art is something which has to be attained, not something from which one starts. It is the summit, not the foundation.

My credo: I believe in a simple, laconic stage idiom which evokes complex associations. That is how I would like to produce *Boris Godunov* and *Hamlet*.

* Ivan Vasilievich Yershov (1867–1943). Wagnerian 'heroic tenor', famous for his singing of Lohengrin, Parsifal and Tristan. Trained at the St Petersburg Conservatoire. Sang at the Mariinsky from 1895 to 1929. Professor at the Conservatoire from 1916 until his death.

I doubt if any director in the world has been criticized as much as I have, but believe me, no one judges me as severely as I judge myself. Of course, I don't particularly care to admit my sins in public; it's a private matter between me and my other self. But private self-criticism is a funny thing. There are triumphs of which one is almost ashamed, and failures of which one is proud.

Critical direct-hits on me have been rather infrequent, not because there was any lack of enthusiasts wanting to shoot me down, but because I am such a fast-moving target.

In my production of Ostrovsky's *The Forest* some things now seem rather coarse and primitive; they are too plain-spoken, too exaggeratedly tendentious. But compare a page from a newspaper of 1924, or a copy of *Krokodil* or *Bezbozhnik** of that time, with a present-day newspaper and a current *Krokodil*. The workers who studied at the Workers' Faculties of the 'twenties aren't like the university students of the 'thirties, either. Our production of *The Forest* was definitely aimed at a contemporary audience, that is, at the audience of the mid-twenties. And it is not surprising that in a number of ways the production is a bit dated. What is surprising is precisely the opposite: that it has dated so little and goes on drawing tumultuous applause from the audience. The explanation for this is that except for a contemporary slant, the production rests on a solid foundation of the best theatrical traditions. By all means let's cut out all the topical allusions which are no longer up to date and obvious. As far as I can see, after many alterations over more than ten years the production has become less and less satirical and more and more romantic. This is due to something like an evolutionary process, which is perfectly legitimate. (*Noted in 1936.*)

Do you know that Salvini and Rossi† played Hamlet differently

---

* 'The Atheist', an anti-religious journal published by the League of Militant Atheists, 1925–43.

† Ernesto Rossi (1827–96). Italian actor and playwright. Rossi's influence on the Russian theatre was considerable, because he made a deep impression on Stanislavsky. Rossi's autobiography, *Quarant' anni di vita artistica*, was translated into Russian in 1896 and is the model for Stanislavsky's *My Life in Art*.

almost every time, sometimes cutting out the philosophical soliloquies and sometimes putting them back again, depending on the type of audience?

The most difficult thing about a production is the casting. When I have to cast a play, I do not sleep for several nights and am almost ill. But if I manage to cope with it without making any obvious compromises, then I can look ahead with assurance.

I don't like starting work on a play with the first act. I like to take the most difficult episode first, and then proceed to the easier ones, like certain French dramatists who began work on the climax and only then turned back to the exposition and the development. I have done most of my work like this.

I went through a period when I would produce a play in small sections, each of which I spent a long time perfecting. Then I noticed that because of this everything used to expand and get distended out of all proportion. I am now reverting to the way in which I used to work long ago: having decided on two or three crucial scenes and having sketched out all the rest, I try to race through all the acts one after another as fast as I can. When one hurries them like this, the whole emerges more quickly. I do not know what technique Wagner used, but I am sure he didn't toil away fashioning little pieces, like bits of mosaic, otherwise his 'endless melody' would never have been created. The overall shape of a production is most easily found by a dynamic approach.

The best of my pre-production ideas—by which I mean those which don't occur to me during a rehearsal—have never been thought out at my desk, but in a crowd, with noise and movement all round, when it seemed that I was not even thinking of my work. One mustn't forget that an artist is always working. Mayakovsky described this perfectly in that slim little book, which sums up all his experience, entitled *How to Write Poetry*. When I come to write about directing plays, I shall try to write as fully and as briefly as he did.

He who has not given everything to his art has not given it anything.

The life of every true artist is the life of a man continuously racked by dissatisfaction with himself. Only amateurs are always pleased with themselves and are not tormented by anything. A master is always strict with himself. Self-satisfaction and conceit are foreign to him. Usually when an artist seems pleased with himself and is self-assured, it is only a pose in self-defence, artificial armour against blows that might hurt him. Mayakovsky was like that. From outside he sometimes seemed to be self-assured, but I knew him well and realized that the rudeness and outward aplomb that Mayakovsky put on were only armour, and, what is more, armour that was infinitely brittle. The life of a true artist is the triumph of a single day, the day when the last blob of paint is flung on to the canvas; the rest is the enormous suffering of the countless other days when the artist can see nothing but his mistakes.

(*To a certain young actor during a break in rehearsal.*) So you didn't manage to see *The Queen of Spades* yesterday? The manager didn't give you a complimentary ticket? What a pity! And the ticket touts were charging too much? Really! And of course you had no money? Yes, I know it's a long time till pay day. So you gave up? You don't know how to get in without a ticket? But when we were young we knew how to! At one time I used to be thrown out of the Maly Theatre almost every night. One evening I would see the first two acts, then the other two on another evening. Of course it's humiliating when you're thrown out in front of everybody, but we would do literally anything to see Yermolova. But you weren't given a complimentary, so off you went. Where did you go — home? You went skating? Well, that's different. Now *that's* even better than *The Queen of Spades.* Good for you. Well done!

Romain Rolland's book on Beethoven lies open on Meyerhold's table. Turning over the pages I see a phrase of Beethoven's which has been underlined: 'There are no rules which cannot be broken for the sake of something still more beautiful ...'

One Day in the Life of Ivan Denisovich *by* Alexander Solzhenitsyn

Novy Mir, 1962/XI

Translated by Max Hayward and Ronald Hingley

The publication of Solzhenitsyn's novella *One Day in the Life of Ivan Denisovich* in the November 1962 issue of *Novy Mir* probably represents the high-water mark of Tvardovsky's courageous editorial policy of making the journal the mouthpiece of liberal dissent within the Soviet Union. The four short stories which constitute the rest of Solzhenitsyn's work to have been passed by the Soviet censor were also published in later numbers of *Novy Mir*. Of all these, *One Day in the Life of Ivan Denisovich* is of the greatest literary interest and has had the most profound moral and political repercussions. Its printing is believed to have been personally authorized by Khrushchev, who regarded it as politically expedient to let it appear as an element in his de-Stalinization campaign, which was then at its height. Although Khrushchev had set this momentous policy going by his famous speech denouncing Stalin at the XX Party Congress of 1956, that speech remained officially 'secret', having been delivered in closed session and not reported in the press or in the official published account of the Congress. Khrushchev judged it necessary to give wider public expression to the de-Stalinizing theme, to which there was still fierce opposition within the party leadership, and indeed in all echelons lower down in the party machine, and he regarded Solzhenitsyn's story as ideal for this purpose.

Its effect was tremendous. For the first time, the facts about Stalin's infamous prison-camp regime were spelt out in print, and the whole Soviet people felt the breath of this wind of truth. The issue of *Novy Mir* was sold out in a matter of minutes and passed from hand to hand until the copies fell to pieces. The story, however, was never reprinted in book form, as were so many others of the best works first published in *Novy Mir*, and when the party's attitude to literature grew more repressive after the fall of Khrushchev, library copies of this issue, and those containing Solzhenitsyn's other works, were withdrawn from the shelves.

After 1966 no more of Solzhenitsyn's writing was published in *Novy Mir*, or anywhere else in the U.S.S.R., although it is known that his novel *Cancer Ward* was accepted by Tvardovsky in 1967 and was actually set up in type, but was banned on party orders by Konstantin Fedin, the secretary of the Union of Soviet Writers, of which *Novy Mir* is an official organ of publication.

The story of *One Day in the Life of Ivan Denisovich* corresponds exactly to its title: it describes a single winter day, from reveille to lights out, as lived by a political prisoner in a Siberian prison camp under Stalin's rule. In form it belongs to the traditional Russian genre of the *skaz*, which concentrates a narrative of wide-ranging significance into a dense, compressed piece of writing that ultimately derives from an oral tradition of story-telling, and which is couched in a popular, colloquial idiom. In his use of this medium, Solzhenitsyn both demonstrated his extraordinary mastery of form and lanlanguage and stressed the manner in which Stalin's arbitrary rule of terror brought suffering and degradation to the remotest, humblest most politically inoffensive members of Soviet society—most of whom, in fact, were incarcerated on grounds which lacked the faintest trace of rationality. In its different context, and on a much more realistic and therefore more widely accessible level, *One Day in the Life of Ivan Denisovich* voices the same kind of despair to which Kafka gave expression in *The Trial*.

Lack of space unfortunately prevents its being included in full, and the following extract constitutes roughly the second half of the narrative. The translation, by Max Hayward and Ronald Hingley, has been chosen as being the one which best reproduces the tone of the original, although the essence of Solzhenitsyn's terse, elliptical but highly expressive style eludes the most skilled translator, largely because it deals with an area of experience for which our culture has virtually no equivalent.

... On his way back Shukhov ran into a warder, took his cap off just to be on the safe side, and ducked into his barracks. There was one hell of a racket inside—somebody's bread ration had been pinched while they were all out at work and everybody was shouting at the orderlies, and the orderlies were shouting back. There was nobody from 104 there.

Shukhov always figured they were in luck if they got back to camp and the mattresses hadn't been turned inside out while they were gone.

He ran to his bunk and started taking his coat off on the way. He threw it up on top and his mittens with the pieces of steel too and felt inside his mattress. That hunk of bread was still there! Good thing he'd sewed it in.

So he dashed out again and went to the mess hall.

He slipped across and didn't run into a single warder—just men coming back and quarrelling about the rations.

The moonlight in the yard was getting more and more bright. The lights in the camp looked dim and there were black shadows from the barracks. There were four big steps up to the mess hall and they were in the shadow too. There was a little bulb over the door and it was swinging and creaking in the freezing cold. And there was a kind of rainbow around all the lights but it was hard to say if this was from the frost or because they were so dirty.

And the Commandant had another strict rule—each gang had to march up to the mess hall two by two. Then the order was—when they got to the steps they had to line up again by fives and stand there till the mess-hall orderly let them up.

This was Clubfoot's job and he wouldn't let go of it for anything in the world. With that limp of his he'd gotten himself classed as an invalid, the bastard, but there really wasn't a thing wrong with him. He had a stick cut from a birch tree and he lashed out with it from the top of the steps if anybody tried to go up before he gave the word. But he was careful whom he hit. Clubfoot was sharp-eyed as they come and he could spot you in the dark from behind. He never went for anybody who could hit back and let him have it in the puss. He only beat a fellow when he was down. He'd let Shukhov have it once.

And this was the kind they called 'orderlies', but if you thought about it they didn't take orders from anybody. And they were in cahoots with the cook.

Today a lot of gangs must have crowded up at the same time or maybe they were having trouble keeping order. The men were all over the steps. There were three of them up there—Clubfoot, the trusty who worked under him, and even the fellow in charge of the mess hall, big as life—and they were trying to handle things on their own, the crapheads.

The manager of the mess hall was a fat bastard with a head like a pumpkin and shoulders a yard wide. He had so much strength he didn't know what to do with it and he bounced up and down like on springs and his hands and legs jerked all the time. His cap was made of white fur soft as down and he didn't have a number on it. There weren't many people 'outside' with a cap like that. He had a lamb's-wool jacket and there was a number on it the size of a postage stamp—just big enough to keep Volkovoy happy—but he didn't have a number on his back. He didn't give a damn for anybody and all the men were scared of him. He had a thousand lives in the palm of his hand. Once they'd tried to beat him up but the cooks all rushed out to help him. And a choice bunch of ugly fat-faced bastards they were too.

Shukhov would be in trouble if 104 had gone in already. Clubfoot knew everybody in camp by sight, and when the manager was there he never let anybody through if he wasn't with his own gang. Just for the hell of it. The fellows sometimes climbed the rails going up the steps and got in behind Clubfoot's back. Shukhov had done this too. But you couldn't get away with it when the manager was there. He'd knock you all the way from here to the hospital block.

Shukhov had to get over to the steps fast as he could and see if 104 was still here—everybody looked the same at night in their black coats. But there were so many of them milling around now like they were storming a fortress (what could they do, it was getting close to lights out?) and they pushed their way up those four steps and crowded at the top.

'Stop, you fucking sonsofbitches!' Clubfoot yelled, and hit out at them with his stick. 'Get back or I'll bash your heads in!'

'What can we do?' those up front yelled. 'They're pushing from the back!'

And it was true, the pushing came from the back but the fellows in front weren't really trying to hold them back. They wanted to break through to the mess hall. Then Clubfoot held his stick across his chest to make a kind of barrier. And he threw all his weight behind it. His trusty got his hand on the stick too and helped him push. Even the manager didn't worry about getting his precious hands dirty and took hold of the stick.

They shoved real hard. They had plenty of strength with all that meat they ate. Those up front were pushed back and fell on the men behind. They went down like tenpins.

'Fuck you, Clubfoot!' some of the guys in the crowd shouted. But they made sure they weren't seen. The others kept their mouths shut and just scrambled to their feet fast so's not to get trampled on. And they got the steps cleared.

The manager went back inside and Clubfoot stood on the top step and shouted: 'How many times do I have to tell you to line up by fives, you blockheads! I'll let you in when we're good and ready.'

Shukhov thought he saw Senka Klevshin's head way up front. He was real glad and started pushing his way through fast. But the men were jammed tight and he couldn't make it.

'Hey, 27!' Clubfoot shouted. 'Get moving!' Gang 27 ran up the steps and inside on the double. The rest rushed the steps again and the men in back pushed hard. Shukhov pushed for all he was worth too. The steps were shaking and the bulb over the doorway was making a sort of creaking noise.

'Won't you ever learn, you scum?' Clubfoot was mad as hell. He hit a couple of the fellows on the back and shoulders with his stick and pushed them over on the others.

He cleared the steps again.

Shukhov could see Pavlo go up the steps to Clubfoot. Pavlo'd taken charge of the gang because Tyurin didn't like to get mixed up in this kind of mob.

'Line up by fives, 104!' Pavlo shouted from up there. 'Let 'em through, you guys up front!'

The hell they'd let 'em through.

'Hey there, let me through! That's my gang!' Shukhov grabbed hold of the man in front of him. The fellow would have been glad to get out of the way but he was wedged in there too.

The crowd weaved from side to side. They were really killing themselves to get that gruel they had coming.

So Shukhov tried another tack. He clutched the rail going up the steps on the left, pulled himself up by his arms, and swung through to the other side. He hit somebody on the knee with his feet. They kicked back at him and called him every name they could think of. But he'd made it. He stood on the top step and waited there. The other fellows from his gang saw him and stuck out their hands.

The manager looked out from the door and said to Clubfoot: 'Let's have another two gangs.'

'104!' Clubfoot yelled. 'And where d'you think you're going, you bastard!' he said to a fellow from another gang and hit him on the neck with his stick.

'104!' Pavlo shouted after him and started letting his own men through.

Shukhov ran in the mess hall and—he didn't wait for Pavlo to tell him—started to pick up empty trays. The mess hall looked the same as ever—great clouds of steam, and men jammed tight at the table like corn on a cob or wandering around and trying to push through with trays full of bowls. But Shukhov had gotten used to this in all his years in the camps. He had a sharp eye and right away spotted S-208 carrying a tray with only five bowls on it for one of the other gangs. The tray wasn't full so it meant this was the last time he'd need it.

Shukhov got over to him and said in his ear from behind: 'Gimme that tray when you're through, pal.'

'But there's another guy over at the hatch waiting for it.'

'Let the bastard wait. He should've been sharper.'

So they made a deal—S-208 put his bowls on the table and Shukhov snatched the tray. But the other guy ran over and grabbed it by the end. He was smaller than Shukhov. So Shukhov shoved it at him and sent him flying against one of the posts holding up the roof. He put the tray under his arm and dashed over to the hatch. Pavlo was standing in line and he was sore because there were no trays. He was glad to see Shukhov. The assistant gang boss of 27 was just in front of Pavlo at the head of the line. Pavlo gave him a shove.

'Get outa the way! Don't hold things up! I've got trays!' Gopchik, the little rascal, was lugging one over too. He was laughing.

'I grabbed it while some other guys weren't looking.'

Gopchik would go a long way in the camp and make a real old hand. He needed a couple more years to learn all the tricks and grow up and then he'd have it made—like cutting the bread rations in the stores. Or even a bigger job.

Pavlo told Yermolayev to take the other tray—Yermolayev was a big Siberian and he'd gotten ten years for being a P.O.W. too—and sent Gopchik to look out for places. Shukhov pushed his tray sideways through a hatch and waited.

'104!' Pavlo called into the hatch. There were five of these hatches—three for dishing out the food, one for men on the sick list (there were ten men with ulcers who got special food, and all the book-keepers had wangled this diet for themselves too), and the fifth for handing back the bowls. Here the men fought to see who'd get to lick 'em out. These hatches weren't very high up—a little above your waist. All you could see through them was hands with ladles.

The cook had soft white hands but they were damn big and had hair all over them, more like a boxer's than a cook's. He picked up a pencil and checked off from his list on the wall: '104—twenty-four!' Panteleyev was here too. Like hell he'd been sick, that sonofabitch!

The cook picked up a great big ladle and stirred the stuff in the cauldron—it'd just been filled nearly up to the top. There were clouds of steam coming out of it. Then he picked up another ladle that held one and a half pints—enough for four bowls—and began to dish out. But he didn't dip down very deep. 'One, two, three, four ... ' Shukhov watched to see which bowls he filled before the good part settled back on the bottom of the cauldron and which had only the watery stuff off the top. He put ten bowls on the tray and went away. Gopchik was waving at him from a place by the second pair of posts. 'This way, Ivan Denisovich, over here!'

You had to be careful carrying these bowls. Shukhov watched his step, sort of gliding along so as not to jolt them, and kept shouting all the time: 'Hey you, K-920, look where you're going ... ! Get out of the way, fellow ... !'

It was tough enough carrying one bowl in that crowd without spilling it, never mind ten. But he got them over to the end of the table Gopchik had cleared off, put the tray down on it real gentle, and didn't spill a drop. And he managed to place it so the two best bowls would be on the side he was going to sit at.

Yermolayev brought over another ten. And then Gopchik ran

back to the hatch and came back with Pavlo. They were carrying the last four in their hands.

Kilgas brought their bread ration on another tray. Today the ration was according to output. Some got six ounces, others eight. Shukhov got ten. He took his ten (it had a lot of good crust on it) and Caesar's six—from the middle of the loaf. Now the men in their gang were coming from all over the mess hall to get their supper. It was up to them to find a place to sit down and eat it. Shukhov handed out the bowls and kept an eye on who'd gotten one, and guarded his corner of the tray. He put his spoon in one of the two good bowls to stake a claim. Fetyukov took his bowl—he was one of the first—and went off. He figured there wouldn't be good pickings in his own gang and it'd be better to snoop around the mess hall and scavenge—there might be somebody who'd left something. Anytime a guy didn't finish his gruel and pushed the bowl away, others swooped down on it like vultures and tried to grab it—a whole bunch of them sometimes.

Shukhov checked over the helpings with Pavlo and everything looked all right. He pushed one of the good bowls to Pavlo for Tyurin. Pavlo poured it in a flat German army canteen—it was easy to carry it pressed close to his chest under his coat.

They gave up their trays to some other fellows. Pavlo sat down to his double helping, and so did Shukhov. They didn't say another word to each other. These minutes were holy.

Shukhov took off his cap and put it on his knee. He dipped his spoon in both his bowls to see what they were like. It wasn't bad. He found a little bit of fish even. The gruel was always thinner than in the morning—they had to feed you in the morning so you'd work, but in the evening they knew you just flopped down and went to sleep.

He began to eat. He started with the watery stuff on the top and drank it right down. The warmth went through his body and his insides were sort of quivering waiting for that gruel to come down. It was great! This was what a prisoner lived for, this one little moment.

Shukhov didn't have a grudge in the world now—about how long his sentence was, about how long their day was, about that Sunday they wouldn't get. All he thought now was: 'We'll get through! We'll get through it all! And God grant it'll all come to an end.'

He drank the watery stuff on the top of the other bowl, poured what was left into the first bowl and scraped it clean with his spoon. It made things easier. He didn't have to worry about the second bowl or keep an eye on it and guard it with his hands.

So he could let his eyes wander a little and look at other bowls around him. The fellow on the left had nothing but water. The way these bastards in the kitchen treated a man! You'd never think they were just prisoners too!

Shukhov started to pick out the cabbage in his bowl. There was only one piece of potato and that turned up in the bowl he got from Caesar. It wasn't much of a potato. It was frostbitten of course, a little hard and on the sweet side. And there was hardly any fish, just a piece of bone here and there without any flesh on it. But every little fishbone and every piece of fin had to be sucked to get all the juice out of it — it was good for you. All this took time but Shukhov was in no hurry now. He'd had a real good day — he'd managed to get an extra helping at noon and for supper too. So he could skip everything else he wanted to do that evening. Nothing else mattered now.

The only thing was he ought to go see the Latvian to get some tobacco. There might not be any left by morning.

Shukhov ate his supper without bread — a double portion and bread on top of it would be too rich. So he'd save the bread. You get no thanks from your belly — it always forgets what you've just done for it and comes begging again the next day.

Shukhov was finishing his gruel and hadn't really bothered to take in who was sitting around him. He didn't have to because he'd eaten his own good share of gruel and wasn't on the lookout for anybody else's.

But all the same he couldn't help seeing a tall old man, Y–81, sit down on the other side of the table when somebody got up. Shukhov knew he was from Gang 64, and in the line at the package room he'd heard it was 64 that had gone to the Socialist Community Development today in place of 104. They'd been there all day out in the cold putting up barbed wire to make a compound for themselves.

Shukhov had been told that this old man'd been in camps and prisons more years than you could count and had never come under any amnesty. When one ten-year stretch was over they slapped on another. Shukhov took a good look at him close up. In the camp you could pick him out among all the men with their bent backs because he was straight as a ramrod. When he sat at the table it looked like he was sitting on something to raise himself up higher. There hadn't been anything to shave off his head for a long time — he'd lost all his hair because of the good life. His eyes didn't shift around the mess hall all the time to see what was going on, and he was staring over Shukhov's head and looking at something nobody else could see. He ate his thin gruel with a worn old wooden spoon, and he took his time. He didn't bend down low over the bowl like all the others did, but brought the spoon up to his mouth. He didn't have a single tooth either top or bottom — he chewed the bread with his hard gums like they were teeth. His face was all worn-out but not like a 'goner's' — it was dark and looked like it had been hewed out of stone. And you could tell from his big rough hands with the dirt worked in them he hadn't spent many of his long years doing any of the soft jobs. You could see his mind was set on one thing — never to give in. He didn't put his eight ounces in all the filth on the table like everybody else but laid it on a clean little piece of rag that'd been washed over and over again.

But Shukhov couldn't spend any more time looking at the old man. When he finished eating he licked his spoon and pushed it in the top of his boot. He jammed his cap on his head, got up, took his own bread ration and Caesar's, and went out. You had to leave through another door. There were a couple of orderlies standing there. They had nothing else to do but unlock the door to let people out and then close it after them.

Shukhov came out with a full belly and he felt good. He thought he might look in on the Latvian, though there wasn't much time to go before lights out. So he headed for Barracks 7 and didn't stop off at his own barracks to leave the bread there.

The moon was way up now. It was all white and clear and looked like it had been cut out of the sky. And the sky was clear too and the stars were as bright as could be. The last thing he had time for now was looking at the sky. But he saw one thing — the cold wasn't letting up. Some of the fellows had heard from the 'free' workers outside that it'd go down to twenty in the night and forty by morning.

From somewhere outside the camp he could hear the noise of a tractor, and a bulldozer was grinding away on the new road they were building. And every time anybody walked or ran through the camp you could hear the crunch of their felt boots in the snow.

There was no wind.

Shukhov would have to pay the same as always for the tobacco— one ruble a mug, though 'outside' it cost three rubles, and even more for the better stuff. Prices in the camp were not like anywhere else because you couldn't have money here. Not many people had any and it was very expensive. In the 'Special' camps they didn't pay you a penny (but in Ust-Izhma Shukhov got thirty rubles a month). And if you got any money from home they didn't hand it over to you but put it in an account in your own name, and once a month you could spend something out of this account in the stores for fancy soap, moldy cookies, and Prima cigarettes. And you had to write to the Commandant beforehand and tell him what you wanted to buy, and if you didn't like the stuff you could either take it or leave it, and if you didn't take it you could say good-by to your money anyway—they'd already taken it out of your account.

Shukhov got his money by doing odd jobs—making slippers (for two rubles) out of the rags the customer gave you or patching up a jacket (you named the price for the job).

Barracks 7 was not like 9, where he was. His had two big halves, but 7 had a long passageway with ten doors off it, and each gang had a room to itself, seven bunks to a room. And each room had its own latrine and the guy in charge of the barracks had his own cubicle. The artists lived here in their own cubicles too.

Shukhov went into the part where the Latvian was. He was lying on a lower bunk with his feet up on the ledge and he was jabbering in Latvian with the fellow next to him. Shukhov sat down on the edge of the bunk and said hello, and the Latvian said hello but didn't take his legs down. In small rooms like these the men pricked up their ears to see who'd come and what he was after. They both knew this. That's why Shukhov sat there talking about nothing very much. ('How're things?' 'Not bad.' 'Very cold today.' 'Yes.')

Shukhov waited till the others got back to their talk—about the war in Korea. They were arguing whether there'd be a world war or not now the Chinese had come in.

And then he leaned close to the Latvian: 'Got any tobacco?'

'Sure.'

'Lemme see.'

The Latvian took his feet off the ledge, dropped them on the floor, and sat up. He was real tight-fisted, this Latvian, and when he put the stuff in the plastic mug he was always scared he'd give you one smoke more than you paid for.

He showed Shukhov his pouch and opened it up.

Shukhov took a little tobacco and put it on his hand. He saw it was the same as last time, the same brownish color and the same cut. He held it to his nose and smelled it. Yes, it was the same stuff, but what he said to the Latvian was: 'Don't look the same to me.'

'Yes it is.' The Latvian got mad. 'I always have the same. It is always the same.'

'Okay,' Shukhov said. 'Pack that mug for me and I'll have a smoke out of it, and then maybe I'll take another mug.'

He said 'pack' because this fellow always sprinkled it in sort of loose.

The Latvian got another pouch from under his pillow—it was fatter than the other one. And he took his mug out of the locker. This mug was made of plastic but Shukhov knew just how much it'd hold and that it was as good as something made of glass. And the Latvian started filling it.

'Press it down now, press it down!' And Shukhov poked his finger in to show him how.

'I know how, I know how.' The Latvian got mad again and pulled the mug away and pressed down himself—but not so hard. Then he went on filling it.

Meantime Shukhov opened his jacket and found the place in the wadded lining where he kept his two-ruble bill. He eased it along through the wadding till he got to a little hole he'd made in another place and sewed up with two stitches. He pushed the bill this far, pulled out the stitches with his nails, folded the bill lengthways, and took it out of the hole. It was old and limp and didn't rustle any more.

Somebody in the room was yelling: 'You think that old bastard in

Moscow with the mustache is going to have mercy on *you*? He wouldn't give a damn about his own brother, never mind slobs like you!'

The great thing about a penal camp was you had a hell of a lot of freedom. Back in Ust-Izhma if you said they couldn't get matches 'outside' they put you in the can and slapped on another ten years. But here you could yell your head off about anything you liked and the squealers didn't even bother to tell on you. The security fellows couldn't care less.

The only trouble was you didn't have much time to talk about anything.

'Hey, you're putting it in loose,' Shukhov grumbled.

'All right, all right.' And the Latvian put a little more on top.

Shukhov took his own pouch out of the inside pocket he'd sewed himself and emptied the mugful of tobacco into it.

'Okay,' he said. 'Give me another mugful.' He didn't bother about trying it out beforehand because he didn't want to have his first sweet smoke in a hurry.

He haggled a little more with the Latvian and emptied another mugful into his pouch. He handed over his two rubles, nodded to the Latvian, and left. Then he chased back to his own barracks so he wouldn't miss Caesar when he came back with that package.

But Caesar was already sitting in his lower bunk and gaping at the stuff. He'd spread it all out on his bed and on the locker, but it was a little dark because the light from the bulb on the ceiling was cut off by Shukhov's bunk. Shukhov bent down, got between the Captain's bunk and Caesar's, and handed over the bread ration. 'Your bread, Caesar Markovich.'

He didn't say, 'So you got it,' because this would've been hinting about how he stood in line for him and that he had a right to a cut. He knew he had, but even after eight years of hard labor he was still no scavenger and the more time went on, the more he stuck to his guns.

But he wasn't master of his eyes. Like all the others he had the eyes of a hawk, and in a flash they ran over the things Caesar had laid out on the bed and the locker. But though he still hadn't taken the paper off them or opened the bags, Shukhov couldn't help telling by this quick look—and a sniff of the nose—that Caesar had gotten sausage, canned milk, a large smoked fish, fatback, crackers with one kind of smell and cookies with another, and about four pounds of lump sugar. And then there was butter, cigarettes, and pipe tobacco. And that wasn't the end of it.

Shukhov saw all this in the time it took him to say 'Your bread, Caesar Markovich.'

Caesar was in a real state like he was drunk (people who got packages were always like this) and he waved the bread away. 'You keep it, Ivan Denisovich.' Caesar's gruel and now his six ounces of bread—that was a whole extra supper—and this, of course, was as much as he could hope to make on that package. And he stopped thinking right away that he might get any of this fancy stuff and he shut it out of his mind. It was no good aggravating your belly for nothing. He had his own ten ounces of bread and now this ration of Caesar's and then there was that hunk of bread in the mattress. That was more than enough! He'd eat Caesar's right away, get another pound in the morning and he'd take some off to work with him. That was the way to live! And he'd leave that old ration where it was in the mattress for the time being. Good thing he'd sewed it in—look how that fellow from 75 had stolen out of the locker, and there wasn't a thing you could do about it.

Some people thought anybody who got packages was well off and fair game, but when you really got down to it, it was gone in no time. And just before a new package came in they were only too glad to pick up an extra bowl of mush and they went around cadging butts. The guy with the package had to give something to his warder, his gang boss, and the trusty in his barracks. They often lost your package and it didn't come up in the list for weeks. When you took it to the storeroom for safe-keeping against thieves and on the Commandant's orders—Caesar would be taking his there before roll call in the morning—you had to give the guy in charge there a good cut or he'd nibble his way through it. How could you keep a check on that rat sitting there all day with other people's food? Then you had to pay off people who'd helped you get it, like Shukhov. And if you wanted the guy in the washhouse to give you back your own underwear from the wash, you had to let him have a little something too. Then there were those two or three cigarettes for the barber so he'd wipe the razor on a piece of paper and not on your bare knee. And what about the guys in the C.E.S. so they'd put your letters aside for you and not lose 'em? Suppose you wanted to wangle a day off and lie around in bed? You couldn't go to the doctor with empty hands. And you had to give something to the fellow next to you in the bunk who shared your locker, like the Captain shared Caesar's. He'd count every little piece you put in your mouth, and even the biggest heel couldn't get out of giving him something.

Some fellows always thought the grass was greener on the other side of the fence. Let them envy other people if they wanted to, but Shukhov knew what life was about. And he was not the kind who thought anybody owed him a living.

He took his boots off and climbed up to his bunk. He got that piece of steel out of his mitten and had a good look at it. He figured he'd look for the right kind of stone tomorrow to grind it down for a knife he could use to mend shoes. And in four or five days, if he worked at it a little mornings and nights, he'd make himself a pretty good knife with a sharp curved blade. But meantime he'd have to hide it. He'd push it between the crosspiece and the boards of his bunk. And while the Captain wasn't in his bunk down below—he wouldn't have wanted any dirt to fall on the Captain's face—he pulled the heavy mattress back (it was stuffed with sawdust, not shavings), and then he hid the thing there. Alyoshka the Baptist and the two Estonians could see him doing it from their bunks. But he didn't have to worry about them.

Fetyukov came through the barracks and he was crying. He was all hunched up and there was blood on his lips. So he must've gotten beat up again for trying to scrounge somebody's bowl. He went past the whole gang, didn't look at anybody, and didn't bother hiding his tears. He climbed up to his bunk and dug his face in his mattress.

You couldn't help feeling sorry for him if you thought about it. He'd never live out his time in the camp. He just didn't know how to do things right.

And now the Captain came along in a good mood with a potful of tea. But it wasn't the kind they got in the camp. They had two tubs with tea in the barracks, but who'd call that tea? It was luke-warm and had the right color, but it was really just slops and it smelled of rotten wood from the tub. But this tea was only for poor suckers. Well, the Captain had gotten a fistful of real tea from Caesar and run off to get some boiling water. He looked pleased with himself and set it up on the locker. 'I nearly scalded my fingers under the faucet,' he said as if he was proud of it.

Caesar was spreading his stuff out on sheets of paper in the bottom bunk. Shukhov could see this through the cracks in the boards, and he put the mattress down again so he wouldn't get upset at the sight of it. But Caesar couldn't do without him.

He stood up and peered over at Shukhov and winked at him. 'I say, Shukhov ... be a good fellow and loan me that "ten days" of yours, will you?' What he wanted was Shukhov's little penknife (you could get ten days in the cooler if they found something like this on you). Shukhov kept it in the boards under his bunk too. It wasn't half as big as his little finger, but it could cut up a piece of fatback ten inches thick like nobody's business. Shukhov had made this knife himself and always kept it sharp. He stuck his hand under the board again and got it out. Caesar gave him a nod and ducked down out of sight.

You could make something on a knife like that, but it meant the cooler if they found it on you. And if anybody borrowed it from you to cut off some sausage or something he'd have to have a heart of stone if all you got out of it was a kick in the ass.

So now Caesar owed him for this too. After all the business with the bread and the knives, Shukhov pulled out his pouch. He took out as much tobacco as he'd borrowed earlier that day, reached it over to the Estonian in the top bunk across from him, and said 'Thanks.'

The Estonian spread his lips and sort of smiled at the other Estonian and jabbered something to him. Then they rolled themselves a cigarette out of it just to see what kind of tobacco Shukhov had. It was no worse than theirs, so why not! Shukhov would have lit up himself to try the stuff out, but he could feel from that time-keeper he had inside of him it was getting very near the night check. Before long the warders would be snooping around the barracks. He'd have to go out in the passageway for a smoke, but it was warmer where he was in his bunk. The barracks was pretty cold and that ice was still up there on the roof. It wasn't so bad right now but he'd get frozen through in the night.

Shukhov started breaking off pieces from one of his hunks of bread, but he couldn't help hearing what the Captain and Caesar were saying while they drank their tea.

'Help yourself, Captain, don't wait to be asked! Have some of the smoked fish, and there's some sausage here too!'

'Thank you, I don't mind if I do.'

'And put some butter on your bread. Real French bread from Moscow, you know.'

'I must say it's hard to believe they still make this sort of bread anywhere. All this luxury reminds me when I was in Archangel once ... '

There was a hell of a racket in their part of the barracks—two hundred fellows talking at once—but all the same Shukhov could hear them pound the rail outside. And he was the only one who did. He saw Snubnose, one of the warders, coming in the barracks. He was a stocky little fellow with a red face. He had a piece of paper in his hand and you could see from this and from the way he walked that he hadn't come to catch smokers or to chase everybody out for the check. He was after somebody. He took a look at his piece of paper and asked: 'Where's 104?'

'Right here,' they told him.

The Estonians hid their cigarettes and waved their hands to get rid of the smoke.

'And where's your boss?'

'What d'you want?' Tyurin said from his bunk and just put one foot down on the floor.

'What's happening about the reports those two guys of yours were supposed to hand in about their extra clothing?'

'They're writing them,' Tyurin said and he didn't bat an eye.

'They should've been handed in already.'

'The trouble is they can't hardly read or write, so it's not easy.' (It was Caesar and the Captain he was talking about! He was a great guy, the boss, he was never at a loss what to say.) 'And they've got nothing to write with. There's no pens and no ink either.'

'There should be.'

'They always take 'em away from us!'

'You better watch what you say or I'll put you in the can,' Snubnose said, but he wasn't too mad. 'But see you get those reports to

the warders' room tomorrow morning! And they should say they've
turned in those things they're not supposed to have to the Personal
Property Stores. Got it?'

'I get you.'

('Looks like the Captain made it,' Shukhov said to himself. The
Captain hadn't heard what was going on. He was too busy telling
his story and eating that sausage.)

'One more thing,' the warder said. 'Is S-311 here? Is that one of
yours?'

'Let me take a look at the list,' Tyurin said, just to stall. 'How can
anybody remember all these damn numbers?' He was playing for
time, trying to drag things out till they called the men for the night
check, and maybe then the Captain wouldn't have to go to the
cooler that night.

But Snubnose shouted out: 'Is Buynovsky here?'

'What's that? Yes, I'm here,' the Captain called out from his
bunk. (Some people move too fast for their own good.)

'Buynovsky? Yeah, that's you all right, S-311. Let's go!'

'Where?'

'You know.'

The Captain just gave a sigh and grunted. It must've been easier
for him to sail his destroyer on a dark night in the stormy sea than
it was to break off talking with his friend now and go to that freezing
cell.

'How many days?' he asked and his voice was kind of low.

'Ten! Come on, make it snappy!'

Just then the orderlies started yelling: 'All out for the night
check! All out for the night check!'

So it meant the warder they'd sent to make the check was in the
barracks already. The Captain looked back at his bunk—should he
take his coat? But they'd only strip it off in the cells and leave him
nothing but his jacket. So he had to go there just as he was. The
Captain thought Volkovoy might have let him off, but Volkovoy
never let anybody off. So he wasn't ready for this and hadn't
managed to hide any tobacco in his jacket. And there was no sense
taking it with him in his hands because that's the first thing they'd
find when they frisked him.

All the same, Caesar slipped him a couple of cigarettes while he
was putting his cap on.

'Well, good-by fellows.' The Captain gave a kind of sheepish look at 104 and he went off with the warder.

Some of them shouted after him: 'Keep your chin up! Don't let 'em get you down!' What could you say?

The fellows from 104 had built the place themselves and they knew how it looked — stone walls, a concrete floor, and no window. There was a stove, but that was only enough to melt the ice off the walls and make puddles on the floor. You slept on bare boards and your teeth chattered all night. You got six ounces of bread a day and they only gave you hot gruel every third day.

Ten days! If you had ten days in the cells here and sat them out to the end, it meant you'd be a wreck for the rest of your life. You got T.B. and you'd never be out of hospitals long as you lived.

And the fellows who did fifteen days were dead and buried.

Long as you were in the barracks you thanked your lucky stars and tried to keep out of the cells.

'Come on, get out!' the trusty in charge of the barracks shouted. 'If you're not all out by the time I count to three I'll take your number and report you to the Comrade Warder!'

This guy was the biggest bastard of them all. He was shut up with them at night in the same barracks but acted like a higher-up and he wasn't scared of anybody. It was the other way around — everybody was scared of him. He could turn you in to the screws or let you have it in the puss. He counted as an invalid because he'd lost one finger in a fight. You could tell from his mug he was a real hood. And that's just what he was. They pulled him in for a real crime, but they hung Article 58/14 on him too. That's why he was in this camp.

And it was no joke. He'd take your number soon as look at you, and give it to the warder. Then you'd land in the cooler for two days with work 'as usual'.

So people started moving and crowding up to the door, and they jumped off the top bunks looking like bears. Everybody was making for that narrow door.

Shukhov hopped down from his bunk and stuck his feet in his felt boots. He was holding the cigarette he'd just made — he wanted it real bad. But he didn't go right away, because he was sorry for Caesar. It wasn't that he wanted to get something out of Caesar again but he was just sorry for him. He thought a lot of himself, Caesar did, and he didn't know a thing about life—he shouldn't have spent all that time fussing with his package and should've gotten it to the storeroom before night check. He could've eaten the stuff later, but what could he do with it now? If he took that damn bag out with him to the check he'd just make a laughing stock of himself in front of five hundred men, but if he left it here it might be pinched by the first man back. (In Ust-Izhma things were even tougher—the crooks always got back from work first and cleaned out all the lockers.)

Shukhov saw Caesar was all in a sweat, but it was too late. He was stuffing the sausage and fatback in his jacket. He thought maybe he'd carry that along with him even if he couldn't save anything else.

So Shukhov was sorry for him and told him what to do: 'Stay here till the last man leaves, Caesar Markovich, and get back in your bunk where it's dark, and don't budge till the warder and the orderlies come through. And then you tell 'em you're sick. I'll go out now and get in the front of the crowd and I'll be the first back ... ' And he ran off.

He had a hard time shoving his way through the crowd at first (and he had to guard that cigarette in his hand so it wouldn't be crushed). But in the passageway that led off both halves of the barracks nobody was in a hurry—they were shrewd as hell—and they stuck to the walls like grim death, two deep on both sides, and all they left clear was the outside door. You could only get out of it one at a time and they didn't mind if any dope wanted to. But most of them liked it better inside. They'd been in the cold all day long and nobody was that eager to freeze out there for another ten minutes. If anybody wanted to die, okay, but the rest of them could wait a little.

Most times Shukhov stuck to the wall too, but now he made straight for the door and turned around and smirked at them: 'What're you so scared of, you nitwits? Never been out in the cold in Siberia before? Come and warm up under the moon like the wolves ... Hey, give me a light, fellow.'

He took a light from somebody and went out on the steps. The 'wolves' sun,' that's what they sometimes called the moon where Shukhov came from.

The moon was real high up now. A little more and it'd be all the way up. The sky was pale—and sort of greenish. The stars were bright and there weren't many of them. The white snow was glistening and the walls of the barracks looked all white too, and the lights in the camp didn't seem very strong now.

There was a great black crowd of men over by another barracks. They were coming out and lining up. And the same outside that other one too. And there wasn't much talk between barracks. All you could hear was snow crunching under people's boots.

Five men came down the steps of Barracks 9, and then another three. Shukhov went in with these three to make up the next row of five. It wasn't so bad standing here when you'd eaten a little bread and had a cigarette in your mouth. The tobacco was all right. The Latvian hadn't lied. It had the right strength and it smelled good.

More men came straggling out the door and there were a couple of rows of fives behind Shukhov now. The fellows coming out were mad as hell at the guys still hugging the walls in the passageway. They had to stand here and freeze till those bastards came out.

The prisoners never got to see a watch or a clock. And what good would it do anyway? They just went by reveille, roll call, the noon meal breaks, and lights out.

But the night check was around nine o'clock, so it was said. Only it never finished at nine. They always kept you hanging around while they double checked, and sometimes it was more than twice. You never got to bed before ten. And reveille, they said, was at five in the morning. No wonder that Moldavian had gone to sleep before the signal to knock off work. If a prisoner found a warm spot any place, he fell asleep right away. They lost so much sleep in the week, they slept like logs in their barracks Sundays. If they weren't chased out to work, that is.

They were all pouring out down the steps now. That trusty and the warder, the motherfuckers, were kicking them in the ass.

The fellows who'd been first in line outside shouted at them: 'Thought you were being smart, didn't you, you bastards? Trying to make cream out of shit or something? If you'd gotten out here before, we'd be through already.'

They were all outside now. There were four hundred men in a barracks, and that made eighty rows of five lined up one after the other. The rows right in front of the barracks kept their lines of five, but the fellows in back were just bunched up any old way.

'Line up by fives, you at the back!' the trusty yelled down from the steps. But the hell they would, the bastards!

Caesar came out of the door all hunched up and doing his best to look sick. There were two orderlies from the other half of the barracks behind him, and two from their half with some lame fellow. They chased Caesar to the back and lined up in front of all the others. So Shukhov was now in the third row of five.

The warder came out on the steps.

'Line up by fi-i-ves!' he shouted to the men at the back and he had a strong voice.

'Line up by fi-i-ves!' the trusty bawled too. And his voice was even stronger.

But they still didn't line up, the bastards.

The trusty shot down the steps, went to the back, and bawled them out real good. And he punched some of the guys. But he was careful who he did it to. He only hit fellows he knew wouldn't stick up for themselves. They all lined up now and he went back to the steps. And he and the warder started yelling together.

'One, two, three ... '

Every row of five shot into the barracks when it was called. They were through now for the day!

If they didn't do another check, that is. Any sheep-herder could count better than these dopes. Maybe he didn't have any book learning, but he could herd his sheep *and* keep count of them. But these bastards couldn't do it even though they'd been taught how.

Last winter there hadn't been any drying room for their felt boots in this camp and they had to keep them in the barracks all night. They were chased outside anywhere up to four times for a recount. So they didn't bother getting dressed even—they went out with their blankets around them. This year they'd put up drying rooms but they weren't big enough for everybody, so each gang could dry out their boots only two nights out of three. And now when they had recounts they let you stay inside and just chased you from one half of the barracks to the other.

Shukhov wasn't the first to get back to the barracks, but he didn't take his eyes off the fellow who was. He ran right over to Caesar's bunk and sat on it. He pulled off his boots, climbed up on another bunk near the stove, and put them on top of it to dry. It was first come, first served here. Then he went back to Caesar's bunk. He sat there with his legs under him and kept one eye on Caesar's package so no one could pinch it from under the mattress, and his other eye was on that stove so nobody'd push his boots off in the rush to put their own there.

'Hey, you there with the red hair!' he shouted to one fellow. 'D'you want that boot in your mug? Put your own boots up there if you like but don't touch other people's!'

The prisoners were pouring back in the barracks. Some fellows in Gang 20 were shouting: 'Hand over your boots for the dryer!'

They let these fellows go out of the barracks with the boots and then locked it. And then they'd come running back and hammer on the door: 'Comrade Warder, let us in!' But by then the warders would be over in H.Q. doing their bookkeeping on those plywood boards to see if anybody'd run away.

But Shukhov didn't give a damn about all that today. Caesar was coming back now. 'Thank you, Ivan Denisovich,' he said.

Shukhov nodded at him and jumped up on his own bunk like a squirrel. He could finish off that bread now or smoke another cigarette or go to sleep if he wanted.

But Shukhov'd had such a good day—he didn't even feel like sleeping, he felt so great.

Making his bed wasn't much trouble—he only had to pull that dark blanket off and flop down on the mattress (he hadn't slept on a sheet since forty-one, it must've been, when he left home, and he wondered why the women bothered so much about sheets—it only meant more washing), put his head on the pillow stuffed with shavings, tuck his feet in the arm of the jacket, and spread his coat on top of the blanket. And that was that, the end of another day! 'Thank God,' he said.

It wasn't so bad sleeping here and he was glad not to be in the cells.

Shukhov lay down with his head to the window, and Alyoshka was on the other side of the bunk with his head the other way so he got the light from the bulb. He was reading the Gospels again.

Alyoshka'd heard Shukhov thank the Lord and he turned to him. 'Look here, Ivan Denisovich, your soul wants to pray to God, so why don't you let it have its way?'

Shukhov looked at Alyoshka and his eyes were narrow. They had a light in them and they were like two candles. And he sighed. 'I'll tell you why, Alyoshka. Because all these prayers are like the complaints we send in to the higher-ups—either they don't get there or they come back to you marked "Rejected".'

In front of H.Q. barracks there were four boxes with seals and one of the security guys came along every month to empty them. A lot of fellows put slips in those boxes and they counted the days— a month or two months—waiting to hear.

Either there was nothing or it was 'Rejected'.

'The trouble is, Ivan Denisovich, you don't pray hard enough and that's why your prayers don't work out. You must pray un- ceasing! And if you have faith and tell the mountain to move, it will move.'

Shukhov grinned and made himself another cigarette. He got a light from one of the Estonians.

'Don't give me that, Alyoshka. I've never seen a mountain move. But come to think of it, I've never seen a mountain either. And when you and all your Baptists prayed down there in the Caucasus did you ever see a mountain move?'

The poor fellows. All they did was pray to God. And were they in anybody's way? They all got twenty-five years, because that's how it was now—twenty-five years for everybody.

'But we didn't pray for that, Ivan Denisovich,' Alyoshka said, and he came up close to Shukhov with his Gospels, right up to his face. 'The only thing of this earth the Lord has ordered us to pray for is our daily bread—"Give us this day our daily bread".'

'You mean that ration we get?' Shukhov said.

But Alyoshka went on and his eyes said more than his words and he put his hand on Ivan's hand.

'Ivan Denisovich, you mustn't pray for somebody to send you a package or for an extra helping of gruel. Things that people set store by are base in the sight of the Lord. You must pray for the

8

things of the spirit so the Lord will take evil things from our hearts...'

'But listen. The priest in our church in Polomnya ... '

'Don't tell me about that,' Alyoshka begged and he winced with pain.

'No. But just listen.' And Shukhov bent over to him on his elbow. 'The priest is the richest man in our parish in Polomnya. Suppose they ask you to build a roof on a house, your price is thirty rubles for plain people. For the priest it's a hundred. That priest of ours is paying alimony to three women in three towns, and he's living with a fourth. And he's got the bishop under his thumb. You should see the way he holds that fat greasy hand of his out to the bishop. And it doesn't matter how many other priests they send. He always gets rid of 'em. He doesn't want to share the pickings.'

'Why are you telling me about this priest? The Orthodox Church has gotten away from the Gospel. And the reason they don't put them in prison is because they have no true faith.'

Shukhov looked straight and hard, and went on smoking. 'Alyoshka,' he said, and he moved the Baptist's hand away and the smoke from his cigarette went in Alyoshka's face. 'I'm not against God, understand. I believe in God, all right. But what I don't believe in is Heaven and Hell. Who d'you think we are, giving us all that stuff about Heaven and Hell? That's the thing I can't take.'

Shukhov lay back again and dropped the ash off his cigarette between the bunk and the window, careful so's not to burn the Captain's stuff. He was thinking his own thoughts and didn't hear Alyoshka any more, and he said out loud: 'The thing is, you can pray as much as you like but they won't take anything off your sentence and you'll just have to sit it out, every day of it, from reveille to lights out.'

'You mustn't pray for that.' Alyoshka was horror-struck. 'What d'you want your freedom for? What faith you have left will be choked in thorns. Rejoice that you are in prison. Here you can think of your soul. Paul the Apostle said: "What mean you to weep and to break my heart? for I am ready not to be bound only, but also to die* for the name of the Lord Jesus".'

* *Translators' note*: The words 'at Jerusalem', which should appear here, are omitted in the Russian text of the novel (Acts 21:13).

Shukhov looked up at the ceiling and said nothing. He didn't know any longer himself whether he wanted freedom or not. At first he'd wanted it very much and every day he added up how long he still had to go. But then he got fed up with this. And as time went on he understood that they might let you out but they never let you home. And he didn't really know where he'd be better off. At home or in here.

But they wouldn't let him home anyway ...

Alyoshka was talking the truth. You could tell by his voice and his eyes he was glad to be in prison.

'Look, Alyoshka,' Shukhov said, 'it's all right for you. It was Christ told you to come here, and you are here because of Him. But why am *I* here? Because they didn't get ready for the war like they should've in forty-one? Was that *my* fault?'

'Looks like they're not going to check us over again,' Kilgas shouted from his bunk.

'Yeah,' Shukhov said. 'We ought to chalk that up on the chimney. Doesn't happen every day.' And he yawned. 'Time we got some sleep.'

The barracks was quiet and there wasn't a sound. Then they heard the grinding of the bolt on the outside door. The two fellows who'd taken the boots to the drying room ran in from the passage-way and shouted: 'Second check!'

The warder was right behind them and he yelled: 'Get out on the other side of the barracks!'

Some of them were sleeping already. They grumbled and started to move and put their feet in their boots (they never took their pants off, it was too cold under the blanket and you got all stiff without them).

'The bastards!' Shukhov said, but he wasn't too angry because he wasn't sleeping yet.

Caesar reached up and gave him two cookies, two lumps of sugar, and a slice of sausage.

'Thank you, Caesar Markovich.' Shukhov leaned over his bunk. 'Now you give me that bag and I'll put it under my pillow here.' (It wasn't so easy to pinch something from a top bunk. And who'd think of looking in Shukhov's anyway?)

Caesar handed up to him his white bag tied with string. Shukhov put it under his mattress and waited a little till they chased most of the fellows out in the passageway—so he wouldn't have to stand there in his bare feet any longer than he had to.

But the warder snarled at him and said: 'Hey, you over there in the corner!'

So Shukhov jumped down on the floor in his bare feet (his boots and foot-cloths were on the stove and they'd gotten nice and warm, and it'd be a shame to take them down). All those slippers he'd made for other people! But never for himself. He didn't mind. He was used to this sort of business and it would soon be over.

And they took these slippers away from you too if they caught you with them in the day.

The gangs who had their boots in the drying room—they didn't mind much either. Some of them had slippers or they went out in their foot-cloths or in their bare feet.

'Get a move on!' the warder yelled.

'Would you like a taste of the stick, you filthy scum?' the trusty said. He was there too.

They were all driven over to the other side of the barracks and the ones who came last had to go out in the passageway. Shukhov stood out there by the wall near the latrine. The floor under his feet was wet and there was a freezing draft from outside.

When they'd gotten them all out from the bunks the warder and the trusty went round and had another look, just to make sure nobody was sleeping in some corner. They were in trouble if they had a man missing, and they were in trouble if they had one too many—it meant they'd have to start checking all over again. They went all around and came back.

'One, two, three, four ... ' They let people back one at a time and it went real fast now. Shukhov was the eighteenth. He shot over to his bunk, put his leg on the ledge, and he was up there in a flash.

It was great! He tucked his legs in the arm of his jacket again and put the blanket and then his coat on top. He'd sleep now. They'd be bringing the guys from the other side of the barracks over here to check them. But that wouldn't worry him.

Caesar came back and Shukhov gave him his bag.

Alyoshka came back too. He was always trying to please people but he never got anything out of it.

'Here, Alyoshka.' Shukhov gave him one of the cookies.

Alyoshka smiled. 'Thank you, but you haven't got very much yourself.'

'Go ahead. Eat it.' It was true he didn't have very much but *he* could always earn something. And he put the piece of sausage in his mouth and chewed it and chewed it. The taste of that meat, and the juice that came out of it! He'd eat the rest of the things before roll call, he thought. And he pulled the thin dirty blanket over his face and didn't hear the guys from the other half of the barracks who were crowding around the bunks waiting to be checked.

Shukhov went to sleep, and he was very happy. He'd had a lot of luck today. They hadn't put him in the cooler. The gang hadn't been chased out to work in the Socialist Community Development. He'd finagled an extra bowl of mush at noon. The boss had gotten them good rates for their work. He'd felt good making that wall. They hadn't found that piece of steel in the frisk. Caesar had paid him off in the evening. He'd bought some tobacco. And he'd gotten over that sickness.

Nothing had spoiled the day and it had been almost happy.

There were three thousand six hundred and fifty-three days like this in his sentence, from reveille to lights out.

The three extra ones were because of the leap years ...

Three Poems *by* Anna Akhmatova

Novy Mir, 1963/1, 1965/1

Translated by April FitzLyon

After the great age of Russian prose – the era of Turgenev, Dostoevsky and Tolstoy – modern Russian literature has above all excelled in poetry. For a number of reasons this form of expression has remained very close to natural Russian speech-rhythms, while expressing a range of thought and emotion that is as complex and wide as human experience itself. The Russian 'Silver Age', corresponding roughly to the first decade and a half of this century, owed its chief impetus to the symbolist movement; but this movement also stimulated a flowering of Russian poetry in the succeeding two generations, of which the best younger descendants today are probably Voznesensky and Brodsky.

It is perhaps not invidious to name the five greatest of the post-revolutionary poets as Mandelshtam, Tsvetaeva, Mayakovsky, Akhmatova and Pasternak, though it would be absurd to attempt to arrange them by merit: their creative personalities and their private fates were all totally distinct, and they stand out as different facets of a whole.

Of the three poets published in *Novy Mir*, Anna Akhmatova (1898–1969) is here represented by three short wartime poems. Together with her husband, the poet Gumilyov (shot by the Bolsheviks in the Civil War for alleged participation in a counter-revolutionary plot), she was the most distinctive of the post-symbolist school of poetry known as acmeism. Their preoccupation with precise, chiselled, highly polished and very succinct verse was exemplified in Akhmatova's early collection usually called *The Rosary* (1913) – a title perhaps more aptly translated *Beads*.

A woman of the utmost artistic integrity, Akhmatova was concerned only to express the truth of universal emotion in intensely personal form, and she firmly refused to bow to the demands of party cultural policy. For this, in 1946 she was branded by Stalin's 'policeman of the arts', Zhdanov, as 'half nun, half whore'. The depth of her suffering under Stalinism, when her son was arbitrarily arrested and imprisoned along with countless other victims, is expressed with great poignancy in her collection *Requiem* (not published in the U.S.S.R.). An edition of her poems has been published in English, translated by Richard McKane (Oxford University Press, London, 1969). In 1965 Oxford University conferred on her the honorary degree of Doctor of Literature; at the ceremony the Public Orator addressed her fittingly as 'the Russian Sappho'.

Quatrain

All gold is doomed to rust, and steel's endurance brief,
And marble crumbles, all is transitory ...
On earth there's nought more durable than grief
Except the royal word's long history.

1945.

(*Novy Mir*, 1963/1)

In memory of V. S. Sreznevskaya

It almost cannot be; why, you were always there:
In lime trees' happy shade, the long blockade, the prison,
And in the hospital; and there, where fell winged creatures
And monstrous undergrowth and terrifying waters were.
All lacked stability; but you were always there.
I feel that half my soul has left me for a season—
The part of me you were—in which I knew the reason
Of something principal. Now suddenly forgotten ...
But from beyond I hear your vibrant voice professing
I should not grieve for you, but wait death as a blessing.
Oh well! I'll try to ...

(*Novy Mir*, 1965/1)

From the cycle 'Tashkent Pages'

Tashkent in bloom

Swift as if some order had been given
All at once the town was full of light—
For there entered into every garden
Apparitions, volatile and white.

And more clearly far than words I hear their breathing,
While their fellow flowers are condemned to lie
On the beds of arid watercourses
Beneath the dazzlingly azure sky.

(*Novy Mir*, 1965/1)

A Journey to the Army *by* Boris Pasternak

Novy Mir, 1965/1

Translated by Halina Willetts

The passage which follows is an unusual and interesting example of Pasternak's prose writing. During the Second World War he became a kind of temporary war correspondent and was invited to join a party of writers who were taken to inspect a newly liberated area of the front line in 1943, when the Red Army had begun to roll the Germans back from the farthest point of their advance into Russia. The object of the excursion was to produce some morale-boosting propaganda in the form of a book based on the writers' experience at the front. Although Pasternak and his fellow literati on that trip wrote several pieces of vivid reportage, of which this is one, the planned book never appeared. If Pasternak's piece is at all representative of the other writers' contributions, it is not difficult to see why. Despite the grimness of much of its subject-matter, it is too gentle, too sharply perceptive of the minutiae of experience, too sensitive in tone to be usable for the kind of crude propaganda which Stalin obviously required.

Fortunately, however, this material survived the war and survived even Khrushchev's displeasure over the *Doctor Zhivago* affair, and was eventually published in *Novy Mir* in 1965, the year after Khrushchev's fall from power, and twelve years after the piece had been written.

There is something peculiarly moving about this passage, in which Pasternak, the great lyric poet, writes something which goes against the grain of his entire sensibility. He has clearly tried manfully to do his job as a journalist, to put in plenty of gritty factual reporting, and to make the right patriotic noises about the Red Army—which he undoubtedly felt sincerely. But everywhere, as if in spite of himself, his poet's eye continually takes over and cannot help pinpointing tiny details which to the propagandist are superfluous trivia, but which give Pasternak's writing a quality of steely delicacy and precision which no blood-and-guts war reporter could ever achieve.

Two of Pasternak's poems, printed in the same issue as 'A Journey to the Army', appear at the end of the article.

Of late we have found ourselves increasingly in the grip of the pace and logic of our magnificent victory. Every day it becomes clearer how its force and majesty have united us all. The whole nation, from top to bottom, has won this victory, from Marshal Stalin down to the rank-and-file workers and private soldiers—who are the real heroes in any war. The victory belongs to the whole people in all its diversity, its joys and sorrows, its dreams and its thoughts. We have won, thanks to our many-sided versatility. We have all won, and now our eyes are being opened to a new and higher stage of our historical existence. A broad sense of community is beginning to pervade everything we do. Its influence can be felt even in our humble occupation.

2

A party of war correspondent, including several literary names, made a trip to the army units which had captured Orel, in the now distant days before Bryansk and Smolensk were taken—although even then their coming fall could be sensed. Light-headed with happiness, we set out one morning on a lorry, reaching such a breakneck speed that the patchwork of the countryside round Moscow flashed towards us like the wind. Our passes, and the fact that we had a faster lorry, allowed us to overtake everyone else, but whenever there was a hold-up our advantage was cancelled out and slower traffic caught us up again. There was one thickset officer with a bit of cigarette paper stuck to his lip which fluttered in the breeze. He overtook us several times in his open jeep, then was left behind again; time went by, the countryside and the view changed, but the paper remained stuck to his lip.

We had lunch in Tula, where street barricades were still standing, signs of civilian resistance from the year before last, and where we listened to a boring, plodding account of it all in the local party offices—until the arrival of Comrade Zhavoronkov, its hero and organizer, who described it to us vividly and colourfully. We drove on. The red-brown, charred remains of Shchokino flashed past. The sun was setting as the immense skeleton of the giant Kosogorsk factory complex was outlined against the sky. One landmark followed another: places renowned for their outstanding resistance, monuments of suffering. Dusk began to fall. We turned off the highway and stopped after driving about fifteen kilometres along a side road.

We were, to all appearances, in some kind of village. It was as silent as a desert island. We were surrounded by something more than the enigmatic silence of a warm August night; it was as if the towering night sky above us was as solid as a stone wall. The seven stars of the Great Bear filled a jagged gash in the wall of some garden or outbuilding. All around us were the shadows of indistinct ruins in the darkness. They were the ruins of Chern, the district town, and they were the beginning of the journey that lay before us, a journey past an endless succession of charred and empty buildings. It was the gateway to that area which in enemy parlance is simply called by that grim euphemism 'deserted zone'.

Suddenly the 'desert' came to life. There was a knock on the window, and footsteps broke the silence. Two female shadows came round a corner and disappeared again. We were given our instructions, and moved off behind the leaders of our party.

Half an hour later we were enjoying the hospitality of the secretary of the Chern Regional Party Committee, A. A. Kukushkina, and her young assistants. The upper floor of a little wooden house which had miraculously survived was brightly lit by a gasoline pressure lamp. Our hostesses, who were members of the Komsomol and local government workers, moved about handing round tea, now and then joining in the conversation or breaking off to disappear into the kitchen and make omelettes. They wore bright blouses, sashes, straight skirts and neat plain hairstyles. Their intelligence and their easy, natural manner aroused memories of the distant past, a very personal kind of emotion. They reminded us of the girl students of 1905, the very best university generation of the past.

The conversation turned on two subjects: the nature of the times and the nature of the place. The nature of the times meant the war. The girls described how they had left Chern when the Germans began to surround it, and what courage and cunning it had needed, because the Germans were advancing from several directions and had already occupied all the surrounding villages. Their greatest danger lay in their being party members, but the local population had protected them. All but two had escaped. These were two most exceptional girls, the kind of person that no one could help liking at first glance. It was unthinkable that anyone should want to harm them, and in fact for a long time they were left undisturbed, because the Germans did not realize the extent of their influence nor that they had been keeping in touch with the Soviets. But one day a German, who had usually behaved decently to them, came in drunk and declared that he had always forgiven them a great deal but this he would not allow—and he ordered them to take down the portraits of Lenin and Stalin from the wall. The girls obstinately refused, so he pulled out his revolver, fired at the portraits and shot the girls.

Kukushkina, an intelligent and energetic woman, simultaneously received us as hostess, organized our supper, arranged our sleeping quarters and gave a lively lead to the conversation. From her we learned not only the harrowing details of the German occupation of Chern, Orel and Mtsensk, but also some fascinating historical facts about the region. The reader will recall that Zhukovsky, Delvig, Tolstoy, Turgenev, Fet, Leskov and Bunin all lived here in their time. I suddenly began to understand the reason for the natural purity of our companions' speech and the ease of their manner. We were at the very source of our greatest national treasure. These are the places where the dialect arose which later became the basis of our literary language, and about which Turgenev spoke with such eloquence. Nowhere else has the spirit of Russian sincerity— the greatest quality we possess—found such full and free expression. Born in these parts, these girls have imbibed the very essence of the Russian genius with their mothers' milk. They are of the very flesh and bone of Liza Kalitin and Natasha Rostov.

When next morning we awoke in a hay-loft, we could see our companions of yesterday more clearly by daylight. Before us were the ruins of the town, which had obviously once sprawled picturesquely over the undulating countryside, smothered in gardens; now the sight of its ruins crying out for revenge evoked savage memories of some Daghestani village in the days of Shamil.* Led by this inspiring woman, these children and guardians of the revolution have set about restoring order in the minutest detail to this war-torn district. They are doing work of the greatest national importance and they do it with the easy, inborn efficiency with which their grandmothers might have bent down to pick up a windfall apple, or to feel under a hen to see if she had laid.

3

In contrast to yesterday's comfortable ride along a tarmac road, today we are bumping along a dirt track. What is more, it has not yet been completely cleared of mines, and is cratered in places. More and more frequently we have to turn off the track and bypass the bridges and river-crossings. Bumping over patches covered by planks, as we jolt along the pot-holed road its changing colours provide us with an extempore course of study in the composition of the region's soil. Now it is a stretch of black earth, parched to a metallic coal-like grey. It began after we had passed the ill-fated town of Mtsensk, whose houses have slithered down the steep bank into the slimy River Zusha, rather as if they had been carrying the town in their arms, slipped, and crashed into the water. The war and the army are getting closer all the time; it is from here onwards that we really begin to be aware of it. More and more of the roadside fields have been wired off and marked with warning notices. To-morrow a file of sappers with mine-detectors will be strung out along the verges of these roads; today they are filled with columns of reinforcements on the march, puny beardless young lads blackened with dust and exhaustion. Now come the first knocked-out tanks among the cabbage fields, the first charred relics of wrecked

*Shamil (1797–1871). Religious and political leader of the North Caucasian Muslim mountain peoples in their resistance to Russian conquest. At the time when Pasternak wrote this piece, Shamil was treated in Soviet historiography as a hero, but a few years later this view was reversed and he was condemned as having been in the pay of Britain and Turkey. The fact that Pasternak's sympathetic reference is permitted here is a small pointer * one aspect of de-Stalinization.

aeroplanes. And so, long prepared for what meets our eyes as we emerge from the forest, we drive into Orel.

It is not immediately obvious that the area we are crossing is the railway station. Here it is just as though reality itself had cracked and the air exploded, scattering lumps of mangled and fragmented metal in all directions as far as the eye can see. The platforms are nothing but endless rows of rusty girders holding up nothing. We drive over ground strewn with writhing lengths of torn-up rail that make the area look as if someone had been chopping up snakes or stamping on centipedes. Bypassing the smashed bridge with its dislocated shoulders and broken spans, we cross a newly made pontoon bridge into the town.

It is a pity that none of us have been to Orel before. Turgenev, Leskov and Bunin have described it several times. The remaining stonework and the layout of the city give the impression of a large European-style town. It was here that Hitler came to rage over his failures, here that he sacked Schmidt, the commander of his panzer armies, and replaced him by General Model.

Orel is no more. It is as if both the town and the River Oka on which it stood are still resting on a field of delayed-action mines: the place continues to explode and collapse before our eyes. We watch this happening from the neglected, overgrown garden beside the headquarters of a reserve infantry regiment where we have stopped for a short rest.

The spectacle is so unnatural that one's mind perversely insists on ascribing it to the light. It is a cloudless afternoon. Mallow blooms in the dry heat, and everything is covered in flies. Across the road, behind the barbed wire of the prison, a visiting commission from Moscow is holding an investigation into the mass executions and tortures committed by the Germans. From somewhere can be heard the nasal whine of a gramophone; draped in sunlight instead of black crepe, cemeteries that were once streets stretch out in lines of broken-backed buildings whose fractured stone limbs clutch their neighbours for support. Isolated brick buildings explode with a dry, crackling sound, and whole blocks of weakened houses collapse and slither to the ground on the edge of the large park, in which stands the modest but noble grave of General Gurtiev, commander of the 408th Rifle Division, hero of Stalingrad and Orel.

That afternoon we tried to make our way out of the tottering ruins of Orel, but we lost our way and kept coming back again and again to the same house, which was gutted from front to back and big enough to hold a whole village. This house was complex and fascinating, a many-storeyed drama in itself, with its three kinds of stairs—front stairs, back stairs and fire escape—its long internal corridors, its multitude of acts and scenes. The pattern on its wallpaper is imprinted on our memories for life; then suddenly, as we drive past it for the third time, we find the right road and roar off.

But having said so much about Orel, what is there left to say about Karachev, which we passed through that evening? The town, once renowned for the eligible daughters of its rich merchants and for its flour-millers, seems to have no end. It requires a monstrous effort to imagine the town as a whole when it is shown to you broken up into tiny fragments. It is one thing to say 'five hundred brick houses and two and a half thousand wooden ones'; you imagine a small provincial town. But it is something totally different when you are simply shown three thousand huge shapeless heaps of rubble and splinters. Your head spins, your sight blurs; you can only pray for mercy and shed tears of outrage and pity.

4

We drive into Pesochnya in deep twilight, the village street crowded with people and vehicles. There are no civilians to be seen, only soldiers, and lorries and carts are strewn across the road at all angles. This is 3rd Army Headquarters, the goal of our journey. Tomorrow, or perhaps tonight if circumstances permit, we shall meet the army commander whose skill has been responsible for the victories we have been winning with such systematic regularity. In the meantime we decide to go for a bathe, to wash off the dust and grime of the journey, even though the night is already pitch black. 'There may be mines,' we are told, 'and in any case the river bottom is covered with jagged metal, so you may get cut if you try and dive.' But when we reach the river we dive into the cold unknown, which flows over us like solid fog ...

5

Here at last are the victors of Orel, the men whose success led indirectly to further victories and who will see to it that the process continues. We are in a large peasant hut at a reception being held for us by the members of the Military Soviet. We are greeted by the friendly, young-looking army commander, Guards Lieutenant-General Alexander Vasilievich Gorbatov, friend and brother-in-arms of the dead Gurtiev. Intelligent and sincere, he is completely without affectation. He talks quietly, slowly and in plain language. His authority is based on the sound common sense of what he says rather than on his tone of voice. This is the best, but also the most difficult kind of leadership. Beside him are the thoughtful, far-sighted General Kononov and General Sabennikov, a brilliant, highly-educated officer. Last night we met General Ivashechkin, a bold and ingenious strategist in moments of difficulty and danger and a delightful off-duty companion at table. He and General Terpilovsky are absent today. Through the little window behind their unoccupied seats we can see the far end of the long village street. It is a dull wet day, and since early morning an endless column of infantry, armed with submachine-guns, mortars and anti-tank rifles, has been streaming past. Company and regimental commanders ride alongside their units on horseback and disappear with them round the bend in the road. This is an army on the march. Since the July breakthrough we have been pushing westward in a constant series of rapid advances.

We go out into the street. An officer on horseback breaks away from a passing column and rides up to our group. Leaning down from the saddle he talks to our 'brigadier', then waves goodbye and trots off to catch up his unit. The brigadier tells me that this officer is a most interesting man, a chemist from Moscow who was called up as a captain in the reserve and is now commanding a regiment. Captain D.'s face sticks in my memory. I have a false impression that it is like the face of someone I saw on the road in the last two days—perhaps the officer with the cigarette paper on his lip. I at once realize my mistake in imagining this apparent similarity, yet am also aware that this is not a chance mistake and that I must retain the memory of that captain's face at any price, for some

reason that will eventually be made clear. Two days later I heard
that he had been killed, blown up by a mine.

6

It had been suggested that we should write a book about the Orel
operation. Having learned of its general features from the men who
directed it, we depart separately to the various regiments and
divisions to meet those who have been directly involved in the
fighting. We are constantly on the move, taking our colleagues to
their destinations. We call on the 267th Division. It is located in a
sparse wood, where the fallen leaves mixed with scraps of torn paper
give the position the look of that particular kind of disorder that is
a sign of imminent departure. And in fact the division is preparing to
move. Everyone is packing and tying things up, they are due to
leave at any minute.

The 380th Division is dispersed among the clearings of a wooded
stretch of countryside. In one of these clearings we find the divi-
sional commander, Colonel Kustov, whose troops, alongside those
of the 129th Division, were the first to break into Orel at dawn on
August 5th, and who, earlier still, on the morning of July 12th,
together with the 308th Division began the famous push which led
to the breach in the German defences.

Although the division is also preparing to move, the colonel has
everything so well under control that he is quite unconcerned with
the minor details of the move. Elegant and sarcastic, he deliberately
plays the part of the nonchalant sophisticate. Having greeted us in
the middle of the forest, he reverts to trading jokes with a pilot who
has been attached to him as liaison officer from a flanking unit to
co-ordinate operations. They both peer into the distance, evidently
awaiting the arrival of a car. A magnificent horse, captured from
the enemy, is led up to Kustov. He vaults lightly into the saddle,
and after giving us a display of dressage he hands the horse back
to the orderly. At that moment the car arrives. With a studied bow,
he excuses himself for being in a hurry and drives off. There is
something in his handsome aquiline profile reminiscent of the
heroes of 1812, something of Tuchkov, of Marshal Bagration.
His uniform tunic fits him immaculately. He expresses himself

elaborately and with refinement. 'Permit me to hasten away,' he says. The soldiers worship him.

7

For ten days we do nothing but drive furiously about the Orel and Kaluga districts. The entire front line is shifting north-west-ward.

I spend three days trying to find Gurtiev's 308th Division, but it is constantly on the move and I am unable to catch up with it. On the way we meet reinforcement units and signals officers who are also looking for the 308th, but the division is not to be found. The search takes me to Zhisdra, Shchigry and Bryn', a village near Sukhinichi. Three times I cross the boundary line between the territory liberated during this summer's campaign and that liberated a year ago. The difference is indescribable. To the south — kilometre after kilometre of scorched desert devoid of the slightest trace of life. To the north — sparkling green countryside dotted with the orange-coloured specks of stone-built villages and farms among the olive-green and whitish-brown expanse of cabbage and potato fields. Finally, convinced that the 308th is too elusive, I decide to return to the 342nd, which took part in the capture of Mtsensk.

8

Once during these travels, our cars stopped in the village of Bely Kolodez'. The village was fortunate in not having been completely obliterated from the face of the earth. When the Germans were leaving, the wheat was only just beginning to sprout ears, and they had no time to trample it down or burn it. The unthreshed stacks were piled up in the middle of the village on the communal threshing-floor by the pond. Across the road from the hillside where we had stopped, several village women had gathered around the entrance to an underground air-raid shelter, while children played on the sites of burned-out cottages where the only things standing were the brick chimney-stacks. We went up to them. The women wore white homespun coats, bordered with red piping, over black-and-

white check skirts, bast shoes and rag puttees wound round their
legs; their headscarves were tied in a knot at the back in the old-
fashioned way. Quietly, and without false pathos, they told us of
the fate of their village, a fate it had shared with thousands of others.
Before pulling out, the Germans had ordered the inhabitants to
prepare for a temporary move westward with all their cattle and
belongings, to await the Germans' return. Most of the people were
forcibly driven away, and only a few managed to hide in the forest.
Holding their hands over their children's mouths, and binding the
cows' jaws so that they could not moo, they waited patiently in the
densest part of the wood. At night they watched from the edge of
the wood as their houses were burnt down and the schoolhouse,
the well, the mill and the barns were destroyed.

Children, smeared in soot, were playing near us in the ashes and
cinders. The sight of the birchwood garden furniture which the
Germans considered so decorative in their billets, and the glittering
empty four-gallon sauerkraut tins from Esslingen-am-Neckar
seemed an affront to these poor people.

9

A campfire in a centuries-old forest of tall oak trees. It is so densely
wooded that despite the approaching night and the black-out
regulations, the fire is not put out. The troops' supper is being
cooked in field kitchens. There is a drizzle of rain.

On one side of the fire a girl soldier, V.F., is sitting beside me on
a rickety bench which threatens to topple over at any moment.
Ostrovskaya, the writer's widow, and a Major K. are sitting on the
other side. The fire leaps about in the wind, and, when fresh
branches are thrown on to it, flings monstrous shadows on to the
brightly lit canopy of leaves over our heads.

I ask V.F. to tell me what life was like in Kaluga under the
Germans and at the same time try to eavesdrop on the loud conversation which is in progress on the other side of the campfire.
V.F. quietly replies to my questions. There is sadness in her voice,
and anger at the Germans. She is also annoyed—with me for not
giving her my full attention, with the major, whose voice disrupts
her story, and with the campfire, for being the focus of two such

discordant conversations. The subject of the talk on the other side of the fire is as follows:

When our troops liberated Turgenev's estate of Spas-Lutovinovo after the capture of Mtsensk, the Komsomol members of the units which had distinguished themselves organized a special celebration in the historic grounds which had been wrecked by the Germans. The meeting was naturally dedicated to the memory of Turgenev and to our literary heritage, and it somehow came to be linked with the name of Nikolai Ostrovsky, the author of *How the Steel was Tempered*. Everyone present swore an oath to follow the example of this Komsomol writer and to fight the Germans as his hero Pavel Korchagin had fought.

They lived up to that oath in the battles that followed, and the name of Korchaginites stuck to them. There were many Komsomol members in the 342nd Division, and especially in the 1150th Regiment, where we attended a meeting the next day.

Ostrovsky's widow was told about this movement, and has come to gather material about it. The information is being given to her by this good-looking major with a brisk, self-assured manner, himself probably a Komsomol and a Korchaginite.

Meanwhile, on my side of the fire the girl soldier, who has herself been listening to the major's story, is at the same time describing her ordeal in a sad, monotonous voice. I can picture it all in my mind's eye.

The savage winter with fifty degrees of frost. Firewood was short, and the inhabitants of Kaluga had to tear down houses and fences for fuel. Thick hoar-frost covered the windows and darkened the rooms. A world of headless people, topless trees, roofless buildings, black days.

'I'll inform on you to the Germans, and nothing will help you, not even if you grovel on the floor in front of me and lick my boots. I can do what I like now, and if I feel like it I'll turn you in,' said their neighbour, a young and normally harmless girl who now spent all her time with German soldiers. 'I don't care if you have already given me your handbag and shoes. I'll have every thread off your back before I'm finished. Whenever I think of that Lenin of yours it makes me so wild I can't control myself, so I'm taking it out on you.'

She stripped them of everything, and made their life a hell; they were blacklisted, denounced, searched. The Komsomol girl left home and went into hiding, where she learned that her mother and sister had been rounded up.

'The way they used to hang people in those days. They used wire. They really did. In a wire noose. But to tell the truth, my people didn't suffer much. They were shot. This was bad enough, but then the other ones came—the punitive detachments with the skull-and-crossbones badges. Again the cold, the bitter, cruel frost. The Germans brought a bell and hung it up in the cathedral. Now, they said, we'll have a real church service, a Lutheran marriage service. And our girls married them, well, of course, only the scum and half-wits, including the one who had informed on my mother and sister. It was freezing, but there they stood on the cathedral steps in their wedding dresses, white lace and all, with their red faces, as bold as brass, laughing their heads off. And there were their German stallions, complete with jackboots and whips and skull-and-crossbone badges. Later, when the Red Army started advancing and getting near, these stupid women started howling, 'Now look what you've done to us! What's to become of us?' The Germans said, 'Of course we won't leave you behind—you're our lawful wedded wives,' and they roared with laughter. This cheered the women up a bit, and they went round saying goodbye: 'We're being flown out to Berlin!'

'Later they were all found on the far side of the forest. They were recognized by their dresses. The Germans had thrown them out of aeroplanes just outside the town.'

These are snatches of the story that was being told on my side of the fire. On the other side, they are having an argument. The major regards acts of courage as merely doing one's duty, something as simple as ABC. There is nothing to tell, he says, although there were, of course, individual cases when a few people, by showing great courage, inspired the rest to follow them and so decided the outcome of the battle. Often the initiative came from Korchaginites. I do not catch everything the major is saying, only occasional words. But an exact account of the Orel offensive is being unfolded before me, and I start to listen attentively.

10

I see it as a chain of events, link following link in the unerring sequence of its moral logic. I try to recall how for the last time (because at some point their lawless aggression must end) the Germans made their frenzied offensive from two carefully chosen points in order to cut off our troops in the Kursk salient from north and south; how for seven days on end they fought and fought, but with very little reward for their amazing, diabolical fury. During the first day they fired as many shells as they had used in the entire invasion of France. We replied with even heavier artillery fire from about two thousand guns over a front of about two kilometres, and by the end of the first week their whole advance had been cancelled out and they were back where they started. Then it was our turn to advance from two points, north and south, to cut off their Orel salient. Everything was reversed – the terms, the roles of the two opponents and their relative strengths. The German attack turned into a defensive action, already a foretaste of the retreat which it was doomed to become. In mathematics and logic this is called cause and effect; in moral terms – retribution.

On the morning of the 12th, Kustov and Gurtiev with the 308th and 380th divisions had broken through the German defences, and by evening their four-kilometre breach was one and a half times as wide. Thereafter everything went in accordance with the strategic calculations of the high command and the skill of individual commanders. More than once the situation was saved by strength of character and quick thinking.

The armies began widening the breach by advancing on Orel from the east, and by July 20th they had reached the River Oka. At this point the enemy beat back our attempts to force a crossing. From July 21st to 23rd German aircraft kept the crossing-site under day and night attack. By then the 342nd Division, pursuing the enemy after capturing Mtsensk the day before, seized a bridgehead at Bagatyshchev and Narykov. This provided an opportunity to advance towards Orel from the north-east. On the 25th the remainder of the army was moved forward to link up with the 342nd Division. But the enemy guessed that we were planning to encircle him. Pulling up his 2nd and 8th Panzer Divisions and the 26th

Motorized Division to join the 56th Infantry Division, he concentrated heavy forces on this flank at the cost of weakening his centre. Lieutenant-General Gorbatov then decided to make another attempt at a frontal assault on Orel. Confident that he would be able to carry out his swift, complex regrouping before the enemy became aware of his intention, he pulled back the 380th and 308th Divisions which were in defensive positions on an extended front, transferred the 17th Tank Brigade from the line of the main thrust to join them, and at dawn on August 5th, Adzhanov, the standard-bearer of Kustov's division, raised the red flag over the liberated town.

II

It is impossible to wreak evil on others without harm to oneself. Wickedness is total. He who breaks the commandment to love one's neighbour is first of all betraying himself.

How much justified anger has been poured out against present-day Germany! Yet the magnitude of her fall is even greater than can be expressed by any amount of righteous indignation.

What is so striking about Hitlerism is that it has deprived Germany of her political primacy. Her dignity has been sacrificed for the sake of playing a derivative role: the country has been forced into becoming no more than a reactionary footnote to Russian history. If revolutionary Russia had ever had need of a distorting mirror for her features to be reflected in, disfigured by a grimace of hate and incomprehension, then here it is: Germany has set about creating it. To have done so was an exercise of utter irrelevance, a relic of the now meaningless rivalry between Teuton and Slav in the Baltic, and its provincialism is all the more obvious for the attempt to invest it with universal significance.

Throughout the nineteenth century, and especially towards its end, Russia made rapid and successful progress. She was imbued with a sense of universal humanity and breadth of vision. The element of genius which underlay our preparation of the revolution as a moral phenomenon on a national scale (the writer does not presume to discuss its political aspect, being unqualified to do so) could be felt everywhere, and it pervaded the atmosphere of the years that led up to the revolution. This spirit of the age was particularly evident in Lev Tolstoy, who used Russian means to express the nature—and the prejudices—of genius, just as the same element, although shared by dozens of his predecessors, was embodied in Shakespeare at the very beginning of England's emergence as a distinctive culture.

Genius is the sense of an undeniable right to measure every thing in the world by one's own yardstick, a feeling of oneness with the universe, the joy of being on intimate terms with history and of feeling an affinity with everything that lives and breathes. Being a primal quality, genius can never be irrelevant or intrusive. The same drive to innovation and creative originality went into the making of our revolution.

But the careless generosity of the self-taught genius inevitably gives rise to its counterpart—dull, envious mediocrity, which sees the deeds and actions of its favoured rival as madness and eccentricity. The ignoramus begins by disapproving and ends with bloodshed.

This was the kind of blinkered, multiplication-table mentality which roared up to our gates mounted on a Tiger tank and a Ferdinand self-propelled gun; to prove in the twinkling of an eye that all these Rudins with their hot air and fancy phrases would collapse when faced with sober German efficiency and a mug of good beer. But oh, horror, it is the 'twice-two-are-four' school of thought which has collapsed, while the sweeping breadth of our spirit has prevailed, will survive this ordeal and many more.

12

We were entering Lyudovino, liberated the previous day. Approaching it, we could see from a distance thick columns of smoke on the horizon. As they retreated, the Germans had managed to destroy the town. Now they were bombing it from the air to set it on fire. As we drew near we could see several Stukas circling steadily round and round in the sky. We drove the car off the road and took cover among the trees on the verge. The army lorries behind us followed our example. Some of the planes began dive-bombing. Explosions shattered the air in front of us and behind us along the road.

Lyudovino was ablaze when we drove into it. The fires had just started and did not reach their full force until the evening. We inspected the ruins of a diesel-engine factory and an officers' cemetery near the cathedral—a bristling forest of Maltese crosses with white inscriptions, they reminded one of the mass of spikes on the back of a hedgehog or a porcupine. As we were due to go back next day, we were invited to write a farewell address to the army. This is what we wrote:

Comrades, soldiers of the 3rd Army—for two weeks we, a group of writers, joined your divisions and marched with you. We passed through places steeped in the imperishable glory of your valiant deeds, tracing the footsteps of a cruel and merciless enemy. We have seen sights of bestial destruction, an endless succession of destroyed and burnt-out villages. The population driven into captivity or, having hidden in the forests until the retreating enemy had done his atrocious work, drifting back in twos and threes, homeless and destitute to the ashes that were once their homes. Our hearts were wrung with pity at the sight, and we wondered what miraculous power could restore these places again and bring them back to life.

Comrades, soldiers of the 3rd Army—you have this power. It lies in your courage and the deadly aim of your guns, in your deserved success and your devotion to duty.

Good sense has taught us throughout the ages, and Comrade Stalin has repeated it: sooner or later, right will prevail. That time has come. Justice has triumphed. It is early yet to say that the enemy is in full retreat, but his ranks have flinched and he is pulling back. Routed by the force of your victorious arms, by pressure from our allies and the intolerable burden of his historic guilt, it is obvious that his defeat is inevitable.

Press him without mercy, and may your good fortune and glory remain with you for ever. Our thoughts and our concern are with you wherever you go. You are our pride, and we admire you.

1943

1917–1942

Number with the magic spell!
You are with me in every transformation.
You've come full circle: you are here.
I did not think you would arrive.

Just as a quarter-century ago,
In that dawn of youth's imaginings,
So now you gild my early sunset
With the glow of the same great exploits.

And now you celebrate your triumph,
Your silver jubilee,
Now, as on that first, that famous morning,
Nothing that I've given you do I regret.

I don't regret my callow work,
And on this autumn morning
I once more greet your coming,
Ready, as before, for new privations.

To me you represent integrity.
You need make no apologies to me
As the war with its spirit of darkness
Casts its shadow on your anniversary.

6 November 1942

(*Novy Mir*, 1965/1)

To the Memory of Marina Tsvetaeva
(A fragment)

Gloomily the dismal day drags on,
Disconsolately run the torrents
Of water past my porch and door
And into open windows.

Beyond the fence and down the road,
The public park is drowning.
Clouds, like beasts in their lair,
Are piled in untidy heaps.

Through the murk, before my eyes, a vision:
A book of this earth and its beauty.
I'm drawing a woodland sprite
For you on its title-page.

Gone, Marina, long gone are those days now
And less heavy now even the task
Of carrying your scattered dust
In a requiem from Yelabuga.

That solemnity of your reburial:
Last year I reflected upon it
By the snows of the lonely river-bank
Where the barges sleep fast in the ice.

December 1942

(Novy Mir, 1965/1)

From the cycle 'Verses to Pushkin' *by* Marina Tsvetaeva

Novy Mir, 1965/III

Translated by Michael Glenny

Marina Tsvetaeva (1893–1941) wrote most of her poetry in emigration. Leaving Russia in 1921, she lived for a few years in a village in Bohemia. Then she and her son and daughter moved to Paris in 1925, where they were followed later that year by her husband, Sergei Ephron. There she stayed, living constantly on the brink of absolute poverty, until she returned to Soviet Russia at Ephron's insistence in 1939; he had already gone back there the year before with their daughter. On arrival in Moscow she found her sister exiled, her daughter in a concentration camp and her husband – who had worked devotedly for the Soviet cause in emigration – in prison. He was shot a year later. Evacuated at the outbreak of war to the provincial town of Yelabuga, she tried and failed to beg some comfort and assistance from the poet Aseyev. The only work she could find was washing dishes in an evacuees' kitchen. She hanged herself on August 31st, 1941.

Tsvetaeva's poetry, some of which is possibly the greatest of its genre written in Russian this century, owes virtually nothing to the influence of the principal schools of the twentieth century – the symbolists, acmeists, futurists. It has something of Mayakovsky's rhythmic drive, but is neither so diffuse nor so colourful, and is much more sparing of neologisms and metric innovation. Tsvetaeva's poetry is, indeed, so passionate yet so condensed, so spartan yet so highly expressive, that most of it must be beyond the skill of any but the rarest translator. A part of her major poem *Krysolov* ('The Rat-Catcher'), a bitter, ironical comment on her time in the form of an updated 'Pied Piper of Hamelin', was also published in *Novy Mir* (posthumously, as was this poem), but proved too daunting to translate. These verses, addressed not so much to Pushkin as to Pushkin's academic embalmers, is very typical of Tsvetaeva's irresistible mastery of rhythm.

252

Scourge of gendarmes, god of students,
Loathed by husbands, loved by wives;
Pushkin as a statue? Never!
No Stone Guest he, with his jibes,

Flashing teeth and saucy grin. What,
Pushkin as *Commendatore*?

Critic nagging, finger wagging:
'But (sob) what of Pushkin's fine
Sense of measure?' You forget his
Sensual pleasure, as the waves

Pounding granite! Can this salty
Pushkin ever be a text-book?

Legs a-straddle by the fireplace,
Warming them: or bounding up,
Leaping on the Tsar's own table!
Self-willed African, the sheer

Comic genius of his age — this
Pushkin in the role of tutor?

Black's ingrained; it can't be whitewashed,
Useless to apply the brush.
Russian classic, yes; but Pushkin
Called the Afric sky his own,

Roundly cursed the grim Nevá; no,
Pushkin's surely no arch-Russian.

Let us too pronounce a speech in
Honour of his jubilee:
'Praise the swarthy, red-cheeked poet,
Handsome does as handsome is;

None more lively, more alive than
Pushkin!' He—a mausoleum?

Sergeant-major-like, they bellow:
'Pushkin present—atten-*shun*!'
Where's the hellfire pouring from his
Lips, or where the coarse abuse?

Pushkin, nature's rebel—how can
Thin-lipped dons claim Pushkin's mantle?

Little midgets! Ah, how dare you
Brand that forehead—olive-blue,
Soaring, boundless—desecrate his
Brow with faded tinsel crowns,

Symbols of those dreary virtues—
'Golden mean' and 'middle way'?

'Pushkin: "toga", Pushkin: "cassock",
Pushkin: "yardstick", Pushkin: "peak" ... '
Pushkin, Pushkin, Pushkin—noble
Surname! Noble as a damnéd
Tinker's curse, you squawking parrots!

Pushkin? Horrors!

1931

On the Borderline of Peace and War *by* Valentin Berezhkov

Novy Mir, 1965/VII

Translated by Hilary Sternberg

The literary and political de-Stalinization campaign which *Novy Mir* pursued with such tenacity under Tvardovsky's editorship was fought at a number of levels, according to circumstances, through such varying media as fiction, oblique scholarly discussion, poetry, book reviews and, in particular, through memoirs of the 'now-it-can-be-told' variety. Of the latter, two of the best known which appeared in *Novy Mir* were the memoirs of the diplomat Ivan Maisky and of Ilya Ehrenburg, both of which are widely available in translation.

A specialized and very interesting subdivision of this literature has been the sometimes muffled but none the less fierce polemic on the subject of Stalin's responsibility for the U.S.S.R.'s disastrous state of unpreparedness when the country was attacked by Hitler's Germany in June 1941. In its military aspect this argument is mainly to be found in the memoirs and other writings of Soviet marshals, generals and admirals, sometimes openly and sometimes in rather cryptic terms. But the anti-Stalinist case on this issue rests at least as much on Stalin's misreading of the political situation and on his alleged ineptitude in the face of ample advance warning of Hitler's intentions. This information was supplied and confirmed by such widely differing sources as Winston Churchill, and Richard Sorge, Stalin's German-born master-spy based in Japan.

Some of the strongest evidence of Stalin's failure to see what was under his nose is contained in the following passage. It is clear from this account of Molotov's last meeting with Hitler in the late autumn of 1940 that if the then Soviet Foreign Minister possessed even a shred of the astuteness generally ascribed to him, then the report that he must have brought back to Stalin after that meeting should at least have put the Soviet government much more on its guard than appears to have been the case. And if Molotov's evidence were not enough, the subsequent dispatches from the Soviet Embassy in Berlin, as we learn from Berezhkov's account, show that Soviet diplomats were doing their duty even if their information was misinterpreted or ignored by the autocrat of the Kremlin.

Valentin Berezhkov, a linguist and expert on German affairs, was a relatively junior official when he served first as Molotov's interpreter with Hitler and then *en poste* in the Soviet Embassy in Berlin, where he was personally involved in the tense diplomatic fencing and bluff which immediately preceded Hitler's attack. As befits a professional interpreter he kept good notes and had a trained memory. Naturally, before accepting his memoir as a leading primary document, it should be remembered that it is subject (like all such writings, from whatever source or country) to potential distortion on at least three counts: Berezhkov's human tendency to show himself and his immediate colleagues—including Molotov—in the best possible light; the Soviet Foreign Ministry's censorship which it undoubtedly exercises over the published writings of all ex-diplomats; and the fact that this account is also a piece of ammunition in a much larger-scale polemical battle concerning Stalin's rule, and his wartime leadership in particular. Furthermore, this English version has had to be somewhat shortened in order to fit it in.

The Molotov-Ribbentrop-Hitler meeting which forms the core of Berezhkov's story has, of course, been documented from the German side as well. The basic papers are to be found in the German Foreign Office Documents captured in 1945, and especially in the personal files of State Secretary von Weizsäcker. Accounts of it have also come from the two German interpreters present, Hilger and Schmidt. Although Schmidt was the senior interpreter, he did not speak Russian, and Hilger was the main channel of communication on the German side. These German sources have been used by William L. Shirer in *The Rise and Fall of the Third Reich*, and anyone with a taste for studying the evidence from both sides of the hill can compare Berezhkov's first-hand account with the German-based interpretation of the same event in Shirer's book. This fills in quite a lot of the political background which Berezhkov leaves out. Directly comparable with Berezhkov, but shorter and less vivid, is Hilger's version, to be found in Hilger and Meyer *The Incompatible Allies* (Macmillan, New York, 1953).

On the evening of November 9th, 1940, a special unscheduled train drew out from a platform of the Byelorussian Station. It consisted of several coaches of the Western European type, and its passengers were members and officials of the Soviet government delegation that was on its way to Berlin for talks with the German government.

Nowadays the Soviet Union has direct rail communications with many countries—a passenger can board his carriage at a Moscow station and remain in it all the way to Warsaw, Berlin or Paris. But before the Second World War Soviet trains only went as far as our frontier. There passengers would board a train which took them to the first station across the border, where they would have to change into a carriage bound for Western Europe. This was because of the difference in gauge; it was not usual to change the bogies under the carriages in those days. In this respect, too, the Soviet delegation's train was special. It was to make the entire journey from Moscow to Berlin; standard-gauge bogies were waiting for our coaches at the frontier.

After a leisurely dinner in the restaurant-car I went back to my sleeper and stretched out on the bed. But sleep was a long time in coming—I was excited by the events of the day. I had learned of the journey only that morning, and I had been obliged to finish off some urgent work, go through the formalities for getting a passport, make hasty preparations and be at the station an hour before departure.

It was not my first trip abroad. In the spring and summer of 1940 I had worked in our trade delegation in Berlin and had explored Germany thoroughly. I had a good knowledge of German in addition to my professional qualifications as an engineer, and my services were frequently called on for important economic talks. In the autumn of 1940 I had been recalled to Moscow and transferred to the German Section of the People's Commissariat of Foreign Trade. Whenever the People's Commissar (who at that

9

time was A. I. Mikoyan) held personal talks with German delegations, I acted as interpreter.

Now, as a member of a team of officials accompanying a Soviet delegation to Berlin, I was travelling in this special train. By nature of my work I knew that in recent months the Germans had been holding back deliveries of important equipment to the Soviet Union, while insisting on increased Soviet supplies of oil, grain, manganese and other commodities. These problems were likely to be discussed in Berlin, but the composition of the Soviet delegation (headed by the People's Commissar of Foreign Affairs, V. M. Molotov) suggested that political talks were going to be the main item on the agenda ...

The question that worried everyone at that time was—what next? How much longer would Hitler keep to his obligations under the Soviet-German non-aggression pact? Might he not turn to the East? In the early autumn of 1940 Berlin had taken a series of steps which had complicated Soviet-German relations: German troops had landed in Finland; a German military mission had arrived in Rumania; Berlin was exerting pressure on Bulgaria. The Germans were systematically failing to meet delivery dates for the supply of equipment to the Soviet Union. It was essential to sound out Hitler's real intentions. This was, in fact, one of the aims of the mission which was making its way to Berlin in November 1940 at the invitation of the German government ...

Outside the carriage windows the forests of Byelorussia flashed past, tinged with crimson. It was still warm in these parts. The sun shone through ragged clouds, the damp grass glistened. At regular intervals of about four or five hundred metres we saw the solitary figure of a Red Army soldier on the embankment, holding his rifle with fixed bayonet. The railway track for the entire route of our train had been placed under a special guard. But only a few of the sentries were standing to attention at their posts; for the most part they were sitting smoking on tree-stumps, or they had spread their greatcoats out on the grass and lay on them chewing a straw and staring curiously at the train with its unusual coaches rushing past them ...

On the morning of November 12th the train reached Berlin. The Soviet delegation was met at the Anhalter Station by various officials. It was drizzling; grey, shaggy clouds hung so low that they seemed to be brushing the rooftops, and there were puddles on the asphalt of the station square. Amongst the welcoming party were the Minister of Foreign Affairs, Ribbentrop, and Field-Marshal Keitel. After an exchange of extremely reserved greetings there was a march-past by a guard of honour. The band struck up. Somehow the atmosphere grew especially quiet during the playing of the 'Internationale'. It was very likely the first time since Hitler's seizure of power in 1933 that this militant proletarian song had rung out in Berlin. The Gestapo had thrown people into death camps for singing it, and now, here on the square in front of the Anhalter Station, Hitler's generals and the highest-ranking officials of the Nazi Reich were standing at attention to the strains of the communist anthem! A detail became engraved on my memory: to the right stood a brick building, part of a factory, and from its windows workers were waving red handkerchiefs and scarves ...

In the Reich Chancellery

The string of black limousines, with an escort of motor-cyclists, pulled out on to the Charlottenburger Allee, passed the Branden-burg Gate and accelerated down the Wilhelmstrasse. Here there were rather more spectators. In some places the entire pavement was filled with Berliners: silently, they peered at the red flag with the golden hammer and sickle fixed to the radiator of the first car. One or two people waved timidly.

The cars slowed down and drove into the inner courtyard of the new Reich Chancellery. This building, designed by the architect Speer in the 'Nazi' style—a mixture of classical, Gothic and ancient Teutonic symbolism—was singularly uninviting. The sombre square courtyard, reminiscent of a barracks or a prison, was framed with tall pillars of dark grey marble and paved with granite slabs of an identical grey. Spread eagles, the swastika in their claws, a blind pediment overhanging the pillars, the frozen figures of the sentries in grey-green helmets—the whole created an ominous impression.

The tall doors of gilded bronze led into a spacious entrance-hall opening into a suite of dimly lit rooms and windowless corridors. Men in various uniforms lined the walls. Like robots, they threw up their right arms and clicked their heels with a hollow sound. We were met at the entrance by State Secretary Otto Meissner, who escorted us by a very long way round, evidently calculated to make the maximum impression on us with all this pomp and protocol.

Finally we found ourselves in a brightly lit circular hall. In the centre stood a table with soft drinks and light refreshments. Long sofas were ranged around the walls. Here were the German experts with their bulky files, and the officers of the guard, waiters moving noiselessly among them. It was here, too, that the officials of our delegation were left. The only persons allowed to enter Hitler's study, which adjoined the circular hall, were the head of the Soviet delegation, V. M. Molotov, his assistants and the interpreters. The Nazis staged this procedure with characteristic theatricality: two tall, tightly-belted SS men—real 'blond beasts' in black uniforms, with death's-heads in their caps—clicked their heels, and with a well-rehearsed gesture flung open the huge, ceiling-high doors. Then, turning their backs to the door-posts and raising their right arms, they formed a kind of living arch through which we advanced into Hitler's study.

It was an enormous room, more like a banqueting hall than a study. The walls were draped with gigantic Gobelin tapestries, and the centre of the floor was covered by a thick carpet. To the right of the entrance was an area resembling a drawing-room—a round table, a sofa and several armchairs. There was a lamp on the table with a tall white shade. At the opposite end of the chamber stood a huge polished writing-desk bearing a large globe on a black wooden pedestal.

Hitler was seated at the writing-desk, his slight figure in its mousy-green uniform tunic barely discernible in this enormous chamber. He gazed fixedly at us, rose abruptly, and with quick short steps came forward into the middle of the room. Here he halted and raised his arm limply, casually, in the fascist salute, turning away his palm in a somewhat unnatural gesture as he did so. Then, still without uttering a sound, he came up and greeted each one of us with a limp handshake. To feel his cold, moist palm was like touching a frog. As he greeted us, his feverishly glittering pupils bored into each one of us like gimlets. His sharp, pimpled nose jutted over his clipped moustache.

After briefly expressing his pleasure at welcoming the Soviet delegation to Berlin, Hitler suggested that we take our seats at the round table in the corner of the study. At that moment Ribbentrop, the Foreign Minister, appeared from behind a tapestry which evidently concealed another entrance. He was followed by Schmidt, Hitler's personal interpreter, and Hilger, a counsellor from the German embassy in Moscow who had a good knowledge of Russian. Everyone sat down around the table, on the sofa or in the armchairs, which were covered with brightly coloured material

The talks began with a lengthy monologue from Hitler. One must give the man his due — he knew how to talk. He possibly even had a prepared text, but he did not use it. His speech was fluent and unfaltering. Like an actor who knew his part perfectly, he rapped out phrase after phrase, with pauses for translation.

The German interpreter, Hilger, had lived in the Soviet Union for many years, knew Russian as well as he knew his native German, and even bore a superficial resemblance to a Russian. When he used to go fishing on the Klyazma river on Sundays in his Russian shirt and straw hat, his pince-nez balanced on his nose, passers-by would take him for a perfect Chekhovian intellectual. Hilger even boasted that when chatting to other anglers he had often acquired some interesting information. Now he sat encased in the black uniform of the Ministry of Foreign Affairs, erect and poker-stiff. Next to him, resting his writing-pad on his knee, the interpreter Schmidt noted down the discussion. Although he had an excellent command of several Western European languages he did not know Russian, and therefore confined himself on this occasion to the role of recorder. Pavlov and I took it in turn to translate the speeches of the Soviet representative and keep the minutes.

The essence of Hitler's argument was that England was already beaten and would very shortly capitulate altogether. Soon England would be destroyed from the air. Then Hitler gave a brief review of the military situation, stressing that the German Reich was already in control of the entire continent of Western Europe. Together with their Italian allies, German troops were carrying out successful operations in Africa, whence the British would soon be finally ousted. From all that he had said, one was to conclude that the defeat of the Western Powers was already assured. Therefore, he continued, the time had come to think about the organization of the world after this defeat.

Hitler then began to develop the following ideas: with the inevitable collapse of Great Britain there would remain her 'unclaimed legacy' — fragments of the empire scattered over the entire globe. We must, he said, dispose of this 'ownerless property'. The Germans, had already exchanged opinions with the governments of Italy and Japan, and would now like to hear the views of the Soviet government. He intended to offer more definite proposals on that score later.

When Hitler had finished his speech, which, including translation, lasted about an hour, it was Molotov's turn. Without embarking on a discussion of Hitler's proposals, he observed that they ought to discuss more concrete, practical questions. Would the Reich Chancellor explain, for instance, what a German military mission was doing in Rumania, and why it had been sent there without consultation with the Soviet government? After all, the Soviet-German non-aggression pact signed in 1939 stipulated consultation on important questions of mutual interest. The Soviet government would also like to know why German troops had been sent to Finland, and why this grave step, too, had been taken without consultation with Moscow?

These remarks affected Hitler like a cold shower. He somehow even seemed to shrink, and for a brief instant his face registered a look of embarrassment. But his histrionic talent gained the upper hand and, clasping his hands dramatically, he threw back his head and fixed his gaze on the ceiling. Then, fidgeting in his chair, he rattled off an explanation: the German military mission had been sent to Rumania at the request of the Antonescu government, for the purpose of training Rumanian troops. As for Finland, the German units had no intention whatsoever of staying there; they were merely passing through that country on the way to Norway.

This explanation, however, did not satisfy the Soviet delegation. The Soviet government, Molotov declared, had received quite a different impression from the dispatches of its envoys in Finland and Rumania. The troops which had landed on the southern coast of Finland had not moved any farther, and were evidently intending to remain in that country for a long period. In Rumania, too, it was not merely a question of a military mission: new German military formations were arriving there all the time. There were already too many of them for one military mission. What was the aim of these movements? Such measures as these inevitably caused unease; the German government must give a precise reply.

At this point Hitler resorted to a well-tried manoeuvre: he pleaded ignorance. He promised to inquire into the questions raised by the Soviet side, though he said that he considered them all matters of secondary importance. Now, he said, returning to his original theme, the time had come to discuss the problems that would arise from the imminent defeat of the Western Powers.

At this, Hitler again began developing his fantastic plan for the partition of the world. England, he assured us, would be crushed within the next few months and occupied by German troops, and it would be many years yet before the United States could represent a threat to the 'New Europe'. Therefore it was time to think about creating a new order over the whole globe. The German and Italian governments had already defined their spheres of interest, which included Europe and Africa, and Japan was showing an interest in certain areas of South-East Asia. In the light of this, Hitler continued, the Soviet Union might well be interested in the territories to the south of its frontier, in the direction of the Indian Ocean, which would give the Soviet Union access to ice-free ports. If a successful settlement could be reached on this point, Hitler added with a sweeping gesture of his arm, the German government was ready to respect these interests of the Soviet Union ...

Here the Soviet delegate interrupted Hitler, remarking that he could see no point in discussing these schemes; his government was interested in safeguarding peace and security in those areas which bordered directly on the Soviet Union.

Hitler made no reaction to this remark, and began again to expound his plan for the apportionment of Britain's 'unclaimed legacy'. The conversation took a curious turn, for the German spokesmen pretended not to hear the Soviet delegation's repeated requests for a discussion of concrete issues concerning the security of the Soviet Union and other independent European states, and the delegates' demands for an explanation of recent German actions threatening the independence of countries bordering directly on Soviet territory. Hitler, however, continually tried to bring the conversation round to his project for the partition of the world, striving to force the Soviet government to commit itself by engaging in a discussion of these wild plans.

The conversation had lasted two and a half hours when Hitler suddenly glanced at his watch, and, mentioning the possibility of an air-raid, suggested that the talks be broken off until the next day.

We rose. The Soviet spokesmen took their leave and went out of Hitler's study, to be once more escorted through the suite of chambers to the inner courtyard of the Reich Chancellery.

The early twilight of autumn had already enveloped the city. A biting wind was blowing, the streets had emptied and the black Mercedes conveyed us speedily to Schloss Bellevue. There behind the heavy curtains bright lights shone in the warmth, and there was the fragrant smell of roses. A report on our talk was compiled immediately and wired to Moscow.

The same evening there was a big reception in our embassy on the Unter den Linden in honour of the Soviet government delegation's visit. In the huge marble hall the tables were arranged in the shape of an enormous letter E. The snow-white tablecloth was set with antique silver and bright-red carnations. A dinner service for fifty people, kept in the embassy for specially solemn occasions, had been brought out. Hitler did not appear at the reception; we inferred that he was 'displeased' with the course the talks were taking. But there were many high-ranking Nazis present—Reich Minister Göring, his chest and stomach adorned with a veritable iconostasis of orders and medals; Rudolf Hess, the Number Three man in the Reich (when war broke out Hitler had announced that should he meet with a sudden death, his successor was to be Göring, and if he too perished Hess was to be Führer); Ribbentrop, Field-Marshal Keitel, and others. But no sooner had the first toast been proposed than the sirens wailed a warning of the approach of British bombers. The embassy building had no shelter, so the guests began hastily to disperse, most of them down the Unter den Linden to the Brandenburg Gate, where they took cover in the underground station.

The Soviet delegation returned to Schloss Bellevue. In the cellars a comfortable air-raid shelter had been fitted out, its walls hung with valuable paintings and Gobelin tapestries, as were the rooms of the Schloss itself. Waiters served drinks. Two hours later came the all-clear, and we dispersed to our quarters.

Next day our second meeting with Hitler took place. A dispatch reached us from Moscow before it began. The report of the previous day's talks had been studied in the Kremlin, and the delegation received instructions for the next round. The Soviet government categorically rejected Hitler's attempt to draw us into negotiations regarding the 'division of British property'. The instructions again emphasized that we should insist on an explanation from the German government on the matters which concerned European security and directly affected Soviet interests.

On this occasion the conversation with Hitler lasted almost three hours, and it included some extremely sharp remarks.

After greetings had been exchanged, and we had all taken our places at the round table in the Reich Chancellor's study, Molotov spoke. In line with Moscow's instructions, he set out the Soviet government's position, and then returned to the question of the presence of German troops in Finland. According to information at the disposal of the Soviets, these troops had no intention of proceeding to Norway. On the contrary, they were strengthening their positions along the Soviet frontier. The Soviet government therefore insisted on their immediate withdrawal.

Now, twenty-three hours later, Hitler could not avoid the issue by pleading ignorance. He did, however, deny that German troops were stationed in Finland, and continued to assert, without adducing any evidence, that the military units were merely in transit to Norway. Then, resorting to an old device—attack is the best defence—he tried to represent the affair as a case of the Soviet Union threatening Finland.

'A conflict in the region of the Baltic Sea', he declared, 'would complicate German-Russian collaboration ... '

'But the Soviet Union has absolutely no intention of disturbing the peace in that region, and in no way represents a threat to Finland,' the Soviet spokesman rejoined. 'We are concerned with ensuring peace and genuine security in the region. The German government must take this into consideration if it wishes Soviet-German relations to develop normally ... '

Hitler replied evasively, repeating that the measures he had taken were intended to safeguard the security of the Wehrmacht in Norway, and that a conflict in the region of the Baltic might have 'far-reaching consequences'. This was nothing less than a direct threat, and could not be left unanswered.

'It seems as though a new factor has been introduced into the
9*

discussions which might seriously complicate the situation,' said the Soviet delegate. Thus Hitler was given to understand that the Soviet Union intended to persist firmly in its demand that the German troops be withdrawn from Finland.

The Soviet side had good cause to raise this question so insistently. Government circles in Finland at that time were openly stating that they regarded the peace treaty made with the Soviet Union in March 1940 as a mere truce, a respite, which, they said, should be used to prepare for a new war against the Soviets, to be waged this time jointly with Hitler's Germany. In October 1940 the Ryti-Tanner government had signed an agreement with Berlin regarding German troops being stationed on Finnish territory. At about the same time a campaign had been started in Finland to recruit volunteers for a 'Schützkorps'; they were sent to Germany, where it was proposed to form a so-called 'Finnish SS Battalion'. Preparations like these gave grounds for believing that with the connivance of the Finnish government Hitler was preparing to use Finland as a springboard for his operations against the Soviet Union. Indeed, immediately before Hitler's attack on the Soviet Union was launched, an army consisting of four German and two Finnish divisions was concentrated in northern Finland. Its task was to occupy Murmansk. Further south, from the Oulujärvi lakes to the shores of the Gulf of Finland, the Karelian and the South-East Finnish Armies were deployed; these consisted of fifteen infantry divisions (one of them German), two infantry brigades and one cavalry brigade. By advancing towards Leningrad and the River Svir, they were to assist the German Northern Army Group in the capture of Leningrad.

When Hitler invaded our country, the German forces advanced from Finland to cross the Soviet frontier alongside Finnish troops ...

But to return to the negotiations in the Reich Chancellery. During the discussion on the German troops in Finland the atmosphere had become so heated that Ribbentrop, silent until then, felt it necessary to relieve the tension. Breaking into the conversation he remarked casually, 'Actually, there is no reason to make an issue of the Finnish question. There has evidently been a misunderstanding of some sort ... '

Hitler took advantage of this remark by his Foreign Minister to change the subject quickly, making yet another attempt to draw the

Soviet delegation into a discussion of the allocation of world spheres of influence.

'Let us turn to the cardinal problems of the present day,' he said in a conciliatory tone. 'After the defeat of England, the British Empire will become a gigantic auction room of forty million square kilometres. Countries which might have an interest in this bankrupt property ought not to quarrel over petty, inessential issues, but should come to grips with the problem of the partition of the British Empire. This concerns above all Germany, Italy, Japan and Russia ... '

The Soviet spokesman observed that he had heard all that the previous day, and that at present it was much more important to discuss matters relevant to European security. The Soviet government was still waiting for an answer on the question of the German troops in Finland, and would like to know the German government's plans for Turkey, Bulgaria and Rumania. Moreover, the Soviet government considered the German-Italian guarantees recently offered to Rumania to be directed against the interests of the Soviet Union. These guarantees must be annulled.

Hitler at once declared that this demand was unacceptable, whereupon the Soviet delegate put the following question:

'What would Germany say if the Soviet Union, in view of her interest in the security of the area bordering on her south-western frontier, gave Bulgaria a guarantee similar to the one Germany and Italy have given Rumania? ... '

At this, Hitler finally lost his equanimity. He shouted shrilly, 'Has Tsar Boris asked Moscow for guarantees? I have heard nothing of the sort. Anyhow, I shall have to consult the Duce. Italy also has an interest in affairs in that part of Europe. If Germany needs to look for sources of friction with Russia', he added menacingly, 'she can find them elsewhere.'

The Soviet spokesman replied calmly that it was the duty of every state to see to the security of its own people as well as the security of friendly neighbouring countries. And it was precisely this which formed the basis of the Soviet government's foreign policy.

Then the Soviet delegate proceeded to other matters. He said that there was considerable dissatisfaction in Moscow over the delay in deliveries to the Soviet Union of important German equipment. It was all the more inexcusable because the Soviet side was fulfilling its obligations in accordance with the Soviet-German economic agreements. The failure to keep to agreed delivery dates was creating serious difficulties.

Once more Hitler tried to dodge the issue. He declared that the German Reich was waging 'a life-and-death struggle' against England, and mobilizing her entire resources for this final engagement with the British.

'But we have just heard that England is already virtually defeated. So which of the sides is fighting for death and which for life?' Molotov remarked sarcastically.

'Yes, it is true, England has been defeated,' replied Hitler, failing to notice the irony, 'but there are still one or two things we need to do ... '

Then Hitler stated that in his opinion this topic of conversation had been exhausted, and since he had an engagement for that evening, the talks would be concluded by Reich Minister Ribbentrop.

So ended the last meeting between the Soviet delegation and Hitler. It was clear by then that Hitler refused to consider the Soviet Union's legitimate requirements regarding national security. But we were as yet unaware that long before the Berlin encounter, Hitler's government had decided to attack the Soviet Union, and was already making specific preparations to do so. From secret German government archives, from the diaries of high-ranking Nazi officials and from documents disclosed during the Nuremberg Trials, we know that after the signature of the Soviet-German non-aggression pact, in the autumn of 1939, Hitler continued to make plans for war against the Soviet Union. Two months after signing the pact, Hitler instructed his army commanders to regard the German-occupied Polish territories as 'an assembly-area for future German operations'. There is a note to this effect in General Halder's diary for October 18th, 1939 ...

At a conference of the services Chiefs of Staff on July 29th, 1940, Hitler declared, this time with no reservations, that he intended to take action against the Soviet Union in the spring of 1941. Clearly, he inclined towards the idea of attacking the Soviet Union before the final defeat of England. At a meeting with officers of the Wehrmacht at his Berghof residence on July 31st, 1940, Hitler announced his decision to postpone the invasion of the British Isles, and declared:

'All Britain's hopes lie in Russia and America. If her hope in Russia fades, her hope in America will fade too, because the withdrawal of Russia from operations will make an enormous difference to Japan's role in Eastern Asia. When Russia is crushed, England's last hope will be shattered … '

Thus Hitler was playing a double game. Having already decided to attack the Soviet Union, he was playing for time by attempting to give the Soviet government the impression that he was ready to discuss the peaceful development of Soviet-German relations. This was evidently the purpose of the Berlin meeting, which Hitler's government had promoted so energetically since the summer of 1940.

In the correspondence between Berlin and Moscow during those months, we find hints that it would not be amiss if high-ranking spokesmen from both countries were to discuss urgent problems. In one German letter it was plainly stated that since Ribbentrop's last visit to Moscow, serious changes had occurred in Europe and indeed in the world, and that it was desirable that a plenipotentiary Soviet delegation should come to Berlin for talks. The Soviet government, always favouring the peaceful settlement of international problems, agreed to the German proposal to hold a conference in Berlin in November 1940.

In Ribbentrop's Bunker

The same evening, after the talks with Hitler were over, a meeting took place in Ribbentrop's residence on the Wilhelmstrasse. His office, though considerably smaller than Hitler's, was luxurious. The patterned parquet floor reflected everything in the room like a mirror. Old masters hung on the walls; the windows were adorned with curtains of costly tapestry, and bronze and porcelain figurines stood around the walls on tall pedestals.

Ribbentrop invited the participants in the discussion to a corner table decorated with bronze statuettes and Greek ornaments, and when everyone had taken their seats he announced that in accordance with the Führer's wishes, it would be expedient to review the progress of the talks and reach an agreement on something 'in principle'. Then out of the breast pocket of his green tunic he pulled a sheet of paper folded into four, and, slowly unfolding it, said, 'Here is a draft of several proposals by the German government ... ' Ribbentrop read out the proposals from the paper before him. They were, in effect, the same boastful arguments that the inevitable collapse of Great Britain made it necessary, according to the Germans, to consider the reorganization of the world. The German government proposed that the Soviet Union should accede to the pact signed by Germany, Italy and Japan. Furthermore, Germany, Italy, Japan and the Soviet Union should pledge themselves to respect each other's interests, and withhold their support from any combination of Powers directed against any of the four signatories. At some future date the members of the pact, taking account of each other's interests, were to solve the problem of the definitive reorganization of the world ...

After listening to the statement, the Soviet delegate said that there was no sense in reopening a discussion on that subject, but might he not be given a copy of the text he had just heard? Ribbentrop replied that he only possessed one copy and did not intend to communicate the proposals in written form, and hastily put the paper away in his pocket.

At that instant the air-raid sirens began to whine. People exchanged glances, and silence fell. A muffled explosion nearby set the panes rattling in the tall windows.

'It's not safe to stay here,' said Ribbentrop. 'Let us go down into my bunker. It will be quieter there ... '

We went out of the office and down a long corridor to a spiral staircase, by which we descended to the cellar. At the entrance to the bunker stood a sentry. He opened the heavy door for us, and after we had gone into the shelter, closed and barred it from the inside.

One of the underground rooms had been fitted out as Ribbentrop's second office. Several telephones stood on the polished writing-desk, and behind it were a small round table and deep, soft armchairs.

When the conversation re-commenced, Ribbentrop began once more to expatiate on the need to study the question of the allocation of world-wide spheres of influence. There was every reason to believe, he added, that England was virtually smashed. To this Molotov retorted, 'If England has been smashed, then why are we in this shelter? And whose bombs are those, falling so close that we can hear the explosions even in here?'

Ribbentrop was embarrassed and said nothing. To dissipate the awkwardness, he summoned his aide-de-camp and ordered coffee. When a waiter had laid the coffee-service on the table, poured out the coffee and gone, the Soviet delegate inquired when he might expect an explanation of why German troops were in Rumania and Finland.

With unconcealed irritation Ribbentrop replied that if the Soviet government were still interested in these 'immaterial questions', as he called them, then they should discuss them through the normal diplomatic channels.

Once more silence reigned. There was nothing more to say, but we were obliged to remain in the bunker, since English planes were continuing their massed air-raid on Berlin. Again and again we heard the muffled thuds of bombs exploding at close range. We were served with dry wine. Ribbentrop started to tell us about his vine-yards, and asked what brands of wine were produced in the Soviet Union. Time passed slowly. It was late at night when the all-clear finally sounded and we were able to return to Schloss Bellevue.

Next morning the Soviet delegation left Berlin. Once again a guard of honour was drawn up on the station square, but Ribbentrop was the only high-ranking official present. At the platform we saw our own train. Two German carriages had been attached to it, a restaurant car and a saloon-car, to accommodate officials of the protocol department of the German Ministry of Foreign Affairs who were to accompany the Soviet delegation as far as the frontier.

The Nazis' Secret Aims

What lay behind Hitler's and Ribbentrop's verbose plans for co-operation with the Soviet Union? Did the German government really assume that there would be no conflict between Germany and the Soviet Union for some time? Had Hitler temporarily abandoned the plans for aggression against the U.S.S.R. which he had pro-pounded in *Mein Kampf*? Of course not.

Hitler regarded the Berlin meeting as merely another diversionary manoeuvre. Proof of this is to be found in particular in the secret Directive No. 18 issued by him on November 12th, 1940 – the day the Soviet delegation arrived in Berlin. This directive stated:

> Political discussions have been initiated with the aim of clarifying Russia's attitude to the immediate future. Irrespective of the outcome of these discussions, all previously stipulated preparations for the East should be continued. Further instructions on this will follow, as soon as the basic provisions of the operational plan have been approved by me ...

We already know what was meant by these 'preparations for the East'.

As for the Soviet government, it did everything possible to avert a war, or at least delay a clash with Hitler's Germany, as long as possible.

The Soviet government continued to maintain diplomatic contact with the German government and to sound out its intentions. On November 26th, 1940, less than two weeks after the Berlin meeting, the German ambassador in Moscow, Schulenburg, was informed that if the talks initiated in Berlin were to be continued, the German side would have to guarantee the fulfilment of a number of conditions; in particular, German troops were to be immediately withdrawn from Finland, and within the next few months the security of the Soviet Union was to be guaranteed by the conclusion of a mutual-assistance pact between the U.S.S.R. and Bulgaria.

Schulenburg promised to convey the Soviet declaration at once to his government. But there was no reply from Berlin. Even then this silence seemed significant; now we know its cause. Hitler was simply ignoring the Soviet demands, and was preparing in earnest for aggression against our country. In his diary General Halder quotes the following comment made by Hitler on Schulenburg's telegram: 'Russia must be brought to her knees as soon as possible' ...

Hitler proposed that his General Staff should speed up their work on the final elaboration of a concrete plan of attack on the Soviet Union. After a four-hour conference with Brauchitsch and Halder on December 5th, Hitler approved the plan, at that time referred to as 'Operation Otto', but soon to be renamed. On December 18th, Hitler signed Directive No. 21 headed 'Operation Barbarossa'. It began as follows:

> The German armed forces must be prepared to crush Soviet Russia in a swift campaign before the end of the war against England. For this purpose the army will have to employ all available units, with the exception of those required to guard the occupied territories against surprise. Preparations are to be completed by May 15th, 1941. Special attention is to be devoted to ensuring that preparations for this attack are not detected.

Recalling now the course of the Soviet-German talks held in Berlin in the autumn of 1940, one cannot help remembering the insinuations which were circulating at the time, and which still appear in the Western press, concerning this meeting. It is asserted, for instance, that on that occasion in Berlin the Soviet side itself had shown some 'territorial aspirations in the direction of the Indian Ocean'. This is either the product of idle fantasy or a deliberate falsification. The Soviet side regarded the Berlin meeting of 1940 as a real opportunity to sound out the position of the German government.

The stand Hitler took during these talks, in particular his obstinate unwillingness to take account of the Soviet Union's natural interest in its own security and his categorical refusal to discontinue the virtual occupation of Finland and Rumania, indicated that despite his demagogic statements on the subject of the 'global interests' of the Soviet Union, Germany was in practice engaged in preparing an Eastern European bridgehead. There can be no doubt that Hitler sought the Berlin meeting with the aim of using his talks with Soviet spokesmen to mask his real intentions, and thereby to place the Soviet government in an unfavourable position. This would tie our hands in the future and simultaneously give Germany the freedom to act, and hence the opportunity to come to terms with England.

When he attempted to foist upon the Soviet delegation at the Berlin meeting a discussion about the 'reorganization' of the world and the apportionment of 'British property', Hitler evidently reckoned on isolating the Soviet Union in the world arena and thus dealing it an insidious blow. But he miscalculated.

Diplomatic Receptions

The gala reception which the German government customarily held for the diplomatic corps on New Year's Day was cancelled 'because of the war'. In its place, diplomats accredited in Berlin went and signed a special book on January 1st at the Reich Chancellery, where they were welcomed on behalf of the Reich Chancellor by the dry, elongated, lath-like Hans Lammers, head of the Chancellery.

However, there were no fewer embassy parties in Berlin – in fact, there were rather more. Diplomats seized every opportunity of meeting with their colleagues to exchange information, rumours and forecasts. And there were incredible numbers of rumours floating about Berlin during the first months of 1941. Most of them were speculations on the future course of the war. Who would be the next victim of German aggression? When would the invasion of England start? Would the United States enter the war soon? Where would Japan move? Would the neutrality of Sweden and Turkey be violated? Would the Germans capture the oil-producing areas of the Middle East? ...

At big receptions any new rumour would fly around the room with lightning speed, although it was, of course, passed on 'in strict confidence'. These receptions were invariably crowded and noisy, and it was impossible to cross the room without pushing and sometimes even elbowing one's way through the guests. One might make the acquaintance of prominent industrialists, high-ranking members of the Nazi hierarchy, or such screen celebrities of the day as Olga Chekhova, Pola Negri and Willi Forst. But conversations with these people were likely to be strictly 'social'. Much more interesting were the meetings in a more intimate circle, where the participants usually tried to pump the latest sensation out of each other, although at times such 'sensations' were two a penny.

The Turkish ambassador Gerede, in particular, loved to spread all kinds of 'news'. However, he never insisted on the authenticity of his information, and usually added, 'I can't guarantee that it's true, but anything's possible, and so I decided to inform you confidentially ... '

Gerede, a tall, foppish man, with wide black brows and a massive nose, always treated his guests to fragrant Turkish coffee, so thick that the spoon would almost stand upright in the cup, Turkish delight and the celebrated Izmir liqueur. Gerede was amazingly loquacious, and a conversation developed more often than not into a monologue by him. A map of the Middle East hung in his study, and his pet subject was to analyse the various possible German moves to capture the oil regions of Iraq and Saudi Arabia.

'Turkey', Gerede's argument would begin, 'has stated more than once that she will not allow the Germans to cross her territory. If Germany starts anything like that, we shall resist. And they know it ... '

'Do you mean they have already approached you with a proposal along those lines?'

'Good heavens, no! I didn't say that. It's just that they know we won't let them in. But they desperately need fuel for their tanks, their aircraft and their submarines. Consequently they will have to land parachute troops to capture Mosul. And to do so they need bases—Greece, the Aegean Islands, Egypt. If the Germans land in Iraq, Turkey will be pressed from two sides. Then things will be difficult for us, very difficult ... '

'Are you implying that in a situation like that Turkey would make concessions to Berlin?'

'No, I wasn't saying that. We don't want to quarrel with anybody. The English are our friends, the Germans are our friends. The English are saying that to capture Iraq the Germans are prepared to insist on the Russians agreeing to allow them to pass through the Caucasus. That is nonsense. You would not allow any such thing. And they will do nothing. You have a non-aggression pact with Hitler, and I know from trustworthy sources that he firmly intends to observe the pact. That is obvious. And there is no point in the Germans attacking us, either. Believe me—they'll concentrate on Egypt, now, help Mussolini to seize Greece and then land troops in Iraq. Those are their plans!'

As he developed his idea, Gerede would go over to the map and try to convince his interlocutor that a landing in Mosul was Hitler's most probable next move. Bidding his guests farewell, he would say,

'If you hear anything about Germany's plans for the Middle East, tell me. It's very important ... '

But Ambassador Gerede was not such a simpleton as he seemed at first glance, and he was close to the Nazi leadership. It is even possible that by prearrangement with the Wilhelmstrasse he was playing a role in Hitler's misinformation campaign: by discussing impending operations in the Middle East, he distracted attention from Berlin's real aims ...

One day, at the end of April 1941, I was invited to a cocktail party by Patterson, the First Secretary of the U.S. Embassy in Berlin. He was said to be wealthy; he rented a luxury three-storey house in Charlottenburg, and could invite two or three dozen people to an informal dinner or organize a cocktail party for three hundred guests.

Since Patterson lived some distance away and his guests usually left late, I borrowed from the embassy garage an Emka — a small car then being produced by the Gorky Motor Works. The streets of Berlin were always pitch dark in the blackout, but there was a moon that night, and it was easy to drive along the deserted streets. There was already a string of cars parked outside Patterson's house.

The drawing-room was crowded, and it was impossible to see the guests clearly at first — the room was lit solely by a log fire, which crackled merrily in the fireplace, and a few dim candle-shaped electric sconces on the opposite wall. When my eyes had grown accustomed to the semi-darkness, I noticed that the guests had already separated into groups and were talking animatedly, wineglasses and tumblers in their hands.

Patterson greeted me and said, 'There's someone here I'd like to introduce you to.' Taking my arm he led me to the fireside. Surrounded by a group of American diplomats whom I already knew, there stood a tall, lean officer in the uniform of a major of the German Air Force, holding a glass of whisky. I was struck by his very sunburned face.

'Allow me to introduce you,' said Patterson, presenting me to the major. 'The major is just home on leave from Africa ... '

The major gave the impression of being an experienced fighter pilot. He had a fund of stories, which he enjoyed telling, about operations in Western Europe and North Africa. He did not hide the fact that contrary to the triumphant accounts put out by the Wehrmacht High Command, the Germans were having a hard time in the African theatre of war. It seemed to me slightly odd that this Nazi officer was so much at home in the house of an American diplomat. Perhaps it was because he had known Patterson for a long time; certain of his remarks suggested that they had met before the war in the United States.

At the end of the evening the German major and I were alone for a time, standing apart from the other guests. Puffing at his cigar and looking me straight in the eyes, he lowered his voice slightly and said, 'Patterson wants me to tell you something. The fact is, I'm not here on leave. My squadron was recalled from North Africa, and yesterday we received orders to transfer to Eastern Europe, to the Lodz area. Perhaps there's nothing in it, but I do know that many other units have recently been transferred to areas near your frontiers. I have no idea what this might mean, but personally I would not like anything to happen between my country and yours. Naturally I am telling you this in confidence.'

For an instant I was confused. It was an unheard-of situation: an officer of Hitler's Wehrmacht was passing on to a Soviet diplomat information which, if genuine, was highly secret. But at that time our greatest fear was of giving any kind of provocation. To be on the safe side I decided to make a discreet and stereotyped reply:

'Thank you for your information, Herr Major. It is extremely interesting. But I believe that Germany will observe the non-aggression pact. Our country, too, is interested in keeping the peace between us. Let us hope for the best ... '

'It should be easy enough for you to check up on what I've told you ... ' said the major. Shortly afterwards we said goodbye.

Like everything else of interest, this conversation was included in the ambassador's next dispatch.

Alarm Signals

For several months we officials of the Soviet Embassy in Berlin witnessed Germany's preparations for military operations in the East. That these preparations were under way was clear from information which reached our embassy from a variety of sources.

First and foremost, it came to us from our friends within Germany itself. Within the Nazi Reich, and even in Berlin, there were anti-fascist groups working deep underground – the so-called 'Rote Kapelle', the Rabi group, and others. In the face of unimaginable difficulties, and sometimes at risk of their lives, the German anti-fascists found ways of warning the Soviet Union of the danger hanging over her. They passed on information about the threatening situation along the frontiers of the Soviet Union, and about Nazi Germany's preparations for an attack on our country.

In mid-February a German printer appeared at our consulate in Berlin, bringing with him a copy of a Russian-German phrasebook that was being published in a huge edition. The contents of the phrasebook left its purpose in no doubt. For instance, in Russian, but transliterated into Roman type, were such phrases as 'Where is the chairman of the collective farm?', 'Are you a communist?', 'What is the name of the district committee secretary?', 'Hands up or I'll shoot!' 'Give yourself up' and so on. We at once sent the phrasebook to Moscow …

In the middle of May Berlin was shaken by the news of the unexpected flight to England of Rudolf Hess, Hitler's deputy as leader of the Nazi party. Piloting a Messerschmitt–110 plane, Hess had taken off from Augsburg in southern Germany on May 10th and headed for the Scottish estate of the Duke of Hamilton, whom he knew personally. But Hess miscalculated his fuel supply, and, only fourteen kilometres short of his target he was forced to bale out by parachute in the region of Eaglesham, where the local people handed him over to the authorities.

For a few days the British government maintained silence about this event. Berlin, too, was silent. But when the British authorities issued a statement about Hess's landing, the German government realized that his secret mission had failed. It was then decided at Hitler's Berghof headquarters to present Hess's action as a sign of mental derangement. In an official communiqué on the Hess affair it was stated: 'Party member Hess was evidently obsessed with the idea that through his personal action he could bring about an understanding between England and Germany.' In clearly inspired commentaries, the German press went even further, alleging that the Nazi leader was 'a deranged idealist, suffering from hallucinations traceable to injuries received in the First World War.' The commentators obviously failed to observe the devastating irony that this 'insane' individual had until recently been second man to Hitler in the Nazi Party.

Hitler fully realized the moral damage Hess's abortive mission had done to himself and his regime. In order to cover up the traces he gave orders that members of Hess's retinue should be arrested, had Hess himself stripped of all his offices and instructed that he should be shot if he returned to Germany. Then he appointed Martin Bormann as his deputy in the party leadership.

There is no doubt, though, that the Nazis had great hopes of Hess. German imperialism was counting on his successfully persuading Germany's adversaries, above all England, to join an anti-Soviet campaign. The Hitlerites were trying to transform their planned attack on the Soviet Union into a 'crusade' against the 'Bolshevik peril'.

Using his connections with leading pro-Munich personalities in England, Hess had made advance arrangements for his visit to England. Initially it was to have taken place in December 1940, but the visit was postponed until after the completion of Hitler's territorial expansion into south-east Europe. When at the end of May 1941 Hess finally flew into England and commenced his talks with high-ranking British spokesmen, both the internal political situation and the whole international climate prevented the Munichites from implementing their plan to co-operate with the Nazis.

The more far-sighted politicians in England and the U.S.A. realized that Hitler only wanted to make a temporary peace so that he could attack them again later, at some time more convenient to the Nazis. By then it was clear to the English ruling class that German imperialism, in its aspiration to rule the entire world, represented a threat to their position and interests, and so they were sceptical of negotiating with Germany, especially as in the past such political experiments had invariably turned to their disadvantage.

After the war Hess was to face the Nuremberg tribunal as one of the chief Nazi criminals. But he escaped the gallows—medical opinion declared him psychologically abnormal—and was sentenced to life imprisonment.

But in May 1941 we did not, of course, know everything that lay behind Hess's flight to England, although it was clearly an attempt to reach an agreement with London against the Soviet Union. It is significant that in those same days in May the tables of the anteroom in the German Ministry of Foreign Affairs were ostentatiously scattered with pre-war journals and brochures glorifying Anglo-German friendship and its importance for the destiny of Europe and the whole world. (At one time, during the Munich period, the Nazis had cherished this idea.) Naturally, all the diplomats who came to the Wilhelmstrasse on business noticed these brochures at once and regarded them as some sort of 'gesture' towards England. This kind of thing caused much gossip, conjecture and speculation.

During this time our military attaché General Tupikov and our naval attaché Admiral Vorontsov had acquired a great deal of important information. According to their intelligence, trains loaded with troops and military equipment had been making their way eastward since the beginning of February 1941. In March and April, tanks, artillery and ammunition followed, by now in a continuous stream, and towards the end of May all reports had it that the build-up area was completely saturated with manpower and equipment.

Meantime the Nazis were openly and brazenly prodding the Soviet defences along the frontiers of the Soviet Union. The end of May and the first few days of June saw a marked increase in the number of provocative actions by the Germans. The embassy received almost daily instructions from Moscow to deliver a protest at yet another violation of the Soviet frontier zone. Not only German frontier guards, but soldiers of the Wehrmacht, too, were systematically intruding into Soviet territory and opening fire on our frontier guards, even causing some loss of life. Aeroplanes bearing the swastika insolently flew deep into Soviet territory. All this was reported to the German Ministry of Foreign Affairs, with precise details of place and time; on receiving our protests, the Wilhelmstrasse would first promise to carry out an inquiry, and then assert that they had been 'unable to confirm this information'.

Finally, another curious fact. Not far from the embassy, on the Unter den Linden, was the luxurious photographic studio of Hoffmann, Hitler's 'court' photographer. It was here that Eva Braun, who later became the Führer's mistress, at one time worked as a model. Since the beginning of the war a large map usually hung in one of the windows of Hoffmann's studio above his official portrait of Hitler. It was his custom to display a map of the part of Europe where military operations were being conducted or projected. In the early spring of 1940 the map was of Holland, Belgium, Denmark and Norway, and for a considerable time after that a map of France hung in the window. By April 1941 passers-by were stopping to gaze at a map of Jugoslavia and Greece. Then suddenly, at the end of May, there appeared a large map of Eastern Europe. It included the Baltic States, Byelorussia and the Ukraine—the territory of the Soviet Union from the Barents Sea to the Black Sea. Hoffmann was unashamedly indicating the location of the next theatre of war, saying, in effect, 'Now it is the turn of the Soviet Union!' ...

From March onwards, persistent rumours of Hitler's impending attack on the Soviet Union circulated in Berlin. The dates mentioned were many and various—evidently in order to confuse us: April 6th, April 20th, May 18th and, finally, the correct date, June 22nd; all were Sundays. All these alarm signals were reported regularly by the embassy to Moscow. At the beginning of May a group of our diplomats was specially appointed to study, evaluate and draw conclusions from the information at the disposal of the embassy concerning Hitler's preparations for war on the Eastern front.

Towards the end of May, a detailed report was drawn up, including, among other things, relevant extracts from *Mein Kampf*. The basic conclusions of the report were that Germany had already completed her practical preparations for an attack on the Soviet Union, and that the scale of these preparations left no doubt that the meaning of this concentration of troops and equipment was—war. It was unlikely that the intention was merely to exert political pressure on our country. Therefore a German attack on the Soviet Union was to be expected at any moment.

During those weeks we lived in a curiously divided state of mind: we were faced with information that pointed unequivocally to the impending outbreak of war; and yet, nothing out of the ordinary seemed to be happening. It was resolved not to send home the wives and children of Soviet employees in Germany; indeed, new officials were arriving almost daily from the Soviet Union with large families and even with wives in the last stages of pregnancy. Deliveries of Soviet goods to Germany continued uninterrupted, despite the fact

that the Germans had virtually ceased to honour their trade obligations. On June 14th (a week before Nazi Germany's attack on the
Soviet Union!) the Soviet press published this TASS communique:

> According to information at the disposal of the U.S.S.R.,
> Germany is observing the conditions of the Soviet-German
> non-aggression pact as strictly as the Soviet Union. In view of
> this, rumours of Germany's intention to violate the pact and
> launch an attack against the Soviet Union are, in the opinion of
> Soviet circles, completely without foundation ... '

By means of this statement, which had been handed the previous
evening to Schulenburg, the German ambassador in Moscow,
Stalin hoped to test the intentions of the German government and
exert some influence upon it. He was evidently calculating to avert
Hitler's attack on the U.S.S.R. at the eleventh hour. But Berlin's
response to the TASS statement of June 14th was an ominous silence;
not a single German newspaper so much as mentioned it.

On June 21st, when Hitler's attack on the U.S.S.R. was only a
few hours away, the embassy received a directive to deliver another
statement to the German government, containing proposals for a
discussion of Soviet-German relations. The Soviet government was
indicating to the German government that it knew of the German
troop concentrations on the Soviet border, and that any military
adventure might have dangerous consequences. But the contents
of this dispatch also testified to something else: that Moscow still
hoped to be able to avert the conflict by holding talks.

The Night of June 22nd

Saturday June 21st was a fine day in Berlin. From early morning it
promised to be hot, and in the afternoon many people set out on
excursions from the city – to the Potsdam parks, or to the lakes of
Wannsee or Nikolassee where the bathing season was in full swing.
Only a small group of diplomats was obliged to remain in the city.
That morning a telegram had arrived from Moscow: the embassy
was to deliver immediately to the German government the statement referred to above.

I was entrusted with the task of contacting the Wilhelmstrasse, where the Ministry of Foreign Affairs occupied an imposing palace dating from the Bismarck era, and with arranging a meeting between embassy spokesmen and Ribbentrop. The official on duty in the ministry secretariat answered that Ribbentrop was away, and my call to State Secretary Baron von Weizsäcker, the minister's deputy, yielded no results either. Hour after hour went by, and I could not contact any responsible officials. Towards midday I eventually got through to Wehrmann, director of the ministry's political department, but he merely confirmed that neither Ribbentrop nor Weizsäcker were in the ministry.

'I believe the Führer is holding an important meeting. That is where everyone seems to be at the moment,' Wehrmann explained. 'If your business is urgent, tell me, and I will try to contact my superiors ... '

I replied that that was impossible, since I had been instructed by my embassy to deliver the statement to the minister in person, and I requested Wehrmann to inform Ribbentrop of this ...

Moscow telephoned us repeatedly during the day, urging us to carry out our instructions. But no matter how often we called the Ministry of Foreign Affairs, the reply was the same: Ribbentrop was not there, and it was not known when he would return. He was out of reach, and it was apparently impossible even to inform him of our request.

Towards seven o'clock everyone went home. I, however, was required to stay on in the embassy and try to arrange the meeting with Ribbentrop. Setting my clock on the table beside me, I decided pedantically to ring the Wilhelmstrasse at precise half-hour intervals.

Through the open window which looked out on to the Unter den Linden I could see Berliners taking their usual Saturday stroll down the middle of the boulevard, which was fringed with young lime trees: there were girls and women in brightly-coloured dresses, and men, for the most part elderly, in their dark, old-fashioned suits. At the embassy gates a policeman in his ugly 'Schutzmann' helmet was leaning against the wall and dozing ...

One of my regular telephone calls to the Ministry of Foreign Affairs received from the official who lifted the receiver his polite stock answer: 'I still have not succeeded in contacting the Herr Reich Minister. But I have noted your request and I am taking steps ... '

To my remark that I would have to continue disturbing him since I wished to discuss an urgent matter, the man replied affably that it was absolutely no trouble to him as he would be on duty in the ministry until morning. Again and again I rang the Wilhelmstrasse, but to no avail ...

Suddenly, at three o'clock in the morning (five o'clock Moscow time)—it was by then Sunday June 22nd—the telephone rang. An unfamiliar, barking voice informed me that Reich Minister Joachim von Ribbentrop was expecting the Soviet spokesmen in his study at the Ministry of Foreign Affairs on the Wilhelmstrasse. The mere tone of this unfamiliar voice, speaking in ultra-officialese, aroused feelings of a sinister foreboding. However, I phrased my reply as if we were referring to the Soviet embassy's request for a meeting with the minister.

'I know nothing about your request,' I heard him say. 'I have merely been instructed to inform you that Reich Minister Ribbentrop requests the Soviet spokesmen to present themselves immediately.'

I said that we would need some time to notify the ambassador and prepare a car.

To this he replied, 'The Reich Minister's personal car is already waiting outside the Soviet embassy. The Minister hopes that the Soviet spokesmen will come without delay ... '

Driving along the Wilhelmstrasse, we could see while still at a distance a crowd of people outside the Ministry of Foreign Affairs. Although dawn had already broken, the entrance, with its wrought-iron porch, was brightly illuminated by spotlights. Reporters, film cameramen and journalists were milling around. An official jumped out of the car ahead of us and flung open the door. We got out, dazzled by the glare of the floodlights and magnesium flash-bulbs. Reporters and cameramen dogged our heels and ran ahead, clicking their shutters, as we ascended the thickly carpeted staircase to the second floor. A long corridor led to the minister's apartments. All along it uniformed men stood to attention. When we appeared, they clicked their heels noisily and threw their arms up. At last we turned off to the left and entered the minister's vast office. In one corner stood a writing-desk, and in the opposite corner there was a round table with an unwieldy lamp topped by a tall shade. Around the table several armchairs stood in disarray.

Ribbentrop, wearing his ordinary greyish-green ministerial uniform was sitting at his writing-desk. Glancing about us, we noticed a group of officials standing to the right of the door. When we crossed the room towards Ribbentrop these people did not move; in fact they stayed there throughout our interview, though they were apparently unable to hear what Ribbentrop was saying as they were a considerable distance away.

When we approached his desk, Ribbentrop rose, nodded silently, shook hands and invited us to follow him to the round table in the opposite corner. His face was bluish-red and puffy; his eyes were dull, their lids inflamed. He walked in front of us, his head lowered, swaying slightly. The thought flashed through my mind, is he drunk?

When we had taken our seats at the round table and Ribbentrop had begun to speak, my guess was confirmed: he was obviously quite far gone.

We never did deliver the statement we had brought with us. Raising his voice, Ribbentrop said that he wanted to talk about an entirely different matter now, and, stumbling over almost every word, he embarked upon a somewhat muddled explanation. The German government allegedly had information about a heavy concentration of Soviet troops along the German border. Ribbentrop feigned total ignorance of the fact that for the past few weeks the Soviet embassy had repeatedly drawn the German government's attention to flagrant violations of the Soviet frontier zone by German soldiers and aircraft. He declared that Soviet servicemen had been violating the German border and intruding into German territory, although in reality there had been no such incidents. Ribbentrop explained that he was summarizing the contents of a memorandum by Hitler, which he then presented to us. He went on to say that at this juncture, when Germany was waging a life-and-death war against the English, the German government regarded this situation as a threat. The government and the Führer himself took it as an indication that the Soviet Union intended to stab the German people in the back. The Führer could not tolerate this threat and had resolved to take measures to safeguard the life and security of the German nation. The Führer's decision was final. An hour ago, German troops had crossed the Soviet frontier.

Ribbentrop then launched into assurances that Germany's action was in no sense an act of aggression, but merely a defensive measure.

He rose to his full height, and stood at attention in an attempt to give himself an air of solemnity; but his voice obviously lacked firmness and confidence as he uttered his final phrase: 'The Führer has instructed me to make an official statement concerning this defensive measure ... '

We rose too. The conversation was over. Now we knew that shells were already exploding along our frontiers. The criminal attack had already begun by the time war was officially declared. It was too late to change anything. Before leaving, the Soviet ambassador said, 'This is an outrageous, utterly unprovoked act of aggression. You will regret that you ever attacked the Soviet Union. You will pay dearly for this ... '

We marched to the door. Then something unexpected happened. Ribbentrop came scurrying after us and assured us in a whispered gabble that he personally had been against the Führer's decision. He had even, so he said, tried to dissuade Hitler from attacking the Soviet Union; he, Ribbentrop, thought it madness. But he could do nothing. Hitler had taken his decision and refused to listen to anyone ...

'Tell them in Moscow that I was against the attack,' were Ribbentrop's last words when we were already in the corridor.

Once more the shutters clicked and the movie cameras whirred. Outside we were met by a crowd of reporters, and the sun was shining brightly. We went over to the black limousine that was still waiting for us at the porch.

On the way back to the embassy we were silent. But our thoughts kept returning involuntarily to the scene that had just been enacted in the Nazi Minister's office. Why had he been so nervous, that arrant fascist? After all, like all the rest of Hitler's ringleaders, he was a fierce enemy of communism, and his attitude to our country and to the Soviet people was one of pathological hatred. What had become of his brazen self-assurance? Of course, his assertion that he had tried to dissuade Hitler from attacking the Soviet Union was a lie. But what could have been the motive for his final words? At that time we had no means of answering that question. But now, when I recall the whole incident, I begin to think that perhaps at that fateful moment when he announced officially the decision which, in the final analysis, led to the downfall of Hitler's Reich, Ribbentrop experienced a dismal foreboding of some sort ... And might this not explain why he had taken a drop too much that night?

As we drove up to the embassy we noticed that the building had been placed under reinforced guard. Instead of the single police-man who usually stood at the gates, a whole cordon of SS men now lined the pavement.

The embassy staff was waiting for us impatiently. No one had known exactly why Ribbentrop had summoned us, but one sign had put everyone on the alert: as soon as we had left for the Wil-helmstrasse, the embassy's communication with the outside world had been cut off—not one of the telephones was working.

At six o'clock that morning we switched on the radio to hear what Moscow would say. But all our stations began by broadcasting gymnastic exercises, then 'Pioneers' Dawn', and then at last the latest news, which began as usual with farming items and reports about the achievements of champions of labour. Alarming thoughts flickered through our minds—was it possible that no one in Moscow knew that war had already started several hours earlier? Had the action on the frontier been classed as border clashes, even though they were on a larger scale than the clashes in the last few weeks? ...

Since our telephone link was not yet restored, and we could not count on being able to talk to Moscow, we decided to telegraph a report of our conversation with Ribbentrop. An employee of the consulate was instructed to take the dispatch to the main post office in an embassy car with a diplomatic number-plate. It was our big ZIS-101, which was ordinarily used for journeys to official receptions. He drove out of the gates and away, but fifteen minutes later returned alone and on foot. He owed his safe return solely to the fact that he had been carrying his diplomatic passport. They had been halted by a patrol of some kind, and chauffeur and car had been put under arrest.

Besides ZIS and Emka cars, the embassy garage also had a small yellow Opel-Olympia. It was decided to use this car to get to the post office and dispatch a telegram without attracting attention. This little operation had been worked out earlier. I took the wheel, the gates flew open and the nimble little Opel shot out into the street at full speed. I glanced around quickly and breathed a sigh of relief: there were no cars outside the embassy building, and the SS guards, who were on foot, watched in bewilderment as I dis-appeared.

I did not manage to send off the telegram at once. In the main Berlin post office all the counter-clerks were clustered round loudspeakers, through which I could hear Goebbels shouting hysterically. He was saying that the Bolsheviks had been prepared to stab the Germans in the back, and the Führer, by his decision to send his troops into the Soviet Union, had saved the German nation.

I called one of the clerks and gave him the text of the telegram. When he saw the address he exclaimed, 'To Moscow? Are you mad? Haven't you heard what's happening? ... '

I refused to discuss it, and asked him to accept the telegram and write me a receipt. Later, back in Moscow, we discovered that the telegram was never delivered. But we did all we could ...

Returning from Friedrichstrasse to the Unter den Linden I saw four camouflage-painted armoured cars standing outside the embassy. Obviously the SS men had learned a lesson from their negligence ...

In a second-floor room a few people were still grouped around the radio receiver. But Moscow radio still made absolutely no mention of what had occurred. I went downstairs, and from my office window I saw small boys running along the pavement waving special editions of the newspapers. I went out of the gates, stopped one of them and bought several papers. They already carried the first photographs from the front: with heavy hearts we gazed at our own Soviet soldiers, wounded, killed ... A communiqué from the German command stated that German planes had bombed Mogilev, Lvov, Rovno, Grodno and other towns during the night. It was clear that Nazi propaganda was trying to create the impression that this war was going to be a walk-over ...

Again and again we returned to the radio set. It was blaring out folk music and marches. Not until twelve noon Moscow time did we hear a Soviet government announcement:

'Today, at four a.m., without presenting any demands to the Soviet Union, without a declaration of war, German troops attacked our country ... Our cause is just. The enemy will be crushed. Victory will be ours.'

... 'Victory will be ours' ... 'Our cause is just' ... These words, coming from our distant homeland, reached us in the very lair of the enemy.

Black Snow: A Theatrical Novel *by* Mikhail Bulgakov

Novy Mir, 1965/VIII

Translated by Michael Glenny

Mikhail Bulgakov is one of the classic instances of a major Soviet writer whose work was suppressed under Stalin, and who re-emerged (in Bulgakov's case posthumously) in the pages of *Novy Mir* during the 'sixties. *Black Snow*, the novel from which this extract is taken, was written between 1936 and 1939. It is unfinished, and is one of his last works; Bulgakov fell ill in 1939 and died in March 1940 of an extremely painful kidney complaint which in its final stages induced total blindness lasting for six months. Although he was spared physical destruction during Stalin's terror, by 1936 he had been effectively silenced as a writer: none of Bulgakov's early novels and stories had been printed since the 'twenties; his major prose works had not been published at all; and his plays ceased to be staged after February 1936.

Novy Mir's bold publication of *Black Snow* began the re-discovery of Bulgakov which is still in progress. His long-suppressed plays were reissued shortly afterwards, some of his short stories, his biography of Molière and an early novel were published for the first time or republished after a forty-year time-lag. But the finest of all Bulgakov's works to appear (in the pages of another literary journal, *Moskva*, in 1966–7) was his masterpiece, the novel *The Master and Margarita*, in which he performed the extraordinary feat of combining supernatural fantasy and knockabout farce with a profound statement of moral conviction expressed in a reinterpretation of the trial and crucifixion of Christ.

The son of a professor at Kiev Theological Academy, Bulgakov was born in 1891. He studied medicine, qualified and practised for a while, but in 1919 he abandoned doctoring and set out to be a professional writer. After five years of stultifying hack-work in the Soviet equivalent of Grub Street, the breakthrough came in 1924 when a literary magazine called *Rossiya* ('Russia') published the first two instalments of his novel *The White Guard*, about Kiev in the Civil War. The magazine closed down before the last instalment could be printed, but the first two parts were sufficient to catch the sharp eye of P. A. Markov, then literary editor of the Moscow Art Theatre; the following year, dramatized, much altered, and re-titled *The Days of the Turbins*, it was given its successful premiere at that theatre. Since then, apart from intermittent bans, Bulgakov's first play has remained one of the classics of the Soviet stage reper-toire. Altogether Bulgakov wrote fourteen plays, of which eleven have been performed, but nothing else of his has ever surpassed *The Days of the Turbins* in the affections of Soviet audiences.

Black Snow is the story, in transparent fictional guise, of the author's tribulations in writing *The White Guard* and re-casting it as a play. It is a work of ironic, often bitter satire which spares few of the characters and certainly not the author himself, who is given the name of 'Sergei Leontievich Maxudov'. But the target of the full force of Bulgakov's acid wit is none other than the great sacred cow of the theatre himself—Konstantin Stanislavsky. In the story Bulgakov renames him 'Ivan Vasilievich'—a wicked and quite intentional use of the name and patronymic of Ivan the Terrible!

Far from being captivated by Stanislavsky's legendary charm and genius, Bulgakov depicts him as vain, tyrannical and devious. Although prepared to acknowledge his talent as an actor, he re-morselessly tears every other element of Stanislavsky's reputation to shreds. His charm is shown up as a mere tool with which to manipulate people, his hypochondria, and neurotic affectations are derided, his dedication to the theatre unmasked as pure ego-mania, his fostering of talent as sheer favouritism; even his famous 'Method' has ossified into a set of idiosyncratic mannerisms. The harmony which outwardly characterized the Moscow Art Theatre company is debunked as a sham, concealing a network of feuds of Byzantine complexity.

The following extract, Chapter 12 of *Black Snow*, which des-cribes 'Maxudov's' first meeting with 'Ivan Vasilievich', when he reads him the script of his play, has been chosen as being one of the wittiest and most exquisite pieces of literary hatchet-work in the Russian language. Compared to the earnest bombast and slabs of congealed ideology which pass for literature in the depressing majority of most Soviet publications, the cool, ironic venom with which Bulgakov knocks this establishment figure off his pedestal is immeasurably refreshing.

Sivtsev Vrazhek

I did not even notice that Toropetzkaya and I had finished transcribing the script. Nor had I time to reflect on what might happen next, before fate itself prompted the next move.

Klyukvin brought me a letter.

My dear Leontii Sergeyevich ... [*Why in heaven's name does he think I'm called Leontii Sergeyevich? Probably because it's easier to pronounce than Sergei Leontievich. Anyhow, who cares.*]

... You must read your play to Ivan Vasilievich. Go to Sivtsev Vrazhek on Monday the 13th at twelve noon.

Yours sincerely,

THOMAS STRIZH.

I was thrilled, as I realized the exceptional importance of this letter. I decided to wear a starched collar, a light-blue tie and a grey suit. It was not difficult to decide on the latter, as the grey one was the only decent suit I possessed. I would behave politely but with dignity and — God forbid — without a hint of servility. The 13th, as I well remember, was the following day, and in the morning I saw Bombardov at the theatre. His advice struck me as curious in the extreme.

'As you pass a big grey house,' said Bombardov, 'you turn left into a little cul-de-sac. From there you'll find it easily. Wrought-iron gates and a colonnade along the front of the house. There's no entrance from the street, so you must turn the corner and go in through the courtyard. There you'll see a man in a sheepskin coat who will ask you, "What do you want?" and you must reply with a single word: "Appointment".'

'Is that the password?' I asked. 'What if the man's not there?'

'He'll be there,' said Bombardov and went on coldly, 'In the corner, opposite the man in the sheepskin coat you'll see a jacked-up motor-car without any wheels, beside it a bucket and a man washing the car.'

'Have you been there today?' I asked in amazement.

'I was there a month ago.'

'Then how do you know that there'll be a man washing a car?'

'Because he takes the wheels off and washes it every day.'

'But doesn't Ivan Vasilievich drive in it sometimes?'

'He never drives in it.'

'Why not?'

'Where would he go?'

'Well, to the theatre, for instance?'

'Ivan Vasilievich drives to the theatre twice a year for dress rehearsals, and then they hire Drykin's coach.'

'How extraordinary! Why hire a coach when he's got a car?'

'And if the chauffeur dies of a heart attack at the wheel and the car drives into a shop window, what happens then, might I ask?'

'But supposing the horse bolts?'

'Drykin's horse never bolts. It never goes faster than a walk. Opposite the man with the bucket there's a door. You will go in and walk up a wooden staircase. Then there's another door. Go in. There you'll see a black bust of Ostrovsky. Opposite it are some little white columns and a black, black stove. Squatting beside it and stoking it will be a man in felt boots.'

I burst into laughter.

'Are you quite sure that he'll be there, and actually squatting?'

'Absolutely,' replied Bombardov dryly, with a straight face.

'It will be interesting to see if you're right!'

'Try it and see. He will ask you anxiously, "Where are you going?" and you will reply ... '

'Appointment?'

'Mm'hm. Then he'll say to you, "Take off your coat here, please." You'll find yourself in the hall, and a nurse will meet you and ask, "What have you come for?" and you will reply ... '

I nodded.

'First of all Ivan Vasilievich will ask you who your father was. What was he?'

'Deputy-governor of a province.'

Bombardov frowned.

'Er ... no, that won't really do. No, no. Say that he worked in a bank.'

'I don't like that at all. Why should I start telling lies the moment I see him?'

'Because it might upset him, and ... '

I could only blink.

' ... and it can't matter to you to say he worked in a bank, or something like that ... Then he'll ask what you think of homoeopathy. And you'll say that you took a homoeopathic remedy for stomach trouble last year and it did you a lot of good.'

Just then a bell rang and Bombardov had to hurry off to a rehearsal, so he gave me the rest of his instructions very briefly.

'You don't know Misha Panin, you were born in Moscow,' said Bombardov rapidly, 'and if he asks you about Thomas Strizh you must say you don't like him. Whatever he says about your play, don't object. Don't read that bit in Act III where there's a shot ... '

'How can I avoid reading it when the character shoots himself?'

The bell rang again. Bombardov ran off into the semi-darkness, his muffled cry reaching me from the distance:

'Don't read about the shot! And you haven't got a cold!'

Completely staggered by Bombardov's puzzling instructions I turned up at the cul-de-sac in Sivtsev Vrazhek a minute before noon.

There was no man in a sheepskin coat in the courtyard, but in his place stood a peasant woman in a headscarf. She asked:

'What do you want?' and stared suspiciously at me. The word 'appointment' satisfied her completely, and I turned the corner. On the precise spot described by Bombardov stood a coffee-coloured motor-car, but with its wheels on. A man was wiping down the bodywork with a rag. Beside the car was a bucket and a bottle of something.

Following Bombardov's directions I found my way unerringly and reached the bust of Ostrovsky. 'Oho,' I thought, remembering Bombardov: although some birch logs were burning merrily in the stove, there was no sign of anyone squatting beside it; but before I had time to laugh an old, dark, varnished oak door opened and through it came a little old man carrying a shovel and wearing patched felt boots. Catching sight of me he looked startled and blinked.

'What do you want, citizen?' he asked.

'Appointment,' I replied, revelling in the power of the magic word.

The little old man brightened and waved his shovel towards the

other door, where an old-fashioned lamp hung from the ceiling. I
took off my coat, stuck my script under my arm and knocked on the
door. At once there came the sound of a chain-bolt being withdrawn, then a key was turned in the lock and a woman in nurse's
uniform looked out.

'What do you want?' she inquired.

'Appointment,' I replied.

The woman moved aside, ushered me in and gave me a searching
stare.

'Is it cold outside?' she asked.

'No, the weather's fine, it's an Indian summer,' I answered.

'You haven't got a cold, have you?' asked the woman.

I gave a start, remembered Bombardov and said:

'No, I haven't.'

'Knock on that door over there and go in,' said the woman
sternly, and vanished.

Before knocking on the dark, metal-panelled door I glanced
round. A white stove; several enormous cupboards. There was a
smell of mint and some other agreeable herb. Utter silence reigned,
to be suddenly broken by the hoarse note of a clock. It struck
twelve times and then from behind a cupboard a cuckoo cuckooed
alarmingly.

I knocked at the door, then gripped the enormous, heavy ring
and the door opened into a large bright room.

I was so excited that I noticed almost nothing except the divan
on which Ivan Vasilievich was sitting. He was exactly like his
portrait, though slightly fresher and younger-looking. His black
moustache, only faintly tinged with grey, was beautifully shaped.
A lorgnette hung by a gold chain on his chest. Ivan Vasilievich
surprised me by his captivating smile.

'Delighted,' he said, with the faintest trace of a throaty pronunciation, 'do sit down.'

I sat down in an armchair.

'What is your name and patronymic?' asked Ivan Vasilievich
with a friendly look.

'Sergei Leontievich.'

'How nice! Well now, and how are you, Sergei Pafnutyerich?'
As he gazed at me with a charmingly solicitous expression, Ivan
Vasilievich drummed his fingers on the table; on it were the stub

of a pencil and a glass of water covered, for some reason, with a sheet of paper.

'I'm very well indeed, thank you.'

'You haven't got a cold?'

'No.'

Ivan Vasilievich gave a sort of groan and asked:

'And how is your dear father?'

'My father is dead.'

'How terrible,' replied Ivan Vasilievich, 'and whom did he see? Who looked after him?'

'I can't remember exactly, but it was a professor, I think ... Professor Yankovsky.'

'Useless,' rejoined Ivan Vasilievich. 'He should have gone to see Professor Pletushkov and all would have been well.'

I assumed an expression of regret that he had not consulted Pletushkov.

'Better still would have been ... h'm, h'm ... homoeopathic medicine,' Ivan Vasilievich went on. 'It is really extraordinary how much good homoeopathy can do ... ' Here he gave a passing glance at his glass, 'do you believe in homoeopathy?'

Bombardov—you're incredible, I thought, and began to say vaguely:

'Of course, on the one hand ... I personally ... although many people don't believe in it ... '

'They're wrong!' said Ivan Vasilievich. 'Fifteen drops—and all pain ceases.' He gave another one of his groans and went on, 'And what, Sergei Panphilych, was your dear father?'

'Sergei Leontievich,' I said gently.

'A thousand pardons!' exclaimed Ivan Vasilievich. 'And what was he?'

I'm not going to lie, I thought and said:

'He ended his civil service career as a deputy-governor.'

This news banished the smile from Ivan Vasilievich's face.

'I see, I see, I see,' he said in a worried tone, then was silent, drummed on the table and said, 'Very well, shall we begin?'

I opened my script, coughed, felt faint, coughed again and began reading.

I read the title, then the long list of the cast and started on the stage directions for Act I: 'Lights in the distance, a courtyard powdered with snow, the side door of a house. From it can be heard the strains of *Faust* being played on a piano ... ' \

Have you ever had to read a play alone with one other person? It is extremely difficult, I assure you. Now and again I glanced up at Ivan Vasilievich and wiped my forehead with a handkerchief. Ivan Vasilievich sat completely motionless, fixing me with an unwavering stare through his lorgnette. I was extremely upset by the fact that he never once smiled, even though there were quite a few funny lines in the first act. The actors had laughed a lot when they had heard it read; one had laughed till he cried. Ivan Vasilievich not only refrained from laughing but even stopped groaning. Every time I looked up at him I saw the same thing—the lorgnette trained firmly on me, and behind it those unblinking eyes. As a result I began to think that my funny lines weren't funny at all.

I reached the end of the first act and started on the second. As I listened in the total silence to the sound of my own monotonous voice it sounded like a deacon reading the litany for the dead.

I was seized with apathy and a desire to close the thick, bound typescript. I felt that Ivan Vasilievich was saying grimly to himself, Will this ever finish? My voice grew hoarse, and I occasionally cleared my throat with a cough. I read first in a tenor then in a deep bass; twice, my voice broke into an unexpected squeak, but none of this wrung so much as a smile from either of us.

A slight relief came with the sudden appearance of the woman in white. She entered without a sound and Ivan Vasilievich glanced rapidly at his watch. The woman handed Ivan Vasilievich a tumbler. He drank his medicine, chased it down with water from his glass, covered it with its lid and gave another look at his watch. The woman bowed to Ivan Vasilievich with a deep, old-fashioned Russian bow and marched haughtily out.

'Shall we go on?' said Ivan Vasilievich, and I started reading again. From far off came the cry of the cuckoo, then the telephone rang behind the screen.

'Excuse me,' said Ivan Vasilievich, 'a call from the institute on a matter of the greatest importance ... Yes,' his voice could be heard from behind the screen, 'yes ... h'm ... h'm ... it's the same gang at work. I order you to keep it all in the strictest secrecy. A reliable man will be here this evening and we will work out a plan ... '

Ivan Vasilievich returned and we reached the end of Scene v.

It was at the beginning of Scene vi that the most extraordinary event occurred. I heard a door slam somewhere, then the sound of loud and apparently sham weeping; a door, not the one by which I had entered but one which evidently led into the inner rooms, was flung open and into the room there flew, in a state of satanic terror, a fat tabby cat. It dashed past me towards a tulle curtain, gripped it with its claws and climbed up. The tulle couldn't bear its weight and immediately began to tear. Still tearing the curtain into strips, the cat climbed to the top, and from there it gazed round in frenzy. Ivan Vasilievich dropped his lorgnette as Ludmilla Silvestrovna Pryakhina appeared in the door. The mere sight of her was enough to make the cat climb even higher, but it was stopped by the ceiling. The animal fell from the rounded cornice and clung, numb with terror, to the curtain.

Pryakhina came in with eyes closed, pressing a fistful of damp, crumpled handkerchief to her forehead and holding in her other hand a second lace handkerchief which was dry and clean. Running to the middle of the room she dropped on to one knee, bowed her head and stretched her arm forward like a prisoner surrendering her sword to the victor.

'I shall not move from this spot,' cried Pryakhina shrilly, 'until you, my teacher, give me protection. Pelikan is a traitor! God sees all, all!'

Just then the tulle gave a ripping sound and an eighteen-inch split opened up above the cat.

'Shoo!' Ivan Vasilievich suddenly shrieked despairingly, and clapped his hands.

The cat slithered down the curtain, tearing it all the way and bounded out of the room. Pryakhina started sobbing in a thunderous voice and covering her eyes with her hands she exclaimed, choking with tears:

'What do I hear? Do my ears deceive me? Is my teacher and benefactor driving me out? O God! O God, be my witness! !'

'Look round, Ludmilla Silvestrovna!' cried Ivan Vasilievich in despair.

An old woman now appeared in the doorway and cried:

'Come back, dear—there's a stranger here!'

Ludmilla Silvestrovna opened her eyes and saw my grey suit in the grey armchair. Her eyes bulged at the sight of me and her

10*

tears, I noticed, dried up instantly. She jumped up from her knees, muttered, 'Oh Lord! ... ' and rushed out. The old woman vanished with her and the door was shut.

Ivan Vasilievich and I sat in silence. After a long pause he drummed his fingers on the table for a while.

'Well, how did you like that?' he asked, and added wearily, 'The curtain's ruined.'

Another silence.

'I suppose that scene surprised you?' Ivan Vasilievich inquired, and groaned.

I too groaned and fidgeted in my chair, at a complete loss what to reply: the scene had not, in fact, surprised me at all. I fully realized that it was a continuation of the scene which had taken place in the changing-room, and that Pryakhina had been carrying out her promise to throw herself at Ivan Vasilievich's feet.

'We were rehearsing,' Ivan Vasilievich suddenly announced. 'I suppose you thought that was simply a piece of scandal, didn't you?'

'Astounding,' I said, concealing my expression.

'We like to refresh our memories with some little scene like that now and again ... h'm, h'm ... these études are very important ... You mustn't believe what she said about Pelikan. Pelikan is a most useful and accomplished man!' Ivan Vasilievich gazed sadly at the curtain and said, 'Well, let us continue!'

We could not continue because the same old woman had re-appeared.

'My aunt, Nastasya Ivanovna,' said Ivan Vasilievich.

I bowed. The charming old lady beamed at me, sat down and inquired:

'And how are you?'

'Thank you very much,' I replied with another bow, 'I am quite well.'

There was a further short silence while Ivan Vasilievich and his aunt looked at the curtain and exchanged a bitter glance.

'And what, pray, brings you to Ivan Vasilievich?'

'Leontii Sergeyevich,' remarked Ivan Vasilievich, 'has brought me a play.'

'Whose play?' asked the old woman, gazing at me sorrowfully.

'Leontii Sergeyevich has written the play himself.'

'What for?' asked Nastasya Ivanovna anxiously.

'What do you mean—what for? ... H'm ... h'm ... '

'Aren't there enough plays already?' asked Nastasya Ivanovna in a tone of kindly reproach. 'There are such lovely plays, and so many of them! If you were to start playing them you couldn't get through them all in twenty years. Why do you want to write? It must be so upsetting!'

She was so convincing that I could find nothing to reply, but Ivan Vasilievich drummed his fingers and said:

'Leontii Leontievich has written a modern play!'

This disturbed the old lady and she said, 'We don't want to attack the government!'

'Why should anyone want to?' I said in her support.

'Don't you like *The Fruits of Enlightenment*?' asked Nastasya Ivanovna shyly and anxiously. 'Such a nice play ... and there's a part in it for dear Ludmilla ... ' She sighed and got up. 'Please give my respects to your father.'

'Sergei Sergeyevich's father is dead,' put in Ivan Vasilievich.

'God rest his soul,' said the old lady politely. 'I don't suppose he knew you were writing a play, did he? What did he die of?'

'They called in the wrong doctor,' said Ivan Vasilievich. 'Leontii Pafnutyevich has told me the whole distressing story.'

'I didn't seem to catch your Christian name,' said Nastasya Ivanovna. 'One moment it's Leontii, then it's Sergei! Do they allow people to change their Christian names too, nowadays? One of our people changed his surname and now I never know who he is.'

'I am Sergei Leontievich,' I said in a husky voice.

'A thousand pardons!' exclaimed Ivan Vasilievich. 'My mistake!'

'Well, I won't disturb you,' said the old lady.

'That cat should be whipped,' said Ivan Vasilievich, 'it's not a cat—it's a bandit. We suffer from bandits of all kinds,' he added confidentially, 'so badly that we don't know what to do!'

With the advancing twilight catastrophe struck.

I was reading:

' "Bakhtin (To Petrov): Farewell. You will be following me soon ...

'Petrov: What are you doing?

'Bakhtin shoots himself in the temple, falls. From afar comes the sound of an accordion ... " '

'That won't do at all!' exclaimed Ivan Vasilievich. 'Why did you write that? You must cross it out without a second's delay. Why, pray, must there be shooting?'

'But he has to die by committing suicide,' I replied with a cough.

'Very well—let him die, and let him stab himself with a dagger.'

'But you see the action takes place during the Civil War ... nobody used daggers by then ... '

'Yes, they were used,' objected Ivan Vasilievich, 'I was told it by ... what was his name ... I've forgotten ... what they used ... You must cross out that shot!'

I was temporarily silenced by having made such an awful mistake, and then read on:

' ... accordion and isolated shots. A man carrying a rifle appears on the bridge. The moon ... '

'My God!' cried Ivan Vasilievich. 'Shots! More shots! What a disaster! Look here, Leo ... Look here, you must cut that scene, it's superfluous.'

'I thought,' I said, trying to speak as calmly as possible, 'that this scene was the main one ... In it, you see ... '

'Quite wrong!' Ivan Vasilievich cut me off. 'That scene is not only not the main one, it is unnecessary. Why? That character of yours— what's his name? ... '

'Bakhtin.'

'M'm, yes ... yes, he stabs himself offstage,' Ivan Vasilievich waved his hand towards the vague distance, 'then another character enters and says to his mother, "Bakhteyev has stabbed himself!" '

'But there's no mother in the play,' I said, gazing stupefied at the covered glass.

'Then there must be one! You must write her in. It's not difficult. It may seem difficult at first—there was no mother and suddenly there she is; but that's an illusion, it's very easy. There's the old woman sobbing at home and the man who brings her the news ... You can call him Ivanov ... '

'But Bakhtin's the hero! He has a soliloquy on the bridge ... I thought ... '

'Then Ivanov can speak his soliloquies. Your soliloquies are good, they must be kept. Ivanov can say, "Petya has stabbed himself and before he died he said such and such ... " It will make a very powerful scene.'

'But how can I do that, Ivan Vasilievich? You see, there's a crowd scene on the bridge ... The two sides clash ... '

'Then you can make them clash offstage. We mustn't on any account see it. It's terrible when people clash onstage! You're lucky, Sergei Leontievich,' said Ivan Vasilievich, getting my name right for the first and only time, 'that you don't know a man called Misha Panin!' (I turned cold.) 'He is, I assure you, the most extraordinary person! We save him up for a rainy day, suddenly something happens and we let him loose! ... He got us a new play recently and I may say that he did us no good with it—Stenka Razin. I arrived at the theatre and as I was driving up I could hear from a considerable distance—the windows were open—crashing, whistling, shouts, curses and gunfire! The horse nearly bolted and I thought there was a revolt in the theatre. Horrible! It transpired that Strizh was rehearsing! I said to Augusta Avdeyevna, "What have you done? Do you want me to get shot? Here's Strizh raking the theatre with gunfire and nobody, I suppose, has thought about the danger to me, have they?" Augusta Avdeyevna, who is an admirable woman, replied, "Punish me if you like, Ivan Vasilievich, I can't do a thing with Strizh. That man Strizh is like a plague in this theatre." If you ever see him I advise you to run a mile.' (I turned cold again.) 'Well, of course, all this had been done with the blessing of someone called Aristarkh Platonovich. Luckily for you, you don't know him, thank God ... But shots—in your play! Very well, let us continue.'

So we continued, and as darkness fell I said in a hoarse voice, 'The end.'

Immediately I was seized by horror and despair. I had the impression that I had built a little house and as soon as I had moved into it the roof had collapsed.

'Very good,' said Ivan Vasilievich when the reading was over, 'now you must start working on this material.'

I wanted to scream 'What?!'

But I didn't.

Now, Ivan Vasilievich, warming increasingly to his job, began telling me exactly how I should re-work my material. The sister in the play should be changed into the mother. But since the sister had a fiancé and as a fifty-year-old mother (Ivan Vasilievich christened her Antonina) could not, of course, have a fiancé, a character had to be eliminated, and, what is more, a character I was very fond of.

Dusk crept into the room. The nurse appeared again, and once more Ivan Vasilievich took some drops. Then a wrinkled old woman brought in a table-lamp and it was evening.

My head was in a whirl. Hammers were beating at my temples. I was so hungry that something seemed to be exploding inside me, and now and again the room swam before my eyes. But worst of all the scene on the bridge had gone and my hero with it. No, on second thoughts, the worst thing of all was that some ghastly kind of misunderstanding had occurred. I suddenly saw in my mind's eye the poster announcing my play; I could feel the last uneaten ten roubles of my advance royalties crackling in my pocket; Thomas Strizh seemed to be standing behind my back and assuring me that the play would start running in two months' time: yet now it was quite obvious that there was no play at all and that I would have to start all over again and rewrite it from start to finish. A wild witches' chorus of Misha Panin, Eulampia and Strizh were dancing in front of me, I had visions of the scene in the changing-room, but of my play there was not a shred left.

But then there occurred something completely unforeseen and even, to my mind, unimaginable ...

Having demonstrated (and demonstrated very well) how Bakhtin —whom Ivan Vasilievich had firmly renamed Bakhteyev should stab himself—he suddenly gave one of his little groans and announced:

'Now I'll tell you what sort of a play you should write ... You could make a fortune with it overnight ... A profound psychological drama ... The fate of an actress ... Let's say that in a certain country there lives an actress and a gang of enemies is torturing her, persecuting her and giving her no peace ... And her only response is to pray for her enemies ... '

'And make scenes,' I thought to myself in a sudden access of malice.

'Does she pray to God, Ivan Vasilievich?'

The question put Ivan Vasilievich in a dilemma. He groaned and answered:

'To God? H'm ... h'm ... No, on no account. You mustn't put in anything about God ... Not to God, but to ... art—art, to which she is profoundly dedicated. This gang of villains persecutes her and they are egged on by a wicked old wizard. You must describe how he has gone away to Africa and transferred his magic powers to a certain Madame X. A terrible woman. She sits behind a counter and is utterly unscrupulous. If you sit down to tea with her, look carefully and you'll see that she puts a special sort of sugar into your cup ... '

'Heavens above, he's talking about Toropetzkaya!' I thought.

' ... and when you drink it, it knocks you out. She and another frightful villain called Strizh ... I mean, h'm ... a certain producer ... '

I sat there staring vacantly at Ivan Vasilievich. The smile gradually slipped from his face and I suddenly saw that there was not a trace of kindness in his face.

'You, I can see, are a stubborn person,' he said extremely gloomily, and chewed his lips.

'No, Ivan Vasilievich, it's simply that the artistic world is so remote to me and ... '

'Well, you must study it! It's very easy. There are personalities in our theatre whom you cannot fail to admire. There's at least an act and a half's worth material ready made for you! Then there are others who only wait for you to turn your back before they'll filch your shoes from the cloakroom or stick a Finnish knife in your ribs.'

'How awful,' I said as I tapped my forehead.

'I see that you don't find it amusing ... You are a man of firm principles! Your play is a good one, too, by the way,' announced Ivan Vasilievich looking searchingly at me, 'all you have to do now is to write it ... and everything will be ready ... '

On tottering legs, with a pounding head, I went out, staring resentfully at the black bust of Ostrovsky as I went. Muttering to myself, I stumped down the creaking wooden staircase; my play, which I had come to hate, hung in my hands like lead. As I walked out into the courtyard the wind blew off my hat and I had to pick it up out of a puddle. The Indian summer was gone without a trace.

Rain was slanting down, water squelched underfoot, damp leaves were torn from the trees in the garden. A trickle ran down inside my collar. Muttering incoherent curses at life in general and at myself in particular, I walked on, glancing at the street lamps glowing dimly through the cobweb of rain.

Rhinoceroses in New York *by* Alexander Anikst

Novy Mir, 1965/VIII

Translated by Jacqueline Mitchell

Alexander Anikst is the Soviet Union's leading theatre critic, writer on drama and Shakespearean scholar. As a general rule *Novy Mir* does not print straightforward dramatic criticism or play scripts although it has published some outstanding theatrical memoirs, for example the Meyerhold reminiscences which are included in this volume. The best theatre reviews, together with the scripts of new plays, are usually to be found in the monthly magazine *Teatr* ('The Theatre'), of whose editorial board Anikst is a member. The same arrangement applies to music, the cinema and ballet, which have their specialized publications. Anikst, however, occasionally contributes to *Novy Mir* on subjects that straddle the borderline between theatre, literature, and criticism in a wider sense.

The essay that follows is an example of this type of criticism. It takes as its point of departure a long, leisurely review of a performance of Ionesco's *Rhinoceros* (Calder, London, 1958), which Anikst saw in New York, and includes generous extracts from the play's text. Then, rather curiously, and without any real pretext (which Anikst disarmingly admits), it launches into the analysis of two American bestsellers of the 'fifties which appear to have nothing whatever to do with Ionesco and indeed no detectable connection with the theatre: William H. Whyte's *The Organization Man* (Cape, London, 1957) and Herman Wouk's *The 'Caine' Mutiny* (Cape, London, 1951).

Odd though this apparently tortuous combination may seem to the Western reader, its genre is instantly recognizable to a Russian. There is in Russia a long and honourable tradition, extending at least as far back as the 1840s, of using literary criticism as a vehicle for comment much wider in scope, reaching out into sociology, politics and ideology. The reason is fairly plain: under both tsarism and communism, criticism of the social structure and of the government policies which shape it has been suppressed by censorship reinforced by terror; so dissident views, however constructive, have generally had to be cloaked in ostensibly innocent, non-political subject-matter. For a century and a half, Russian intellectuals have had to exploit with cunning the minimal leeway available to them in the media of literature, drama, scholarship and criticism to put across in oblique, coded form ideas which in a more open society are the common coin of social and political debate in parliaments, press, radio, television and books.

Over the years there have developed certain quite well-defined techniques for doing this. The genre as a whole is usually defined as 'Aesopian': you talk in one set of categories, knowing that your listeners will realize that you are referring to another set, i.e. to an area where explicit critical comment is tabu. There are a number of such Aesopian forms. The playwright Yevgeny Schwartz, for instance, wrote plays based on the fairy tales of Hans Andersen (or made up his own), imbuing his apparently childlike, humorous, fantasies with subtle critiques of Stalinism. One of his best plays, *The Naked King*, can in fact be taken equally well as a brilliant satire on both Nazism and Stalinist Communism. Other writers have used the analysis of historical characters or events to draw telling parallels with the present. Literary and dramatic criticism, with its vast range of subject-matter and the ability to invoke foreign literature, has always provided a great deal of scope for the clever practitioner of the Aesopian mode.

In the present essay, Anikst uses yet another technique (although also drawing on techniques already mentioned); this is the device of what one might call 'mirror-writing'. The method consists in holding up the mirror to other countries, in particular to capitalist countries whose politics and social systems are condemned by the doctrines of Marxism-Leninism and which are therefore a legitimate object of critical analysis by any conscientious Soviet writer. Here the author holds up his mirror to the wicked capitalist world, describes its evils with much display of righteous horror and usually concludes with a comforting homily on the lines of 'It can't happen here, comrades'—although Anikst dispenses with even this formality.

In devoting so much space to Ionesco's *Rhinoceros*, Anikst actually has two aims, one fairly direct, to do with the Soviet

Communist Party's cultural policy on the theatre, the other oblique and more general. In his perceptive and absolutely 'straight' exposition of Ionesco's criticism of Western society, Anikst is making a plea for the works of Ionesco to be performed in the U.S.S.R.; that they are not is due to the hidebound incomprehension and philistinism of the Soviet cultural bureaucrats, who are baffled by the Theatre of the Absurd and write it off as decadent bourgeois rubbish, unsuitable for Soviet audiences. In his attempt to puncture this dully restrictive policy, Anikst even manages to quote Lenin and Gorky in support of his case! (Though unsuccessfully, it must be said; Ionesco is still unperformed in Russia.) He also makes a wider and less explicit point: while apparently explaining the deadening frustrations and pressures towards mediocrity and conformism pilloried by Ionesco, Anikst is, by being carefully selective in his illustrations and exegesis, actually describing phenomena which *mutatis mutandis* are rife in Soviet society too—as his readership will known only too well.

Similarly, when stressing the social and political tensions set up by the behaviour of giant American corporations so ably analysed by W. H. Whyte, Anikst is making a damning comment on dominant Soviet 'Organizations' which exert their monopoly far more effectively than General Motor or U.S. Steel. Finally, when he discusses *The 'Caine' Mutiny*, this story of cowardice, incompetence and dubious moral behaviour in the U.S. Navy is an even more deadly parable of the recent situation in Soviet Russia. The lieutenant in the story forcibly relieved his incompetent, and probably temporarily insane captain of his command in an emergency; the clear implication is that Stalin's fellow leaders displayed criminal cowardice by not removing the monstrous tyrant from control when he was obviously drunk with power and steering the Soviet ship of state to disaster.

I happened to be in New York just at the time when *Rhinoceros*, a play by the French playwright Eugène Ionesco, was on at one of the theatres on Broadway. We saw the premiere announced in a publicity leaflet giving the New York theatre programmes for the current week. I must admit my curiosity was roused, and I thought to myself, This I must see!

In some of our literary circles Ionesco's plays have been firmly labelled Theatre of the Absurd, and there the matter ends. This is obviously the reason why not one of his plays has been either translated or performed in the Soviet Union, although they are shown throughout the world, including Czechoslovakia and the country of Ionesco's birth, Rumania.

I had already read Ionesco's plays and knew what they were about, but I still wanted to see at least one of them on stage in order to test my impressions of them.

I do not, in short, share the prejudice against this playwright held by some of my fellow writers. I like the use of comedy, paradox and eccentricity in art, and I do not believe that they are incompatible with realism. Whenever I come across a work of this type I always remember what Lenin once said to Maxim Gorky 'about the eccentric as a form of theatrical art': 'One finds in it a certain satirical or sceptical attitude towards accepted conventions, an attempt to turn them inside out, to distort them somewhat and to show the illogicality of everyday life. A bit complicated—but interesting!'*

Ionesco's use of absurd comedy is not merely funny—otherwise he would not have called some of his plays 'tragi-farces'. All the originality of Ionesco's dramatic method is contained in *Rhinoceros*, and this play demonstrates with particular force that the absurd lies not so much in the writer's style as in the very fundamentals of life in contemporary bourgeois society.

There are many more traditional elements in Ionesco's works than one might think at first sight. One may argue about the aesthetic value of his farces and tragi-farces, but one must be careful not to reject the whole tradition of popular 'tuppence-coloured' melodrama, the 'commedia dell' arte' and all the classical playwrights who had no scruples about making the audience laugh by portraying monstrously unrealistic, grotesque but nevertheless basically real-life situations. One must not look for full-blooded characters in Ionesco: his characters are types, essentially one-dimensional. There is a good deal of the absurd in Ionesco's

---

* M. Gorky, *Collected Works,* 30 vols (Russian edition, Moscow, 1949–55), vol. 17, p. 16.

comedies—but then what would comic art have done over the past centuries if life had not supplied such a wealth of subjects for satire ... ?

And so, accompanied by an American guide, our group of Soviet tourists set off for the Longacre Theatre on New York's West 48th Street. I noticed that once again John, our guide, had brought with him the book which he was reading in every spare moment.

'What are you reading?' I asked curiously. He handed me one of those cheap paperback editions which are now very common in Western countries. On the black, red and blue cover was written *The Organization Man*, by W. H. Whyte.

'How would you translate the title?' I asked, ' "the organized man"?'

Apparently it meant more 'the organizing man', 'the organizer' or, closer still, 'a person serving an Organization'. By 'Organization' is meant an establishment belonging to some large corporation. In short, it means people working on the staff of one of the great monopolies as an administrator. This has nothing to do with the civil service, but refers to people working for the real masters of the U.S.A., i.e. the owners of the large monopolies.

'Just a minute,' my readers will interrupt, 'I thought you were going to the theatre. Tell us about the production of *Rhinoceros*. Why this digression on American organization men?'

The fact is that there is a connection between them and *Rhinoceros*, which I shall attempt to explain.

On the stage in front of us is the square of a small provincial town; in the background, a two-storey house. On the ground floor is a grocery shop window. On the left (looking from the auditorium) is a small café, with tables set out on the square. On the right a narrow side-street goes off into the distance. It is warm and sunny and people are lightly dressed, some even in their best clothes because today is Sunday. A housewife crosses the square carrying a basket of food in one hand and holding a cat in the other.

A sleepy, boring little town where nothing ever happens and where all that occupies the inhabitants' minds is scandal and gossip. The few intelligent people in the town are suffocated by its oppressive atmosphere. One of them is Jean, a tall, stout, balding man with a round face, with a nose like a potato but lively eyes and a sharp tongue. (This part was played by Zero Mostel, one of New York's best character-actors.) Jean is sitting in his best clothes at one of the tables in the café. He has arranged to meet his friend Bérenger, who is late. Eventually he appears—unshaven, without a hat, his hair untidy, and slightly drunk. When Jean reproaches him, Bérenger answers that he is fed up with this monotonous, senseless life.

While the two friends are bickering the sound of some ponderous animal is heard in the distance. The noise comes closer and we realize that the animal has passed quite nearby.

Jean is the first to shout, 'Oh, a rhinoceros!' and, like an echo, all the other characters repeat the phrase: the waitress in the café, the grocer's wife, her husband, an elderly, scholarly-looking gentleman, and the housewife who went by with a basket and a cat at the beginning of the play.

Suddenly a clatter of hooves and an animal's roar are heard again, and when the noise dies down all the characters start talking at once and interrupting each other. The small square is full of people discussing where the rhinoceros could have come from. Bérenger says with a yawn; ' ... perhaps the rhinoceros escaped from the zoo.'

' ... there's been no zoo in our town since the animals were destroyed in the plague ... ages ago,' answers Jean.

With the same bored expression Bérenger suggests, 'Then perhaps it came from a circus.'

But the town has no circus either. Jean is resentful of his friend because he thinks Bérenger is making fun of him with his ridiculous suggestions as to where the rhinoceros could have come from.

At that moment two new characters appear on stage: the Old Gentleman and the Logician. The Logician is explaining the fundamentals of his subject to the Old Gentleman. And here begins a passage of 'pure Ionesco'—two simultaneous conversations, one between Jean and Bérenger and the other between the Old Gentleman and the Logician.

LOGICIAN (*to the Old Gentleman*): Here is an example of a syllogism. The cat has four paws. Isidore and Fricot both have four paws. Therefore Isidore and Fricot are cats.

OLD GENTLEMAN (*to the Logician*): My dog has got four paws.

LOGICIAN (*to the Old Gentleman*): Then it's a cat.

BERENGER (*to Jean*): I've barely got the strength to go on living. Maybe I don't even want to.

OLD GENTLEMAN (*to The Logician, after deep reflection*): So then logically speaking, my dog must be a cat.

LOGICIAN (*to The Old Gentleman*): Logically, yes. But the contrary is also true.

BERENGER (*to Jean*): Solitude seems to oppress me. And so does the company of other people.

JEAN (*to Bérenger*): You contradict yourself. What oppresses you — solitude, or the company of others? You consider yourself a thinker, yet you're devoid of logic.

OLD GENTLEMAN (*to The Logician*): Logic is a very beautiful thing.

THE LOGICIAN (*to The Old Gentleman*): As long as it is not abused.

BERENGER (*to Jean*): Life is an abnormal business.

JEAN: On the contrary. Nothing could be more natural, and the proof is that people go on living.

BERENGER: There are more dead people than living. And their numbers are increasing. The living are getting rarer.

JEAN: The dead don't exist, there's no getting away from that! ... Ah! ... Ah! ... (*He gives a huge laugh.*) Yet you're oppressed by them, too? How can you be oppressed by something that doesn't exist?

BERENGER: I sometimes wonder if I exist myself.

JEAN: You don't exist, my dear Bérenger, because you don't think. Start thinking, then you will ... '

Lecturing his friend and advising him to change his way of life, Jean convinces him that education is the best way to counteract the squalor of one's environment. ' ... visiting museums, reading literary periodicals, going to lectures,' says Jean. 'That'll solve your troubles, it will develop your mind. In four weeks you'll be a cultured man ... '

The 'culture' which Jean is advocating is not genuine but superficial. From his very words it is obvious that this is not the kind of culture which will in fact resolve the contradictions of life, but something which will 'remove' them by means of sublimation. With this attitude, there is a complete rift between life and culture. Life remains vulgar, trivial and drab, but a 'culture' that is divorced from life and even opposed to it will inevitably be a mere substitute for genuine activity.

The idea that Ionesco is anti-intellect has become a cliché among critics. It is based on his first plays, *The Bald Prima Donna*, *The Lesson* and *The Chairs*. His comedy *Rhinoceros* is perhaps the first play to reveal with clarity the reasons and essence of Ionesco's anti-intellectualism. He is against empty intellectuality and against all philosophizing—the pastime of intellectuals who fail to use their minds to solve the urgent problems of life.

In the 'quartet' that I have just quoted, the Logician epitomizes intellectual activity devoid of any aim; Jean expresses a morality that is equally aimless. Why should Bérenger be cultured, if his culture is a sterile acquisition and serves no useful purpose in his work and his daily life?

Rationalism was the philosophy of nascent bourgeois society. Anything that did not answer the demands of reason was condemned to annihilation. Now that this society has fallen into decadence, its spiritual culture is degenerating. Descartes would undoubtedly have turned in his grave at the abuse of logic parodied by Ionesco in the character of the Logician. Is it surprising, now that reason has so degenerated that logic serves as an excuse for absurdity, that a rhinoceros should appear on the scene?

The arguments of Ionesco's characters are again interrupted by the clatter of a rhinoceros's hooves. This time the cat, which has slipped from the housewife's arms, is trampled on and killed by the beast. The Logician and the Old Gentleman have just been discussing the problem: what is a cat, how many legs does it have, could a cat have more or less than four legs and could a cat have no legs at all? The cat they are busy discussing is an abstraction. But real cats exist, and one of these ordinary cats was the rhinoceros's first victim. The Old Gentleman and the Logician have a ready-made consolation: 'What do you expect, Madam, all cats are mortal!' While they are consoling the owner of the squashed cat, an argument starts up as to who killed the cat—the rhinoceros who appeared the first time or some other one? Jean insists, 'No, it was not the same rhinoceros. The one that went by first had two horns on his nose, it was an Asian rhinoceros, this only had one, it was an African rhinoceros.' Bérenger disagrees with Jean and says the rhinoceros ran past too quickly to have been seen clearly, and adds, 'You're ... a pedant who's not certain of his facts in the first place, because it's the Asian rhinoceros with only one horn on its nose, and it's the African with two.' The two friends quarrel.

The Logician undertakes to solve the problem which has arisen and the logical abracadabra begins again. First of all he establishes that they could have seen:

1. The same rhinoceros with one horn both times;
2. the same rhinoceros with two horns both times;
3. a rhinoceros with one horn the first time and with two the second time;
4. or with two horns the first time and one the second time.

Furthermore, if a rhinoceros with two horns ran past the first time and with one horn the second time, this still gives no grounds for a definite conclusion. 'For', says the Logician, 'it is possible that since its first appearance the rhinoceros may have lost one of its horns, and that the first and second transit were still made by a single beast ... It may also be that two rhinoceroses both with two horns may each have lost a horn.'

Thus, concludes the master of deduction, the first rhinoceros was either Asian or African and the second was either African or Asian, 'for good logic cannot entertain the possibility that the same creature be born in two places at the same time.' Bérenger remarks that this was already obvious, and that anyway it does not solve the problem. Then the Logician explains to him with a significant smile, 'Obviously, my dear sir, but now the problem is correctly posed.'

'Well, it may be logical,' the grocer announces, 'but are we going to stand for our cats being run down in front of our very eyes by one-horned rhinoceroses *or* two, whether they're Asian *or* African?' The others agree with him.

Meanwhile Bérenger, who is sorry he quarrelled with Jean over some stupid rhinoceros, in his annoyance orders a double brandy:

'I feel too upset to go to the museum. I'll cultivate my mind some other time.' With this the first act ends.

Compared with Ionesco's early works, this is not an anti-play but a real play, a comedy, written in the classical French tradition. Ordinary people like these are found in many French comedies. The Logician is directly descended from Molière's pedants, and reminds one of the teacher of logic in *Le Bourgeois Gentilhomme*. Vulgar, empty provincial life has been ridiculed more than once in literature. Chevalier's *Clochemerle*, which we laughed at on the screen, is just as ridiculous as the town portrayed by Ionesco. However, Ionesco is not just portraying some godforsaken little country town and comparing it with the capital, but is showing the whole of bourgeois society as wallowing in the mire of vulgarity and provincialism. It is a society characterized by spiritual stagnation, mental backwardness, petty interests and dull egotism.

What of the people living in this world who have managed to preserve some of their higher aspirations? Some, like Jean, amuse themselves with a semblance of cultural life, with high-sounding intellectual activity which has nothing serious behind it. Others, like Bérenger, lapse into bohemianism and live without interests or belief, completely indifferent not only to petty cares but also to the great problems of our time. So much for Western 'culture' in the first act of *Rhinoceros*.

In American theatres there are no foyers where people can walk about in the interval, so we remained seated. I asked John:

'What does the author of your book say about organization men?'

'He is describing a particular group of people who have run the country for decades. "It is from their ranks", Whyte says, "that most of the first and second echelons of our leadership are drawn." '

'Tell me about it in more detail.'

'Sure. Whyte is writing about the people who control industry, finance and trade. Not about the owners, but about the men who actually *control* everything. These are the organization men. They are the employees of corporations or, as Whyte calls them, 'Organizations' (with a capital O). They are not just clerks. Each one of them is involved in the management of a large firm and controls huge amounts of fixed capital. They don't own these firms, but in function they virtually are the owners.'

'What are they, then—capitalists without capital, owners without property?'

'It seems paradoxical, but it is so. They are the administrators who have complete charge of large manufacturing and trading divisions of big corporations, and psychologically they have every reason to feel like wealthy capitalists.'

'Where do they come from?'

'As a rule they come from middle-class origins. But instead of carrying on their fathers' business or setting up on their own they prefer to get jobs in large corporations. This gives them a guaranteed income, which is more secure than being the owner of a small firm.'

'Tell me, then, are organization men only found in the business world?'

'No, not exclusively. Of course, the majority is made up of managers of industrial and commercial firms. But you must also include as organization men the lawyers who work in those corporations, and certain other white-collar professions. The design engineers, the chemists and physicists in the laboratories of the Organizations, the doctors in the clinics belonging to the corporation—all these are organization men. Even a priest can be an organization man if he's in charge of some church Organization.'

'What's the difference, then, between these organization men and the old-style businessman?'

'You see, the old businessmen ran their own firms, whereas the new men manage the business of large Organizations. They don't think of themselves in terms of private enterprise.'

'In other words, the ruling class of your society has created a special bureaucratic stratum to organize production and trade. The capitalists are in fact verging on the point where they even hire brains to do their work for them. And would you say that these organization men are influential?'

'Whyte thinks that they are virtually in control of everything now. This means that a major change has taken place in our society. This should have been reflected in our ideology, too, but in fact it has not, if one can put it that way, kept pace with the real structure of social relations.'

'Is that your opinion?'

'No, I'm still quoting from Whyte. One of the main theses of his book is that the forms and practice of our social life have remained the same but the ideology is quite different, in that it differs radically from the characteristics of the "system", Whyte's name for our ruling class.'

'What's the difference between conditions as they really are and the ruling ideology?'

'Everyone knows that the American ideology has always been individualism. The official view is that even now our society is based on the principles of individualism, in other words, that it's founded on individual initiative.'

'And isn't it really like that?'

'That's the point, it isn't. The reality of contemporary America can only be understood if you realize that all forms of activity have in one way or another been drawn into the orbit of large Organizations. The very way these Organizations work demands a new moral philosophy. "The Protestant ethic", the philosophy of individualism, still remains the official moral philosophy of bourgeois society. But this individualism no longer has any basis in economic reality.'

In Whyte's opinion, what amounts to a new ideology has already arisen. He states frankly that his task is to persuade us to look at life in terms of the *real* conditions of contemporary American society. The time has come to discard antiquated ideas about the value of the individual, and the individual being the centre around which life revolves. It is similar to the medieval belief that the sun and the planets revolved round the earth. It is time we adopted the Copernican system. It is not society which serves man but man who serves society, by means of the Organization in which he works.

'In other words Whyte comes to the conclusion that if you want to serve society, you must serve the monopolies.'

'But your Communist morality also demands that man should serve society.'

'How can there be any comparison? The difference lies in where the profits go. In your society it goes to the monopolies. Whyte tries to mystify us by using the vague term Organization instead of the word capital.'

Whyte has a chapter called 'A Generation of Bureaucrats' about the people who have chosen to work in the large Organizations as their career. 'The bureaucrat as hero is new to America,' writes Whyte, 'but a considerable number of young people in America now see this as their ideal.'

Organization men try to live apart from the rest of the population. Housing estates are already growing up in the suburbs of large towns where whole colonies of these bureaucrats live in villa-like houses. The inhabitants of these rich suburban districts see themselves as an exclusive caste. They only associate with each other. Contemporary society is going through a revival of the corporate principle, which Whyte calls 'the social ethic'.

'Why do Americans think "the social ethic" is something new? It was devised earlier and applied in the Old World.'

'Who by?' asked John

'The "theorists" of Italian and German fascism. The corporate state has already existed and has collapsed, like the system built on feudal loyalties.'

'Excuse me, but Whyte is writing about something quite different —'

'No, he's not. Whyte admits quite frankly that the age of free capitalism is over. True, the bourgeoisie of the U.S.A. is still trying to preserve the outward trappings of democracy, but not much of it has remained if "the social ethic", the ethic of slave-like devotion to the monopolies, the ideology of loyalty to the "system", has become the last word in bourgeois moral philosophy ... '

The bell. The second act of *Rhinoceros* awaits us.

The room of a firm which publishes law books. There are still a few minutes before the working day begins, and the employees are discussing yesterday's incident: the appearance of the rhinoceros in the town. Botard, a former schoolteacher, thinks it is all nonsense, mere newspaper sensationalism. He is fifty, but has kept his vitality and clarity of judgment. A self-assured man, he knows everything, understands everything and passes judgment on everything. He wears a beret, a long grey overall and spectacles on his long nose, and a pencil is stuck behind his ear. He is arguing with Dudard, a much younger man of about thirty-five who has the advantage of being the manager's favourite and most trusted assistant. Nine o'clock strikes, and it is time to start work. At the last moment, Bérenger runs in panting. They are all busy arguing about the rhinoceros: was it true, and how many were there? Botard exclaims, 'An example of collective psychosis, Mr Dudard. Just like religion — the opiate of the people!'

The manager of the department, Monsieur Papillon, a man of forty with a moustache, a high, starched collar, a black tie, and the red ribbon of the the Legion of Honour in the buttonhole of his jacket, orders them to stop their futile argument. But no sooner has he gone into his office with some proofs than the squabbling breaks out afresh. Meanwhile a stout lady is climbing the stairs leading to the office. She comes in quite out of breath and they sit her down on a chair in the middle of the room. It is Madame Boeuf, the wife of one of the employees. She tells them that her husband could not come to work. Why was she so out of breath? She had had to run because she had been chased all the way from her house by a rhinoceros! It had followed her here. Just then stamping noises are heard on the stairs, then there is a dreadful crash: the staircase has collapsed. Now the rhinoceros is no longer a myth: one of them is prowling around this very building and roaring. They can all see him from the window. Madame Boeuf joins the spectators and suddenly lets out a fearful shout.

'It's my husband! Oh Boeuf, my poor Boeuf, what's happened to you?'

Monsieur Boeuf has changed into a rhinoceros. His wife faints. When they bring her round she announces that she will never abandon her husband and Botard assures her that he and his trade union will not leave Boeuf in the lurch now that this misfortune has befallen him. When Papillon announces that he is giving Boeuf the sack for being late for work and for turning into a rhinoceros, Botard protests against the illegal dismissal in the name of the trade union.

The lure of the rhinoceros's growling has such an effect on Madame Boeuf that she leaps down the broken flight of stairs, and falls straight on to the rhinoceros's back; the office employees watch the animal from the window, trumpeting for all it's worth and carrying off its wife in triumph.

The meaning of Ionesco's farce becomes clearer and clearer; in an atmosphere of stuffiness, torpor and complacency things begin to run wild. Man reverts to his primitive savagery. We see this not only when Monsieur Boeuf turns into a rhinoceros but also when his wife decides to follow her husband.

In Act II, Scene ii, which I think is the best scene of the play, we see the house in which Jean lives. On the same landing live two old people, husband and wife. Jean is lying on the bed with his back to the audience and to Bérenger, who enters the room. Jean answers his friend's questions peevishly and curtly. He eventually turns round to face him and says he feels ill. He has grown hoarse, and, what is more, a bump has appeared on his forehead, right above his nose. Jean rushes off into the bathroom to look in the mirror and admits, Yes, a bump has come up. He touches it with his fingers and can feel it growing under his fingertips. At the same time his skin takes on a greenish tinge.

While he talks to Bérenger, Jean keeps rushing off into the bathroom. Each time he comes back he turns greener and greener. This was the stage direction in the play. In the New York production they avoided this too straightforward, obvious device. Jean still runs out from time to time to look at himself in the mirror. He thinks he is changing outwardly. In fact he is changing inwardly, while outwardly he remains normal.

Bérenger, who still does not understand what is happening to Jean, wants to call a doctor. There follows some Molièresque humour:

JEAN: Doctors invent illnesses that don't exist.
BERENGER: They do it in good faith — just for the pleasure of looking after people.
JEAN: They invent illnesses, they invent them I tell you.
BERENGER: Perhaps they do — but after they invent them they cure them.
JEAN: I only have confidence in veterinary surgeons.

At this moment we do not yet understand why Jean has suddenly started believing in vets. But it will soon become clear to us.

Bérenger assures him that his concern was aroused solely by friendly feeling. Jean replies grumpily in his hoarse voice: 'There's no such thing as friendship, I don't believe in your friendship ... I am misanthropic, very misanthropic indeed. I like being misanthropic.'

A little later Jean adds, 'It's not that I hate people. I'm just indifferent to them — or rather, they disgust me; and they'd better keep out of my way, or I'll run them down.' And then, 'I've got one aim in life. And I'm making straight for it.'

Then Berenger tells him that his fellow worker Boeuf has turned into a rhinoceros. Jean reassures him.

JEAN: I tell you it's not as bad as all that. After all, rhinoceroses are living creatures the same as us; they've got as much right to life as we have.
BERENGER: As long as they don't destroy ours in the process. You must admit the difference in mentality.

JEAN: (*pacing up and down the room and in and out of the bathroom*): Are you under the impression that our way of life is superior?

BERENGER: Well, at any rate, we have our own moral standards which I consider incompatible with the standards of these animals.

JEAN: Moral standards! I'm sick of moral standards! We need to go beyond moral standards.

BERENGER: What would you put in their place?

JEAN: Nature ... Nature has its own laws. Morality's against nature.

BERENGER: Are you suggesting we replace our moral laws by the law of the jungle?

JEAN: It would suit me, suit me fine.

BERENGER: You say that, but deep down, no one ...

JEAN (*interrupting him, pacing up and down*): We've got to build our life on new foundations. We must get back to primeval integrity.

BERENGER: I don't agree with you at all.

JEAN (*breathing noisily*): I can't breathe.

BERENGER: Just think a moment. You must admit that we have a philosophy that animals don't share, and an irreplaceable set of values, which it's taken centuries of human civilization to build up ...

JEAN (*in the bathroom*): When we've demolished all that, we'll be better off! (*Jean comes out of the bathroom*) ... Don't talk to me about mankind!

BERENGER: I mean the human individual, humanism ...

JEAN: Humanism is all washed up! You're a ridiculous old sentimentalist.

He gets more and more heated, and Bérenger tries in vain to calm him down. Bérenger watches his friend's transformation with horror. 'Oh, your horn's getting longer and longer—you're a rhinoceros!'

Jean leaps out of the bathroom and snarls, 'I'll trample you, I'll trample you down!' At this point he thrusts forward his right hand, as the Nazis did, shouting, 'Heil!'

Bérenger wants to call the porter to catch his friend who has turned into a rhinoceros. He rushes down the stairs and returns horrified: 'There's a whole herd of them in the street now! An army of rhinoceroses, surging up the avenue ... A whole herd of them! And they always said the rhinoceros was a solitary animal.

That's not true, that's a conception they'll have to revise. They've smashed up all the public benches.'

Bérenger rushes about in despair, wringing his hands: 'What's to be done? Rhinoceros! Rhinoceros!'

A terrifying crash is heard. It is Jean, who has rushed out into the bathroom, made a hole in the door with a violent thrust of his head and forced his snout through the hole. The very image of a rhinoceros! Interval.

To tell the truth, I invented my conversation with John. The only truth in it is that John was there and I saw him carrying William Whyte's *Organization Man*. I found the book in the library on my return to the Soviet Union, and I used this device to set forth some of the author's propositions.

One of the chapters, entitled 'Love That System', deals with the literature of conformism. Here Whyte describes the effect that the ideology of the capitalist bureaucracy in the U.S.A. has had on literature and art. He tells a hypothetical story which reflects, 'as in a drop of water' as he puts it, the whole ideology of the organization men:

A middle-management executive is in a spot of trouble. He finds that the small branch plant he's helping to run is very likely to blow up. There is a way to save it; if he presses a certain button the explosion will be averted. Unfortunately, however, just as he's about to press a button his boss heaves into view. The boss is a scoundrel and a fool, and at this moment he's so scared he is almost incoherent. Don't press the button, he says.

An organization man is generally not a rebel by nature. He knows that his boss, although he is stupid, is the representative of the Organization. Nevertheless, our hero would like to save everyone from destruction. He is in a dilemma: if he presses the button, then he would be acting like a bad employee but the Organization and the factory would be saved; if he does not press the button, he will demonstrate that he is a good organization man and they will all be blown to smithereens.

Whyte admits, of course, that the dilemma is idiotic:

11

A damn silly dilemma, you might say. Almost exactly this basic problem, however, is the core of one of postwar America's biggest-selling novels, Herman Wouk's *The 'Caine' Mutiny*, and rarely has a novel so touched a contemporary nerve. The book was printed in hundreds of thousands of copies and it was made into a film. Much of its success, of course, was due to the fact it is a rattling good tale, and even if the author had ended it differently it would still probably have been a success. But it is the moral overtones that have made it compelling. Here, raised to the *n*th degree, is the problem of the individual versus authority, and the problem is put so that no reader can duck it. There is no 'Lady or the Tiger' ending. We must, with the author, make a choice, and a choice that is presented as an ultimately moral one ...

The man caught in the dilemma is one the reader can identify himself with. He is Lieutenant Maryk, the executive officer of the minesweeper *Caine*. Maryk is no scoffer, but a stolid, hard-working man who just wants to do his job well. He likes the system and all his inclinations lead him to seek a career in the Regular Army.

Ordinarily he would lead an uneventful, productive life. The ship of which he is executive officer, however, is commanded by a psychopath named Queeg. At first Maryk stubbornly resists the warnings about Queeg voiced by Lieutenant Keefer, an ex-writer. But slowly the truth dawns on him, and in a series of preliminary incidents the author leaves no doubt in Maryk's — or the reader's — mind that Queeg is in fact a bully, a neurotic, a coward and, what is to be most important of all, an incompetent.

The *Caine* is struck by a typhoon.

Terrified, Queeg turns the ship south, so that it no longer heads into the wind. Maryk pleads with him to keep it headed into the wind as their only chance of survival. Queeg, however, now virtually jabbering with fear, refuses to turn the ship around into the wind. The ship is on the verge of foundering.

What shall Maryk do? If he does nothing he is certain that they are all lost. If he takes advantage of Article 184 in Navy Regulations and relieves Queeg temporarily of command for medical reasons, he is in for great trouble later.

Maryk makes his decision. With as much dignity as possible he relieves Queeg of command and turns the ship into the wind. The ship still yaws and plunges, but it stays afloat. As if to punctuate Maryk's feat, the *Caine* passes the upturned bottom of a destroyer that hadn't made it.

Eventually there is a court martial for Maryk and his fellow officers. The defence lawyer, Barney Greenwald, makes what appears to be highly justified points about Queeg and, through skilful cross-examination, reveals him to the court as a neurotic coward. The court acquits Maryk. Queeg's career is finished.

Then the author pulls the switch. At a party afterwards, lawyer Greenwald tells Maryk and the junior officers that *they*, not Queeg, were the true villains of the piece. Greenwald argues that Queeg was a regular officer, and that without regular officers there would be no going system for reserves to join later. In what must be the most irrelevant climax in contemporary fiction, Greenwald says that he is a Jew and that his grandmother was boiled down for soap in Germany and that thanks to the Queegs who kept the ships going. He throws a glass of champagne at Keefer.

'I see that we were in the wrong,' one of the junior officers writes later, with Wouk's blessing. 'The idea is, once you get an incompetent ass of a skipper—and it's a chance of war—there's nothing to do but serve him as though he were the wisest and the best, cover his mistakes, keep the ship going, and bear up.'

This is the slavish morality of conformism.

Fiction cannot survive without conflict. What then do bourgeois writers do? According to Whyte's definition, they avoid the difficulty this way: the hero begins by being unaware that all is for the best; the author's task is to throw off the veil which prevents the hero from seeing that everything about him is not merely all right but marvellous! So in this kind of fiction, which relies on mass consumption, one of the characters comes forward as an accredited representative of the 'system' in which the characters live and act. Through this mouthpiece, the 'system' resolves all the hero's dilemmas, and helps him understand the conformist moral philosophy better with a few didactic pronouncements towards the end of the book.

One can therefore establish the following natural law governing the moral nature of the characters: since the 'system' is good, then its representatives express the highest moral principles. They play the part of the chief benefactors. They are a source of good, wisdom, justice and everything that makes life worth living.

It is no accident that the ranks and grades of the characters are important in fiction of this kind. And it is significant that bourgeois writers are especially fond of using war-time situations. This is linked with the U.S.A.'s violent militarism, the propagation of war and the ideological preparation for it.

Whyte says nothing of this. Surely he is not ignorant of the militaristic bias of many of the ruling class? The militarists, i.e. the generals and officers, are, after all, organization men too.

Both military and civilian organization men are equally inimical to the individual and to humanism. And when I heard Ionesco's character in that New York theatre snarl the words, 'Don't talk to me about mankind ... I'll trample you!' it struck me that the play was not too divorced from reality.

On the day before the premiere of his play in New York, Ionesco said in an interview with the *New York Times*:

Why did I decide to turn my heroes into rhinoceroses? Because the rhinoceros is the stupidest, most malicious animal in the world, and also the ugliest. You saw how the people of Nazi Germany turned into rhinoceroses. They dehumanized themselves and became a horde of terrifying, destructive beasts. That's why the play is such a success in Germany, where it has played in sixty towns. The Germans recognized themselves at once. Totalitarian doctrine and mass psychosis made them stupid and fanatical.

As everyone knows, far from all the fascist rhinoceroses were exterminated. Many of them recovered and, with the support of the American monopolies (the same Organization which Whyte writes about), they are once more stamping about in West Germany. It is not only on German soil, however, that rhinoceroses can breed. The facts of present-day life show that monopoly capital has created and is consolidating its own system of totalitarianism elsewhere.

It would be wrong to think that fascism can only be found in the form that it took in Nazi Germany, for there was also the Italian version of it. Fascism creates a new basis for the old system of class inequality.

The following description of the philosophy which justifies the supremacy of the parasitic minority is taken from a reliable, scholarly work of reference:

> The antidemocratic ideology of fascism, rejecting the 'myth' of equal political rights for all, advances the theory of the elite, the 'heroes' as opposed to the 'crowd', which must, according to the ideologists of fascism, submit to and believe implicitly in the 'historical mission' of fascism.
>
> The reactionary concept of nation and state occupies a most important place in this social 'philosophy'. Fascism, the ideology of extreme nationalism and chauvinism, raises the state to an absolute. The state, according to the definition of fascist 'theorists', is the highest form of expression of the universal spirit, the 'immanent consciousness', the 'will' of a nation. The nation itself, according to the concepts of Italian fascism is the outcome of the state. The individual must merge entirely with the state and subordinate his will to it.*

Whyte's 'social ethic' is merely the American version of individual subordination to the state. There is an excellent book which fully reveals the nature of the ruling class in totalitarian America by the American sociologist, C. Wright Mills, called *The Power Elite*.† Although it was translated some time ago in the Soviet Union, it has attracted less attention than it deserves. This book makes it clear that fascism has become a fact of life in the U.S.A. It is, of course, concealed by demagogic phraseology: America has her 'historic mission' — to save 'Western civilization', in other words to maintain the privileges of the ruling class, the elite. Vietnam has shown the world just what a 'civilizing' force America really is.

There is a semblance of democracy in the U.S.A. But a journalist called Christopher Lasch thinks the reality is otherwise: he shows that honest, thinking people in American society are completely powerless, since the ruling elite controls all the means of exerting influence through the mass media. He writes that American

* Dynnika, M. A. (ed.), *Contemporary philosophy and sociology in Western Europe and America* (Moscow, 1964), p. 159.
† Oxford University Press, New York, 1956. (Editor's note.)

326 ALEXANDER ANIKST

intellectuals feel despairing and impotent 'in a huge country where political debates are subject to the mass media of communication, where public opinion, misinformed and put on the wrong track, is absolutely powerless when the government should be persuaded to conduct a more liberal policy but is all-powerful when it is being stirred up to conduct an even more anti-liberal policy than it already intends to ... '*

Whilst the real intelligentsia, prompted by humanity and justice, might try to make a totalitarian government act for the good of the nation, the pseudo-intelligentsia stirs up all the reactionary feelings of the governing elite which is concerned solely with keeping its privileged position intact. The ideologists of the elite warn everyone of the likelihood of a 'liberal backlash', and create a semblance of public opinion by making a stir in the press and on radio and television. They shout louder than everyone else, so that the government (whose point of view they express) can conduct a reactionary policy and still say, We are doing what the people want.

Ionesco, to whom we must return now, is obviously aware that these shameless, loud-mouthed ideologists of the reactionary ruling elite are to be found in France, the U.S.A., the German Federal Republic and other countries of the 'free' West. In the interview which I mentioned earlier Ionesco said, 'In my opinion the ordinary man is superior to the semi-intellectual. Nazi slogans were thought up by semi-intellectuals – Nazi journalists, novelists, artists, ideologists.'

He is right, for these semi-literates are capable only of demagogy and vicious slogan-mongering. The sense of their slogans is immaterial, what matters is that they should appear to contain some principle. Fascist-type demagogy does not appeal to the conscious mind: it simply promises to fill people's bellies and purses. Every demagogy has its fanatics, and this type is represented by Jean in Ionesco's play.

At first Jean was afraid of other people seeing that he was turning into a rhinoceros. But the more he altered, the more aware he was of his own dignity as a rhinoceros: a rhinoceros should consider himself the salt of the earth. This compensates for his inferiority, which he wants to hide from himself and others by

* Lasch, C., *The New Radicalism in America 1889–1963: The Intellectual as a Social Type* (Chatto and Windus, London, 1966).

demonstrating his power as a rhinoceros: he can trample things down, and this, he thinks, makes him superior to other decent people.

Jean began by lecturing Bérenger and advising him to acquire some culture. Yet at his first encounter with mass psychosis, Jean surrendered without resistance, and now this erstwhile *Kulturträger* is snarling at culture louder than all the other rhinoceroses who are threatening to trample it down.

The third bell. The last act begins.

How will Ionesco's tragifarce end? Surely not in victory for the rhinoceroses and their regime?

We now see Bérenger's modest little flat, a solitary island of human life in a world where the rhinoceroses have triumphed.

Bérenger is asleep on the sofa, and is having a nightmare. He cries out in his sleep, 'The horns, mind the horns!', turns over clumsily and slides off the sofa on to the floor. The first thing he does is touch his forehead to make sure no bump has come up. Bérenger heaves a sigh of relief: there is nothing on his forehead.

The stamping of the rhinoceroses is heard. They have filled the whole town, and Bérenger has taken refuge from them in his flat. He is afraid of contact with the outside world and of the contagion affecting everybody. Bérenger is not a hero but an ordinary man, sincere if somewhat naive. But he is most definitely human ...

Bérenger's friend from work, Dudard, comes to visit him. Dudard is not afraid of the rhinoceroses. On the whole he sees no point in Bérenger's panic over them. 'They won't attack you,' Dudard consoles him. 'If you leave them alone, they just ignore you.' He advises Bérenger not to think about them; after all, what is it all to do with him?

BERENGER: I feel responsible for everything that happens. I feel involved. I just can't be indifferent.

DUDARD: Judge not lest ye be judged. If you start worrying about everything that happens you'd never be able to go on living.

BERENGER: If only it had happened somewhere else, in some other country, and we'd just read about it in the papers, one could discuss it quietly, examine the question from all points of view and come to an objective conclusion. We could organize debates with professors and writers and lawyers, and blue-stockings and artists and people.

And the ordinary man in the street, as well — it would be very interesting and instructive. But when you're involved yourself, when you find yourself up against the brutal facts, you can't help feeling directly concerned — the shock is too violent for you to stay cool and detached.

Dudard persuades him not to worry, since they can't do anything about it anyway:

DUDARD: My dear Berenger, one must always make an effort to understand. And in order to understand a phenomenon and its effects you need to work back to the initial causes, by honest intellectual effort. We must try to do this because, after all, we are thinking beings. I haven't yet succeeded, as I told you, and I don't know if I shall succeed. But in any case one has to start out favourably disposed — or at least, impartial; one has to keep an open mind — that's essential to a scientific mentality. Everything is logical. To understand is to justify.
BERENGER: You'll be siding with the rhinoceroses before long.
DUDARD: No, no, not at all. I won't go that far. I'm simply trying to look the facts unemotionally in the face. I'm trying to be realistic. I also contend that there is no real evil in what occurs naturally. I *don't* believe in seeing evil in everything. I leave that to the inquisitors.

Just think: the existence of even the most narrow-minded rhinoceros regime in the world is justified by the need to keep an open mind about it!

Ionesco has given a masterly demonstration of how semi-intellectuals can adapt themselves unconsciously to what can be described as 'conformity to evil'. Gorky embodied this brilliantly in the character of Klim Samgin. Ionesco is not trying to emulate Gorky — he might not even have read his novel; but that is unimportant, as similar types exist not only in literature but, in even greater numbers, in real life.

Modern Samgins have become the spokesmen of an ideology which excuses evil and injustice. Their philosophy rests on relativism and scepticism, which enable them to question the genuine, positive values of normal, human coexistence. For example, listen to Dudard arguing:

DUDARD: What could be more natural than a rhinoceros?

BERENGER: Yes, but for a man to turn into a rhinoceros is abnormal beyond question.

DUDARD: Well, of course, that's a matter of opinion ...

BERENGER: It is beyond question, absolutely beyond question!

DUDARD: You seem very sure of yourself. Who can say where the normal stops and the abnormal begins? Can you personally define these conceptions of normality and abnormality? Nobody has solved this problem yet, either medically or philosophically. You ought to know that.

And so here we see this 'higher reason' of modern man questioning even what is clear and obvious! Here intellect serves to disarm man. Reason serving madness, reason denying rationality — surely this is what modern bourgeois irrationalism has come to, and it has all been done with the full panoply of 'logic'.

During the argument there suddenly appears beneath the window a rhinoceros's head, wearing the straw boater of someone we recognize from the first act, the Logician. 'That's the bloody limit! The Logician's turned into a rhinoceros!' Bérenger's exclamation sums up his argument with Dudard. Any cruelty or injustice can be justified by logic and philosophy. Or they can simply be disregarded at will: does the man in power need any excuse for persecution and oppression?

But how in all this can humanity be preserved? According to Ionesco, in our primitive state. In the play, Bérenger epitomizes 'natural man'. 'The hero of my *Rhinoceros*', explained Ionesco, 'is more or less a child. He is the only one who preserves his common sense. And only he is aware of the horror that is taking place. He is conscious as a human being and this consciousness provides a basis for fundamental human truths.'

Everyone knows that the philosophy of 'natural man' is not new. It inevitably accompanies an acute crisis within the social system. Back to nature, simplicity and plain living is the cry of those honest people who strive to break away from the bonds of the false civilization which has thwarted mankind's hopes. But Ionesco should have pointed out that the enemies of progress also summon us to revert to simplicity. For example, Jean, when he is turning into a rhinoceros, cries out that he is returning to the bosom of nature.

11*

Significant, too, are Ionesco's attempts to differentiate between the two concepts of back to nature, i.e., on the one hand, by instinct (the rhinoceros and Jean), and on the other by intuition (Bérenger). Both concepts tend towards those sides of human nature which are independent of consciousness. It is sometimes difficult to distinguish between instinct and intuition, and a man turning into a rhinoceros can plead that he is prompted by intuition.

Ionesco is right only in so far as the simplest yet greatest fundamentals of humanity, namely truth, goodness, justice and beauty, do exist. They have been monstrously distorted. We must purge life of the sophistry which turns lies into truth, cruelty into justice and calls the grotesque beautiful.

It is easy enough to say 'purge'. But we saw that the rhinoceroses — or the 'system', as Whyte calls it — won. Can one fight a 'system' of rhinoceroses? Whyte says one must recognize the victory of the 'system', but thinks there is still a place left for individuality: at first the Organization adapts the individual to itself, but later the individual can adapt the Organization to himself. However, this verbal juggling cannot hide the fact that there is no place left for the freedom of the individual in the so-called free world. Whyte's approach is that of the time-server who relies on the illusion that once inside the Organization, and having asserted oneself in it, one can triumph over it and bring about reforms. This is obviously naive. Whyte himself is fully aware of just how powerful the 'system' is. No sniping from within can change it. It can be altered only if the very foundations of the 'system' are shattered. This truism has long since been established and proved by Marxism-Leninism.

The fictitious character Dudard adapted himself to the 'regime' of the rhinoceroses. He genuinely sympathizes with Bérenger, and advises him for his own good not to jib but to reconcile himself to the rhinoceroses. 'I'll never follow you!' shouts Bérenger to Dudard.

Meanwhile, fewer and fewer people remain. Not only the Logician but also Botard the 'radical' has turned into a rhinoceros. Bérenger finds this out from his girlfriend Daisy, who comes and tells him the news. 'Did he give any reasons?' Bérenger asks her. 'What he said was: we must move with the times! Those were his last human words.' Daisy adds that her cousin and his wife, and as far as she knows, a good quarter of the town have turned into rhinoceroses.

Botard is a minor character in Ionesco's play. However, we must give the author his due: through him he portrayed a tragic development which is occurring among some of the Western left-wing intelligentsia. It is common knowledge that a considerable number of the German intelligentsia of the 'thirties went over to the fascists because they feared the Nazi concentration camps. But it was not only there that 'rhinocerization' of the intelligentsia took place. In the early 'forties, a significant rightward shift took place among intellectuals in countries under bourgeois democracy who had supported the Popular Front in the 'thirties and whose ideals were linked with those of communism. Under the strain of McCarthyism in the 'fifties in the U.S.A., some of the American left-wing intelligentsia renounced their past. A number of them, when questioned by the House Un-American Activities Committee, betrayed their friends who had taken part in the progressive movement.

Nowadays, some people who formerly paraded their left-wing views are among the keenest supporters of 'Western civilization' and the so-called free world. That intelligent, cultivated people can forget the duty they owe the nation and humanity as a whole, and lend their names to this reactionary injustice, is one of the greatest tragedies of the twentieth century.

But let me continue with the story of the rhinoceroses, which I have still not finished.

The dreadful stamping of the rhinoceros horde can be heard. Their numbers are increasing every minute, and everything in their path is thrust aside. Dudard decides he would rather join the rhinoceroses than stay here. Bérenger tries to stop him: 'Man is superior to the rhinoceros.' Dudard replies evasively, 'I didn't say he wasn't. But I'm not with you absolutely, either. I don't know. Only experience can tell.' Bérenger and Daisy stand at the window and see Dudard joining the rhinoceroses. He merges with them so well that he is indistinguishable from the rest. 'They all look alike, all alike,' exclaims Daisy.

Bérenger and Daisy are the only ones left in a town full of rhinoceroses. For a while it seems as if love will protect them from danger. But Daisy can hold out no longer. She does not want 'to regenerate the human race', as Bérenger suggests. She begins to change. When she has changed, Daisy says, 'Those are the real people. They look happy. They're content to be what they are.'

Bérenger tries to argue with her, but she answers back just like Dudard: 'There's no such thing as absolute right. It's the world that's right—not you and me.' Daisy begins to find the rhinoceroses attractive, even beautiful creatures. She quarrels with her boy-friend and joins the rhinoceroses.

Bérenger is left on his own. He is suddenly seized by doubt—might it not be better to join the rhinoceroses after all? He looks at himself in the mirror: perhaps Daisy was right and man is a monster compared to the rhinoceroses. Yes, man is not very beautiful, Bérenger reflects; but still he will not surrender. It is too late to change. 'I'll put up a fight against the lot of them, the whole lot of them! I'm the last man left, and I'm staying that way until the end. I'm not capitulating!'

Bérenger's last words are directed at the audience. He throws them at the public like a challenge, an appeal to leave the world of the rhinoceroses and make a stand for humanity.

The play is over.

When asked by reporters why he wrote the play, Ionesco answered:

> In *Rhinoceros* I wanted to say that any kind of fanaticism is wrong. When critics ask me, 'What are you going to put in its place? What's your answer?' I reply, 'The writer is not God Almighty. He doesn't know everything. He's a man like every-one else. You can't demand answers from him. He puts the questions and asks others to explain things to him. Like everyone else, I'm searching for the answer.'
>
> I wrote *Rhinoceros* to inspire people to resist this mass psychosis so that they wouldn't suffer from a feeling of their own isolation ... I'm not going to suggest answers, and in any case there aren't solutions to all life's problems. Truth is a highly subjective, individual thing; it is something everyone should work out for himself on the basis of his own experience of life.

These words might well have been spoken by Ionesco's hero, Bérenger, the same person whom Ionesco called 'more or less a child'. The hero may argue like a child, but his creator, even if he hides his true feelings, should not offer childish ideas to his readers and public. Ionesco's weakness is that he tries to leave politics out of his arguments. The reason for this bias is obvious. Corruption, duplicity, treachery, mass-murder, wars great and small lie behind the political slogans with which bourgeois governments excuse their actions.

Ionesco would appear to agree with those whose motto is 'A plague on both your houses!' But nowadays one cannot leave politics out when deciding the problems of mankind, the individual, freedom and culture. Sartre is right in this respect when he says that even those who avoid a direct answer to the question of their position are still 'engagé', whether they like it or not; that is, they follow one trend or another in contemporary politics. There is no doubt that a pure love of humanity would be a wonderful thing were it not an illusion. Sweet resignation is just what the rhinoceroses need, they want everyone else to be passive in order to keep them under control. Nowadays, just as twenty or thirty years ago, the only possible way of resisting the rhinoceroses is to fight for peace, socialism, national independence and genuine democracy.

Ionesco's early plays were rather pessimistic, but nevertheless witty, farces on the theme of the complete absence of logic in bourgeois morals, concepts and institutions. In *Rhinoceros*, in a new vein, he creates a hero who refuses to be dehumanized. He still does not know what to do, and has no idea of how to fight a world of malice and stupidity, but one thing is clear to him: the only people who remain human are those who do not join the horde of rhinoceroses, but try to remain true to themselves.

One need scarcely say that the problems facing Ionesco's hero cannot be solved within the bounds of a capitalist society. As long as economic inequality exists, the problem of the individual can never be solved, because economic inequality is increased and made worse by political inequality. What kind of a democracy can exist when, despite the outward signs of freedom of expression, all power is in the hands of a small clique who have lost touch with the people?

There is not even a convincing semblance of freedom left in the U.S.A. Not so long ago, the American press assured us that Macarthyism was over, whereas in fact, the obvious forms of political repression have simply been replaced by more subtle, cunning methods. But as soon as the domestic and foreign political situation took a slight turn for the worse, the Macarthy machine was dragged out again. The Negro's civil rights movement and growing protest against aggression and the suppression of other countries' national liberation movements has greatly disturbed the government. And then we heard in the summer of 1965 that the House Un-American Activities Committee had been revived with new vigour. When the three-day sessions of this shabby little fascist tribunal were held in Chicago they were guarded by two hundred policemen. And so the people of the 'free world' are not free, either economically or politically. That leaves us with culture.

In *Rhinoceros*, Ionesco presents two types of bourgeois culture. On the one hand there are the 'free' philosophers, like the Logician, who draw on a limited set of ready-made truisms whether they are relevant or not. They perform mental gymnastics and manipulate their set of ideas without even bothering whether they make sense or not. Their stream of words is devoid of a single inspiring thought or of anything which might help one to come to grips with reality. Ionesco portrays the second type of intellectual activity in the place where Bérenger works, a kind of ideology-factory. Monsieur Papillon is in charge of it, although he is not the real boss. We learn from the text that the factory belongs to another 'director'. Thanks to this hierarchy of big and little bosses, thought and culture have been bureaucratized.

Whyte has a chapter called 'The Bureaucratization of the Scientist', which explains how the thinking individual becomes part of the machinery of government. Individual freedom, interests and inclinations are sacrificed to what Whyte calls the 'group' interest. Basically, thinking *people* turn into thinking *machines* which do the work for the monopolists. What individual freedom is there in a society so bureaucratized that the people responsible for organizing science cannot appreciate outstanding talent? Whyte's chapter on 'The Fight against Genius' sums up the situation in the U.S.A.: the system prefers mediocre people who can be easily harnessed to specific jobs.

This is the position of the individual in bourgeois society today. I have quoted two opinions, a playwright's and a journalist's. Both are far removed from Marxism. Whyte's book is my source for the point of view of a man wholly devoted to the system, who wants to resolve its contradictions. It is as if Whyte were saying, 'Let's stop getting on each other's nerves by talking about individualism, the freedom of the individual and other things which have been dead for a long time, and let's work out an ideology in keeping with the real state of things.' A small fraction of Whyte's diatribe is true; but bourgeois politicians show no sign of modifying their brand of demagogy to take account of it. They go on saying, as they always have done, that their world is the 'free world'. We cannot expect anything else from them since the ideology of the exploiting classes was and always will be false.

Ionesco is sick of this lie, which the ruling classes exploit in order to cramp people's lives. Like Whyte, he wants to say, 'Stop trying to fool us.' Whereas Whyte is attempting to exchange an ideology based on an imaginary state of affairs for one based on reality, Ionesco is rejecting ideology altogether. His ideas reflect the phenomenon which, as the bourgeois writer Daniel Bell puts it, is the 'end of ideology'. Laughter is the last resort of people who cannot believe in anything—God, reason or the sacred rights of the individual—and Ionesco is a playwright whose work reflects the spread of this attitude in the West today. He is a pessimist, although his farces make the audience laugh. I would not compare him to Beckett, who maintains that one cannot overcome life's absurdity. There is one character in *Rhinoceros* who embodies Ionesco's only hope: Bérenger. He has not been as corrupted, as have the others, by false civilization, he is both naive and helpless, but nevertheless he still preserves genuine human characteristics.

Despite his seeming intellectual sophistication, Ionesco is naive. Yet although he fails to find solutions to the contradictions of modern life, he is honest and sincere; this distinguishes him from Western writers who share and support the illusions of the petty bourgeoisie.

I suppose I was lucky to see *Rhinoceros* in New York, for it is here that the contrast between the power of the totalitarian system of monopoly capital and the attempts of the individual to assert himself is most keenly felt.

Poor Bérenger; as long as this callous system of mercenary interests exists, you will find it hard to live in a world of rhinoceroses. But at least you were not afraid of them, and did not go over to their side. Although we are miles apart from you, we can share your hatred for the rhinoceroses and your faith that man will one day overcome these pachydermatous beasts. But he will overcome them not by naivete, or by going 'back to nature', but by arming himself with the power of the human intellect to make life worth living for everyone. Passive rejection of the world of the rhinoceroses is now largely a thing of the past, and more and more people are beginning to realize this.

A great progressive upheaval is becoming more and more apparent among young people in the United States.

The mass involvement of America's youth started with the battle for civil rights for Negroes, which was seen as a great moral question.

It has now been swept over to the peace issue, especially against Johnson on the American invasion of South Vietnam and the Dominican Republic.

The latest involvement of the young people is against the new witch-hunt by the Congressional Committee on Un-American Activities, which recently spent three hectic days in Chicago.

'The youth movement is certainly something to see,' says a letter I have just received from Gilbert Green, well-known American Communist leader.

Referring to the Un-American Committee's meeting in Chicago, he writes: 'How different from when they were last here in 1959 ...

'All the key civil rights and youth organizations were participants at the mass meeting and at the picket-line. Youth came from all the surrounding universities.

'The militant youth are not pro-Communist but they are definitely not anti-Communist. This is the most hopeful development in American life.'*

But, Monsieur Ionesco, you will achieve nothing by intuition. The irony is that ultimately even the rhinoceroses are forced to have recourse to an intellect which they do not themselves possess. But this will not save them. Reason may be suppressed or jeopardized, but it still exists, and can never be reconciled to the rhinoceroses' regime.

* *Daily Worker*, London, June 7th, 1965, p. 3.

Will their reign come to an end? Yes. Not as quickly as people living under its oppression might wish, but there is no doubt that it will end. In the history of humanity there have been frequent periods of utter darkness. They have all come to an end.

The 'mole of history' burrows on unseen. The dark night of Nazi-style fascism has come to an end. Its other forms will also cease to be. It is towards this goal that the best minds are working, as well as all those honest people who, like Ionesco's hero, say no to the rhinoceroses.

Recollections of Lord Rutherford *by*
P. L. Kapitza

Novy Mir, 1966/VIII

Academician Pyotr Leonidovich Kapitza (b. 1894) is the Soviet
Union's leading nuclear physicist. After graduating in electrical
engineering at the Petrograd Polytechnical Institute he came to
England in 1921 as a research assistant at the Cavendish Laboratory,
Cambridge, under Lord Rutherford, one of the great pioneers of
modern nuclear physics. In 1925 Kapitza became a Fellow of
Trinity College, Cambridge, and in 1930 Director of the Mond
Laboratory. There he worked until 1934, when after one of his
holidays with his family in Russia he was ordered not to return to
England. He was given his own laboratory and put at the head of
the Institute of Physical Problems of the U.S.S.R. Academy of
Sciences; his work here led directly to the construction of the
Soviet atomic and hydrogen bombs, and was also concerned with
the strategic use of cosmic ray energy.

For some undisclosed political misdemeanour Kapitza was
placed under house arrest from 1946 to 1955, but allowed to continue his researches. Now a member of the Presidium of the U.S.S.R.
Academy of Sciences and a professor of Moscow University, the
list of his honorary degrees, fellowships, memberships and appoint-
ments is too long to produce.

Although he was elected a Fellow of the Royal Society as long
ago as 1929, the following reminiscences of Lord Rutherford were
delivered as an address to the Royal Society in London only in 1966.

I am greatly honoured by the invitation of the President of the
Royal Society to speak to you on my reminiscences of Lord Rutherford. But this is a very difficult task and I accepted it after long

deliberation. At first sight I thought that to speak about the scientific achievements of so great a scientist as Rutherford would be easy. The greater the achievements of a scientist the more exactly and briefly can they be described. Rutherford created the modern study of radioactivity; he was the first to understand that it is the spontaneous disintegration of the atoms of radioactive elements. He was the first to produce the artificial disintegration of the nucleus and finally he was the first to discover that the atom has a planetary system. Each of these achievements is sufficient to make a man a great physicist. But nowadays these achievements and their fundamental values are well known not only to research students but even to schoolboys. Equally we all know the very simple and beautiful classical experiments by means of which Rutherford made his great discoveries. To come from the Soviet Union to speak about all this to the Fellows of the Royal Society would scarcely be appropriate.

You are all well aware that from research into radioactivity there grew up an independent science which is now called nuclear physics, and of all the papers published on physical research one-fifth relate to the investigation of nuclear phenomena. Both nuclear energy and the use of artificial radioactivity in science and technology are developing quickly and simultaneously. All these fields absorb the main bulk of the monetary resources spent on science and which now reaches the sum of thousands of millions of pounds, dollars and roubles. And all this for the last thirty years grew out of one modest domain of physics which in the old days was called radioactivity and of which Rutherford is justly called the father. To speak of the development of nuclear technology and physics which came from the work of Rutherford and his school is very interesting and very instructive. But I am sure that such Fellows of the Royal Society as our President Professor Blackett, Sir James Chadwick, Sir John Cockcroft, Sir Charles Ellis and Sir Mark Oliphant who in the old days were the most active members of Rutherford's school and who themselves in this domain have made fundamental discoveries and researches are certainly more qualified than I to speak on these matters.

The only way in which I can satisfy the interest of the Fellows of the Royal Society is to speak of Rutherford the man, of how I remember him during my thirteen years' work in the Cavendish Laboratory, of how he worked, how he trained us young scientists and also of his relations with the scientific world. My task is therefore to draw you a portrait of a great scientist and of a great man. Frankly, this is the job of a writer and not of a scientist. If I have now decided to do so, this is mainly for the following reasons. When I look back and see myself as a young man coming to England in 1921 and starting work at the Cavendish Laboratory and, after thirteen years, growing into a scientist, I feel that these years of my work were the happiest, and for all that I have been able to achieve I feel immensely grateful for the attention and kindness which Rutherford showed me, not only as a teacher but as a very kind and sympathetic man for whom I have a sincere affection and with whom I eventually became great friends.

However imperfect my recollections of Rutherford may be, this is the only way in which I can express my deep gratitude to this great and remarkable man.

As is well known, Rutherford was not only a great scientist but also a great teacher. I can recall no other scientist contemporary to Rutherford in whose laboratory so many outstanding physicists were trained. The history of science tells us that an outstanding scientist is not necessarily a great man, but a great teacher must be a great man. Therefore my task is even more difficult: I must give you a portrait not only of a scientist but of a man. I will attempt to make my portrait of Rutherford as alive as possible and for this purpose I shall illustrate my talk with episodes which I most vividly remember. From my many recollections I shall select the ones which characterize different sides of Rutherford's nature. I hope this will help you to reconstruct a lifelike picture of Rutherford in your imagination from all these fragments.

I would like to begin my recollections with a small episode which happened in 1930 in the Cavendish Laboratory. At that time a small conference was being held in Cambridge to commemorate the centenary of the birth of Maxwell, the first director of the Cavendish Laboratory. He was succeeded by Rayleigh, J. J. Thomson and Rutherford, four great physicists of the last and present century. After the official part of the meeting in which some of Maxwell's pupils talked of their reminiscences, Rutherford asked me how I liked the speeches. I answered that they were very interesting, but I was surprised that all the speakers spoke only of the positive side of Maxwell's work and personality and made a

'sugary extract' [*sic*] of him and I said that I would like to see
Maxwell presented as a living figure with all his human traits and
faults which of course every man possesses however great his
genius. Rutherford as usual laughed and said that he charged me
after his death to tell future generations what he was really like.
Rutherford was joking and I was laughing too. And now when I
try to fulfil his behest and I imagine Rutherford as I have to present
him before you, I see that time has absorbed all his minor human
imperfections and I can only see a great man with an astounding
brain and great human qualities. How well I now understand
Maxwell's pupils who spoke about him in Cambridge.

There are numerous books and articles on Rutherford as a scientist.
It is widely recognized that the simplicity and clarity of his thinking,
his great intuition and great temperament were very characteristic
of his creative ability. Studying the works of Rutherford and
observing how he worked I think the basic characteristics of his
thinking were great independence and hence great daring.

The basic method by which science is developing consists of
experimental investigations into natural phenomena and the continuous verification of the consistency of the results of our investigations with our theoretical conceptions. The progress of our
knowledge of nature appears in cases when we find contradictions
between theory and observation, and these contradictions, as they
compel us to develop our theories, enable us to widen our knowledge of nature. The more acute these contradictions are, the more
they lead us to further fundamental changes in understanding the
laws of nature, on the basis of which we may use nature for our
cultural development. In science, as in history, definite stages of
development demand their particular kind of genius. A definite
period of development requires men with corresponding mental
abilities. In the history of the development of physics, as in any
other experimental science, the most interesting periods are those
in which we are brought to revise our fundamental scientific
conceptions. Then not only deep thinking and intuition are required
from the scientist but also a daring imagination. As an illustration
I shall remind you of two well-known cases in the history of physics.
They made a great impression on me personally. The first case
concerns Franklin's creation of the study of electricity. On the basis
of this study Franklin stated that electricity has a material origin

and can impregnate metal and freely move in it. In his day this concept was in fundamental contradiction to the concept of the continuous nature of matter. But Franklin's view was eventually accepted as it gave a simple and complete explanation of all the electrostatic phenomena observed in his day. It is only recently, 150 years later, after J. J. Thomson discovered the electron, that Franklin's concepts were completely justified. But the most striking thing in this story is how it could have happened that Franklin, who had never before done any scientific work, could, in the course of a few years in a small remote American town when he was already a middle-aged man, find the right way by which this most important branch of science should be developed. And this happened in the middle of the eighteenth century when science was developing on the level of Newton, Huygens and Euler. How could Franklin achieve such results which were beyond the reach of professional scientists?

The other similar case in which the fundamental concepts of electricity had to be revised in the light of experiments is also well known. This is Faraday's concept on the electrical field. It is difficult to find a more revolutionary and original idea than Faraday's. He advanced the concept that electrodynamical processes must be explained by the phenomena happening in the space surrounding the conductor. I mention this case mainly because Faraday was a scientist who had no traditional scientific education, even though at that time its level was high for an average English scientist. I mention these two well-known cases only to show that at a particular stage of the development of science, when new fundamental concepts have to be found, wide erudition and conventional training are not the most important characteristics of a scientist required to solve this kind of problem. It appears that in this case imagination, very concrete thinking and, most of all, daring are needed. Strict logical thinking which is so necessary in mathematics hinders the imagination of a scientist when new fundamental concepts must be found. The ability of a scientist to solve such scientific problems without showing a logical trend of thought is usually called 'intuition'. Possibly there is a way of thinking which takes place in our subconscious but the laws by which it is governed are at present unknown. If I am not mistaken, even Freud, a pioneer in the study of subconscious processes, was not aware of it. But if intuition exists as a powerful creative thinking process then doubtless Franklin and Faraday mastered it thoroughly. I am sure that Rutherford mastered it too and he has rightly been called the Faraday of our time.

When at the beginning of our century Rutherford started studying radioactivity it had already been proved experimentally that these phenomena contradicted the most fundamental law of nature, the law of conservation of energy. The explanation of radioactivity which Rutherford gave, namely the disintegration of matter, at once provided not only the key to the understanding of these phenomena but also led all investigation in the right direction. The same thing happened when Rutherford created the planetary model of the atom. At first sight this model completely contradicted laws of classical electrodynamics since in its circular motion an electron was perpetually bound to lose by radiation its kinetic energy. But the experiments of scattering the α-particles, performed by Rutherford's pupil Marsden in 1910, definitely showed the existence of a heavy nucleus in the centre of the atom and Rutherford imagined the collision of particles so clearly that even these contradictions with the fundamental laws of electrodynamics could not prevent him from establishing the planetary structure of the atom. We know that only three years later Bohr, on the basis of the developing quantum theory of light, evolved his brilliant theory of the structure of the atom which not only justified Rutherford's planetary model but also quantitatively explained the spectra of atomic radiation.

The peculiar character of Rutherford's thinking could easily be followed when talking to him on scientific topics. He liked being told about new experiments but you could easily and immediately see by his expression whether he was listening with interest or whether he was bored. You had to talk only about fundamental facts and ideas without going into the technical details in which Rutherford took no interest. I remember, when I had to bring him for approval my drawings of the impulse generator for strong magnetic fields, for politeness sake he would put them on the table before him, without noticing that they were lying upside down, and he would say to me, 'These blueprints don't interest me. Please state simply the principle on which this machine works.' He grasped the basic idea of an experiment extremely quickly, in half a word. This struck me very much, especially during my first years in

Cambridge, when my knowledge of English was poor and I spoke it so badly that I could only vaguely explain my ideas, yet in spite of this Rutherford caught on very quickly and always expressed very interesting opinions.

Rutherford also liked talking about his own experiments. When he was explaining something he usually made drawings. For this purpose he kept small bits of pencil in his waistcoat pocket. He held them in a peculiar way — it always seemed to me a very inconvenient one — with the tips of his fingers and thumb. He drew with a slightly shaky hand, his drawings were always simple and consisted of a few thickly drawn lines, made by pressing hard on the pencil. More often than not the point of the pencil broke and then he would take another bit from his pocket.

A number of physicists, especially theoreticians, like to discuss science and apparently the process of argument is a way of thinking. I never heard Rutherford argue about science. Usually he gave his views on the subject very briefly, with the maximum of clarity and very directly. If anybody contradicted him he listened to the argument with interest but would not answer it and then the discussion ended.

I greatly enjoyed Rutherford's lectures. I followed the course of general physics which he gave to the undergraduates as Cavendish Professor. I did not learn much physics from this course since by that time I already possessed a fair knowledge of the subject, but from Rutherford's approach to it I learnt a great deal. Rutherford delivered his lectures with great enthusiasm. He used hardly any mathematical formulae, he used diagrams widely and accompanied his lectures with very precise but restrained gestures from which it could be seen how vividly and picturesquely Rutherford thought. I found it interesting that during the lecture he changed the topic as his thoughts, probably following some analogy, turned to a different phenomenon. This was usually connected with some new experiments made in the field of radioactivity which fascinated him and he then proceeded to speak with enthusiasm on the new subject. In this case he usually put his assistant in a difficult position by asking him to give a demonstration which was not part of the original planned version.

About the same time I also attended the lectures of J. J. Thomson in his special course on the conductivity of electricity through gas.

It was interesting to notice how differently these two great scientists, approached scientific problems. If Rutherford's way of thinking was inductive, then the way of thinking of J. J. Thomson was deductive.

I think it useful when training young scientists to ask them to follow a course of lectures, even an elementary one, but delivered by an eminent scientist. Listening to these lectures they will learn something that they will never find in any textbooks. In this connection I remember a conversation which I had with Sir Horace Lamb. He was telling me how he had attended Maxwell's lectures. Maxwell, he said was not a brilliant lecturer; he usually came to lectures without any notes. When he was doing mathematics on the blackboard he often made mistakes and sometimes got muddled. From the way in which Maxwell tried to disentangle and correct his mistakes Lamb learned more than from any textbooks he ever read. Lamb told me that for him the most precious parts of Maxwell's lectures were those in which he made mistakes. No doubt the mistakes of a genius are sometimes as instructive as his achievements.

When I came to Cambridge Rutherford did no more experimental work by himself; he worked chiefly either with Chadwick or with Ellis. But in both cases he took an active part in experiments. The setting up of the apparatus was done mainly by his laboratory assistant, Crow, whom he treated rather severely. But I sometimes saw how Rutherford himself, despite his slightly shaking hands, dealt quite skilfully with the finewalled glass tubes filled with radium emanation. Although Rutherford's experiments are well known, I cannot refrain from saying a few words about them. The most attractive thing about these experiments was the clarity of setting the problem. The simplicity and directness of approach to the solution of the problem were most remarkable. From my long experience as an experimenter I have learned that the best way of correctly evaluating the capacity of a beginner as well as of a mature scientist is by his natural inclination and ability to find a simple way of solving problems. There is an excellent saying by an unknown French author which applies perfectly to Rutherford: 'La simplicité c'est la plus grande sagesse.' I should also like to quote the profound saying of a Ukrainian philosopher, Gregory Skovoroda. He was by origin a peasant and lived in the second half of the eighteenth century. His writings are most interesting but probably

346 P. L. KAPITZA

quite unknown in England. He said, 'We must be grateful to God that He created the world in such a way that everything simple is true and everything complicated is untrue.' Rutherford's finest and simplest experiments concerned the phenomena of scattering by nuclear collisions. The methods of observation of scintillations by counters were worked out by Rutherford in collaboration with Geiger in 1908. Since then more than half a century has passed and this method and the Wilson chamber invented about the same time remain the fundamental methods for studying nuclear phenomena, and only the optical and resonance methods for determining nuclear moments have since been added. And up to now all nuclear physics possesses no experimental possibilities other than those used by Rutherford and his collaborators. The present development of nuclear physics is proceeding not by the invention of new experimental possibilities of investigating nuclear phenomena but thanks to the possibility of investigating nuclear collisions of a *larger* number of elements; and these collisions are studied in the domain of larger energies which are reached mainly by the use of powerful modern accelerators. But even now the way which leads us to the knowledge of the nucleus is still the method discovered by Rutherford, and he was the first to appreciate its fundamental value. I am referring here to the investigation of the collision of nuclei. Rutherford always liked to say, 'Smash the atom!'.

Even now, in the process of investigating nuclear collisions, there is one great weakness: the necessity of using statistical methods in the interpretation of experimental results. Great care is required to deduce correct general laws from limited statistical data. Someone once said about statistics: 'There are three kinds of lies: lies, damned lies and statistics.' In fact this was said about the application of statistics to social problems. But to some extent it is true of statistics in physics. I do not think that in any other branch of physics so many mistakes and faulty discoveries were made as in the course of the interpretation of statistical data obtained from experiments on nuclear collisions. Nearly every year new particles of resonance levels are still discovered, some of which may not exist. Rutherford was well aware what danger lies concealed in the interpretation of experimental data of statistical origin, especially when the scientist anticipates definite results. Therefore Rutherford was very careful to exclude the personal element and took the following precautions during the course of these experiments: the counting of scintillations was usually done by undergraduates who did not know the purpose of the experiment; the curves were drawn by persons who did not know what results were expected. As far as I remember, Rutherford and his pupils never made a single such mistake, while in the same line of investigation a number of mistakes were made in other laboratories. I remember that in those days the most critical approach in the interpretation of statistical data was that of Chadwick on whose judgment Rutherford usually relied completely.

I did not work with Rutherford because my investigations were not connected with nuclear physics and therefore I did not see him working in his laboratory. But I know that up to the very end of his life the main bulk of his time was taken up by his personal scientific research. I expect he gave the same amount of attention and strength to directing the work of young research pupils working in the Cavendish Laboratory. The detailed guidance of scientific work he left to one of the senior scientific workers, usually Chadwick. But he himself always took an interest in the choice of problem for experiment and of the experimental approach. Until the research student began obtaining results Rutherford showed no marked interest in his work. He never bothered about detailed guidance.

He often came to the laboratory but only for a short time; just to make remarks like, 'Why don't you get a move on—when are you going to get some results?' When I started working in the Cavendish Laboratory such remarks made a great impression on me, especially as they were made in a thundering voice, and with a severe expression. But eventually I found out that such utterances were automatic, maybe customary for a New Zealand farmer who when going through the fields found it useful to stimulate the workers with a few 'kind' words. That it was actually so was proved by an episode which happened a few years later in the Cavendish. One day it was necessary to break a hole through a stone wall to put through a cable needed for some experiment. The work was urgent and it happened that at that time there was a building strike and it was exceptionally difficult to find a bricklayer who would consent to work. Finally a man was found and he started work but after a while he came and said that he refused to go on. When asked why, he replied that twice a gentleman had passed by him and both times had asked him when he would finally start work and get the job done. These remarks offended the workman. When asked who this gentleman was, his description showed without a doubt that it was Rutherford. When we reproachfully pointed out to Rutherford that during a strike one should be a little careful we were surprised that Rutherford denied having said anything to the bricklayer. Obviously when he likewise grumbled at us in the laboratory for our slow work, he did it unconsciously; it was a kind of conditional reflex.

The greatest quality of Rutherford as a teacher was his ability to direct research work in the right direction, then to encourage the beginner and to give just appraisal of his achievements. What he valued most in a pupil was independent thought and originality in his work. Rutherford did his utmost to develop in his pupil an individuality. I remember how in the first years of my work in the Cavendish I once said to Rutherford, 'You know that the work of X is pretty hopeless; don't you think he's wasting his time and apparatus?' Rutherford replied that he too knew that the man was working on a hopeless problem, 'but', said Rutherford, 'it is a problem of his own and even if the work cannot be accomplished it will lead him to another original research problem which will be successful'. The future showed that Rutherford was right. As I said, Rutherford would do his utmost to develop in his pupils independence and originality of thought and as soon as a pupil showed these qualities Rutherford would pay close attention to his work. As an example of Rutherford's ability to direct the research of his pupils I remember the story, as Rutherford told it himself, of the discovery made by Moseley. In 1912 Moseley worked with Rutherford in Manchester. He was very young and Rutherford spoke of him as one of his best pupils. When Moseley came to Manchester he at once accomplished some minor research work and then eventually he came to Rutherford and told him of three different topics he would like to investigate. One of these researches was the classical work which had made Moseley's name so well known—the dependence of the wavelengths of Roentgen rays on the position of atoms in the periodic system. Rutherford at once advised Moseley to choose this work for his investigation. The future showed that Rutherford made the right choice, but he always pointed out that the idea of the experiment belonged to Moseley.

Rutherford was very particular to give credit for the exact authorship of any idea. He always did this in his lectures as well as in his published works. If anybody in the laboratory forgot to mention the author of the idea Rutherford always corrected him. He was also very particular not to give a beginner technically difficult research work. He reckoned that, even if a man was able, he needed some success to begin with. Otherwise he might be disappointed in his abilities, which could be disastrous for his future. Any success of a young research worker must be duly appreciated and must be duly acknowledged.

Once, in one of our outspoken talks, he told me that the most important thing a teacher must learn is not to be jealous of the successes of his pupils—which is not so easily done as the teacher gets older! This profound truth made a great impression on me. No doubt the greatest quality of a good teacher should be generosity. Rutherford was undoubtedly very generous and I think this is one of the main secrets which explains why so many first-class scientists came from his laboratory. There was always an atmosphere of freedom and efficiency there.

Rutherford well understood the importance that his pupils had for him. It was not merely that young research students increased the scientific productivity of the laboratory, but, as he said, 'My pupils keep me young.' This is very true, since pupils do not permit a teacher to lag behind new achievements in science. How often do we notice that when a scientist is ageing he starts opposing new ideas and underestimates the significance of new trends in science. Rutherford, with great ease and generosity, always accepted new ideas in physics like wave quantum mechanics, while a number of distinguished scientists of his generation were sceptical of the same ideas. Such conservatism is characteristic of scientists who work by themselves without having pupils to be directed and encouraged.

Rutherford was very sociable and loved talking to the scientists who came to visit him and the Cavendish Laboratory. Usually there were many such visitors. His attitude to other people's work was kind and considerate. In conversation Rutherford was very lively; he was fond of jokes and often made them himself. He laughed easily, his laughter was sincere, loud and infectious. His face was very expressive: you could see at once what mood he was in, good or bad, or whenever he was worried by anything. You always knew he was in a good temper when he good-naturedly teased the person he was talking to. The more he teased him, the more he liked him.

This was particularly noticeable when he talked to Bohr or to Langevin to both of whom he was especially attached. His kindest jokes often concealed a deeper sense. I remember one occasion when he brought Professor Robert Millikan to my room in the laboratory. Rutherford said to me, 'Let me introduce you to Millikan; no doubt you know who he is. Show him your installation to produce strong magnetic fields and tell him about your experiments. But I doubt whether he will let you speak as he himself will tell you about his own experiments!' There followed loud laughter in which Millikan joined with rather less enthusiasm. Rutherford then left us, and I soon found out that his prophecy was correct.

I shall not describe the way in which Rutherford read his papers. I always liked them very much as regards both their content and their exposition. He attached great importance to the way in which his papers were presented and evidently prepared them very carefully. He taught me how to read papers to the Royal Society, and one of his instructions I still remember very clearly: 'Don't show too many slides. When it is dark in the lecture room some of the audience take the opportunity to leave!'

Rutherford's interests were not limited narrowly to physics; they were much wider. He was well read, he liked books on geography and history and liked to discuss what he had read. He absorbed all knowledge enthusiastically and always extracted the essentials.

Later on, when I became a Fellow of Trinity and used to accompany him home after dinner on Sundays, we often discussed politics. On the first day I started work in the Cavendish I was surprised to hear him saying to me that in no circumstances would he tolerate my making communist propaganda in his laboratory. At this time this remark came quite unexpectedly. It not only surprised me, but also shocked me and to a certain extent even offended me. Undoubtedly it was a consequence of the current atmosphere of acute political struggle and was connected with the propaganda which existed in those days, only four years after the Russian revolution. Before coming to England, I was so absorbed by my research work in Russia that I was completely unaware of what was happening in Western Europe and could not appreciate the scale of the bitter political controversy which then existed. Later on when my first experimental research was published I presented Rutherford with a reprint and I made an inscription on it that this work was proof that I had come to his laboratory to do scientific work and not to make communist propaganda. He got extremely angry with this inscription, swore and gave me the reprint back. I had foreseen this and I had another reprint in reserve with an extremely appropriate inscription with which I immediately presented him. Obviously Rutherford appreciated my foresight and the incident closed. Rutherford had a characteristically hot temper but cooled down just as quickly.

Eventually we had many conversations on political questions: we were especially concerned about the growth of fascism in Europe. Rutherford was an optimist and thought that all would soon be over. We know now that this was not the case. Rutherford, like most scientists who work in the exact sciences, had progressive political views. I involved Rutherford in some political activity on two occasions.

The first of these was connected with Langevin. In his younger days Rutherford had worked with Langevin in the same room at the Cavendish. A deep friendship developed between them. Indeed it was practically impossible not to be friendly with a man of such brilliant intelligence and exceptional moral qualities. In Paris my friends, pupils of Langevin, were greatly shocked that Langevin, undoubtedly the best French physicist, had not been elected to the French Academy as a result of his left-wing political views. Langevin had taken part in a number of progressive organizations, had been the founder of the League of the Rights of Man (*Ligue des droits de l'homme*) and had fought anti-semitism in the Dreyfus case. I told Rutherford of the difficulties Langevin had encountered in France and asked him whether a man who held such leftist views as Langevin could be a Foreign Member of the Royal Society. Rutherford said something I could not quite follow, then started to tell me what a really good man Langevin was, and then recalled that during the war Langevin had been very active in inventing supersonic beams propagated in water by which he had established communication between England and France across the Channel. At this point the conversation ended. I learnt later that at the next election in 1928 Langevin was elected a Foreign Member of the Royal Society and this was much earlier than his election to the French Academy.

The second example occurred much later, when Hitler started to come into power. We were very anxious about the fate of such distinguished physicists as Stern, Frank, Born and a number of others in the conditions of active and increasing anti-semitism in Germany. About this time Zillard came to England and we were faced with the question of how to get these scientists out of Germany without raising suspicion. I spoke to Rutherford and he was very willing to help, writing personal letters to these scientists, and inviting them to come to lecture in Cambridge.

Rutherford took an interest in a great variety of people, but he particularly liked people with strong personalities. When Rutherford was elected President of the Royal Society and often had to attend dinner parties with distinguished politicians, businessmen and statesmen, he was fond of telling stories afterwards about the conversations he had had with them and always gave descriptions of them. I specially remember that Churchill made a great impression on Rutherford. His description of Churchill was, like all his descriptions, short and clear, and in due course I found out that it was quite correct. I well remember that Churchill in those days already regarded Hitler as a real danger to peace and called him 'a man riding a tiger'. Possibly this conversation somewhat altered Rutherford's optimistic view of the future. Rutherford's interest in understanding human psychology and his kindness to others was undoubtedly felt by them. This explains why Rutherford's excessively direct way of speaking which was sometimes not very tactful, was completely compensated for by his kindness and cordiality.

Of course Rutherford's correct evaluation of people and his understanding of them was due to the fact that he was a subtle psychologist. People interested him and he had the faculty of understanding them. His assessments of people were always very outspoken and direct. As in his scientific work, his description of a man was always brief and very accurate. I was always convinced that his descriptions were correct. Possibly his approach to people was also a subconscious process and could be called intuitive.

I should like to illustrate his interest in psychology with the following two episodes. In Cambridge there was a small but progressive theatre which produced Chekhov's play *Uncle Vanya*. Rutherford went to this play and was greatly taken with it. As in all Chekhov's works, it deals with a psychological problem complicated by the fact that all the people in the play are highly intellectual and therefore their acceptance of life is very complex. In the play a certain retired professor comes to live on the estate of his wife. Uncle Vanya, who manages the estate, has devoted his whole life to supporting the professor. Soon Uncle Vanya finds that the professor is a fake celebrity, scholastic and pedantic in his work. Against a background of complex psychological situations Uncle Vanya fires a pistol at the professor but misses him. I remember how vividly, clearly and simply Rutherford told me this plot and his sympathy was completely on Uncle Vanya's side. The fact that Rutherford was so attracted by the play shows that he undoubtedly enjoyed disentangling complicated psychological cases of this kind.

A great impression was made on me by the following case which demonstrates Rutherford's skill in handling complicated psychological problems. I think enough time has now passed and I can tell you about this case which involved the then well-known physicist, Paul Ehrenfest.

Ehrenfest was born in Austria. On one of his mountaineering excursions he met a Russian woman scientist and followed her to Russia where he married her. In Russia he published a number of outstanding theoretical works on thermodynamics. Eventually he was invited to Leiden University to take the chair of theoretical physics vacated by the great Lorentz, creator of the electronic theory of metals and one of the founders of the theory of relativity. In Leiden Ehrenfest and his house became one of the world centres of theoretical physics. Ehrenfest's main quality was his precise critical mind. He was not only a very good teacher of young scientists, who were very fond of him, but his criticisms were regarded as profound and of such high quality that leading theoretical scientists like Einstein and Bohr often came to Ehrenfest to discuss their work. Ehrenfest always noticed even the smallest contradiction or mistake. His critical remarks were made very readily, with great spirit and even sharply, but always very good-naturedly. The quality of his criticism was greatly appreciated. Despite our difference in age we became friends and I often visited his very hospitable and very charming family and more than once was present at his scientific discussions.

Ehrenfest's exceptionally strong critical mind evidently acted as a restraint on his creative imagination and he did not succeed in producing scientific work which he himself would have considered

12

of sufficiently high standard. In those days I did not know that in his acute nervous condition Ehrenfest suffered greatly when he could not in his work attain the level of the friends he criticized. I learnt about his feelings in the following manner. In the beginning of 1933 I received a long letter from him in which he described in detail his state of mental depression and spoke of the futility of his achievements. He had come to the conclusion that it was not worth living any more. The only way to save himself, he thought, was to leave Leiden and settle somewhere away from his friends. He asked me to help him to find a chair at some small university in Canada and to ask Rutherford, who doubtless had connections in Canada, to assist him. I was, of course, very upset by this letter. We all liked Ehrenfest and all knew that his influence as a teacher and critic in the development of modern physics was colossal. I translated the letter from German into English and came to Rutherford, who had little personal acquaintance with Ehrenfest. I handed Rutherford the letter and told him that we were very worried about Ehrenfest's future as, without any doubt, the letter showed that he was mentally unbalanced; perhaps, I said, this state was only temporary and everything possible should be done to help him out of his state of depression. Rutherford said I must not worry and he would handle the case himself. I do not know what Rutherford wrote to Ehrenfest but shortly afterwards I received a letter telling me that he was once again in a happy frame of mind. He said that Rutherford had explained what a great role he was playing in physics and he added that of course there was now no need for him to go to Canada. This story shows how skilfully Rutherford dealt with a very complicated psychological case, probably better than a professional psychiatrist.

A few months later, while I was on a visit to Russia, the state of depression returned to Ehrenfest and on September 25th, 1933, he committed suicide.

I should now like to recall quite a different and rather amusing case characteristic of Rutherford's attitude to the young. Once Rutherford called me into his study and I found him reading a letter and roaring with laughter. It appeared that the letter was from some Ukrainian schoolboys. They had written to say that they had organized a physics club and were proposing to continue Rutherford's fundamental work on the study of the nucleus of the atom and ask him to be an honorary member and to send them reprints of his scientific work. In the part of the letter in which they described Rutherford's achievements in nuclear physics, instead of using the correct term in physics they used a corresponding term which in slang has a different meaning. In this way the description of the structure of the atom acquired a property of the living organism. Its character is such that one does not speak about it in polite society, and it made Rutherford laugh heartily. I explained to Rutherford that the schoolboys were apparently not very well versed in English and the writing of the letter was mostly done with the use of a dictionary and the mistake was bona fide. Rutherford said that he appreciated this. He sent the boys a reply, thanking them for the honour of being elected a member of the club and promising to send them reprints.

Finally, I should like to discuss a question I have come across several times in descriptions of Rutherford's activities. The question is: did Rutherford foresee the great practical consequences which would emerge from his scientific discoveries and investigations into radioactivity?

The immense reserves of energy which are hidden in matter was understood by physicists a long time ago. The development of his view took place side by side with the development of the theory of relativity. The question which was not clear at that time was: would it eventually be possible to find technical means of making practical use of these reserves? We know now that the actual possibility of obtaining energy from nuclear collisions was becoming more and more real as nuclear phenomena were better understood. But up to the last moment it was not certain whether it would be technically possible to produce nuclear reactions with a great yield of energy. I remember only rare occasions on which I discussed this question with Rutherford and in all these conversations he expressed no interest in it. From the beginning of my acquaintance with Rutherford I noticed that he never took any interest in technical problems and I even had the impression that he was prejudiced about applied problems. Possibly this was because such problems were connected with business interests.

I am by training a chartered engineer and naturally I always took an interest in solving technical problems. During my stay in Cambridge I was approached several times to help in solving technical problems in industry. In these cases I used to take advice from Rutherford and he always said to me, 'You cannot serve God and Mammon at the same time.' Of course he was right. Once I remember Rutherford telling me about Pupin who as an able young physicist had come to Cambridge and done successful scientific work in the Cavendish Laboratory. Pupin was somewhat senior to Rutherford so they met only occasionally. Eventually, Pupin turned to commercial activity in the U.S.A. and made a lot of money. Rutherford spoke disapprovingly of Pupin's activities. So I think that Rutherford's opinions on the practical applications of nuclear physics had no real value as they lay outside the scope of his interests and tastes.

In connection with Rutherford's views on industry I remember a conversation I had with him during a high table dinner at Trinity College. I do not remember how the conversation started, maybe it was under the influence of Lombroso's book, *Genius and Madness*. I was telling my neighbour that every great scientist must be to some extent a madman. Rutherford overheard this conversation and asked me, 'In your opinion Kapitza, am I mad too?'

'Yes, Professor,' I replied.

'How will you prove it?' he asked.

'Very simply,' I replied. 'Maybe you remember a few days ago you mentioned to me that you had had a letter from the U.S.A., from a big American company. (I do not remember now which one it was, possibly General Electric Co.) In this letter they offered to build you a colossal laboratory in America and to pay you a fabulous salary. You only laughed at the offer and would not consider it seriously. I think you will agree with me that from the point of view of an ordinary man you acted like a madman!' Rutherford laughed and said that in all probability I was right.

The last time I saw Rutherford was in the autumn of 1934 when I went as usual to the Soviet Union to see my mother and my friends and unexpectedly was deprived of the possibility of returning to Cambridge. I did not hear his voice again, nor hear him laugh. For the next three years I had no laboratory to work in and was unable to continue my scientific work and the only scientist with whom I freely corresponded outside Russia was Rutherford. At least once every two months he wrote me long letters which I greatly valued. In these letters he gave me an account of life in

Cambridge, spoke about the scientific achievements of himself and his pupils, wrote about himself, made jokes, gave good advice and invariably cheered me up in my difficult position. He understood that the important thing for me was to start my scientific work which had been interrupted for several years. It is no secret that it was only due to his intervention and help that I was able to obtain the scientific installation and apparatus of the Mond Laboratory and in three years time I was able to renew my work in the domain of low-temperature physics.

I am sure that in the course of time all Rutherford's letters will be published but even so I should like here and now to quote three short extracts which require no comment.

On November 21st, 1935, he wrote:

... I am inclined to give you a little advice, even though it may not be necessary. I think it will be important for you to get down to work on the installations of the laboratory as soon as possible, and try to train your assistants to be useful. I think you will find many of your troubles will fall from you when you are hard at work again, and I am confident that your relations with the authorities will improve at once when they see that you are working wholeheartedly to get your show going. I would not worry too much about the attitude or opinions of individuals, provided they do not interfere with your work. I daresay you will think I do not understand the situation, but I am sure that chances of your happiness in the future depend on your keeping your nose down to the grindstone in the laboratory. Too much introspection is bad for anybody! ...

On May 15th, 1936, he wrote:

... This term I have been busier than I have ever been, but as you know my temper has improved during recent years, and I am not aware that anyone has suffered from it for the last few weeks! ...

... Get down to some research even though it may not be of an epoch-making kind as soon as you can and you will feel happier. The harder the work the less time you will have for other troubles. As you know, 'a reasonable number of fleas is good for a dog' — but I expect you feel you have more than the average number!

You see what short and clear and fatherly advice he gave me. The last letter is dated October 9th, 1937. He wrote in great detail about his proposed journey to India. In the last part of the letter he said: ' ... I am glad to say that I am feeling physically pretty fit, but I wish that life was not quite so strenuous in term time ... ' Ten days before his death he did not feel that it was so near.

For me the death of Rutherford meant not only the loss of a great teacher and friend; for me, as for a number of scientists, it was also the end of a whole epoch in science.

Obviously we should attribute to those years the beginning of the new period in the history of human culture which is now called the scientific-technical revolution. One of the greatest events in this revolution has been the use of atomic energy. We all know that the consequences of this revolution may be very terrible — it may destroy mankind. In 1921 Rutherford warned me not to make any communist propaganda in his laboratory, but it now appears that just at that time he himself together with his pupils were laying the foundations for a scientific-technical revolution.

We all hope that in the end people will have sufficient wisdom to direct this scientific revolution to the benefit of humanity.

But nevertheless the year that Rutherford died there disappeared forever the happy days of free scientific work which gave us such delight in our youth. Science has lost her freedom. Science has become a productive force. She has become rich but she has become enslaved and part of her is veiled in secrecy.

I do not know whether Rutherford would continue nowadays to joke and laugh as he used to do.

People and Situations: An Autobiographical Essay *by* Boris Pasternak

Novy Mir, 1967/1

Translated by Jacqueline Mitchell

People and Situations is an autobiographical essay by Boris Pasternak. It was written in 1956 as the preface to a book of his verse which was never published. He later revised the essay, gave it its present title and completely rewrote the concluding section. The subject matter deals only with the first half of his life, up to 1935. No doubt from an understandable wish to spare the feelings of many of his friends and relatives, Pasternak remains silent about the worst years of Stalin's oppression, which began with the first 'great purge' in 1936. Indeed, by the late 'thirties most of his contemporaries to whom he refers in any detail, such as the poets Yesenin, Mayakovsky Mandelshtam, Tsvetaeva, Sergei Tretyakov, Yashvili and Tabidze had died either by suicide or as a result of the Stalinist terror, while a minority such as Akhmatova and Pasternak himself managed by sheer good fortune to survive. Others, like Aseyev and Ehrenberg, owed their survival to varying degrees of compromise with the dictates of the regime.

Pasternak's aim in writing this essay was a limited one. As he himself described it: 'I have purposely restricted myself to the central core of the circle of my life. What I have written is sufficient to provide an understanding of how, in my particular case, life was transmuted into art, of how my art grew out of my destiny and experience.'

This conscious curtailment of its scope means that no mention is made of his later poetry, of his translations from Georgian poetry, his remarkable translations of Shakespeare, his dramatic fragment *The Blind Beauty*; nor, above all, is anything said of the work by which he is probably best known outside the U.S.S.R., the novel *Doctor Zhivago* and its accompanying poems. Nevertheless, in its modest compass it remains a frank, carefully distilled and wholly delightful exercise in self-revelation by one of the greatest writers of the century.

For its publication in *Novy Mir*, this piece of autobiography was edited by the author's son, Yevgeny Pasternak; thanks to his access to his father's papers and other archives, he has been able to correct the few minor chronological errors and other small lapses of memory. The footnotes supplied by Yevgeny Pasternak are indicated in the text by numbers; those inserted by the present editor, by asterisks. The editor is greatly indebted to the poet's sister, Mrs Lydia Pasternak-Slater, for her invaluable comment and assistance.

Childhood

1

In my autobiography *Safe Conduct*, written in the 'twenties, I examined the circumstances of my life which had made me what I was. Unfortunately the book was spoilt by being excessively mannered, a common defect of that time. Although I shall have to retell the story to some extent in this essay, I shall try to avoid repeating myself.

2

I was born in Moscow on January 29th, 1890 (Old Style),* in the Lyzhin's house opposite the theological seminary in Oruzheiny Street. Strangely enough I can still remember something of those autumn walks with my wet-nurse in the park alongside the seminary —the paths, sodden beneath piles of dead leaves, the ponds, the small mounds and the spiked, painted fence round the seminary, the games, fights and roars of laughter of the seminarists during their breaks from study.

Directly opposite the gates of the seminary stood a two-storey stone-built house with a yard where cab-drivers stabled their horses; our apartment was over the arch of the vaulted gateway.

3

My childhood sensations were a combination of fear and ecstasy, whose fairy-tale colours can be traced to the two chief impressions

* February 10th, according to the New Style or Gregorian calendar, which Russia did not adopt until 1918.

which dominated and linked them all; one was the image of the stuffed bears in the carriage-makers' workshops on Karetny Street, and the other was the image of the publisher P. P. Konchalovsky, that round-shouldered, shaggy, friendly giant with his deep, booming bass voice, his family, and the drawings in pencil and pen by Serov, Vrubel and the Vasnetsovs, father and brothers, which used to hang in the rooms of his apartment.

Our neighbourhood—Tverskaya-Yamskaya, Truba and the streets around the Tsvetnoy Boulevard—was most disreputable. I was often pulled away by the hand from things which I was not supposed to know about or to hear, but nannies and wet-nurses could not bear being alone, and whenever I was with them we were always surrounded by a gay and motley company. At midday the mounted police recruits did their training on the open square in front of the Znamensky Barracks.

From this contact with beggars and vagabonds, and from living in such proximity to the world of outcasts on the nearby boulevards, with their hard-luck stories and hysterical behaviour, I developed a precocious feeling of heartrending pity for women, which has lasted throughout my life, and an even more unbearable pity for my parents, who would die before me and for whom, to save them from the torments of hell, I would have to perform some impossibly saintly, unheard-of feat.

4

When I was three we moved to an official government apartment near the College of Painting, Sculpture and Architecture in Myasnitskaya Street opposite the post office. The apartment was in a small wing in the yard outside the main building.

This building, ancient and beautiful, was remarkable in many ways. It had survived the fire of 1812. A century earlier, under Catherine the Great, the Freemasons had used the house as a secret meeting-place for their lodge. On the side which curved around the corner of Myasnitskaya and Yuskov Streets there was a semicircular colonnaded balcony. This spacious balcony was recessed into the wall and communicated with the College's main assembly hall. From the balcony one could see the whole length of Myasnitskaya Street, stretching out into the distance towards the railways stations.

From this balcony the people living in the house had watched the ceremonial procession when the ashes of the Emperor Alexander III had been laid to rest in 1894, and two years later they had witnessed part of the celebrations held for the coronation of Nicholas II.

A crowd of students and teachers were standing there to watch. My mother held me in her arms in the crowd at the balcony railings. At her feet was a yawning abyss at the bottom of which the empty street, strewn with sand, lay silent in expectation. Officers bustled about issuing loud orders at the tops of their voices, although the sound could not be heard by the spectators up on the balcony, and it seemed as if the silence of the townspeople, standing with bated breath and being pressed back on to the pavement by cordons of soldiers from the road, swallowed up every sound as completely as sand swallows up water. The bells began to toll slowly and mournfully. From the far distance there swept past us and away a rolling wave of hands raised to heads: all Moscow bared its head and crossed itself. The head of the endless procession appeared, to the tolling of funeral bells which filled the air—troops, clergy, plumed horses caparisoned in black, the unbelievably ornate catafalque, and heralds dressed in the wondrous costumes of a bygone age. On and on went the procession, the house-fronts shrouded in long strips of crêpe and festooned in black, the funeral banners dipped in dejection.

A certain sense of pomp was inseparable from the College, which came under the jurisdiction of the Ministry of the Imperial Court. The Grand Duke Sergei Alexandrovich was its patron, and he used to attend its speech days and exhibitions. The Grand Duke was a tall, lanky man. Covering their albums with their hats, my father and Serov would draw caricatures of him at parties given by the Golitsins and the Yakunchikovs, which the Grand Duke used to attend.

5

Our wing of the building was situated among the outhouses and coach stables in the courtyard, facing the gate which led into a small garden full of ancient trees. Down below in the cellar, hot lunches were served to the students. The smell of greasy pies and puddings and fried meatballs lingered permanently on the staircase.

The door to our apartment was on the first-floor landing. The College secretary lived on the floor above.

Fifty years after it happened, in the Soviet era, I read about an incident in N. S. Rodionov's book *The Place of Moscow in the Life and Work of L. N. Tolstoy*. On page 125, describing the year 1894, he writes:

> On November 23rd, Tolstoy and his daughters went to see the artist L. O. Pasternak at his home in the College of Painting, Sculpture and Architecture, of which he was the Principal, to attend a concert in which Pasternak's wife and two professors from the Conservatoire, the violinist I. V. Grzhimali and the 'cellist A. A. Brandyukov, were performing.

This is all correct, apart from one slight error: Prince Lvov, and not my father, was the Principal of the College.

I well remember the evening that Rodionov described. I woke up in the middle of it with a delicious twinge of pain, stronger than I had ever felt before. I began shrieking and crying with loneliness and fear, but the music drowned my weeping, and only when they had finished playing the movement of the trio which had woken me was I heard. The curtain behind which I lay and which divided the room into two was drawn apart. My mother appeared, bent down over me and soon calmed me down. I think I must have been carried in to see the guests, or perhaps I caught a glimpse of the drawing-room through an open doorway. It was full of tobacco smoke. The candle flames fluttered like lashes, as if they were eyes and the smoke was making them smart. They cast a brilliant light on the polished mahogany of the violin and 'cello. Beside them loomed the black shape of the grand piano. Black, too, were the men's frock-coats, and the ladies' necks and shoulders seemed to sprout out of their dresses like flowers in a birthday posy. Smoke rings were wreathed about the grey heads of two or three old men. Later I got to know one of them well and saw him often. This was the artist N. N. Gué. The other old man was to affect my whole life, as he affected most people's, but mine especially because my father did some illustrations for him, used to visit him and respected him; and because his spirit pervaded our whole household. This man was Lev Nikolaevich Tolstoy.

Why, I wonder, did I cry so much, and how is it that I can

remember my distress so well? I was, after all, used to hearing the piano in the house, for my mother was an accomplished pianist. The sound of the grand piano was to me inseparably bound up with the very notion of music. The tone of stringed instruments, however, especially in a chamber ensemble, I found strange and disturbing, as if they were really cries for help or omens of disaster floating in from outside through the open window.

Two people died during that winter, I seem to remember — Anton Rubinstein and Tchaikovsky. They were probably playing Tchaikovsky's famous piano trio at the time.

That night marked a kind of watershed that divided the blurred impressions of my early infancy from my later childhood. It is from that night that my memory comes into play and from then on my consciousness began to function, without any very great gaps or interruptions, as in an adult.

6

In the spring, exhibitions of the Peredvizhniki school of painters were held in the halls of the College. The crates of paintings were brought during the winter from St Petersburg, and were stored in the row of sheds facing the windows at the back of our apartment. Then before Easter the crates would be brought out into the court-yard and unpacked out of doors in front of the sheds. The College staff opened the crates, unscrewed the pictures from their heavy frames where they were fastened to the bottoms and tops of the crates and carried them two at a time across the courtyard for the exhibition. We children would squeeze on to the window ledges and watch it all avidly. Thus the greatest works of Repin, Myasoye-dov, Makovsky, Surikov and Polyonov, a good half of the paintings to be found in the galleries and state collections of today, passed before our eyes.

At first my father and other artists close to him exhibited in these Peredvizhniki exhibitions, but not for long. Very soon Serov, Levitan, Korovin, Vrubel, Ivanov, my father and others formed an association of younger artists known as the Union of Russian Artists.

In the late 'nineties the sculptor Pavel Trubetskoy, who had lived all his life in Italy, came to Moscow. He was given a new studio with a skylight, which was built out from the wall of our house and which enclosed our kitchen window, having previously looked out on to the courtyard, it now opened into Trubetskoy's studio. From the kitchen we used to watch him and his caster, Robecchi, at work, and we also used to watch his models, who were anything from children and ballerinas, to two-horse carriages and mounted cossacks, for whom there was ample space to ride through the wide doors of his vast studio.

My father's wonderful illustrations to Tolstoy's *Resurrection* were dispatched to St Petersburg from this same kitchen. In its finally revised form, the novel was printed chapter by chapter in the journal *Niva*, published by Marx in St Petersburg. Work on this was a feverish affair, and I shall always remember how my father had to hurry over it. The issues of this journal always came out on time, so my father had to meet the deadline for every one.

Tolstoy took a long time correcting the proofs and made endless alterations. There was always the danger that the drawings, which had been based on his original text, would not match up with his subsequent alterations. But my father made his sketches from the very places from which Tolstoy himself had drawn his observations: the court-room, the transit prison, the countryside and the railway. The risk of deviating from the original was averted by the wealth of vivid detail and by the sense of realism which they both shared.

Because of the urgency, they seized every possible opportunity to dispatch the drawings in time. All the guards of the express trains on the Moscow–St Petersburg railway were pressed into service. My childish imagination was deeply impressed by the sight of a guard in his uniform greatcoat as he stood waiting in the doorway of our kitchen, as though he were on a station platform standing beside the carriage door of a train about to depart.

Joiner's glue would be heated up on the stove, the drawings would be given a quick rub down, dried with fixative, stuck on to sheets of cardboard, wrapped up and tied. When the packages were ready they were sealed with sealing-wax and handed over to the guard.

Scriabin

I

The first and second decades of my life were very different from each other. Moscow in the 'nineties still looked like a fabulously picturesque but remote provincial town, with its legendary associations with the days when it had been called 'the Third Rome', or the fabled capital of ancient epic tales in all the splendour of its celebrated forty times forty churches. The old customs were still observed. In the autumn, horses were blessed in Yushkov Street, into which the college courtyard opened, in front of the church of Sts Frol and Lavr, who were by tradition the patron saints of horse-breeding. With the drivers and grooms who had brought them to be blessed, the horses filled the whole street as far as the College gates, as though it were a horse fair.

In my childhood memories, everything seemed to change as if at the wave of a magic wand when the new century began. Moscow was seized by the same fury of business activity which gripped the chief capitals of the world. Tall blocks of rented apartments were built with tremendous speed, to give a quick return on investment. On every street these brick giants shot skywards almost before one had time to notice it. With them, outpacing Petersburg, Moscow created a new style of Russian art—the fresh, youthful, modern art of the big city.

2

The feverish style of the 'nineties was also reflected in the College. Government funds did not suffice for its upkeep, and business experts were called in to find means of increasing the College's income. It was decided to build some multi-storey blocks of rented apartments on College land, and in the middle of the grounds, where the garden had been, to build a glass exhibition hall that would be leased out. In the late 'nineties demolition began on the houses and sheds inside the courtyard, and deep trenches were dug on the site of the uprooted garden. These pits filled with water and became ponds where drowned rats floated and frogs jumped about and dived into the water. Our wing, too, was scheduled for demolition.

One winter we were given a new apartment made out of two or three classrooms and lecture halls in the main building. We moved into it in 1901. Since the apartment had been converted from a number of rooms, one of which was circular, and another was of an even more arbitrary shape, our new home, where we were to live for ten years, had a crescent-shaped pantry and bathroom, an oval kitchen and a dining-room with a semicircular protrusion jutting into it. Muffled sounds could always be heard from the College studios and corridors, and from the end room adjacent to the College we could hear Professor Chaplygin lecturing to the architecture class on heating installation.

In the past, when we had been in the old apartment, my mother and sometimes a private tutor had looked after my pre-school education. At one time I was coached for the Sts Peter and Paul High School, and I was made to learn the whole initial syllabus in German.

Of these tutors, whom I recall with gratitude, I would particularly like to mention my first one, Ekaterina Ivanovna Boratynskaya, who wrote children's stories and translated children's books from English. She taught me reading, writing, elementary arithmetic and the rudiments of French through the method of telling me how to sit in my chair and how to hold a pen in my hand. I used to be taken to her furnished apartment for my lesson. Her room was dark, and the walls were lined from top to bottom with books. It smelt of cleanliness, discipline, boiled milk and roasted coffee. Outside the windows with their crocheted lace curtains, dirty creamy-grey snow would fall, looking like a loose knitting pattern. This used to distract me and I would reply absentmindedly to Ekaterina Ivanovna's remarks to me in French. At the end of the lesson Ekaterina Ivanovna would wipe her pen-nib on the inside of her jersey and wait until someone came to fetch me before letting me go.

In 1901 I started in the second form of Moscow's Fifth High School, which had kept the classical syllabus after Vannovsky's reform, and in addition to natural sciences and the other new subjects which he had introduced, Greek was still on the curriculum.

3

In the spring of 1903 my father rented a *dacha* in Obolenskoe near Maloyaroslavets, on the Bryansk, now the Kiev railway. Our neighbour, as it turned out, was Scriabin. Until then we had not known the Scriabins. Our dachas stood on a hillside some distance apart from each other on the edge of a forest. As usual, we arrived at our dacha early in the morning. The sun still hung low over the house, its rays filtering through the leaves of the forest. The bales of matting were ripped open and the stitching unpicked as our bedding, provisions, pans and buckets were taken out. I ran off into the forest.

Good Lord above, what a place the forest was that morning! The dappled sunlight, the shifting forest shadows ever on the move like someone trying to keep his hat straight in a gale, the birds swaying up and down on the branches as they poured out that chirruping song that is always unexpected and fresh, loud and irregular at first, and then becoming part of the background, until its fervent persistence becomes as beautiful as the trees of the forest as they retreat into the distance. And just like the interplay of light and shade in the wood, just as the birds flew from branch to branch, and sang, so odd snatches of the Third Symphony of the 'Poème de l'Extase', which were being composed at the piano in the neighbouring dacha, floated and echoed through the air.

God, what music that was! The symphony was continually collapsing in ruins like a city under artillery fire, only to rise again, rebuilt from the wreckage and destruction. It was bursting with fantastically new and elaborate musical ideas, just as the forest with its vitality and freshness was new on that morning, clothed, if you understand me, in the spring foliage not of 1803 but of *1903*. Just as no leaf in that forest was made out of corrugated paper or painted tin, so the symphony was utterly free of pseudo-profundity or borrowed rhetoric; there was nothing in it that was 'like Beethoven', 'like Glinka' or like anybody else at all, but the tragic power of the music expressed a magnificent scorn of everything that was drably derivative, pompous and dull, and instead was joyously daring to the point of madness, mischievous, elemental and as free as a fallen angel.

One might imagine that the man who had composed such music must acquire a great insight into his own nature, and that when his work was over he would be lucid, clear-headed, calm and rested, like God when he rested from his work on the seventh day. Such indeed was Scriabin.

He and my father often used to go for walks along the Warsaw highway which passed nearby. Sometimes I went with them. Scriabin used to like to take a run and then jump, moving forward with a kind of hopping motion as though propelled by his own momentum like a stone ricocheting across the water, and one felt that if he had gone on much longer he would have taken off and floated through the air. Indeed, he cultivated several variants of this kind of inspired agility and the lithe movement that bordered on flight. These displays are to be put down to his entrancing elegance, the sophisticated manner with which in society he avoided anything that smacked of seriousness and tried instead to seem vapid and superficial. So his paradoxical character seemed all the more astounding when it was revealed on those walks at Obolenskoe.

He would argue with my father about life, about art, and about good and evil; he would attack Tolstoy, and preach Nietzsche's philosophy of amoralism and the Superman. They agreed on one thing—their views on the nature and obligations of the creative artist. On all else they disagreed.

I was twelve years old and did not understand half their arguments, but Scriabin won me over by his freshness and vitality. I was deeply fond of him, and although I could not fully understand his views, I was on his side. Soon afterwards he left to spend six years in Switzerland.

Our return to town that autumn was delayed because I had an accident. My father had planned a painting which was to be called 'To the Night Pasture'. It depicted some girls on horseback from the village of Bocharovo driving a herd of horses as fast as they could gallop towards the bogland pasture at the foot of our hill at sunset. Once I joined up with them, and while jumping a wide stream fell from my galloping horse and broke my leg, which set shorter than the other one. This later exempted me from all military service.

Even before that summer in Obolenskoe I used to strum on the piano a little and could just about pick out a tune of my own. Now, influenced by my adoration for Scriabin, I became passionately keen to improvise and compose. From that autumn onwards I spent my six high school years learning the fundamentals of the theory of composition, at first under the guidance of that noble man Y. D. Engel, a noted musicologist and critic of the time, and then under Professor R. M. Glière.

No one had any doubt about my future. My destiny was agreed upon, my path rightly chosen. I was intended for a musician, and was forgiven everything for the sake of my music—all my beastly ingratitude towards my elders, to whom I was not fit to hold a candle, my obstinacy, disobedience and my thoughtless, eccentric behaviour. Even at school, when I was asked a question in a Greek or mathematics lesson and was caught solving problems of fugue and counterpoint in the music book which lay open on my desk, I would stand rooted to the spot and unable to answer while the whole class covered up for me, and the teachers invariably let me off. And yet in spite of this I abandoned music.

I abandoned it when by rights I should have been rejoicing, and when all around were congratulating me. My God and idol had returned from Switzerland with his 'Poème de l'Extase' and his other most recent works. Moscow was celebrating his victorious return. At the very height of his triumph I was bold enough to go and see him and play him my compositions. Scriabin's reception of me passed all expectation; he listened to it all and then gave me support, encouragement, inspiration and his blessing.

But no one knew about my secret plight, and even if I had told anyone about it they would not have believed me. Although my composing was making progress, my practical skill was abysmal. I could barely play the piano and could not read music fast enough, having to pick it out almost note by note. The discrepancy between my free-ranging musical ideas and their inadequate technical execution turned this natural talent, which might have been a source of delight, into a constant torture which, in the end, I was unable to bear. How was this discordance possible? Fundamentally it was caused by an improper attitude on my part, something which was bound to evoke a reprisal, an unforgivable adolescent arrogance, the nihilistic scorn of the semi-educated for every worthwhile, accessible goal. I despised everything that depended on hard work rather than creativity, having the cheek to believe that I understood such things. I imagined that everything in life should be like a miracle, preordained from above, and that nothing should be deliberate, intentional or the product of the conscious will.

This was the reverse side of Scriabin's influence, which had become decisive for me in everything. His egocentricity was appropriate and justifiable only in his own case, but the seeds of his opinions, misinterpreted by my callow mind, fell on fertile ground.

Since early childhood I had inclined towards mysticism and superstition, and felt attracted by anything that smacked of pre-destination or prophetic fate. Almost from the night of the concert Rodionov describes I had believed that there was some higher, heroic plane of existence which had to be served with rapture even

PEOPLE AND SITUATIONS 371

though it brought suffering. Many times at the ages of six, seven or eight I was near to suicide.

I suspected that I was surrounded by every kind of mystery and deception, and I would have believed any piece of nonsense. Sometimes when I was very young—the only time of life when such absurdity is conceivable—remembering perhaps the first little smocks which I had been dressed in as a baby, I used to imagine that once upon a time I had been a girl, and I would pull in my belt so tightly that I nearly fainted in the attempt to regain my other more charming and fascinating self. At other times I would imagine that I was not my parents' son but some foundling they had taken in and adopted.

In the same way the causes of my failure at music were indirect and imaginary, conjectures based on chance circumstance, the expectation of signs and portents from above. I did not have perfect pitch, the ability to identify any note chosen at random—a skill which was in any case quite unnecessary for my work. The lack of this particular ability grieved and humiliated me, and I saw it as proof that my music was not pleasing to fate or to heaven. Under this multitude of blows I lost heart and gave up.

I wrenched myself away from music, from that beloved world of six years of toil, hope and anxiety, feeling as people do who part with their most treasured possession. For some time my habit of improvising on the piano remained with me, but it was a knack which gradually disappeared. I then decided to make my renunciation of music more drastic; I no longer touched the piano or went to concerts, and I avoided meeting musicians.

4

Scriabin's notion about the Superman was a form of the Russian yearning for extremes. He thought that not only should music be super-music in order to have any significance, but everything on earth should transcend itself in order to be wholly true to its nature. Man and his deeds must contain an element of the infinite if they were to attain the truth of their finite selves.

Because I have now abandoned music, and my links with it have faded and died so completely, the Scriabin of my memories, the Scriabin who was the mainstay of my existence, who had nourished me like my daily bread, has remained the Scriabin of his middle period, approximately from his third to his fifth sonata. The flashing harmonies of 'Prometheus' and of his last works are nothing more to me than evidence of his genius, and not the everyday nourishment of the mind; but I had no need of this evidence because I already believed in him without it.

People who died young, such as Andrei Biely, Khlebnikov* and a few others, were searching before they died for new means of expression, dreaming of a new language, groping and feeling their way in their search for its syllables, vowels and consonants.

I have never understood the need for this search. For me, the most startling developments occur when an artist is so bursting with what he has to say that he has no time to think, and utters his new words in the old language without caring whether it is old or new. Thus Chopin, using the old idiom of Mozart and John Field, still had something so shatteringly new to say that it became the start of a new age in music. In the same way Scriabin, at the very beginning of his career, used the means of his predecessors to bring about a fundamental renewal of the perception of music. In such early works as his Etudes, opus 8, or his Preludes of opus 11 his music is entirely modern, full of purely musical analogies with the outside world, with the environment in which people of those days lived, thought, felt, travelled and dressed.

The melodies of those works of his are so affecting that tears at once start from the corners of your eyes and run down your cheeks to the corners of your mouth. The melodies, mingling with your tears, flow straight along your nerves to your heart, and you cry, not because you are sad but because he has pierced you to your heart with such unerring poignancy.

Suddenly the melody will be interrupted by an answering or a conflicting note in a woman's voice in a higher register, then by another in a simpler and more conversational tone. An unexpected clash, a momentary discord quickly resolved. He introduces a note of such utter naturalness into the work, the kind of naturalness which is decisive in any work of art.

* For a note on Andrei Biely see the introduction to his *Reminiscences of Blok*, pp. 57–9. Viktor Khlebnikov (1885–1922). One of the leaders of the futurist movement in poetry, Khlebnikov was remarkable for his radical, iconoclastic treatment of words and verse-forms. Contributor to the futurist manifesto of 1922 called *A Slap in the Face to Public Taste*.

Art is full of commonplaces and everyday truths. Although they are there for all to use, simple things often wait in vain to be used. Only rarely does fortune smile on an obvious truth; perhaps once in a hundred years it will find its proper expression. Scriabin was such a stroke of fortune as this. Just as Dostoevsky was not merely a novelist, just as Blok was not merely a poet, so Scriabin was not only a composer but a cause of everlasting delight, the zenith and the personified triumph of Russian culture.

The Nineteen Hundreds

I

In response to student demonstrations after the manifesto of October 17th, [1905],* a turbulent mob sacked the University and the Technical College. The College of Art was also threatened with attack. On the landings of the main staircase piles of cobblestones were prepared under the Principal's orders, and hoses were screwed on to the fire hydrants in readiness for the assailants.

Demonstrators from passing street processions came into the College, organized meetings in the assembly hall, took over the premises, appeared on the balcony and made speeches to the people in the streets below. The College students formed armed detachments and manned their own brigade to patrol the building at night.

Some notes made at the time have been preserved among my father's papers: 'Mounted dragoons charge at the crowd and fire from below at a woman agitator speaking from the balcony. She is wounded, but goes on speaking, clutching a pillar to stop herself from falling.'

At the end of 1905 Gorky arrived in Moscow. The city was paralysed by a general strike. The nights were freezing, Moscow was plunged in darkness and lit only by bonfires. Stray bullets whistled about the streets and mounted Cossack patrols dashed furiously across the silent untrodden snow. My father met Gorky to discuss the satirical political magazine *Bich* ('The Scourge') and

* The October Manifesto, issued by Nicholas II in response to the pressures of the 1905 revolution, granted Russia a limited form of constitutional government.

Zhupel ('The Bugbear'), and others to which he had been invited to contribute.

It must have been at that time or a little later, after the year I spent in Berlin with my parents, that for the first time in my life I saw some lines written by Blok. I cannot remember what the poem was—it may have been his 'Willow Branches' or something out of 'To The Children', dedicated to Olenina d'Alheim, or something revolutionary, something about St Petersburg—but I can remember my impression so clearly that the memory can be revived and I shall try to describe it.

2

What is literature in the most widespread, everyday sense of the word? It is a world of eloquence, of generalities, of neatly turned sentences, written by respected names who saw something of life when they were young but who on achieving fame lapse into abstractions, clichés and commonplaces. And when someone who is far more than a mere phrase-maker opens his mouth in this world of entrenched and therefore unnoticed artificiality, and when this someone knows something and intends to say it, it seems revolutionary. It is as if doors are flung open to let in the tumult of life outside, as if this is not a man talking about what is happening in the city but the city itself speaking through the lips of this man. So it was with Blok. Such was the unique, childlike, unspoilt nature of his message; such was the strength of what he did.

The paper seemed to contain some kind of news. It was as though the news itself had spread unbidden across the printed page, but that no man had composed or written these verses. It seemed that what covered the page were not verses about the wind, about puddles in the street, about street lamps and stars, but that the lamps and puddles themselves were spreading their windswept ripples across the surface of the paper, impressing their great wet marks upon it.

3

I and several others whom I shall mention later spent the days of our youth with Blok. In Blok there was everything which makes a man a great poet—fire, tenderness, insight, his own image of the world, his own special touch which transformed everything, a consciousness of his own secret, withdrawn, yet all-embracing destiny. Of these qualities, and many others besides, I shall dwell on the one which perhaps influenced me most, and which therefore seems to me pre-eminent: the urgency of Blok's restless gaze, the fluency of his observation.

> Flicker of light in a window.
> Half-lit, alone
> By a doorway, Harlequin
> Whispers to the dark ...
>
> A snowstorm lashes the streets,
> Swirling, staggering.
> A hand reaches out to me
> And someone smiles ...
>
> A hand's wave, a tantalizing light.
> Winter's night on a porch,
> A shadow like a silhouette,
> A face swiftly hidden.

Adjectives without nouns, predicates without subjects, a game of hide-and-seek, disjointed phrases, figures which flit past in a trice, abruptness—how well this style fitted the spirit of the age, the furtive, secretive, underground spirit as yet hardly emerged from the cellars and which spoke the language of conspiracy, whose chief plotter was the city itself and whose chief event was the street.

These characteristics are the essence of Blok's being, the essential, fundamental Blok, the Blok of the second volume published by Alkonost,* the Blok who wrote 'Terrible World', 'The Last Day', 'Deception', 'A Tale', 'Legend', 'The Meeting', 'The Unknown Woman', and the poems: 'In the mist above the sparkling dew'; 'In taverns, in side streets and in the winding lanes', and 'A girl was singing in the church's choir'.

Traces of reality whirl through Blok's works like a current of air carried on the whirlwind of his sensitivity, as well as elements so remote as to seem like mysticism, concepts of what one might call

* A publishing house founded in 1918 in Petrograd by S. M. Alyansky. Published almost all of Blok's post-revolutionary poetry, also works by Biely, Akhmatova, Remizov and others. After 1923 Alkonost left Russia and continued publishing in emigration.

the 'divine'. These are not metaphysical fantasies but snatches of everyday church language which permeate his poetry, passages from the litany, the prayers before communion and requiem psalms, known by heart and heard a hundred times in church services.

The totality of his world, the spiritual and physical expression of that reality was the city of Blok's poetry, the principal character in his life and his art. This city, Blok's Petersburg, is the most real of all the Petersburgs described by modern artists. Its existence in the imagination is indistinguishable from its existence in life, it is charged with that everyday prose which nourishes poetry with its drama and its anguish, and in its streets there sounds the ordinary humdrum colloquial speech which so invigorates the language of poetry.

At the same time the image of this city is composed of elements picked out by such a sensitive hand and subjected to an inspiration of such power that it is wholly transformed into a captivating picture of the rarest kind of inner world.

4

I was fortunate enough to be able to know many of the older poets who lived in Moscow—Bryusov, Andrei Biely, Khodasevich, Vyacheslav Ivanov and Baltrushaitis.* I was first introduced to Blok during his last visit to Moscow, in the corridor or on the staircase of the Polytechnic Museum, when he was speaking one evening in the Museum lecture-hall. Blok was very kind to me and said that he had heard favourable reports of me. He complained of feeling unwell and asked me to postpone our next meeting until his health had improved.

That evening he was giving a poetry-reading in three different places—the Polytechnic Museum, the Press House and the Dante Society, where his keenest admirers had gathered to hear him read his 'Italian Verses'.

---

* Valery Bryusov. See note p. 69.

Vladislav Khodasevich (1886–1939). Russian poet of Polish origin, who combined mysticism with a style of refined classicism.

Vyacheslav Ivanov (1886–1949). A prominent symbolist poet who welcomed revolution in the abstract, but was disillusioned by its violence and destruction. Emigrated in 1924; died in Rome.

Yurgis Baltrushaitis (1893–1944). Symbolist poet who wrote in Lithuanian and Russian. Lithuanian ambassador to U.S.S.R., 1921–39. Died in Paris.

Mayakovsky was at that poetry-reading in the Polytechnic Museum. In the middle of it he told me that the audience at the Press House was planning to give Blok a so-called 'benefit night' by hissing him and shouting him down—all under the guise of 'critical integrity'. He suggested that we go there together in order to thwart this disgraceful plan.

We left Blok's poetry-reading and set out on foot. Blok was taken to the second meeting by car, and by the time we got to the Press House in Nikitsky Boulevard, the reading was over and Blok had moved on to the Society for Italian Literature. In the meantime the scandalous scene that we had feared had already taken place. After his reading in the Press House, Blok had been subjected to a barrage of monstrous insults by people who dared to reproach him with having outlived his time and with being spiritually dead, to which he calmly agreed. All this was said only a few months before he actually died.*

5

In those early years of our first brash experiments, only two people, Aseyev† and Tsvetaeva, had achieved a mature and fully developed poetic language. The much praised originality of the others, including myself, sprang only from the fact that we were unoriginal and derivative, which nevertheless did not prevent us from writing, translating and being published. The most appalling of the painfully inept work which I did at that time were my translations of Ben Jonson's *The Alchemist* and Goethe's *Die Geheimnisse*. Among the reviews which Blok wrote for the World Literature publishing house, and which can be found in the last volume of his collected works, is one about these translations of mine. I agree that his devastatingly uncomplimentary criticism is wholly justified. However, I must stop running ahead of events and return to my account which I left in the 'nineties, those years now so long past.

6

When I was in my third or fourth year at high school, I travelled alone to St Petersburg from the Christmas holidays on a free ticket

* Blok died in August 1921.

† Nikolai Aseyev (b. 1889). A romantic poet of the revolution, one of the founder members of the 'LEF' group of futurists (q.v. below, p. 404). Later became an official propagandist in verse.

given to me by my uncle, who was in charge of the freight yards at the Petersburg end of the Moscow–Petersburg railway. For days I wandered through the streets of that immortal city, as though devouring with my eyes and legs some work of genius written in a stone book, and in the evenings I would go to Komissarzhevskaya's Theatre. I was completely in thrall to avant-garde modern literature, infatuated with Andrei Biely, Knut Hamsun and Przybyszewski.*

I learned much more about what travelling really means when our whole family went to Berlin in 1906. This was my first journey abroad.

Everything was so strange and different. It was as though one were not really living through it but dreaming it, voluntarily taking part in some made-up theatrical show. You knew no one and there was no one to tell you what to do. There was a long row of opening and slamming doors along the whole length of the railway carriage with a separate door for each compartment. Four-track railway lines on the city's elevated railroad, suspended over streets, canals, racing stables and the backyards of the gigantic city. Trains racing and overtaking each other, trains travelling side by side and then branching off in different directions. Lines of street lamps under the bridges, doubling, intersecting and crossing each other, lights in the second and third storeys of buildings on a level with the fly-overs, automatic machines in station buffets lit up with different colours and selling cigars, sweets and sugared almonds. I soon got used to Berlin, and would stroll along its countless streets and its vast, seemingly boundless park; I spoke German imitating a Berlin accent and breathed in a mixture of locomotive smoke, gas and beer fumes, and listened to Wagner's music.

Berlin was full of Russians. The composer Rebikov used to play his 'Christmas Tree' to his friends, and divided music into three periods: 'animal music' up to Beethoven, 'human music' since then and 'the music of the future' which was to begin after him.

Gorky was also in Berlin. My father drew a picture of him. Andreyeva† did not like the fact that his cheekbones looked so

* For note on Knut Hamsun, see above, p. 192. Stanislaw Przybyszewski (1868–1927). Polish poet and playwright whose erotic, decadent 'modernism' was fashionable in St Petersburg at the turn of the century.

† Maria Yurkovskaya, alias Andreyeva (1868–1953). Distinguished actress; early member of Bolshevik Party. For many years Gorky's secretary, interpreter and mistress.

prominent in the drawing, because it made him look too angular. She said, 'You haven't understood him. He's *gothic*.' That was how people used to talk in those days.

7

It must have been after my return to Moscow from this trip that another great lyric poet of this century entered my life. This was the German poet Rainer Maria Rilke, who, although he is famous throughout the world today, was scarcely known at the time.

In 1900 he visited Tolstoy at Yasnaya Polyana, knew and corresponded with my father, and spent the summer with the peasant poet Drozhzhin at Zavidovo near Klin.

In those far-off days he gave my father his early collection of poetry and inscribed them affectionately. Many years later two of these books came into my hands during one of the winters I have described, and they gave me as much of a shock as I had received on first reading the verses of Blok: I was astounded by the urgency, conviction, inevitability and seriousness of his poetry, the directness of his language.

8

Rilke is quite unknown in Russia. The few attempts to translate him into Russian have been unsuccessful. It is not the translators' fault; they are accustomed to reproduce the sense and not the tone of what is said, but with Rilke everything depends on the tone.

When Verhaeren* was in Moscow in 1913, my father drew his portrait. Sometimes he used to ask me to entertain his sitters so that their faces would not become too set and expressionless. I once had to entertain the historian V. O. Klyuchevesky in this way, and I was called upon to do the same with Verhaeran. With pardonable enthusiasm I told him how I admired him, and then asked him tentatively whether he had ever heard of Rilke. I had not supposed that Verhaeran would know him, but his face changed immediately. My father could have hoped for nothing better.

* Emile Verhaeren (1855–1916). Leading Belgian poet and playwright, who wrote in French. His works, popular in Russia, were translated by Blok and Bryusov.

This one name brought the sitter to life more than anything else I had to say. 'He is the greatest poet in Europe,' said Verhaeren. 'And he is, as it were, my favourite brother.'

For Blok, prose remained the ultimate source of his poetry; but he never used it as a means of expression. For Rilke, the pictorial and psychological methods of modern novelists (Tolstoy, Flaubert, Proust and the Scandinavians) were inseparable from the language and style of his poetry.

Yet analyse him as I may, I cannot give a true picture of him unless I quote some examples of his work which I have translated especially for this chapter.

9

The Reader

I'd long been reading. Since with rush of rain
this afternoon first dimmed the window-pane.
The wind outside had passed from my regard:
my book was hard.
And, as I turned its pages, I would con them
like features darkened by reflectiveness;
time's flow was stemmed around my studiousness.
Then of a sudden something overshone them,
and, ousting anxious verbal maziness,
stood: Evening, Evening ... everywhere upon them.
I do not yet look out, but the long lines
have split in two, and words from their combining
threads roll away wherever they're inclining ...

And then I know: above the serpentining,
glittering gardens, there's a spaciousness;
yes, once again the sun must have been shining.
Now summer-night is all encompassing:
small groups are formed by what lay scatteredly,
people on long walks wander darksomely,
and strangely far, as though more meaningly,
is heard the little that's still happening.

And when I gaze up now from what I've read,
everything's great and nothing's unakin.
Out there exists what I live here within,
and here and there it's all unlimited;
save that I weave myself still more therein
when on to outward things my glances fly
and gravely simple masses formed thereby —
there far beyond itself the earth's outswelling.
It seems to be embracing all the sky,
and the first star is like the farthest dwelling.

Westerwede, September 1901

The Spectator

I watch the storms in the trees above:
after days of mild decaying
my windows shrink from their assaying,
and the things I hear the distance saying,
without a friend I find dismaying,
without a sister cannot love.

There goes the storm to urge and alter,
through forest trees and through time's tree;
and nothing seems to age or falter:
the landscape like an open psalter,
speaks gravely of eternity.

How small the strife that's occupied us,
how great is all that strives with us!
We might, if, like the things outside us,
we let the great storm over-ride us,
grow spacious and anonymous.

We conquer littleness, obtaining
success that only makes us small,
while, unconstrained and unconstraining,
the permanent eludes us all:
that angel who, though loath, yet lingers
to wrestle with mortality,

and, when opponents' sinews settle
in strife and stretch themselves to metal,
can feel them move beneath his fingers
like strings in some deep melody.

The challenger who failed to stand
that trial so constantly rejected
goes forth upright and resurrected
and great from that hard, forming hand
that clasped about him and completed.
Conquests no longer fascinate.
His growth consists in being defeated
by something every-grandlier great.

Berlin-Schmargendorf, mid-January 1901

10

From about the year 1907 onwards, new publishing houses began
to crop up like mushrooms, there were frequent concerts of modern
music and one art exhibition after another opened: The World of
Art, The Golden Fleece, The Knave of Diamonds, the Donkey's
Tail, The Blue Rose. Among such Russian names as Somov,
Sapunov, Sudeikin, Krymov, Larionov and Goncharova, French
names such as Bonnard and Vuillard began to appear.

In the grounds of one of the new apartment-houses in the
Razgulyai district an old wooden building had remained intact
in the courtyard; it was owned by a general. Here in the attic his
son, the poet and painter Julian Pavlovich Anisimov, used to hold
gatherings of young people who shared his interests. He suffered
from weak lungs and spent his winters abroad. His friends would
gather at his home in spring and autumn when the weather was
good. There they used to read, make music, draw, argue, eat and
drink tea laced with rum. I made many friends there.

Our host, who was a highly talented man of great taste, educated
and well read, spoke several foreign languages as fluently as Russian.
He himself was the very embodiment of poetry, but although he had
all the charm of an amateur, he was not by nature vigorously
creative, and did not have the character of the true artist. We had

interests in common and shared the same favourite writers. I liked him very much.

One of the habitués was the late Sergei Nikolaevich Durylin, who was then writing under the pseudonym of Sergei Raevsky. He it was who lured me from music to literature and who was kind enough to find something worthwhile in my first attempts at poetry. He was very badly off and had to support his mother and aunt by giving lessons. His keen, direct manner and ardent convictions reminded one of the image of Belinsky which has been handed down to us by tradition.

It was here that K. G. Loks, a friend of my student days whom I had known earlier, first introduced me to the poetry of Innokenty Annensky,* because he saw some similarity between my rambling efforts and the work of that marvellous poet, until then unknown to me.

The group had its own name. It was christened the Serdarda, although no one knew what this meant. Apparently one of the group's members, a poet and bass singer called Arkady Guryev, had heard the word one night, on the Volga, during the confusion which arose when two steamers arrived at a landing-stage simultaneously. After one steamer had been moored alongside the other, the passengers and luggage from the second boat crossed to the landing-stage over the first arrival, mingling chaotically with the passengers and baggage of the first steamer.

Guryev came from Saratov. He had a powerful, mellow voice which he used with great artistry to bring out all the dramatic and vocal subtleties of whatever he sang. Like all naturally gifted people, he could amaze one equally with his endless buffoonery and with a capacity for genuine feeling which showed through his clowning. His remarkable poetry anticipated the unrestrained candour of the later Mayakovsky, as well as Yesenin's clear-cut, strikingly direct imagery. He was a polished operatic and stage performer, with one of those bred-in-the-bone actor's temperaments which Ostrovsky portrayed in several of his plays.

He had a round, onion-shaped head, with a broad forehead, a barely perceptible nose and signs of incipient baldness all the way

* Innokenty Annensky (1856–1909). Early symbolist lyric poet; terse and epigrammatic. Translator of Euripides and Horace. Teacher and poetic exemplar of Akhmatova (q.v. below pp. 230–31).

from his brow to the back of his head. His whole being was expressive and mobile. He did not gesticulate or wave his arms about, but whenever he stood up to discuss something or to recite, his whole torso would move, act and speak. He would incline his head forward, lean back with his body and stand with his feet apart as if he had been caught in the middle of stamping his heels in a Russian dance. He was rather prone to drink, and when drunk he would start believing in his own fantasies. At the end of his performances he would pretend that his heel had stuck to the floor and he could not pull it away, assuring everyone that the devil had caught him by the foot.

Poets and painters used to frequent the Serdarda; B. B. Krasin, who set Blok's 'Willow Branches' to music; Sergei Bobrov,* who collaborated with me on my earliest work and whose arrival at Razgulyai was preceded by rumours that he was the new Russian Rimbaud; A. M. Kozhebatkin, the publisher of *Musagetes;* and Sergei Makovsky, publisher of *Apollo,*† who paid occasional visits to Moscow.

I myself became a member of the Serdarda in my old capacity of musician. At the start of the evening I would improvise on the piano, describing in music each person as he arrived until everyone had assembled.

The short spring night used to pass quickly, and the cold of morning would waft through the open window, making the bottoms of the curtains billow; the candle-flames guttered and the sheets of paper lying on the table would rustle softly. Everything and everyone yawned — the guests, our host, the empty distance outside, the grey sky, the rooms and staircases. We went home, overtaking the sewage carts loaded with barrels as they rumbled through the broad streets, streets which looked all the longer for being deserted. 'Centaurs', someone said, in the typical idiom of that time.‡

* Sergei Bobrov (b. 1889). Poet, scholar and novelist. Belonged to the futurist group known as the Centrifuge. Author of utopian science fiction. Translator of George Bernard Shaw.

† *Apollo*: the leading literary journal of the symbolist movement. Published 1909–1917. *Musagetes*: a symbolist journal, rival to *Apollo*.

‡ The word 'centaurs' was a kind of in-joke among the younger disciples of the symbolist movement in the early 1900s. For them these mythical figures, by their dual nature, epitomized the mysterious link between the ideal and the real worlds which symbolism strove to evoke.

II

A kind of academy formed itself around the editorial office of *Musagetes*. Andrei Biely, Stepun, Rachinsky, Boris Sadovsky, Emil Medtner, Shenrok, Petrovsky, Ellis and Nilender used to talk with young admirers on problems of rhythm, the history of German romanticism, Russian lyric poetry, the aesthetics of Goethe and Richard Wagner, Baudelaire and the French symbolists, and the pre-Socratic philosophy of ancient Greece.

Andrei Biely was the life and soul of all these undertakings. In those days he was undoubtedly the most authoritative figure of the group, a first-rate poet and the brilliant author of the *Symphonies* in prose and the novels *The Silver Dove* and *St Petersburg*, which brought about a total change in the literary taste of his pre-revolutionary contemporaries and which laid the foundations of the earliest Soviet prose writing.

Andrei Biely had all the makings of genius, untrammelled by any of the frustrations of everyday life, family or uncomprehending friends. Yet he dissipated his genius, and its creative power changed into a sterile and destructive force. This fatal excess of inspiration did not spoil him, however — on the contrary, it made one sympathetic towards him, and this tragic streak in him added to his charm.

He gave a course of instruction on the classical Russian iambic, and examined the various rhythmic patterns of the metre with his students by statistical analysis. I did not attend the course because I have always maintained, and maintain to this day, that the music of words does not depend on acoustics nor on the euphony of individual vowels and consonants, but on the relation between meaning and sound.

The young members of *Musagetes* sometimes met in other places besides the editorial office, for example in the studio of Kracht, the sculptor, in the Presnya district.

The upper half of the studio, which was used as living quarters, was not partitioned and consisted of a platform that jutted out over the room. Down below stood casts of fragments of antique sculpture, plaster masks and pieces of Kracht's own work, all festooned with ivy and other ornamental plants.

In this studio late one autumn I read a paper on 'Symbolism and Immortality'. Some of the company sat downstairs, some

13

listened from above, sprawled out on the floor of the mezzanine platform with their heads leaning over the edge.

The theme of my paper was the subjective nature of our perceptions, and that there was a correlation between the sounds and colours of nature as we perceive them and their purely objective existence in the form of vibrations of sound and light waves. I put forward the idea that this subjectivity is not a characteristic of the individual but is a generic function independent of the individual, that this subjectivity is a factor common to the whole human race. In my paper I suggested that a portion of this collective racial subjectivity, which is contained in each person while they live and which enables them to partake of the totality of human existence, remains alive even when that particular individual dies. My main aim was to advance the hypothesis that this universal human quality of subjectivity constitutes both the age-old arena of art and the chief source of its subject-matter. I also suggested that although the artist is of course mortal like everyone else, the joy of existence which he has experienced is immortal, and that others, centuries later, can through his works attain a certain degree of insight into the vital, personal nature of his original perceptions.

The paper was called 'Symbolism and Immortality' because it affirmed the symbolic, conventionalized nature of all art, in the same general sense in which one can speak of the symbolism of algebra.

My paper made a certain impression, and people talked about it. I arrived home late that night. There I heard that Tolstoy had fallen ill after leaving Yasnaya Polyana and had died on Astapovo Station. My father had been summoned there by telegram. We quickly got ready and set off for the Paveletsky Station to catch the night train.[1]

12

In those days, leaving the city was much more noticeable than it is now; the countryside was more sharply distinguished from the town and began more abruptly. From early morning onward and throughout the day the carriage window was filled with the view of the flat expanse of fields under winter wheat or lying fallow,

[1] The death of L. N. Tolstoy (November 7th, 1910) and the reading of the paper (February 1913) are erroneously described as having taken place on the same night.

only very occasionally relieved by the sight of villages—these were the thousands and thousands of acres of the arable land of rural Russia, which toiled for those relatively few Russians who lived in cities and which fed them. The ground was already silvered by the first frosts, the meadows framed by the still unshed gold of the birch trees. The silver of the frost and the gold of the birch trees delicately adorned the humble, blessed soil of age-old Russia like sheets of gold leaf and silver foil.

The sleeping ploughland rushed by the carriage windows, unaware that nearby its last great hero had died, a man noble enough to have been tsar, a man of subtle mind who though seduced by all the most refined pleasures of this world, the most spoilt of all spoilt darlings, lord and master of all other lords, had nevertheless out of love and compassion for this land himself followed the plough dressed as a peasant.

13

It had presumably been announced that a drawing was to be made of the deceased, and that a moulder from Merkurovs was coming to make a death-mask of him, for all the mourners were sent out of the room. It was empty when we entered. The tear-stained widow, Sofia Andreyevna, came quickly towards my father from the far corner. She seized him by the hands, choking back her tears, and blurted out: 'Oh, Leonid Osipovich, what I have suffered! You must know how much I loved him!' And she began to tell us how she had tried to commit suicide by drowning herself when Tolstoy had left her and how they had dragged her out of the pond half-dead.

A mountain the size of Mount Elbruz lay in that room, and she was one of its peaks. A towering thundercloud filled that room and she was one of its flashes of lightning. Yet she did not know that the mountain peak and lightning had a right to silence, a right to say nothing about her distraught behaviour, and that she had no need to enter into arguments with the Tolstoyans, who were in reality the most un-Tolstoyan creatures on earth, that there was no need for her to get involved in the squabbles of these pygmies. Yet she tried to justify herself, and called my father to witness that she surpassed all her rivals in her devotion to Tolstoy and in intellectual comprehension of his ideas, and that she would have cared for him better than they did. Oh God, I thought, how far can a human being be driven—and the wife of Tolstoy, too.

It is strange indeed. A man of our time, who rejects duelling as an out of date practice, writes an enormous book on the theme of the duel and death of Pushkin. Poor Pushkin! He should have married Shchegolev and all subsequent Pushkin scholars, and all would have been well. He would have lived on to our day, added a few sequels to *Eugene Onegin* and would have written five *Poltavas* instead of one. But I have always thought that I should cease to understand Pushkin if I had ever admitted that he needed our understanding more than he needed Natalya Nikolaevna.*

14

It was no mountain lying there, but a wrinkled little old man, one of those created by Tolstoy himself, which he had so often described and scattered throughout his works. The whole place was full of branches of evergreen. Four shafts of light from the setting sun slanted across the room, and the dark cross-like shadow thrown by the lattice-work on the windows and the tiny childish crosses woven from the fir trees bestowed a blessing on the corner where the body lay.

That day the little village around Astapovo Station was like a noisy, disorderly camp full of journalists from all over the world. The station buffet did a brisk trade, and the waiters were run off their feet trying to keep pace with the orders, dashing about serving fried beefsteaks. Beer flowed in torrents.

Tolstoy's sons Ilya and Andrei were at the station. Sergei arrived on the train which came to take Tolstoy's body back to Yasnaya Polyana. Students and young people sang 'Eternal Memory' as they carried the coffin with the body across the station yard and garden to the platform for the special train, where they placed the coffin in a freight car. The crowd of people on the platform bowed their heads, and as the singing began again the train slowly moved off in the direction of Tula.

It was somehow natural that Tolstoy should find his last rest, like a travelling pilgrim, beside the railway, then Russia's main means of transport, the railway along which his heroes and heroines

* 'Natalya Nikolaevna' was Pushkin's wife, Natalya Goncharova, whose behaviour brought about the duel in which Pushkin was mortally wounded.

still rushed whirling past, looking out through the carriage windows at the insignificant little station as it flashed by, not knowing that it was here that the eyes which had looked upon them all their lives, had caressed and immortalized them by their glance, were now closed for the last time.

15

If one were to take a single quality of every writer—Lermontov's passion, Tyutchev's creative intensity, Chekhov's ability to evoke the poetry of life, Gogol's dazzling genius, the power of Dostoevsky's imagination—what would one say about Tolstoy if one were to limit oneself to a single aspect of him?

The main quality of this moralist, this spiritual leveller and preacher of a law intended to embrace the whole of mankind without concession or exceptions, was his unique, indeed paradoxical originality.

At all times throughout his life he had the gift of seeing events and phenomena in the definitive finality of each separate moment, as a kind of comprehensive statement that stood out in relief, a kind of vision that we only have in rare moments such as in childhood, or on the crest of a surge of rejuvenating happiness, or when we experience a great spiritual triumph.

To see things in this way, our eyes must be guided by passion. For it is passion which illuminates things with its momentary brilliance and increases our perception of them. This passion, the passion of creative vision, was always with Tolstoy. It was the light of passion which enabled him to see everything in its pristine freshness, to see things anew and as if for the first time. The truthfulness of what he saw is so different from what we are used to that it may seem strange to us; yet Tolstoy did not seek for strangeness, nor did he pursue it as an aim; still less did he consciously employ it in his writings as a form of artistic method.

Before the First World War

1

The spring and summer of 1912 I spent abroad. Our Russian university vacations coincide with the summer term in Western

Europe, and I spent this term in the ancient university town of Marburg. It was in this university that Lomonosov studied under the mathematician and philosopher Christian Wolf. Half a century earlier Giordano Bruno, on his way home to his death at the stake in Rome, lectured at Marburg on his new theory of astronomy.

Marburg is a little medieval town. In those days it had twenty-nine thousand inhabitants, half of them students. It clings picturesquely to the hillside from which is quarried the stone used for building its houses and churches, its castles and university, and it is smothered in the dense greenery of its gardens which cast a shade as dark as night.

I still had some remnants of the money laid out for my board and tuition in Germany, and with that unexpended sum I travelled to Italy. I saw Venice, brick-red, pink, aquamarine and green, looking like a cluster of translucent pebbles thrown up on the shore by the sea; I visited Florence, that dark, cramped, but handsome city — a living quotation from Dante's *terza rima*. My money did not stretch to seeing Rome.

Next year I graduated from Moscow University, with the help of Mansurov, a young historian who had stayed on at university after graduation. He supplied me with a whole collection of essential textbooks which he had used to take the state examination the previous year. This professorial library was more than I needed to satisfy the examination requirements, for apart from general textbooks, it contained specialized reference works on classical antiquity and a number of monographs on various topics. I was scarcely able to carry away this wealth of books in a cab.

Mansurov was a relative and friend of the young Trubetskoy and Dmitry Samarin. Although these two used to study at home, they came to sit the external examinations every year at the Fifth High School, where I first met them.

The elder Trubetskoys, the father and uncle of the student Nikolai, were both distinguished men. One was the professor in charge of editing the encyclopaedia of law, the other was Rector of the University and a famous philosopher. Both were markedly corpulent and looked rather like frock-coated elephants as they lumbered up on to the rostrum. They delivered their brilliant lectures on a note of what sounded like entreaty, almost of beseeching, in their hoarse, slightly guttural, aristocratic voices. The young

Trubetskoys were of the same breed. Tall, talented young men with eyebrows that met in the middle, loud voices and famous names, they always attended the university as an inseparable trio.

The people in this circle thought highly of the Marburg school of philosophy. Trubetskoy wrote about it and sent his most gifted pupils there to complete their education. Dmitry Samarin had been there before me; he came to feel quite at home in the little town and felt very much a Marburger. I went there on his advice.

Dmitry Samarin was a member of the famous Slavophil family, whose former estate now houses the writers' village of Peredelkino and the Peredelkino children's tuberculosis sanatorium. Philosophy, the dialectic and knowledge of Hegel were in his blood, inherited from his forebears. He lacked singleness of purpose, his manner was vague and he was probably not quite normal. The strange escapades with which he amazed everyone when the mood was on him made him a difficult person, and quite intolerable in the students' hostel. One cannot blame his relatives, who never managed to get on with him either and with whom he was always quarrelling.

At the beginning of N.E.P.,* when he arrived in Moscow from Siberia where he had served for a long time in the Civil War, he had developed into a much less eccentric and more intelligent person. He was bloated with hunger and covered with lice, which he had picked up on the journey. Although themselves exhausted with privation, his relatives gave him every care and attention, but it was too late: before long he caught typhus and died, just as the epidemic was abating.

I do not know what became of Mansurov, but Nikolai Trubetskoy became a world-famous philologist and died quite recently in Vienna.

2

I spent the summer after my final examinations with my parents at their country house in Molody, near Stolbovaya Station on the Moscow–Kursk railway line. Tradition had it that Cossacks of the retreating Russian Army had used our house as cover from which to fire at the vanguard of Napoleon's troops who were pressing them hard. Deep in the park, where it merged with the cemetery, their graves still stood, neglected and overgrown.

* New Economic Policy—see p. 47.

Within the house the rooms were rather narrow in relation to their height and the windows were tall. A paraffin table-lamp threw gigantic shadows across the corners of the dark, claret-coloured walls and the ceiling. Below the park meandered a small stream. Over one of the pools, a huge old birch tree had been partly up-rooted, but continued to grow in its overturned position. The green tangle of its branches formed a kind of aerial summerhouse hanging over the water. In its thickly intertwined branches one could make oneself quite comfortable sitting or half-lying down, so I made it into my study. There I read Tyutchev and for the first time in my life began writing poetry, not as an occasional pastime but persis-tently, with the same absorption with which painters or composers throw themselves into their work. I spent the two or three months of that summer among the thick branches of that tree and wrote my first book of poetry.

The title of the book, *A Twin in the Clouds* was ridiculously pretentious, and came from my attempt to imitate the aesthetic cosmological language much used by the symbolists for their book titles and the names of their publishing houses. Writing this poetry, crossing out lines and then restoring them, satisfied a profound need in me and gave me an incomparable pleasure which brought me close to tears.

I tried to avoid romantic affectation and any kind of external subject-matter. I had no need to thunder out my verses from a plat-form to make intellectuals shy away from them and say disapprov-ingly, 'What decadence! What barbarity!' I did not want their modest elegance to make the flies drop dead, nor did I intend to read them in a circle of six or seven admirers so that afterwards that professors' wives should come up to me and say: 'Allow me to shake your worthy hand.' I was not striving for dance-like or song-like rhythms, whose effect would be to make people's arms and legs start moving almost without the help of the words. I was expressing nothing, reflecting nothing, representing nothing, depicting nothing.

Later, as part of various futile attempts to bring me closer to Mayakovsky, people began finding oratorical and incantatory elements in my work. This was quite wrong; there was no more of this in me than there is in any other person who has the gift of speech. On the contrary, my abiding concern was for the content, and my chief aim was that a poem should say something, that it should contain some new thought or new image. I wanted my poem in every particular to be, as it were, engraved into the book, and to speak from the pages in all its silence, with all the colours of its black, colourless print.

Take for example my poems 'Venice' and 'The Station'. Venice, the city built on water, stood before my eyes, and the circles and figures-of-eight of its reflections floated, multiplied, and swirled on the water like rusks dipped in tea. Likewise, in 'The Station' I could see rising up far beyond the tracks and platforms the cloudy, smoky, horizon of departure, whither the trains would vanish; it encompassed a whole world of relationships, meetings, partings and the chains of events which happened before them and after them.

I made no demands on myself, on my readers, on any theory of art. All I asked was that one poem should contain the city of Venice, and the other should contain the Brest railway station, nowadays known as the White Russian Station. Bobrov liked this line from 'The Station':

The west opens up in the shunting of sleepers and rain.

Aseyev, myself and a few other beginners all pooled our resources to form a small publishing house. Bobrov, who knew something about printing from having worked on the Russian Archives, used to print and publish our work with his own. He published my *Twin in the Clouds* with a kind foreword written by Aseyev.

Maria Ivanovna Baltrushaitis, the poet's wife, used to say: 'One day you will regret having published an immature book.' She was right. I have often regretted it.

3

During the hot summer of 1914, with its drought and its total eclipse of the sun, I lived with the Baltrushaitis in their country house on a large estate beside the River Oka, near the town of Aleksin. I coached their son and translated Kleist's comedy *Der zerbrochene Krug* for the newly founded Kamerny Theatre, of which Baltrushaitis was the literary director.

There were many people from the artistic world living on the estate: the poet Vyacheslav Ivanov, the painter Ulyanov, and the wife of the writer Muratov. Not far away from us, in Tarusa, Balmont*

* Konstantin Balmont. See note p. 69.

13*

was translating the play *Sakuntala* by the Sanskrit poet Kalidasa for the same theatre.

I received my mobilization papers in July and went to Moscow where I was given a 'white ticket', i.e. total exemption from military service, because one of my legs was shorter than the other. After this I went back to the Baltrushaitis on the Oka.

I well remember an evening soon after that, when the sound of an army band playing polkas and marches came wafting towards us over the river, shrouded in a mist which clung to the reeds. Then a small steam tug pulling three barges came into sight round the bend. They had no doubt seen the estate up on the hillside and had decided to moor their boat for the night. The tug turned round to face upstream and towed the barges to our bank. There were soldiers on board—a large detachment of a grenadier regiment. They disembarked and lit their camp fires at the foot of the hill. We invited the officers up to the house to dine and spend the night with us. They set off again in the morning—a tiny incident from the advance mobilization plan which was being put into effect. War had begun.

4

I then spent two periods which lasted, with breaks, for about a year, in the family of a rich businessman, Moritz Philipp working as private tutor to his son, a pleasant and affectionate boy called Walter.

During the anti-German riots in Moscow that summer, when large firms like Einem, Verein and others were looted, Philipp's offices and private house were also ransacked. This was a planned piece of destruction, carried out with the knowledge of the police. Only the owner's property was destroyed, that of the employees being left untouched. My underwear, clothes and other belongings were rescued from the resulting chaos, but my books and manuscripts vanished in the general disorder.

Later I was to lose many more things under more peaceful circumstances. I do not like my style up to the year 1940, I reject half of what Mayakovsky wrote, and I do not like everything of Yesenin's either. The general decadence of form, the impoverishment of ideas, and the cluttered, uneven style of that time is alien to me. I do not regret the loss of faulty, imperfect works; but there is an entirely different reason why I have never been upset by the loss of anything.

In life it is more important to lose than to acquire. A grain will not germinate unless it first dies. One must live and never tire, one must look ahead and feed on the living substance provided by oblivion and memory working together.

At different times and for a variety of reasons I have lost many things: the text of my paper 'Symbolism and Immortality', articles written during my futurist period, a children's fairy tale written in prose, two long poems, a notebook full of verse written between my collection *Above the Barriers* and *My Sister, Life*, the rough draft of a novel in several looseleaf notebooks, the opening section of which was printed separately as a short story called *The Childhood of Luvers*, and finally my complete translation of a tragedy by Swinburne from his dramatic trilogy about Mary Queen of Scots.[2]

We moved out of the ruins of the Philipps' half-burnt house into a rented apartment, where I again had a room to myself. I remember it well. The rays of the setting autumn sun were tracing furrows across the room and across the book I was looking through. Two aspects of that evening were summed up in the book: one was the pale rosy colour which tinged the pages, the other was the meaning and the soul of the poetry written on them. I envied that author's ability to crystallize with such simple means the particles of reality captured in that book. It was one of the first books of Akhmatova's[3] poetry, probably *Plantain*.

5

During those same years, in between working for the Philipps, I visited the Urals and the Kama river country. I spent one winter

---

[2] Of this list of lost works, two articles of the author's futurist period have been found. They have been preserved in the archives of S. P. Bobrov. These were reviews of a book by Mayakovsky and of N. Aseyev's *Oxana*. Also found were the drafts for a poem called 'A Poem about a Friend'. The main themes of his paper 'Symbolism and Immortality' are preserved in the Central State Archives of Literature in the R. M. Glière papers, f. 2085, No. 1, ed. khr. 1143, 1. 8. The translation of Swinburne's *Chastelard* was lost at the printing works, a fact which emerged from a questionnaire dating from 1919, preserved in the Manuscript Department of the Lenin Library.

[3] *Plantain* was not published until 1921. Obviously the author refers to her volume entitled *Beads*, which appeared in 1913.

in Vsevolodo-Vilvo in the north of the Perm province, in a place
which, according to A. N. Tikhonov's account of this region in his
memoirs, was once visited by Chekhov and Levitan. I spent another
winter in the Tikhiye Mountains, at the Ushkov chemical factories
on the Kama.

I worked in the factory office and for a time I was in charge of
the paperwork for dealing with conscription. I exempted whole
districts of reservists, men attached to the factories and those
engaged on defence work. In winter, communications between the
factories and the outside world depended upon the most antedilu-
vian method. The mail was brought by troika from Kazan, about
160 miles away, just as it is described by Pushkin in *The Captain's
Daughter*. I once made the journey during that winter. In March
1917, when we heard in the factories that revolution had broken
out in St Petersburg, I left for Moscow. I had to go to the Izhevsky
factory to find a remarkable man called Zbarsky, an engineer recently sent there to take charge; there I was to put myself at his
disposal and work under him from then onwards.

I spent an evening, a night and part of the following day travelling from the Tikhiye Mountains in a *kibitka,* a covered sledge on
runners. Wrapped in three long coats and buried deep in hay, I
rolled about on the bottom of the sledge like a heavy sack, being
quite unable to control my movements. I dozed, nodded off, fell
asleep and woke up again, opened and closed my eyes. I could
see the road through the forest and the stars of the frosty night.
Mountainous snowdrifts made huge bumps along the narrow path,
and the top of the covered sledge often hit the lower branches of
overhanging fir trees, shook the hoar frost off them, rustled past
them and pulled them down behind it. The white shroud of snow
reflected the twinkling of the stars and lighted our path. In the
depths of the forest there was something frightening about the
gleam of this blanket of snow, which sometimes looked like a
burning candle set among the trees.

The sledge was drawn by three horses harnessed one behind the
other. Every so often first one and then another would spoil the
formation by pulling to one side. Our driver was always trying to
keep them in line, and whenever the *kibitka* rolled over to one side
he would jump off and run alongside, supporting it with his shoulder
to prevent it from falling over.

I fell asleep again and lost all concept of what was happening until I was woken up with a jolt as we came to a sudden halt.

The posting-station in the forest was exactly as it is always described in stories about brigands: a light in the hut, the samovar hissing and the tick of a clock. While my driver took off his coat and recovered from the cold, he talked in a low hushed voice, out of consideration for the other people probably sleeping behind the partition, to the woman in charge of the station who was getting him something to eat. Meanwhile our new driver wiped his mouth and his moustache, buttoned up his thick woollen coat and went out into the freezing cold to harness a fresh troika.

Then off again at full speed to the swish of the runners, drowziness and sleep. Later the next day, there in the far distance were factory chimneys, the boundless snowy desert of the great frozen river and the railway line.

6

Bobrov's attitude towards me was undeservedly warm. He watched over my futuristic purity with tireless energy, and protected me from harmful influences. Among these he included the sympathy of my elders. The moment he noticed any signs of their interest in me he was terrified lest their attention made me turn to academicism, and he hastened to use every possible means to destroy any such incipient relationship. Thanks to him I never ceased quarrelling with everybody.

I was very fond of the Anisimovs, Julian and his wife Vera Stanevich, and I played an involuntary part in their break with Bobrov. Vyacheslav Ivanov had written a touching inscription in a book which he gave me. When Bobrov was with Bryusov and his circle, he poured scorn on the inscription in a way which implied that it was I who was responsible for his sneer. Vyacheslav Ivanov stopped speaking to me.

The journal The Contemporary published my translation of Kleist's comedy Der zerbrochene Krug. The translation was immature and pedestrian, and I should have gone down on my knees to thank the magazine for publishing it. I should have shown even more gratitude to the editorial staff for the fact that an unknown hand had edited the manuscript, greatly to its benefit and improvement.

But a sense of fairness, modesty and gratitude were not rated very highly by the young left-wing artists of the day, and were considered to be signs of sentimentality and weakness. It was the fashion to turn up one's nose at everything, to strut about and be insolent, and however much it sickened me I could not help following the crowd in order not to lose the esteem of my friends.

Something happened to the proofs of the comedy. They were delayed, and when they did arrive they contained some irrelevant additions which had nothing to do with the text and which had been inserted by the type-setters.

To do Bobrov justice I must admit that he knew nothing of the whole affair and that in this case he really did not know what he was doing. He said something had to be done about this disgraceful tampering with proofs and these unwanted corrections to the style of the original, and that I should go and complain to Gorky who, according to him, was unofficially connected with running the magazine. And this is what I did. Instead of expressing my gratitude to the editor of *The Contemporary*, I wrote a stupidly naive letter to Gorky which was full of affected arrogance and in which I was in reality complaining about their kindness and decency towards me. Years went by before I found out that I had complained to Gorky about himself. It was he who had suggested that the play should be published and had corrected it.

Even my friendship with Mayakovsky began through a controversial meeting between two hostile futurist groups, of which I belonged to one and he to the other. According to the organizers, some kind of brawl was bound to take place, but from the first few words that we spoke our obvious mutual understanding prevented any quarrel from flaring up.

7

I shall not describe my relations with Mayakovsky. We were never on intimate terms. People tend to exaggerate his acknowledgment of me and to distort his opinion of my work.

He did not like my '1905' and 'Leiutenant Schmidt', and thought they were both a mistake. But he liked my two books *Above the Barriers* and *My Sister, Life*.

I am not going to give a list of our meetings and our differences of opinion, but I shall try as far as possible to describe Mayakovsky's general characteristics and his significance. My opinions will naturally be somewhat subjective and biased.[4]

8

To begin with the main thing: we have no idea of the mental torment people go through before they commit suicide. People who suffer physical torture on the rack frequently lose consciousness, for the pain is so great that their inability to withstand it hastens the end. But the man sentenced to be executed is still not destroyed in the spiritual sense when he falls unconscious from pain, for he is present at his own end, his past belongs to him, his memories are with him; if he wishes to he may draw strength from them, they may still comfort him before he dies.

But people who start thinking about committing suicide have given themselves up as failures, have declared themselves bankrupt and reject their memories as meaningless. Their memories are impotent to help or support them; the continuity of the suicide's inner life has been broken and his personality destroyed. Perhaps in the final analysis people do not kill themselves because they want to stick to their decision to do so, but because they are unable to bear the spiritual anguish which seems to belong to no one, this suffering without a sufferer, this empty expectation which is not filled by the continuing process of life.

[4] Pasternak wrote about Mayakovsky several times. His views on the poet's work were complex and changed with time. A review that he wrote of Mayakovsky's collection *As Simple as Mooing* began with the words, 'What a joy that Mayakovsky exists and is not just an invention' (*Literaturnaya Rossiya*, 1965, no. 13). Their relations — or more precisely Pasternak's relation to Mayakovsky —take up the third part of his autobiographical work *Safe Conduct*, which was written in the summer of 1930 under the immediate impression caused by Mayakovsky's suicide. 'I worshipped him. My entire spiritual horizon was contained within him,' wrote Pasternak in *Safe Conduct*. Nevertheless, in the same chapter Pasternak wrote how Mayakovsky's work from his poem '150,000,000' and up to the introduction to his poem 'At the Top of my Voice', was alien and incomprehensible to him. Referring to the subjectivity and biased nature of his views, Pasternak wrote later in a letter to N. Vachnadze: 'Yes, long ago I underestimated him and I failed to understand Mayakovsky's later work and much else besides.' (Letter to N. G. Vachnadze, December 31st, 1949. *Voprosy Literatury*, 1966, no. 1, p. 184.)

I think that Mayakovsky shot himself out of pride, out of condemnation of something within himself or around him which his self-respect could not accept. When Yesenin hanged himself he did not think rationally about the consequences and say to himself in the depths of his soul, 'Who knows? Perhaps this isn't the end? Who knows what'll happen, nothing's ever definite.' Throughout her life Marina Tsvetaeva shielded herself from day-to-day reality by working; but when she realized that this was an impermissible luxury, and that for a time she must sacrifice her absorbing passion for the sake of her son and take a sober look around her, she saw chaos as it really was, untransfigured by art, stagnant, immovable and unfamiliar to her; she started back in fear, and, not knowing how to escape from this horror, she hastily took refuge in death, putting her head into a noose as though hiding under a pillow. I believe that Paolo Yashvili was unaware of what he was doing ... when he watched his daughter asleep one night and decided that he was no longer worthy to look at her, and next morning went to his friends and blew his brains out with buckshot from a double-barrelled shotgun. I think too that Fadeyev, with that apologetic smile on his face which he never lost throughout his years of cunning political scheming, said goodbye to himself in the last moment before pulling the trigger with something like these words, 'Well, it's all over. Goodbye, Sasha.'*

But they all suffered indescribably, suffered to such a degree that their feelings of anguish reached the intensity of a mental disease. Leaving aside for a moment their talent and the bright image of their personalities, let us also bow our head in compassion before their suffering.

9

It was in the summer of 1914 that a confrontation was supposed to take place between two literary groups in a café on the Arbat. There were Bobrov and myself on our side and Tretyakov and Shershene-

---

* Alexander Bulyga, alias Fadeyev (1901–56). One of the best of the proletarian writers who emerged after the revolution. General Secretary of the Union of Soviet Writers from 1946 to 1955. Although an obedient Stalinist in cultural policy, he was criticized for his novel *The Young Guard* in 1947 and forced to re-write it. Already an alcoholic, Fadeyev committed suicide after Khrushchev's denunciation of Stalin at the XX Party Congress.

vich on their side. But they brought Mayakovsky along with them.[5]

Unexpectedly, it turned out that the young man's face was familiar to me, as I had seen him around the corridors of the Fifth High School, where he had been a pupil two years junior to me; at symphony concerts, too, he had caught my eye in the foyer during the intervals.

Shortly before this, someone who was to become one of his most uncritical admirers showed me something from Mayakovsky's first printed work. At that time this person not only failed to understand his future idol, but was even scornful and indignant when he showed me this early printed poem as being a purposely, crude, meaningless piece of nonsense. Nevertheless I was extremely taken with the poem. It was one of his most brilliant first attempts, which later appeared in the collection *As Simple as Mooing*.

I was no less attracted by the author himself on seeing him now sitting in front of me in the café. He was a handsome young man with a gloomy look, the bass voice of an archdeacon, the fist of a boxer and an inexhaustible, devastating wit—something between one of Alexander Grin's* mythical heroes and a Spanish toreador.

I guessed at once that the chief thing about him was not his good looks, his wit or his talent—perhaps a supreme talent—but his iron self-control, a kind of noble imperative and a sense of duty which forbade him to be any less handsome, witty or talented than he was.

His decisive manner, and his tousled mane, which he kept on ruffling with his hand, reminded me immediately of the image of the young revolutionary compounded from several of Dostoevsky's younger provincial characters.

The fact that the provinces lagged behind the capital cities was not always a bad thing. Sometimes when the main centres were in decline, places in the depth of the country were saved by virtue of their lingering traditions. What Mayakovsky brought to the world of tangos and skating rinks from the dense forests of his native Transcaucasia was the conviction, still firmly held in his provincial

[5] Here the mention of Tretyakov is obviously a mistake. In describing this meeting in *Safe Conduct*, Pasternak names the third person as K. Bolshakov, who was in fact present.

* The pseudonym of A. S. Grinevsky (1880–1932). Russian writer of Polish origin. Author of a number of tales of romantic mystery somewhat after the manner of Edgar Allan Poe. Their locales and characters, totally divorced from conventional reality, have a compelling fascination.

birthplace, that the modernization and enlightenment of Russia could only come by way of revolution.

The young man had very effectively added to his natural good looks by assuming the pose of the slovenly artist, rough and ready, careless and unwieldy in body and mind, the rebellious bohemian; he dressed and played the part with great style.

10

I am very fond of Mayakovsky's early lyric poetry. His seriousness — grave, menacing, accusing — was something most unusual against the background of buffoonery of those years. His poetry was brilliantly moulded, proud and demonic, but at the same time profoundly aware of impending fate, doomed, almost as if it were crying out for help.

> Time, you limping ikon-painter;
> Paint if you will my image
> On the triptych of this hideous age!
> I am lonely, lonely as the last good eye
> Of a man who walks among the blind.

Time obeyed him and did what he asked. His image has indeed been painted on triptych of this age. But what powers one must have to be able to foresee this! In another lyric he writes:

> Who can comprehend the reason
> Why amid a storm of mockery I
> Should bear my soul upon a dish
> To the banquet of the passing years ...

One is bound to recognize here certain parallels with the liturgy: 'Let all mortal flesh keep silence and stand with fear and trembling, thinking no earthly thoughts. For the King of Kings and Lord of Lords approaches, to die for us and to give himself as sustenance to the faithful.' Unlike the classic writers who regarded the meaning of hymns and prayers as important — from Pushkin, who retold Efrem Sirin in *The Hermit Fathers*, to Aleksei Tolstoy, who turned the requiem chants of St John Damascene to poetry — Blok, Mayakovsky and Yesenin on the other hand regarded quotations from liturgical responses as having a purely evocative value, as being the stuff of everyday life on a par with streets, houses and familiar colloquial speech.

These relics of an ancient literature suggested to Mayakovsky the parodic structure of his longer poems. One can see in them many analogies with the concepts used in canonic literature, analogies that are both concealed and sometimes openly stressed. They demanded grandiloquent treatment and a firm hand, and thus taught Mayakovsky to be bold.

It is a very good thing that Mayakovsky and Yesenin wrote about what they knew and remembered from their childhood; good that they brought these familiar buried layers of experience into the light of day and made use of their inherent beauty instead of leaving it hidden.

II

When I got to know Mayakovsky better we discovered that there were unexpected congruences in our techniques, a similar way of constructing images and rhyme-schemes. I loved the beautiful precision with which his verse moved. I could ask for nothing better. I did not want to echo him, and so as not to appear as his imitator, I began to suppress any tendencies I had in common with him — for example, the heroic tone and a certain striving for effect which would have sounded artificial in me. This narrowed the range of my style and made it purer.

Mayakovsky had his companions and fellow-travellers. He was not alone in a poetic desert. On the pre-revolutionary stage his rival was Igor Severyanin,* and in the revolutionary arena and in the hearts of the people it was Sergei Yesenin.

Severyanin lorded it over the concert halls, and, to use show-business expressions, he always played to full houses and was usually a sell-out. He used to sing his poetry to two or three popular tunes from French operas, without ever slipping over into vulgarity or offending the ear. His lack of polish and good taste and his demotic neologisms, combined with his enviably pure, free-flowing, poetic diction, produced a strange but quite distinct style which underneath all the banality amounted to the belated arrival of Turgenevism in poetry.

* I. V. Lotaryov, alias Igor Severyanin (1887–1942). A self-styled futurist poet, disdained by Mayakovsky as a charlatan. His brilliant if superficial charm of style earned him a certain following. Emigrated in the Civil War; died in Esthonia.

Since Koltsov's day the soil of Russia has produced nothing more genuine and natural, more utterly native to it than Sergei Yesenin, to whom it granted perfect freedom without burdening its gift with the deadweight of militant populism. At the same time Yesenin was a living, pulsating bundle of that unique kind of artistry which since Pushkin coined the phrase has been known as 'the Mozart principle' – that elemental fount of creativity epitomized by Mozart.

Yesenin thought of his life as a fairy tale. Like Ivan Tsarevich he crossed the ocean mounted on a grey wolf and caught Isadora Duncan, like the Fire-Bird, by the tail-feathers. His way of writing poetry, too, was like something out of a fairy tale, sometimes laying out his words like cards in a game of patience, at other times writing them with his heart's blood. The most precious thing about him is the image of his native countryside, the forests of Ryazan in Central Russia, which he conveys with a stunning freshness retained from childhood. Compared with Yesenin, Mayakovsky's technique is weightier and coarser, but on the other hand it has, perhaps, greater profundity and scope. Where Yesenin wrote about nature, Mayakovsky writes about the labyrinth of the great city, the place where the lonely soul of modern man wanders in despair and moral confusion. He is the poet of our desperate, inhuman, yet always dramatic situation.

12

As I said before, people have exaggerated the closeness of our friendship. Once when we were having a discussion at Aseyev's, and our disagreement had reached an intense pitch, he defined the contrast between us with his usual sombre humour: 'Well, we're different, all right. You like lightning in the sky, I like it in an electric iron.'

I never did understand his enthusiasm for propaganda, his aggressive intrusion into the social arena, his passion for company and for group work, his obedience to the voice of topicality.

Even more incomprehensible to me was the magazine LEF*

* The name LEF is a contraction of the words Left Front, the journal's full title being Left Front of Art. LEF was the journal of the left wing of the futurist movement, of which Mayakovsky was the guiding spirit. It was published from 1923 to 1925, then was revived for a year in 1927–8 under the title New LEF.

of which Mayakovsky was in charge. I could understand neither the people who contributed to it nor the ideology which they purveyed. The only consistent and honest man in that clique of negators was Sergei Tretyakov,* who carried his anarchy to its natural conclusions. Tretyakov agreed with Plato that there was no place for art in a new socialist state, or at least not in its very early stages. But the kind of uninspired, hack pseudo-art which flourished in *LEF*, crippled by being forced to conform with the modish style of the time, was not worth the effort and labour spent on it and one felt its departure as no loss.

Apart from that immortal document 'At the Top of my Voice' which Mayakovsky wrote just before he died, his later works from *Mysteria-Bouffe* onwards are simply beyond me. I cannot understand this clumsy doggerel, this tortuous way of saying absolutely nothing, these platitudes and truisms put into such involved, artificial and pedestrian language. For me this Mayakovsky does not exist, yet amazingly it is this non-Mayakovsky who is thought of as the revolutionary.

People have always made the mistake of thinking of us as friends. Yesenin, for example, when he was going through an anti-imagist phase, asked me to make peace between him and Mayakovsky, thinking that I was just the right person to do this. Although I was on more familiar terms with Yesenin than I was with Mayakovsky, I actually saw much less of Yesenin. I can count the number of times we saw each other on the fingers of one hand, and our meetings always ended up in storm and fury. Sometimes, drenched in tears, we would swear eternal loyalty to each other; at other times we would fight, and even draw blood, and people would have to drag us apart by force.

13

During the last years of Mayakovsky's life, when all poetry, his own as well as everyone else's, had come to a standstill, and when Yesenin had hanged himself ... it was Aseyev, an excellent man,

---

* Sergei Tretyakov (1892–1940?) was one of the most consistently left wing of the futurist poets. In a style reminiscent of Mayakovsky but rather more four-square, he wrote poetry and verse-plays on social and political themes. Accused of Trotskyism, he was arrested in 1938 and is presumed to have died in prison.

intelligent, gifted, clear-sighted and without emotional ties who was Mayakovsky's mainstay and close friend.

I had broken with Mayakovsky once and for all. The reason was that although I had stated I was no longer a contributor to *LEF*, and had told them that I did not belong to their circle any more, they still went on printing my name on the list of contributors. I wrote Mayakovsky a brusque letter which must have made his blood boil.

Earlier, when I was still under the spell of his genius, of his inner strength, his limitless possibilities and his artist's prerogative, and when he reciprocated my feelings, I wrote him an inscription in a copy of *My Sister, Life* which included the following lines:

> Your concern is with our balance-sheet
> And the failures of the national plan;
> You hover like the Flying Dutchman,
> Your warning voice o'ershadows all our verse.
> I know you are sincere in what you do—
> But, honest as you are,
> What can have brought you
> To spend your time in matters so mundane?

14

Two well-known sayings were current then: 'Life is getting better, life is more fun,' and, 'Mayakovsky is and will remain the best, most talented poet of the epoch.'* I wrote to the author of these words thanking him for the second one, which spared me from exaggerating my own importance, a thing I tended to do in mid-thirties around the time of the Writers' Congress. I love my life and am content with it. I do not need any extra gilt on it. I cannot conceive of a life which has no privacy and seclusion, the kind of life lived in the mirror-like glitter of a showcase.

Mayakovsky is being forced down people's throats in a manner reminiscent of the compulsory introduction of potatoes in the reign of Catherine the Great. It is his second death, and of this he is not guilty.

* The two catch-phrases quoted by Pasternak were coined by Stalin. The Writers' Congress took place in 1934.

Three Shades

I

In July 1917 Ehrenberg took Bryusov's advice and came to see me. It was then that I first made the acquaintance of this clever writer, a hard-working, gregarious man whose way of thinking was totally different from mine.

That time was the beginning of a great influx of political émigrés returning from abroad, of people who had been caught in a foreign country by the war and interned there. Andrei Biely came back from Switzerland, and Ehrenburg also returned home.

Ehrenburg started singing Tsvetaeva's praises and showed me some of her poetry. At one of our evening meetings at the beginning of the revolution I was present when she, among others, came to read her poetry. One winter during the years of War Communism I went to see her on some errand, when we simply exchanged trivialities. Tsvetaeva made no impression on me at all.

At that time my mind's ear had been spoilt by the fashion for oratorical extravagance and by the complete break-up of the world as I had known it. I had become incapable of speaking normally and had forgotten that words by themselves could mean something besides the gaudy finery in which they were being decked.

The very harmony and clarity of meaning of Tsvetaeva's poetry, the fact that it contained only merit and no faults was a stumbling-block for me and prevented me from understanding what it was about. I kept on looking for some irrelevant stroke of wit and over-looked the poetry's essential meaning.

For a long time I underestimated Tsvetaeva just as, for a variety of reasons, I had underestimated many others such as Bagritsky, Khlebnikov, Mandelshtam and Gumilyov.*

As I said before, among all the younger writers who were unable

---

* Eduard Bagritsky (1895–1934). After early symbolist influence, Bagritsky developed into a writer of colourful, if brash, heroic verse on revolutionary themes. Osip Mandelshtam (1891–1938). A 'poet's poet', writer of verse of extreme compression, intensity of feeling and complex imagery, Mandelshtam is probably the single most influential poet of his contemporaries. Persecuted by Stalin, he died in a prison camp. Nikolai Gumilyov (1886–1921). Co-founder with Mandelshtam and Akhinatova (Gumilyov's wife) of the 'acmeist' school of poetry. Although primarily a lyric poet, he used his verse to denounce the revolution. Shot for counter-revolutionary activity.

to express themselves intelligibly, who made a virtue out of being inarticulate, and who could not help being eccentric, there were only two, Aseyev and Tsvetaeva, who spoke like human beings and wrote in the classical language and style.

And yet at some point they were both to reject their talent. Aseyev was attracted by Khlebnikov's example, while Tsvetaeva underwent some inward change. But the early Tsvetaeva, who still belonged to the great tradition, succeeded in captivating me before the metamorphosis set in.

2

One had to read her poetry very carefully, but when I did so the unfathomable depths of purity and strength which it revealed took my breath away. Nothing of the kind existed anywhere else around me. But let me be brief. I am committing no sin when I say that with the exception of Annensky, Blok and, with a few reservations, Andrei Biely, the early Tsvetaeva was what all the other symbolists together aimed for but failed to be. Where their poetry floundered helplessly in a world of factitious devices and lifeless archaisms, Tsvetaeva took all the problems of true art in her stride, solving all the difficulties with her incomparable technical brilliance as though they were child's play.

In the spring of 1922, when she was already living abroad, I bought in Moscow her little book entitled *Versts*. I was immediately won over by the lyrical force of Tsvetaeva's style; expressive of profound experience, it was at the same time pared to the bone and condensed, a style which did not run out of breath at the end of each line but which embraced whole stanzas without a break in the rhythm by the sheer strength of its periodic structure.

I sensed a kind of kinship to me behind all these features: perhaps it was the result of shared influences, or of the same kinds of stimuli which had formed our characters; perhaps family and music had played similar roles in our lives; or perhaps we shared points of departure, aims and preferences.

I wrote a letter to Tsvetaeva in Prague, full of rapture and astonishment that I had overlooked her for so long and discovered her so late. She answered me, and we began corresponding with particular frequency during the mid-twenties when her poem 'The Craft' was published, and when manuscript copies of her wide-ranging, brilliant and original works 'The Poem of the End', 'The Poem of the Mountain' and 'The Pied Piper' achieved fame in Moscow. We became friends.

In the summer of 1935 I was unwell and on the edge of a nervous breakdown after almost a year of insomnia, when I arrived in Paris for the Anti-Fascist Congress. There I got to know Tsvetaeva's son and daughter, as well as her husband, a sensitive, charming and utterly steadfast man whom I came to love as my own brother.

Tsvetaeva's family insisted that she should return to Russia. It was partly homesickness and their sympathy for communism and the Soviet Union which made them say this, and partly the thought that it was no life for Tsvetaeva in Paris and that her talent was waning because she lived in a vacuum, without a response from her readers.

Tsvetaeva asked me what I thought about this suggestion, but I had no definite ideas. I did not know what to advise her, and was much too afraid that she and her remarkable family would find life hard and unsettling in Russia. The tragedy which befell the whole family was infinitely greater than even I had feared.*

3

At the beginning of this introductory essay, in the part referring to my childhood, I described actual scenes, things I saw and events I lived through, but from the middle onwards I started generalizing and limiting myself to more fleeting, summary descriptions. I had to do this in order to be as concise as possible.

If I were to narrate step by step how it was that similar aims and interests brought Tsvetaeva and myself together I should far exceed the limits which I have set myself.

I could write a whole book about how much we experienced in common, how many vicissitudes we shared, both joyful and tragic, which though always unexpected often served to enlarge our horizons. But here and in the remaining chapters I shall avoid what is purely personal and restrict myself to the essential and the general.

Tsvetaeva was a woman with a practical, masculine mind; she was decisive, militant and indomitable. In her life and work she

* See above, p. 252.

was impetuous, avid and almost rapacious in the way she strove for finality and certainty, in pursuit of which she went so far that she outstripped everyone.

Besides the little of her work which is known to us, she also wrote a large quantity of poetry which we have not seen; vast, turbulent works, some in the style of Russian folk tales, others on themes from familiar historical legends and myths. Their publication would be a great triumph and a revelation for Russian poetry, for it would at once be enriched by this unique, belated gift.

I think that Tsvetaeva is due for a major reappraisal and that she will be greatly appreciated.

We were friends. I had about one hundred of her letters, replies to mine. Despite all the losses and disappearances which have occurred throughout my life, as I mentioned before, it was simply unimaginable that these carefully preserved, precious letters should ever be lost. Too much care in looking after them was the cause of their destruction.

During the war years when I used to visit my family, who had been evacuated, a woman employed at the Scriabin Museum, who was a great admirer of Tsvetaeva and a great friend of mine, offered to take these letters, together with my parents' letters and several letters from Gorky and Romain Rolland, and put them in safe-keeping for me. She placed them all in the museum safe, except Tsvetaeva's letters which she never let out of her sight, as she did not trust even the solid walls of the fireproof safe.

She lived out of town all the year round, and every evening when she went home after work she would take these letters with her in a small attaché case, bringing them back with her when she came to work in the mornings. Once in winter when she was walking home through the woods, utterly exhausted, she suddenly remembered that she had left the attaché case with the letters in the train. And so Tsvetaeva's letters vanished.

4

Over the decades since the publication of *Safe Conduct*, I have often thought that if I ever had to re-publish it I should add a chapter about the Caucasus and two Georgian poets. But time has gone by and the need to make any other additions did not arise.

Since this chapter is the only omission in the work, I am going to write it now.[6]

One winter in Moscow round about 1930 I was visited by the poet Paolo Yashvili and his wife. He was a very handsome man, cultured in the European sense, brilliant, highly educated, fond of company and fascinating to talk to.

Soon after this, my own family and that of a friend of mine were victims of various upheavals, complications and changes which had an enormous emotional effect on us all.* For some time my companion – who later became my second wife – and I had no roof over our heads and so Yashvili offered us the shelter of his own home in Tiflis.

At that time the Caucasus, Georgia, many of its people, and its national life were a complete revelation to me. Everything was new and astonishing. In the very heart of the streets of Tiflis, dark beetling crags rose up. There the life of the poor people came out of the backyards and on to the streets, and that life seemed somehow vivid and frank, more free and easy and not as secretive as in the north. The folk traditions are full of a mystical and messianic symbolism

[6] Pasternak wrote of his intention to add an extra chapter on Georgia to *Safe Conduct* soon after the book was published. 'That City [Tiflis] with all the people I saw in it and with all the things I had gone to experience and all the things I had brought with me will be the same to me as Chopin, Scriabin, Marburg, Venice and Rilke have been, one of the chapters of my *Safe Conduct* which goes on all through my life, one of the chapters which, as you know, are not numerous; one of these chapters, and it will be the next to be written. I say 'will be' because I am a writer, and all this had to be written down and an expression found for it all; I say 'will be' because so far as I am concerned it has already become a fact.' (Letter to Paulo Yashvili dated July 30th, 1932, *Voprosy Literatury*, 1966, no. 1, p. 173.)

[The English translation of this quotation from Pasternak's letter to Paolo Yashvili is taken from *Letters to Georgian Friends*, translated by David Magarshack [London, Secker and Warburg, 1967]. This book contains the fuller, uncensored version of Pasternak's correspondence with the Georgian poets whose work he translated and with whom he had close ties of friendship; the Russian version, published in *Voprosy Literatury*, was considerably cut by the censor, although it is believed that the uncensored correspondence was published in the U.S.S.R. in Georgian, in a Tiflis literary magazine. As a preface to the *Letters*, David Magarshack's volume also includes his translation of the whole of this section (4) of *People and Situations*. Editor's Note.]

* This refers to Pasternak's estrangement from his first wife and subsequent marriage to Zinaida Neigaus.

whose imaginative power gives the people a life-affirming quality
and makes everyone a poet, as in Catholic Poland. The high culture
of the progressive element of society and the level of intellectual life
that existed in those days have now almost vanished. I loved the
beautiful secluded corners of Tiflis, which reminded one of St
Petersburg, the first-floor balcony railings bent into the shape of
baskets or lyres, and the picturesque little alleyways. Close on one's
heels and following one everywhere was heard the sound of the
tambourine beating out the rhythm of the *lezghinka*. The goat-like
drone of the Georgian bagpipes and other instruments remind me
of the onset of evening in a southern town, full of stars and fragrance
from gardens, confectioners' shops and cafés.

5

Paolo Yashvili was an outstanding poet of the post-symbolist
period. His poetry is built on precise data and sense-impressions.
In the freshness of his unexpected but precise observations, his
poetry is related to the modern European prose of Biely, Hamsun
and Proust. His poetry is extremely rich in content, and is not
crammed with unnecessary effects, but is full of space and air. It
moves and breathes.

When the First World War broke out, Yashvili was a student
at the Sorbonne in Paris. He was returning home to Russia in a
rather roundabout way when on a desolate little station in Norway
his attention wandered and he missed his train. A young Norwegian
farming couple, who had driven to the station by sledge from the
depths of the countryside to collect their mail, noticed what happened as this spirited, southern-looking young man stood day-
dreaming. They took pity on Yashvili, spoke to him in God knows
what language, and took him home to their farm until the next
train, which was not due till the following day.

Yashvili was a marvellous raconteur. He was a born teller of
adventure stories, and unexpected things were always happening
to him in the way they do in novels. He had the knack of attracting
surprise happenings.

His talents visibly seeped out of him. The fire of his soul shone
through his eyes, the fire of his passions burned on his lips. His
face was scorched and blackened by the heat of life so that he
looked battered and experienced, a man older than his years.

On the day of our arrival he had gathered his friends together, members of the group which he headed. I cannot remember exactly who was there, but I expect Nikolai Nadiradze, his next-door-neighbour and a first-rate authentic lyric poet, was there. Titsian Tabidze and his wife were also present.

6

I can see that room as if it was yesterday. How could I ever forget it? Even at the time, during that party, when I was still ignorant of what horrors awaited its members, I stored it up carefully in the depths of my soul so that it would not break together with all the other dreadful things which were to happen later to those friends of mine and those around them.

Why were these two people sent into my life? How should I describe our relationship? They both became an integral part of my private life. I did not prefer one to the other, since they were inseparable and complemented each other. Their fate and that of Tsvetaeva were to become one of the greatest sorrows of my life.

7

If Yashvili was outgoing and centrifugal, then Titsian Tabidze was centripetal, in every line he wrote and in every step he took into the depths of his soul, rich in enigma and foreboding.

The main feature that underlies all his poetry is its inexhaustible lyrical potential, the fact that more is unexpressed and hinted at than is said. This untouched storehouse of emotion forms a kind of backdrop to his poetry, giving it a special mood, an all-pervasive bitter-sweet charm. There is as much of his soul in his poetry as in himself, that complex, secret soul wholly dedicated to good yet fated to clairvoyance and self-sacrifice.

When I think of Yashvili I think of life in Tiflis, of rooms, of arguments, public speeches and Yashvili's marvellous gift of oratory which he displayed at crowded night-time drinking parties.

When I think of Tabidze I think of elemental nature and I imagine the countryside, the great expanse of flower-covered plains, the waves of the sea. Clouds float in the sky, the mountains rise up to them in the distance, and with them merges the solid, stocky figure of that smiling poet. He walks with a slightly jerky gait. His whole body shakes when he laughs. He gets up, stands sideways to the table and taps his glass with his knife before making a speech. He looks slightly lopsided because of his habit of raising one shoulder higher than the other.

The house stands in Kodzhory on a bend in the road. The road passes the front of the house, then skirts around it and passes by the back wall, so that everyone who drives or walks past can be seen twice from the house.

It was the height of the time when, as Biely wittily remarked, the triumph of materialism had done away with material things. There was nothing to eat, nothing to wear, nothing tangible anywhere, only ideas. If we did not perish it was thanks to my friends the miracle-workers of Tiflis, who always managed to get hold of something and to supply us, goodness knows how, with advances from publishers.

We are all gathered together, exchanging news, having supper, reading to each other. The cool air seems to run its fingers through the silvery poplar leaves, their undersides white and velvety. The air is heavy with an intoxicating southern fragrance. Like a railway car gently shunting on to the coupling bolt, the whole night sky slowly turns the coachwork of its lumbering star studded-waggon. And bullock carts and cars pass by along the road and each one can be seen twice from the house.

We may be on the Georgian military highway or in Borzhomi or Abastuman. Or we may have come back from an outing and have seen the beauties of nature, had an adventure or been drinking and have all got something to show for it—I, for example, had a fall in Bakuriany and have a black eye. Or we may be visiting Leonidze, a highly original poet, closest of them all to the mysteries of the language in which he writes and therefore hardest of all to translate. A feast on the grass in a forest at night, the beautiful hostess, her two charming little daughters. The next day a *mestvire* arrives unexpectedly, a wandering folk-singer who improvises on his bagpipes and sings a song extempore in honour of each guest at the table, thinking up suitable words for each one in turn and jumping at the slightest excuse for drinking a toast—to my black eye, for example.

Or else we are by the seaside at Kobulety: rain and storms. Simon Chikovani is in the same hotel as we are, the man who was to become a master of vivid imagery but at that time was still very young. And above the line of all the mountains and horizons is the head of the smiling poet walking along by my side, the radiance of his immeasurable talent and the shadow of sadness and fate in his smile and on his face. And if I bid farewell to him again in these pages let it be through him that I bid farewell to all my other memories.

Conclusion

This is where my biographical essay ends. It will be much too difficult to go on any further. If I continued I should have to speak about the years, circumstances, people and their destinies which belong within the framework of the revolution. Also of the world of previously unguessed-at aims, of aspirational problems and heroic deeds, of new privations, new austerities and new ordeals with which this world has faced the human personality; of honour, pride, hard work and endurance.

That unique, incomparable world has retreated into distant memories and rises up on the horizon like mountains seen from the plain, or like the smoky haze of a distant city glowing in the night.

One should write about this world in a way that makes the reader's heart miss a beat and his hair stand on end. To write about it in a flat, banal way that never shocks, in a manner that cannot compete with Gogol's or Dostoevsky's descriptions of St Petersburg, is not only meaningless and futile: it is base and shameful.

We are still a long way from that ideal.

November 1957